Evaluating Witness Evidence

Evaluating Witness Evidence

Recent Psychological Research and New Perspectives

Edited by

Sally M.A. Lloyd-Bostock
SSRC Centre for Socio-Legal Studies, Oxford

and

Brian R. Clifford
North East London Polytechnic

JOHN WILEY & SONS
Chichester · New York · Brisbane · Toronto · Singapore

Library of Congress Cataloguing in Publication Data:
Main entry under title:

Evaluating witness evidence.

  Based on a conference held in Oxford in 1981 under the auspices of the Centre for Socio-Legal Studies of the Social Science Research Council.
   Includes index.
    1. Psychology, Forensic—Congresses. 2. Witnesses—Congresses. I. Lloyd-Bostock, Sally M. II. Clifford, Brian R. III. Social Science Research Council (Great Britain). Centre for Socio-Legal Studies.
K5462.E825   347′.066   82–7107

ISBN 0 471 10463 9   342.766   AACR2

British Library Cataloguing in Publication Data:

Evaluating witness evidence.
  1. Witnesses
  I. Lloyd-Bostock, Sally M.   II. Clifford,
  Brian R.
  363.2′501′9   HV795

ISBN 0 471 10463 9

Typeset by Inforum Ltd, Portsmouth.
Printed and bound in Great Britain by the Pitman Press, Ltd, Bath.

Contents

Part IV Future Directions

List of Contributors

ALAN BADDELEY — *MRC Applied Psychology Unit, Cambridge, England.*

BRIAN R. CLIFFORD — *Department of Psychology, North East London Polytechnic, London, England.*

GRAHAM M. DAVIES — *Department of Psychology, University of Aberdeen, Scotland.*

KENNETH A. DEFFENBACHER — *Department of Psychology, University of Nebraska, Omaha, Nebraska, USA.*

PATRICIA G. DEVINE — *Behavioral Science Program, SUNY, New York, USA.*

GISLI H. GUDJONSSON — *Institute of Psychiatry, University of London, London, England.*

ERIN C. HEWITT — *Department of Psychology, University of Western Ontario, London, Canada.*

HAZEL P. TRESSILLIAN JONES — *Department of Psychology, University of Guelph, Ontario, Canada.*

KATHERINE KETCHAM — *Department of Psychology, University of Washington, Seattle, Washington, USA.*

R.C.L. LINDSAY — *Department of Psychology, University of Manitoba, Winnipeg, Canada.*

SALLY M.A. LLOYD-BOSTOCK — *Centre for Socio-Legal Studies, Oxford, England.* SSRC

ELIZABETH F. LOFTUS — *Department of Psychology, University of Washington, Seattle, Washington, USA.*

ROY S. MALPASS — *Behavioral Science Program, SUNY, New York, USA.*

DAVID M. SAUNDERS — *Department of Psychology, University of Western Ontario, London, Canada.*

JOHN W. SHEPHERD — *Department of Psychology, University of Aberdeen, Scotland.*

WILLIAM TWINING — *School of Law, University of Warwick, Coventry, England.*

NEIL VIDMAR — *Department of Psychology, University of Western Ontario, London, Canada.*

GARY L. WELLS   *Department of Psychology, University of Alberta,*
                        Edmonton, Alberta, Canada.
MURIEL WOODHEAD   *MRC Applied Psychology Unit, Cambridge,*
                        England.
A. DANIEL YARMEY   *Department of Psychology, University of Guelph,*
                        Ontario, Canada.

Preface

Evaluating witness evidence would seem to be an especially appropriate area for collaboration between psychologists and lawyers. It clearly involves understanding of a variety of psychological processes, including in particular, perception, memory, recognition, and recall. Belief in this potential for collaboration has given rise to a considerable body of psychological research which aims specifically to apply psychology in the area. In this book the most recent developments in research and thinking are presented through the work of leading figures in the field on both sides of the Atlantic. Contributions from psychologists cover work on factors influencing the quality of memory for events, faces, and voices; techniques of maximizing and evaluating the reliability of information provided by witnesses, including lie detection; and the newer topic of juror responses to witness testimony. In addition, a totally new perspective on the field as a whole is provided by an academic lawyer, who discusses the influence of certain trends in legal thought on the definitions of 'the problem' of identification and misidentification which have, perhaps uncritically, been adopted by psychologists.

Although apparently direct and obvious, the relationship between psychology and law in the area of witness evidence has turned out to be exceedingly complex, and the goal of making a practical contribution somewhat elusive. The tenor of the book is therefore critical and cautious. As well as reporting recent empirical findings, contributors devote their attention to analysis of conceptual, theoretical, and methodological issues and to reassessment of conclusions previously drawn from earlier work. There are also crosscurrents in the book which reflect differences of approach and opinion among researchers. Thus the book captures current debates within the field, and indicates new directions which research is taking and could take in the future. The book will interest psychologists with theoretical interests in cognition generally as well as those working in the particular area of witness reliability; criminologists; academic lawyers with interests in evidence and procedure; and practising laywers, the police, and others actively concerned in legal processes surrounding the evaluation of witness evidence. In addition, both the methodological and the substantive content should develop the experimental sophistication of undergraduate and postgraduate students in many fields.

Most of the chapters originated as papers presented at a conference on Law and Psychology held in Oxford, England, under the auspices of the Centre for

Socio-Legal Studies, Oxford, and funded by the Social Science Research Council. We wish to acknowledge the support of these institutions, which made it possible to bring together this group of major researchers in the area and hear papers on their recent work presented and discussed in the lively and stimulating atmosphere which such a meeting of common interests creates. We would also particularly like to thank John Boal and Jennifer Dix for their help in organizing the conference, Jennifer Dix for her painstaking work in the preparation of the manuscript, and Chris Clifford who compiled the index. Last but not least, we would like to thank our contributors for their patience when we kept them waiting and their prompt and good humoured cooperation whenever we asked for it.

February 1982

S.L.-B.
B.R.C.

Chapter 1

Introduction

Sally M.A. Lloyd-Bostock and Brian R. Clifford

Research on the reliability of evidence, or 'witness psychology' is by far the longest established area of law and psychology, having a history dating back to the beginning of the twentieth century. Almost as soon as experimental psychologists began making new discoveries about perception and memory, and about the relationship of physiological measures to various emotional states, the potential relevance of this work to questions of the reliability of witnesses and the detection of deception was realized. Hopes were quickly — and, it turned out, prematurely — raised that psychology could be as useful to law as the other forensic sciences. The psychology of the time could not by a long stretch fulfil this sort of promise. In particular, the development of theory about memory, as distinct from the accumulation of intriguing but puzzling findings, had a long way to go.

While stemming from the same basic view of the potential applicability of psychology in this area, work in the field today as represented in this book has altered radically in character since that early flurry of interest. Theory and methodology have obviously advanced greatly in the intervening years and continue to be refined and modified; and the questions tackled in research have been reformulated. As reviews of more recent work in the field show (e.g. Clifford and Bull, 1978) there has been a fundamental reorientation within psychology in the past 15 years or so, which has profound implications for the way psychological questions about the reliability of witnesses are approached. In particular, earlier, mistaken notions of memory and perception as passive copying processes analogous to those of the camera or tape recorder have given way to a recognition that these are active and constructive processes, shaped and reshaped by a very wide range of factors in the individual, the nature of the stimulus, and subsequent attempts to recall and describe. At the same time psychologists have become aware of the pitfalls in attempts to isolate subprocesses and study them experimentally — that is, that it is impossible to study memory in and of itself, divorced from, for example, social processes. The approach of narrowing down the processes under investigation dominated the study of memory for many years and led to the development of theory applicable only to a narrow range of human functioning specific to the tasks set.

1

Attempts to generalize from this work to practical applications are now seen to be problematic, or frankly misleading. Recognition of these dangers has led psychologists researching in this area to call for research specifically designed to be applicable to legal questions about witness reliability, and in particular to emphasize the importance of using as near as possible 'real life' methods whenever the line of enquiry permits. To a certain extent this represents a return from the laboratory to the earlier 'staged event' methods of Stern and others (see, e.g. Stern, 1910), but equipped with a much more fully developed theoretical structure. Most would feel that the proportion of laboratory studies in the literature on the topic of witness evidence is still unsatisfactorily high when it comes to practical application. Perhaps equally important, psychologists have developed a much clearer idea of what they may be able to offer of practical value and what they cannot. While those who work in the area obviously believe in the value of what they do, this book shows that they are also anxious to retain a proper perspective and restraint and avoid exaggerated claims for the applicability of psychology research.

In addition to theoretical and methodological developments within psychology, the chapters in this book reflect a broadening of focus. The early work concentrated on the courtroom, and the evaluation of evidence presented to the courts — as reflected in the title to Munsterberg's (1908) book *On the Witness Stand*. The emphasis today is far more on the process of gathering and evaluating information from witnesses prior to any court appearance, and indeed without the implication that the information will ever become courtroom evidence. Thus topics discussed in this book include aspects of the process of eliciting and evaluating information from witnesses in the course of an investigation, such as the use of identity parades, Photofit and other techniques, regardless of whether the end result is a prosecution. Attention is now given not only to factors in the event witnessed, but also to factors *subsequent* to it which may relate to the accuracy of memory. Other newer topics in the book include the possibility of improving the ability to recognize through training; and 'earwitnessing'. Twining in Chapter 14 shows that the perspective could be broadened still further and also more systematically and deliberately.

Where court processes are the focus, as in the first three chapters, it is from the new angle of asking how jurors or other court participants will evaluate the testimony of an eyewitness on the basis of common-sense psychology, and how far a psychologists' expert testimony would differ from this common-sense evaluation. The immediate relevance of this question arises from the fact that expert evidence is generally speaking only regarded as admissible in law if it concerns matters which cannot equally well be dealt with on the basis of ordinary common sense. Yarmey and Jones take this as their starting point in Chapter 2. Saunders, Vidmar, and Hewitt in Chapter 4 argue that there is a more fundamental relevance in that, from the practical legal point of view the crucial question about eyewitness evidence in the court is not 'How reliable, in an objective sense, is the evidence?' but rather 'How does it actually influence decisions?' If the (un)reliability of such evidence is accurately assessed and accounted for by participants in making their decisions, then quite aside from the legal rules one can question whether there is any need for *psychologists* to contribute at all.

This is indeed a fundamental question which goes well beyond the issue of admissibility of expert evidence from psychologists or the credulity of jurors, and gets to the heart of the relationship between psychology and law. The idea that psychology may have a contribution to make in the area of witness evidence implies a notion which underlies most psychology and law research, namely that 'scientific' psychology can add to, clarify, or improve on the 'common sense' or 'naive' psychology on which law proceeds. As Wells and Lindsay indicate in their discussion of metamemory, the study of 'naive psychology' in the area of evaluation of witness testimony is related to research within attribution theory in social psychology, which concerns the ways in which people attribute causes of behaviour. Jones *et al.* have described the scope of attribution theory as being a part of 'psychological epistemology' or the processes whereby man knows his world. Attribution theory concentrates on that part which deals with knowledge about people — 'not "naive physics", or "naive cosmology" but a naive version of psychology itself' (Jones *et al.*, 1967, p. x).

It is into this area that the first three chapters of the book move, in asking whether and in what ways 'scientific' psychology in such areas as memory and recognition differs from common-sense psychology; or conversely in what ways common-sense psychology might yield mistaken or biased decisions. The question at this level is not 'Is memory likely to be fallible in such and such circumstances?' but rather 'What is the common-sense answer to this question, and in what ways and why does it differ from the "scientific" answer?' The authors of these chapters phrase their particular questions in more specific terms than this: Saunders *et al.*, for instance are primarily interested in a particular hypothesis about the jury, namely that jurors tend to place too much faith in eyewitness testimony; while Yarmey and Jones are concerned with the legal rules about admissibility of expert evidence from psychologists in this area. Wells and Lindsay's concern (Chapter 3) also arises from the question of whether jurors can accurately assess eyewitness evidence, and hence the proper role of psychologists as experts on this assessment. All, however, have moved to a different level in the general type of questions they raise, as Wells and Lindsay's discussion makes explicit. Loftus and Ketcham in Chapter 9 return implicitly to the same theme in their discussion of the malleability of memory: the very surprisingness of this malleability stems from its divergence from our common-sense beliefs about the nature of memory.

If the experience of attribution research is any guide this type of question is going to turn out to be immensely complex. To begin with, as Yarmey and

Jones's study shows (Chapter 2), there is neither a consensus 'scientific' (or 'expert') view, nor a consensus 'common-sense' view on matters concerning the likely reliability of different sorts of witness evidence under different circumstances. Yarmey and Jones's study seems to tap the process of interplay between psychology as a research discipline on the one hand, and practical beliefs on the other. The extent of contact individuals have with the psychological research literature is clearly reflected in the extent to which the influence of experimental findings and developments in theory is seen in their replies to the survey questions. The importance of this perhaps obvious observation goes beyond the immediate interests of Yarmey and Jones in the question of how far psychology has a special 'scientific' or 'expert' view, and how far ordinary people are informed about advances within psychology. It reflects the filtering through and assimilation of psychological findings to become part of our common-sense understandings — a process which has been rather little studied. Psychology this century has provided us with models, concepts, and findings which have radically changed the way we think about people, frequently with implications for law, since laws, legal procedures, and discussion of law in jurisprudence all involve assumptions about the nature of human beings, their capacities, and their behaviour. This process is not without its dangers. There is, for example, a real danger that theories long since rejected, refined or superseded within psychology itself may survive for much longer in received common-sense wisdom and influence legal decisions. This provides an added reason for caution in applying psychological research in this area. Lindsay and Wells suggest in Chapter 12 for example that psychologists are not yet in a position to offer clear advice to the courts on the issue of cross-race identification. If such advice as has already been given turns out to have been mistaken or to require elaboration or qualification, it may be difficult to undo its influence.

The idea that scientific psychology offers an improvement on the common-sense psychology on which law operates — through jurors or otherwise — is an inextricable part of almost all psychology and law work, but it is clearly not without contention. The implication that psychology can usefully be regarded as a science, on a par with the physical sciences has been widely questioned and the various arguments and discussion surrounding it need not be rehearsed here. None the less this kind of view is still often accepted too uncritically, and it is too often assumed that 'scientific' equals 'better' in this context. It is not uncommon to find psychologists implying that their suggestions ought immediately to be incorporated into the law if only they could persuade lawyers to discard some of their outdated ideas. The range of difficulties which arise from the nature of psychological 'knowledge' of course include all the problems of generalizing from laboratory experiments to other contexts; of operationalizing concepts; of interpreting results; and many more. Ironically the more scientific the approach in psychology in the sense of proceeding through tightly controlled, narrowly focused experiments, the greater the problems often are in applying the research to practical questions concerning the reliability of witnesses. As Rabbitt (1981) clearly shows, such research is simply not designed to answer applied questions.

Contributors to this book are well aware of the provisional and partial nature of psychological knowledge; and much emphasis is now placed on the use of appropriate methodology if research is to be applied. It is characteristic of the field that little is accepted as finally established. Findings are constantly reassessed and alternative interpretations considered, resolution of conflicting findings is sought, experimental procedures are carefully examined, and alternative methodologies proposed. Indeed, two of the chapters in this book, those by Saunders, Vidmar, and Hewitt, and by Lindsay and Wells, are primarily concerned to question the conclusions of earlier studies and to emphasize that the psychological literature does not yet provide a clear basis for claiming that its conclusions ought to be incorporated into legal processes. Deffenbacher, in Chapter 13 seeks to resolve apparent contradictions in research on the effects of arousal on testimony. And Gudjonsson is largely concerned to emphasize the limitations on the practical application of lie detection techniques.

Psychologists naturally concentrate on the difficulties within their own discipline, and see these as the source of any problems in applying their work to law. Twining, as an academic lawyer, is less concerned in his chapter with the nature of psychological research and its findings, but raises some questions of a different type not previously discussed among psychologists, since they are questions which arise from law rather than psychology. Psychologists have tended to proceed on the assumption that the practical legal problems surrounding witness evidence, to which they have directed their attention, are reasonably clearly defined and that there would be broad agreement on this among lawyers. Twining shows us the dangers in such an assumption. There are differing traditions within legal scholarship which involve quite different approaches to and perspectives on legal phenomena, and hence on the nature of such 'problems' as identification and misidentification in legal processes. Contrasting two general approaches to the study of law — the Expository Tradition and the Contextual Approach — he examines how far biases associated with the former, much narrower approach are to be found in the literature (legal and psychological) on identification, and suggests that adopting something closer to the Contextual Approach opens up a very much broader perspective. The full implications of this approach for psychological research in the area of witness evidence have yet to be worked out, but it is apparent that at least some of the questions psychologists have been investigating would be cast in a radically different form, while other quite new questions would be raised. Twining is addressing lawyers as much as psychologists, and it may seem to be more for lawyers to clarify the nature of practical legal problems; but these are none the less issues which psychologists working in the area cannot afford to ignore. If psychologists are implicitly buying into a particular view of legal processes which is widely and increasingly questioned within law, then it is surely essential that they should at least be aware of this.

The complexities of the area are also reflected in the interlocking of issues across chapters in the book. It is clear that no part of the problem of evidence reliability can be isolated from the rest. For instance, Shepherd in discussing recognition performance over delays, makes use of mock identity parades; Malpass and Devine in Chapter 5 raise a range of fundamental questions about the identity parade which might seem to throw some confusion into Shepherd's findings. Yarmey and Jones, for the purposes of their survey, select certain answers to questions about reliability as being 'correct' on the basis of current psychological research, and hence the view an expert witness might put to a court: Lindsay and Wells in Chapter 12 cast doubt on whether the 'correct' answer regarding cross-race identification is indeed the right one, and whether psychologists ought to be putting views on the matter before the courts at all. The book contains numerous such instances where what is taken as a working assumption or not discussed as an issue in one chapter, is fundamentally questioned in another. There are also points of disagreement within the book. It would obviously have been quite inappropriate and out of keeping with the purposes of this book to attempt to iron out these differences of viewpoint and opinion (even had it been feasible to do so) and attempt to present a false united front.

The book is organized in four parts. The three chapters in Part I are concerned in various ways with the impact which eyewitness evidence has on those who must take it into account in making decisions. In Chapter 2 Yarmey and Jones pick up the objection sometimes met in the courts, that the reliability of witnesses is a matter for the jury to decide using its own common sense. They report a survey designed to throw light on the question of how far psychologists as experts would in fact present a different opinion to the court from that which a jury would on its own arrive at. In Chapter 3, Wells and Lindsay develop a metamemory analysis of how lay jurors make judgments about the reliability of memory, and in Chapter 4, Saunders, Vidmar, and Hewitt discuss and challenge previous conclusions concerning the credulousness of jurors, and present results of their own experiments designed to replicate, extend, and clarify the earlier work.

The four chapters in Part II of the book concern the process of eliciting and assessing information from witnesses in the course of an investigation. Malpass and Devine, in Chapter 5, analyse the concept of fairness in identity parades, showing that it comprises two different types of fairness — size and bias. They discuss the empirical basis of these as well as ways in which they might be measured. Davies, in Chapter 6, examines the relative effectiveness of visual versus verbal means of communicating information about appearance, both at the stage of interrogating witnesses, and when passing on descriptions to the public and to fellow police officers. Davies reviews the research evidence with particular reference to the various techniques used in police procedures such as the sketch artist, Identikit, and cued description. The emphasis in these two chapters, as in the literature generally, is on obtaining reliable evidence from cooperating witnesses, or at least on estimating the likely extent of its unreliability. The remaining two chapters in this part, however, turn to questions of a different type which have received much less attention in this context. In Chapter 7, Baddeley and Woodhead are concerned with the way in which we encode faces. They examine the possibility that the performance of witnesses in recognizing a face might be improved through training in strategies whereby one may commit a face to memory in such a way that it will subsequently be readily recognized. Gudjonsson's Chapter 8 provides a full and critical discussion of the various techniques of lie detection and the possible countermeasures a subject might adopt.

These four chapters are in a sense the most straightforwardly applied in the book. They focus directly and closely on actors and techniques within the legal process of investigation itself, with the explicit aim of furthering legally defined goals, and ultimately improving the quality of information obtained and/or accurately assessing its reliability, and avoiding errors. The variables studied fall within what Wells (1978) has termed 'system variables' — i.e. variables which the police can in principle do something about. The output of these researchers vindicates the view that psychology research geared specifically to forensic issues has the potential to yield information which can be applied to make identification procedures more effective and more just: at the least, it can establish limitations on the practical usefulness of techniques and strategies. However, as Malpass and Devine discuss in Chapter 5, psychologists as objective researchers can only go so far in this role: ultimately value judgments need to be made which are not the province of the psychologist. In the case of the fairness of a lineup, or identity parade, judgments need to be made about such issues as what is an acceptable risk of error of identification, given that the lineup can never altogether eliminate this possibility. Their contribution is to show how fairness of a lineup can be defined and quantified; to test the empirical basis of lineups in psychological assumptions about the impact of the similarity of foils on choices; and to suggest how this information might be put to practical use. But they point out that they cannot as psychologists take on the task of deciding what *ought* to be done on the basis of the information they can provide.

Part III concerns various aspects of the 'witnessing event' and its *sequelae*, and individual characteristics of the witness which may influence the quality of memory for the event — the raw material so to speak with which the preceding part operates. Loftus and Ketcham (Chapter 9) review the findings of a continuing programme of research which has shown that factors subsequent to an event may somehow modify or interfere with the original memory for the event, and which seeks a theoretical understanding of these phenomena. Shepherd (Chapter 10) looks specifically at the effect of varying lengths of delay on recognition performance. In terms of Wells's (1978) distinction, these two chapters embrace both estimator and system variables: sometimes factors subsequent to the event may be outside the control of the police or other investigating agents, but others, such as the wording of questions, or delay between an event being witnessed and holding an identity parade, clearly have implications for the kinds of procedures discussed in Part II. The remaining three chapters in Part III are more clearly concerned with estimator variables. Clifford looks in Chapter 11 at the relatively new area of voice identification, reviewing the existing literature on the topic and reporting on his own original work. The realistic conclusion unfortunately is that voice identification is even more troublesome than eyewitness identification. The following chapters by Lindsay and Wells, and by Deffenbacher, review and reassess findings in two major topic areas in the field. Lindsay and Wells (Chapter 12) examine critically the research literature on cross-race identification and suggest a novel theoretical angle which casts doubt on earlier conclusions. Deffenbacher suggests in Chapter 13 that apparently conflicting findings concerning the effects of arousal on memory for an event may arise because different studies relate to different parts of the Yerkes–Dodson curve, and examines the procedures used in all the relevant studies to substantiate this proposition.

In Part IV, Twining looks at the general directions and character of research and discussions by both lawyers and psychologists in the area of identification, arguing that there is a need for a new and more comprehensive model of the process of identification for future work. His viewpoint, as an academic lawyer, is novel and somewhat provocative, especially for psychologists, but also for lawyers; the chapter has far-reaching implications for work in this area.

Lastly, we attempt in our conclusion to draw together the main issues and themes in the book and draw out some tentative possibilities for future directions.

The book as a whole describes recent developments in research and theory and captures current debates as represented in the work of some of the most prominent figures in the field. The continuing rapid advances which are evident in many areas give grounds for satisfaction but not for complacency. Obviously, very great progress has been made since the earliest attempts whose failure is in retrospect unsurprising. But the tenor of the book is critical and realistic, and it is in this that we see much of its value. We hope that the book will encourage implementation of improved methodologies, and lead to more clearly articulated development of the broader perspective which we see emerging.

REFERENCES

Clifford, B.R. and Bull, R. (1978). *The Psychology of Person Identification.* London: Routledge and Kegal Paul.

Jones, E.E., Kanouse, D.E., Kelley, H.H., Nisbett, R.E., Valins, S., and Weiner, B. (1967). *Attribution: Perceiving the Causes of Behaviour.* Morristown, N.J.: General Learning Press.

Münsterberg, H. (1908). *On the Witness Stand.* New York: Clark Boardman.

Rabbitt, P.M.A. (1981). Applying human experimental psychology to legal questions about evidence. In S.M.A. Lloyd-Bostock (ed.), *Psychology in Legal Contexts: Applications and Limitations,* London: Macmillan.

Stern, L.W. (1910). Abstracts of lectures on the psychology of testimony and on the study of individuality. *American Journal of Psychology,* **21**, 270–281.

Wells, G. (1978). Applied eyewitness-testimony research: system variables and estimator variables. *Journal of Personality and Psychology,* **36**, 1546–1557.

PART I

NAIVE/JUROR RESPONSES TO WITNESS TESTIMONY

Evaluating Witness Evidence
Edited by S.M.A. Lloyd-Bostock and B.R. Clifford
© 1983 John Wiley & Sons Ltd.

Chapter 2

Is the Psychology of Eyewitness Identification a Matter of Common Sense?

A. Daniel Yarmey and Hazel P. Tressillian Jones

Many people believe that their years of experience, their maturity and their objective way of looking at things give them a body of knowledge which can be trusted, and which allows them to make good decisions. This information derived from unique, personal experiences is assumed to be general, obvious, and available to everyone. On the basis of common sense, behaviours often are justified regardless of their irrationality and unreasonableness. Even worse, because of their familiarity and uncomplicated conclusions, common-sense arguments can become articles of faith which are used as buffers against scientific analyses and practical applications.

The study reported here is concerned with common-sense knowledge of eyewitness testimony compared with 'scientific' expert knowledge of it. Our interest in this problem dates back to an incident that happened to the first author two years ago. He was not permitted to give expert testimony on eyewitness identification in an Ontario Supreme Court because, to paraphrase the judge, *jurors have been deliberating about questions regarding perception and memory for over 200 years and there is nothing new a psychologist can tell us about these processes*.

The decision whether expert testimony should be admissible in the North American court lies solely with the judge of a particular case. Many reasons have been given for claiming that testimony of the experimental psychologist in the area of eyewitness identification is inadmissible. These reasons are based on the opinion that sufficient legal safeguards to protect against bias are already employed, and that the testimony would invade the province of the jury. It is also claimed that the testimony would consume too much trial time relative to its probative value (Sobel, 1979). Further objections assert that such evidence would merely be partisan (Goldstein, 1977), that most of the substantiating research is purely theoretical in nature (Clifford, 1979), and that the testimony would carry undue weight (Loftus and Monahan, 1980). However, the main legal roadblock by which the admissibility of psychological testimony is denied is under the rules governing the presentation of expert evidence. These rules state that testimony '. . . may not be given upon a subject matter within, what may be described as, the common stock of knowledge' (McDonald, 1978, p. 326). The judge is free to conclude, as many have, that a jury is as competent as a psychologist to form opinions on matters of perception and memory. As 'common knowledge', by definition cannot be classified as expert, it is not exempt under the exclusionary rules for opinions in expert testimony.

Although potential jurors do have opinions about eyewitness identification, it is our contention that they do not necessarily have sufficient knowledge to interpret and evaluate correctly the many variables that affect its reliability. Addressing the claim that psychological findings are within the bounds of common sense, Loftus and Porietas (cited in Loftus, 1979) conducted a study in which 500 potential jurors (University of Washington students) were tested on their comprehension of factors that affect eyewitness identification and testimony. Their results showed a wide variation in accuracy of information and indicated that this knowledge, on the whole, is limited.

We also suspect that neither attorneys nor judges at the present time have sufficient psychological expertise on these issues to direct the necessary questions to witnesses, nor to address the jury effectively. To this end, this investigation examined the general knowledge about eyewitness testimony held by judges, lawyers, and potential jurors. In addition, the sample of respondents included senior law students, who may have sufficient academic knowledge to begin their legal careers, but lack the courtroom experience of practising lawyers. And finally, the study included a sample of experimental psychologists who, because of their academic qualifications and substantial research and publication in this area, we felt it would not be inappropriate within the parameters of this study to term 'expert'. It was predicted that the non-scientific groups in comparison to the 'expert' group would show limited knowledge of the variables involved in eyewitness testimony. These differences would cast doubt on the claims that the adversary system, in and of itself, provides adequate safeguards with respect to issues of eyewitness identification, and that knowledge in this field falls within what is termed 'the common stock of knowledge'.

METHOD

A total of 211 people participated as subjects in this study. A group of legal professionals were selected randomly from the Legal Directory of Canada and were solicited by mail. One hundred and fifty letters were sent to Ontario lawyers practising criminal law and 35 (23%) responded. Forty-five letters were sent to judges of Ontario provincial criminal courts and eight (18%) responded. The mean age of the legal professionals was 47.8 years, and their mean number of years of legal experience was 16.9. Two subjects in the legal professional category were female.

A group of 32 law students were selected from a senior class at Dalhousie University Law School, Halifax, Nova Scotia.[1] Nine females and 23 males with a mean age of 26.6 years completed the questionnaire.

A group of 60 potential jurors (citizens), 14 females and 46 males having a mean age of 31.2 years, was randomly selected from a list of volunteers from the city of Guelph, Ontario. These participants worked at 30 different occupations, e.g. mailman, factory worker, barmaid, salesman, housewife, professor, etc., and all qualified as potential jurors in Canada. Two additional subjects in the citizen-juror sample were not included in the analyses since the demographic information indicated that they were not eligible for jury duty according to the regulations of the Office of the Attorney General. Five other people in the citizen-juror sample refused to participate. They were replaced by five other citizens.

A group of 60 potential jurors (students) was selected randomly from non-psychology students at the University of Guelph. There were 23 females and 37 males, with a mean age of 20.9 years. Five other students in the potential student-juror sample were excluded from the study since they did not qualify as jurors.

Twenty-seven letters were sent to 'expert' psychologists soliciting their assistance. Experts were defined as those psychologists who had published controlled, quantitative studies in refereed journals on eyewitness identification and testimony. All of the experts possessed the PhD degree, and all were employed as university professors. Sixteen experts (59%), 2 females and 14 males having a mean age of 39.7 years and a mean of 14.3 years of professional expertise in their fields, completed the questionnaire.

The multiple-choice questionnaire consisted of 16 items which examined respondents' knowledge concerning several issues related to eyewitness testimony. The specific questions are presented in the Results below. Five of the items were adapted from the questionnaire used previously by Loftus (1979) and two items were adapted from a questionnaire constructed by Deffenbacher (unpublished) (see Tables 2.8 and 2.9).[2]

RESULTS

Since few judges responded to the questionnaire the data for this group and for the criminal lawyers were combined and are referred to as responses of legal professionals. An analysis of variance of scores summed over all 16 items, $F(3,207) = 54.22$, $p < .01$, revealed that the expert psychologists differed significantly in their choices of answers from potential jurors (citizens and students), legal professionals, and law students. None of the other subject groups differed from each other according to the Newman–Keuls test.

A chi-square analysis on each question tested whether there was a significant difference ($p < .05$) between the mean 'correct' scores, as indicated by an asterisk in the tables, for the experts compared to the mean correct scores for legal professionals, law students, and potential jurors (citizens and students). The answer chosen as 'correct' was based on our understanding of the current literature in the field, and its subsequent confirmation by the foremost professionals in that area of research. However, we do not mean this to be taken as an absolute. Citizen-jurors and student-jurors were combined into one category for the chi-square analyses since their results were so similar. The 16 items are presented in Tables 2.1–2.16. The tables show the percentage of subjects in each group selecting a particular response. Although the potential student-juror group and the potential citizen-juror group were similar in their responses separate percentage scores are shown for illustrative purposes.

Cognition and stress

The perception and memory of criminal events often involves stress, violence, weapons, and different durations of time. Four of these types of events are presented in Tables 2.1–2.4. The tables also show the percentage scores for respondents in the Loftus (1979) study on comparable items.

Table 2.1 refers to the Yerkes–Dodson Law (1908) which suggests that extreme stress and anxiety will interfere with a person's ability to acquire and process information (see also, Deffenbacher, this volume). Experts showed high agreement on response (d), and differed significantly from potential jurors and legal professionals but not from law students. The University of Guelph students and the students sampled by Loftus at the University of Washington were very similar in their choices of responses.

Table 2.2. describes respondents' knowledge about memory for criminal events involving violence. Clifford and Scott (1978) found that both males and females have superior recall for information about a non-violent crime compared to recall for a violent crime. Ten of the 16 experts (62%) checked response (a), the correct alternative according to Clifford and Scott. Experts' scores differed reliably from potential jurors and from law students, but not from the legal professionals. Guelph students and Washington students again were similar in their responses. Most errors for all subject groups, with the exception of the experts, occurred on alternative (b), that is, most subjects believed that memory for details of a *violent* crime is best.

Table 2.3 centres on the problem of weapon focus. Loftus (1979) suggests that when a robber holds a gun in his hand victims are distracted by the weapon, which leaves little processing time and attention for other details such as perceiving the robber's face. It is clear that the experts (88%) are aware of the weapon focus factor, although some experts commented that they were not satisfied with the research done to date on this problem. All subject groups differed reliably from the experts. A high proportion of legal professionals (51%) were aware of the interference that weapon focus can cause with facial

Table 2.1 Percentage of subject groups that gave each of the responses to a question about eyewitness testimony and stress

'When a person experiences extreme stress as the victim of a crime, he/she will have:'

Answers	Subject groups					
	'Experts' N = 16	Legal professionals N = 43	Law students N = 32	Student 'jurors' N = 60	Citizen 'jurors' N = 60	Loftus study N = 500
(a) greater ability to notice and remember the details of the event;	0	5	3	12	13	12
(b) The same ability to notice and remember the details of the event under normal conditions;	0	2	0	3	8	3
(c) greater ability to remember the details of the event, but less ability to notice the details of the events as they occurred;	12	42	28	23	27	18
*(d) reduced ability to notice and remember the details of the event.	88	51	69	62	52	67

* 'Correct' answer (see text).

Table 2.2 Percentage of subject groups that gave each of the responses to a question about eyewitness testimony and violence

'Suppose that a man and a woman both witness two crimes. One crime involves violence while the other is non-violent. Which statement do you believe is true?'

Answers	Subject groups					
	'Experts' $N = 16$	Legal professionals $N = 43$	Law students $N = 32$	Student 'jurors' $N = 60$	Citizen 'jurors' $N = 60$	Loftus study $N = 500$
*(a) Both the man and the woman will remember the details of the non-violent crime better than the details of the violent crime.	62	37	16	10	7	18
(b) Both the man and the woman will remember the details of the violent crime better than the details of the non-violent crime.	6	42	78	57	60	66
(c) The man will remember the details of the violent crime better than the details of the non-violent crime, and the woman will remember the details of the non-violent crime better than the details of the violent crime.	25	9	6	22	22	6
(d) The woman will remember the details of the violent crime better, and the man will remember the details of the non-violent crime better.	0	9	0	12	12	10
Invalid	6	2				

* 'Correct' answer.

Table 2.3 Percentage of subject groups that gave each of the responses to a question about eyewitness testimony and weapon focus

'Consider a situation in which a person is being robbed. The robber is standing a few feet away from the victim and is pointing a gun at him/her. The victim later reports to the police officer, "I was so frightened, I'll never forget that face." Which of the following do you feel best describes what the victim experienced at the time of the robbery?'

Answers	Subject groups					
	'Experts' N = 16	Legal professionals N = 43	Law students N = 32	Student 'jurors' N = 60	Citizen 'jurors' N = 60	Loftus study N = 500
(a) The victim was so concerned about being able to identify the robber that he/she did not even notice the gun.	0	2	0	0	3	2
(b) The victim focused on the robber's face and only slightly noticed the gun.	6	16	3	25	15	20
*(c) The victim focused on the gun which interfered with his/her ability to remember the robber's face.	88	51	41	52	63	39
(d) The victim got a good look at both the gun and the face.	6	30	56	23	18	39

* 'Correct' answer.

Table 2.4   Percentage of subject groups that gave each of the responses to a question about eyewitness testimony and time estimation

'If an eyewitness to a crime is asked to estimate the length of time it took for the crime to take place, he/she is most likely to:'

Answers	Subject groups					
	'Experts' N = 16	Legal pro- fessionals N = 43	Law students N = 32	Student 'jurors' N = 60	Citizen 'jurors' N = 60
*(a) overestimate the duration of the crime;	94	65	50	37	33
(b) underestimate the duration of the crime;	0	2	19	18	17
(c) be accurate in his/her estimate of the duration of the crime;	0	0	3	0	2
(d) be equally likely to overestimate as to underestimate the duration of the crime.'	6	33	28	45	48

* 'Correct' answer.

recognition. However, 30% of them believed that witnesses can get a good look at both the gun and the face, whereas 16% claimed the gun is only slightly noticed. Fifty-six % of the law students also believed that victim witnesses can get a good look at both the gun and the face. Potential jurors, in Canada and in the United States, indicated some knowledge of the weapon focus problem, but their responses also suggested that inaccurate explanations were believed.

Table 2.4 summarizes subjects' knowledge regarding time perception for a criminal event. Experts agreed (94%) that the temporal perception of a crime is likely to be overestimated by an eyewitness. This response differed reliably from all other groups. Some of these respondents indicated that time perception probably would be overestimated, but a high proportion also believed that time would be underestimated as often as it is overestimated.

Cross-racial identification

According to Wall (1965) the courts are sensitive to the possibility of errors in identification which may occur when witnesses differ from suspects in skin colour and racial origin. Table 2.5 shows that experts (94%) and law students (81%) were highly knowledgeable of this problem. Experts differed reliably from the legal professionals and potential jurors in their selection of alternative (b). Potential jurors in Washington and in Ontario gave similar responses. It is of some interest that 23% of the legal professionals and 23% of the citizen-jurors thought that Asian women would be superior to white women in identification. Also, 12% of the potential citizen-jurors and 13% of Loftus's potential jurors gave the most inaccurate answer possible. They believed that the white woman would find the black man *easier* to identify than the white man.

Identification by a policeman

Experimental evidence has failed to confirm the police belief that their training and practical experiences make them superior eyewitnesses for details of criminal events (Clifford, 1976). This belief is shared by the courts and by potential jurors if the results of the present investigation are valid. Table 2.6 presents subjects' choices on a question involving differences between policemen and civilians in cross-race identification of suspects. Experts differed reliably from all other subject groups. The clear majority of the experts endorsed the view that the policeman and the civilian will be equally accurate, though it is interesting to note that 2 of the 16 experts indicated that they believed white policemen would be superior to white civilians in identifying a black robber. Approximately 25% of the legal professionals, law students, and potential jurors concurred with the 'experts'. However, most of the legal professionals (63%) and law students (56%) felt that the police are superior to civilians in person identification regardless of the race of the suspect. Forty-three % of potential jurors also held this belief.

Table 2.7 presents additional information about beliefs held by the public regarding policemen and civilians. Interestingly, only 69% of the experts agreed that a policeman and a clerk would be equally accurate in identifying a suspect. However, experts did differ significantly from all other subject groups. Sixty-six % of legal professionals and law students put their trust behind police identification. However, only 47% of potential jurors had such high regard for police evidence. In fact, 28% indicated that if testimony conflicts, neither police nor civilians are likely to be accurate.

Memory for faces

Laboratory studies of memory for human faces indicate that such memory can be quite good (see Yarmey, 1979). But how good is memory for people and the different situational contexts in which they are seen? Are the courts and potential jurors aware that suspects who are seen initially in mugshots, regardless of their guilt or innocence, also are more likely to be identified if viewed again in a lineup (Brown *et al.*, 1977)? Furthermore, what knowledge do legal professionals and others have about the relative independence of witnesses' accuracy of identification and subjective confidence in ability to identify, especially when observations are made under poor viewing conditions (see Deffenbacher, 1980)? Tables 2.8, 2.9, and 2.10 address these issues.

Table 2.8 shows that experts are as divided in their opinions on the evidence on memory for faces as are all other groups. All subject groups gave fairly similar responses to all four alternatives. The majority of all subjects agreed with 50% of the experts that a face seen only once before is difficult to remember after a period of several months. Thirty-four % of the law students claimed memory is poor after a period of only 2 weeks. Of interest is the finding that 19% of the experts, 26% of the legal professionals, and 32% of the potential student-jurors believed that even after several months eyewitness memory for faces will be 90–95% *accurate*.

Whereas the previous table showed some disagreement among experts, Table 2.9 indicates that all 16 experts agreed that a positive identification in a photo spread is likely to lead to a positive identification in a lineup, regardless of guilt or innocence. Most legal professionals (84%) are aware of this probability. Law students (66%) and potential jurors (44%) are reliably less knowledgeable of this effect. Sixteen % and 23% of the latter two groups, respectively, indicated that previous mugshot viewing has *no* effect on lineup identification, which is simply wrong (see Brown *et al.* 1977).

Table 2.10 shows that 88% of experts agreed that under poor lighting conditions a highly confident witness will be equally accurate in identification as a witness with less confidence in his or her ability to make an identification. Contrary to our expectations, legal professionals did not select alternative (a) as their preferred choice. In fact, most legal professionals (42%) believed that

Table 2.5 Percentage of subject groups that gave each of the responses to a question about eyewitness testimony and cross-race identification

'Two women are walking to school one morning, one of them is Asian and the other is white. Suddenly, two men, one black and one white, jump into their path and attempt to grab their purses. Later, the women are shown photographs of known purse snatchers in the area. Which statement best describes your view of the women's ability to identify the purse snatchers?'

Answers	Subject groups					
	'Experts' N = 16	Legal professionals N = 43	Law students N = 32	Student 'jurors' N = 60	Citizen 'jurors' N = 60	Loftus study N = 500
(a) Both the Asian and the white woman will find the white man harder to identify than the black man.	6	5	3	22	17	16
*(b) The white woman will find the black man more difficult to identify than the white man.	94	63	81	48	43	55
(c) The Asian woman will have an easier time than the white woman making an accurate identification of both men.	0	23	9	17	23	16
(d) The white woman will find the black man easier to identify than the white man.	0	5	0	7	12	13
Invalid	0	5	6	7	5	13

* 'Correct' answer.

Table 2.6   Percentage of subject groups that gave each of the responses to a question about eyewitness testimony, cross-race identification and police evidence

'Two white men, one of whom is a policeman, are walking together in front of a large store window. Through this window they see two men, one black and one white, robbing the store owner. The two robbers escape and the two witnesses are shown a number of mugshots of known thieves. Which statement best describes your view of the two men's abilities to identify the robbers?'

Answers	'Experts' N = 16	Legal professionals N = 43	Law 'students' N = 32	Student 'jurors' N = 60	Citizen 'jurors' N = 60
			Subject groups		
(a) The policeman will be superior to the civilian in identifying both robbers.	6	63	56	47	40
(b) The civilian will be superior to the policeman in identifying both robbers.	0	0	3	2	3
*(c) The policeman and the civilian will be equally accurate in identifying the robbers.	81	28	22	28	33
(d) The policeman will be superior in identifying the black robber, but both will be equally accurate in identifying the white robber.	13	9	19	22	23

* 'Correct' answer.

Table 2.7   Percentage of subject groups that gave each of the responses to a question about eyewitness testimony and police identification

'Two eyewitnesses give conflicting evidence about the identification of a suspect, seen earlier for about 10–15 seconds. One of the eyewitnesses is a policeman and the other is a clerk. Which statement best reflects your view about the witnesses' testimony?'

Answers	Subject groups				
	'Experts' N = 16	Legal professionals N = 43	Law students N = 32	Student 'jurors' N = 60	Citizen 'jurors' N = 60
(a) The policeman's evidence is more likely to be accurate.	19	65	66	52	42
(b) The clerk's evidence is more likely to be accurate.	0	0	6	7	5
*(c) It is likely that both the policeman and the clerk will be equally accurate.	69	21	16	17	22
(d) Since the evidence conflicts, neither person is likely to be accurate.	6	14	12	25	32
Invalid	6				

* 'Correct' answer.

Table 2.8 Percentage of subjects that gave each of the following responses to a question about eyewitness testimony and memory for faces

'Which of the following statements do you feel best represents the truth about an eyewitness's memory for faces?'

Answers	Subject groups				
	'Experts' N = 16	Legal professionals N = 43	Law students N = 32	Student 'jurors' N = 60	Citizen 'jurors' N = 60
(a) Even after several months the eyewitness's memory will be 90–95% accurate.	19	26	9	32	15
(b) Physically attractive and unattractive faces are not remembered any better after several months, than average faces.	6	12	9	5	12
(c) After a period of 2 weeks, a face seen only once before becomes indistinguishable from faces never seen before.	12	16	34	22	28
*(d) After a period of several months, a face seen only once before becomes indistinguishable from faces never seen before.	50	46	47	38	45
Invalid	12			3	

* 'Correct' answer.

Table 2.9 Percentage of subjects that gave each of the responses to a question about eyewitness testimony and identification in a lineup

'A robbery is committed. Later, the clerk who was robbed at gunpoint identifies someone from a set of photographs as the person who committed the crime. Still later, the clerk is asked whether the robber is present in a lineup of several somewhat similar individuals. Which of the following statements is most likely to be true?'

Answers	Subject groups				
	'Experts' N = 16	Legal professionals N = 43	Law students N = 32	Student 'jurors' N = 60	Citizen 'jurors' N = 60
*(a) Guilty or not, if the person identified in the photos is present, he/she is likely to be identified from the lineup as well.	100	84	66	43	45
(b) Having seen the photos, the witness (victim) is not likely to choose someone from the lineup if the robber is not present.	0	2	6	17	22
(c) If the robber is present in the lineup, having seen his/her photo previously would not alter the chances of the victim identifying him/her from the lineup.	0	9	16	25	20
(d) The effect of viewing the photos on accuracy of identification later at the lineup, is not affected by how good a look the witness got of the robber.	0	2	12	15	13

* 'Correct' answer.

Table 2.10   Percentage of subjects that gave each of the responses to a question about eyewitness testimony and subjective confidence

'There are two eyewitnesses to a criminal assault which was committed under poor lighting conditions. When giving evidence some time later, one witness is very positive about his ability to identify the criminal. The other witness is not absolutely positive about his ability to identify the criminal. Which statement best reflects your belief in their testimony?'

Answers	Subject groups				
	'Experts' N = 16	Legal professionals N = 43	Law students N = 32	Student 'jurors' N = 60	Citizen 'jurors' N = 60
(a) The positive person is more likely to be accurate than the less positive person.	6	19	22	27	28
(b) The less positive person is more likely to be accurate than the more positive person.	0	42	34	15	23
*(c) Both persons are likely to be equally as accurate as each other.	88	37	44	37	33
(d) If the less positive person's testimony does not agree essentially with the more positive person's, then the less positive person's testimony will be accurate.	6	2	0	20	15
Invalid				1	

* 'Correct' answer.

the *less* positive person would be more accurate. All subject groups differed reliably from the experts, and the legal professionals proved to be as inaccurate as the potential jurors.

Question wording

Loftus (1979) has provided substantial evidence that people are aware that slight changes in the wording of a question can alter the response that a witness gives. Table 2.11 shows that all subject groups, except potential citizen-jurors, were aware of this effect. Only 55% of the citizen-jurors selected the correct answer. University of Guelph students gave similar responses to the University of Washington students. (The question used by Loftus differed slightly from the one used here). Of interest is the relatively high proportion of legal professionals (21%) and citizen-jurors (22%) who felt that a witness would disregard the distinction between *a* scar and *the* scar. We wonder if this is an example of research done in academic settings which is not necessarily relevant to the 'real world' of the courts, and how ordinary civilians understand the implications of the effects of specific word manipulation. Only research testing non-academic subjects can answer this question.

The elderly as eyewitnesses

When the questions presented in Tables 2.12, 2.13, and 2.14 were given to respondents little or no information was published on the performance of the elderly as eyewitnesses. However, some of the experts participating in this survey attended a conference at the University of Alberta (Wells, 1980), and heard a paper on this topic by the first author (Yarmey and Kent, 1980). Consequently, some of the experts (if they stayed awake) may have been familiar with the 'correct' information. Yarmey and Kent (1980) found that elderly witnesses are inferior to young adults in verbally describing criminal events, but they were equally accurate in recognizing a criminal suspect.

Table 2.12 shows that experts were reliably different from the other subject groups on the question of verbal descriptions. However, one-third of the experts thought there would be no difference between the two witness groups. Of interest is the finding that 65% of the legal professionals believed that the elderly witness would be as accurate as the young in verbal descriptions.

Table 2.13 focuses upon differences in recognition memory between the young and the elderly. All groups were equally accurate in choosing the correct answer (b). However, 44% of the experts believed that the young adult would be superior to the older person. In contrast, 37% of the legal professionals thought that an elderly woman would be superior to a young woman. Similarly, more law students believed that if there were differences in recognition performance, they would favour the elderly (22%) rather than the young

Table 2.11 Percentage of subjects that gave each of the responses to a question about eyewitness testimony and question wording

'Suppose a person is mugged in a darkened hotel hallway. He/she is later asked questions about the incident. (1) "Did you see *a* scar on the left side of the assailant's neck?" or (2) "Did you see *the* scar on the left side of the assailant's neck?" Would it make any difference which question the witness was asked?'

Answers	Subject groups					
	'Experts' $N = 16$	Legal pro- fessionals $N = 43$	Law students $N = 32$	Student 'jurors' $N = 60$	Citizen 'jurors' $N = 60$	Loftus study $N = 500$
(a) No, since the witness would know whether or not he/she had seen a scar.	0	2	3	3	13	4
(b) No, there is no difference between the two questions.	0	2	3	3	10	1
'(c) Yes, since question (2) assumes that there was a scar.	94	75	84	80	55	90
(d) No, the witness would disregard the distinction between *a* and *the*.	6	21	9	13	22	5

* 'Correct' answer.

Table 2.12 Percentage of subjects that gave each of the responses to a question about eyewitness testimony and verbal descriptions by the elderly

'If an elderly person is giving evidence as an eyewitness to a crime, which statement best reflects your view of his/her ability to describe the events?'

Answers	Subject groups				
	'Experts' N = 16	Legal professionals N = 43	Law students N = 32	Student 'jurors' N = 60	Citizen 'jurors' N = 60
*(a) It is unlikely that the elderly person will be as accurate in describing what occurred as a younger person would be.	44	9	16	10	10
(b) The elderly person is likely to be just as accurate in describing the events as a younger person would be.	31	65	53	47	37
(c) Immediately after the crime the elderly person will be just as accurate as a younger person in describing details of the events.	12	19	31	28	28
(d) Provided that some time has elapsed after the crime, the elderly person will be able to describe the details of the events that took place as accurately as a younger person.	12	7	0	12	25
Invalid				3	

* 'Correct' answer.

Table 2.13   Percentage of subjects that gave each of the responses to a question about eyewitness testimony and recognition memory by the elderly

'Suppose that two physically healthy women witness a crime. One is elderly (about 70 years) and the other is young (about 20 years). Which statement best represents the witnesses' ability to recognize the criminal?'

Answers	Subject groups				
	'Experts' N = 16	Legal professionals N = 43	Law students N = 32	Student 'jurors' N = 60	Citizen 'jurors' N = 60
(a) The young woman will be better able to recognize the criminal than the elderly woman.	44	12	12	35	25
*(b) Both women are likely to be equally good at recognizing the criminal.	56	49	62	52	48
(c) The elderly woman is likely to be better at recognizing the criminal than the younger woman.	0	37	22	10	20
(d) Women are generally poor at face recognition and so neither is likely to recognize the criminal.	0	2	3	3	7

* 'Correct' answer.

(12%). Is it possible that legal professionals are overly-protective of the elderly, or do these scores reflect practical experiences with elderly witnesses?

Table 2.14 presents an interesting anomaly. Legal professionals were reliably more correct than the experts in 'knowing' that an elderly witness would be reasonably likely to be accurate in recognizing a suspect. It appears to us that legal professionals are sensitive and protective of the elderly. However, this protectiveness should not be generalized to an optimistic view of their cognitive abilities without scientific support.

Children as witnesses

Table 2.15 illustrates that a high percentage (82%) of experts agreed that a young child is likely to answer questions asked by authorities in a way that he or she thinks the authority wants them answered. All groups differed reliably from the experts. Of concern, however, was the belief held by half of the legal professionals that children will be unduly influenced (and inaccurate) by the authority figure, whereas another 40% believed the child will be accurate. A similar split in answers is seen in the selection of responses by potential student-jurors and citizen-jurors. Only one expert out of the 16 believed the child would be accurate.

Earwitness identification

Saslove and Yarmey (1980) found that voice identification is accurate only if the speaker talks in the same tone of voice on both the initial presentation and the identification test. However, Clifford et al. (1980) have recently found that a voice identification test is more accurate if given within minutes of first hearing the speaker as opposed to 24 hours later. Thus, both alternatives (a) and (c) could be considered 'correct' answers. Table 2.16 shows that most experts chose alternative (c), which agrees with the results of Saslove and Yarmey (1980). Since Clifford et al.'s study had not been published before this survey was conducted most experts would have known of their findings only through personal communication or seminar presentations. This may account for the difference in experts' selections between alternatives (a) and (c). However, all subject groups gave similar responses to the experts. This suggests that experts may have answered this question through inference and not knowledge of the experimental research literature on earwitness evidence.

DISCUSSION

The findings of this study strongly support our contention that knowledge about the psychological variables that influence eyewitness identification and testimony does not fall within the province of common knowledge.

Table 2.14   Percentage of subjects that gave each of the responses to a question about eyewitness testimony and person identification by the elderly

'An elderly eyewitness to a crime is unable to describe the criminal to the police when they arrive on the scene shortly after the event. However, when looking through the police files later that day he/she identifies a photograph as being the criminal's. Which statement best reflects your view of his/her identification?'

Answers	Subject groups				
	'Experts' $N = 16$	Legal professionals $N = 43$	Law students $N = 32$	Student 'jurors' $N = 60$	Citizen 'jurors' $N = 60$
(a) Unlikely to be accurate as the elderly person will obviously be confused.	0	2	0	5	5
(b) Unlikely to be accurate as he/she could not describe the person.	19	7	0	8	12
(c) Equally likely to be accurate as inaccurate.	12	9	12	8	13
*(d) Reasonably likely to be accurate because recognizing someone is different from being able to describe them.	69	82	88	78	70

* 'Correct' answer.

Table 2.15 Percentage of subjects that gave each of the responses to a question about eyewitness testimony and responses by children

'If a young child (about 8 years) is questioned by police or in court, which statement best reflects your view of the type of replies the child might give?'

Answers	'Experts' N = 16	Legal professionals N = 43	Law students N = 32	Student 'jurors' N = 60	Citizen 'jurors' N = 60
			Subject groups		
(a) The child is likely to reply accurately.	6	40	28	47	30
*(b) The child is likely to reply the way he/she thinks the questioner wants him/her to.	82	49	53	37	47
(c) The child is unlikely to reply to the questions.	0	0	3	1	1
(d) The child is likely to reply 'I don't know' to the questions.	9	11	16	10	22
Invalid	12			5	

* 'Correct' answer.

Table 2.16 Percentage of subjects that gave each of the responses to a question about earwitness testimony and voice identification

'A female witness overhears a robbery being committed by a woman in the next room. Although she could not see the robber, it is likely that the robber can be positively identified by voice if:

Answers	'Experts' N = 16	Legal professionals N = 43	Law students N = 32	Student 'jurors' N = 60	Citizen 'jurors' N = 60
			Subject groups		
(a) the voice identification test is given within minutes of first hearing the robber's voice rather than 24 hours later;	31	49	38	47	43
(b) the robber speaks in a normal tone of voice during the identification test regardless of the tone of voice she used during the robbery;	0	0	6	5	8
*(c) the robber speaks in the same tone of voice during the identification, as she spoke during the robbery;	69	47	50	42	47
(d) the voice identification test was given within a month of the robbery taking place.	0	2	3	3	0
Invalid	2	2	3	3	2

* 'Correct' answer.

The sample of legal professionals who completed the questionnaire may well have had special interests in these issues. Despite this possibility, their scores were still significantly lower than those of the expert psychologists, offering strengthened support for our contention. Furthermore, it can be argued that as the legal professionals did not have a significantly greater overall degree of knowledge on these issues than did the potential jurors, they would not be in any better position than the jurors themselves to question witnesses effectively, and direct or guide the jury on relevant eyewitness issues. As one criminal court judge commented: 'This questionnaire has forced me to answer questions limited to factors that would never normally occur to me.' One defence lawyer also acknowledged his lack of expertise by stating: 'My conclusions are no more accurate or valuable than any other person's except to the extent that they may affect the manner in which I might conduct a case.' This last comment highlights one of the issues that we raised. How can lawyers be expected to conduct effectively cases involving eyewitness testimony unless they have adequate knowledge themselves, or are able to obtain access to it through an expert adviser or witness?

A comparison of the potential student-juror data from this study and the study undertaken by Loftus and Porietas shows that the two student samples were markedly similar in their pattern of responses on the five questions that were common to both studies. These similarities, especially as they related to cross-cultural samples, indicate that the results are generalizable to a wider population. This is further supported by the fact that there was no significant difference found between the student-juror responses and the citizen-juror responses. As a side issue, this also offers some support for the use of an easily accessible student population in experimentation on eyewitness testimony except perhaps in areas where knowledge, which might be loosely termed 'academic', is concerned. As, for example, in the question-wording issue (see Table 2.11).

The chi-square analyses on mean item differences showed that there were some responses from the three subject groups which did not differ significantly from the expert responses. In particular, the responses to items in Tables 2.8, 2.13, and 2.16 were not significantly different from the expert responses. Rather than suggesting a sophisticated level of knowledge by the 'non-experts', these results reflect a major problem of research in this area — that is, experts may disagree on what actually is the correct answer. That experts do disagree, even on the issues that we believed were straightforward when constructing the questionnaire, can easily be seen by the following scores. Questions in Tables 2.8, 2.13, and 2.16 were widely open to doubt with only 50%, 56%, and 69% concordance with what we had taken to be the 'correct' answer based upon our knowledge of the research literature. Altogether, there were seven questions with less than 70% concordance. Unfortunately, the 'correct' answer may be the result of only one experimental investigation which has not been tested by further research, and, as we know, replication of results is the backbone of science.

This poses a serious problem in terms of the psychologist in court as an expert witness; as one psychologist commented on the questionnaire: 'I would not "swear to" any of the answers, not even the ones supported by my own data.' Nonetheless, this does not invalidate the utility of psychologists as expert witnesses provided that the status of the research in the area in question is honestly and carefully explained. The expert would then be able to say whether he or she would be in a position to evaluate effectively the situation with respect to current research findings. In no way would this usurp the function of the jury, as its responsibility would be to examine the research results as presented, and to decide whether or not they should be considered in that particular case.

The analysis of the questionnaire from the potential juror samples revealed that the scale had a wide variance. The low inter-item correlations (from − .243 to .264) among the questions showed that there was no item redundancy in the questionnaire. Each question posed a different problem sampling from a wide range of the field. Furthermore, it is clear that because of the heterogeneous nature of the field, a correct response on one question was not a good predictor of a correct response on any other question. This is an important point for a judge to consider when deciding whether or not to allow an expert witness on the stand. The fact that the judge may believe that issues raised in one area of eyewitness identification are clear and straightforward and thus within the scope of the knowledge of the jury, does not mean that any of the surrounding issues are also straightforward, nor that they are also within the scope of general knowledge. The issues involved not only cover a very broad spectrum, but also are differentially complex.

As noted already some of the feedback from our subjects proved both interesting and informative. Perhaps the most outstanding was the response from some of the potential citizen-jurors. On seeing questions which concerned racial identifications, there was an immediate assumption that the questions were racist in nature. These face-value misinterpretations also were placed on the questions concerning the elderly. Even one of the lawyers noted that the questionnaire was 'obviously' designed to show up prejudices. It is clear that care must be expended to ensure that the nature of the research and its integrity is fully understood.

It is also important to ensure that the legal profession is aware of the relevance of research in this area. One crown attorney, who refused to complete the questionnaire, commented that: 'As we do not have professional witnesses, what point is there in endeavouring to analyse their attitudes?' This plainly shows that cooperation with the legal profession cannot be expected unless they understand not only the purpose of the research, but also how it directly applies to the court system.

Psychologists also have to be aware that the opinions and belief systems of criminal defence lawyers and prosecutors are not necessarily the same on questions involving eyewitness testimony. In a recently completed study, Brigham (1981) found that prosecutors in Florida appear satisfied with the *status quo* — no change in emphasis is needed by the courts on eyewitness evidence in their opinion. On the other hand, defence attorneys felt that judges and juries place too much emphasis on such evidence.

In conclusion, this study suggests that the adversary system, in and of itself, is not necessarily sufficient to safeguard against miscarriages of justice when the question of the reliability of the eyewitness arises. The professional expertise of the experimental psychologist could be an asset to the judiciary process. It is evident that further research and replication of studies in the applied area of eyewitness identification and testimony are urgently needed. Just as important also is the need for good communication between legal professionals and experimental psychologists. Until such time as the judiciary system accepts both the probative value of psychological testimony and its probity, the positive talents that psychologists are able to apply towards the pursuit of justice in the court system, will never be felt.

If the courts are reluctant to accept evidence on eyewitness identification and testimony from expert psychologists, and prefer to categorize it as common sense, the following story may be of interest:

A London theatre hoping to drum up interest in a film starring Charlie Chaplin decided to run a Charlie Chaplin look-alike contest. Charlie Chaplin entered himself as a contestant. He was placed third.

NOTES

1. We would like to acknowledge our appreciation of Professor Neil Brooks's assistance in gathering these data.
2. We would also like to thank Beth Loftus and Ken Deffenbacher for their assistance.

REFERENCES

Brigham, J.C. (1981). The accuracy of eyewitness evidence: How do attorneys see it? *Florida Bar Journal*, November, 714–721.

Brown, E., Deffenbacher, K., and Sturgill, W. (1977). Memory for faces and the circumstances of encounter. *Journal of Applied Psychology*, **62**, 311–318.

Clifford, B.R. (1976). Police as eyewitnesses. *New Society*, **22**, 176–177.

Clifford, B.R. (1979). The relevance of psychological investigation to legal issues in testimony and identification. *Criminal Law Review*, **5**, 153–163.

Clifford, B.R., Bull, R.H.C., and Rathborn, H. (1980). *Voice Identification*. The Final Report to the Home Office (Res. 741/1/1). Department of Psychology, North East London Polytechnic, November 1980.

Clifford, B.R. and Scott, J. (1978). Individual and situational factors in eyewitness testimony. *Journal of Applied Psychology*, **63**, 352–359.

Deffenbacher, K.A. (1980). Eyewitness accuracy and confidence: Can we infer anything about their relationship? *Law and Human Behavior*, **4**, 243–260.

Deffenbacher, K.A. (1983). The influence of arousal on reliability of testimony. This volume.

Goldstein, A.G. (1977). The fallibility of the eyewitness: Psychological evidence. In B.D. Sales (ed.), *Psychology in the Legal Process*. New York: Spectrum.

Loftus, E.F. (1979). *Eyewitness Testimony*. Cambridge Mass.: Harvard University Press.

Loftus, E.F. and Monahan, J. (1980). Trial by data: Psychological research as legal evidence. *American Psychologist*, **35**, 270–283.

McDonald, D.C. (1978). Opinion evidence. *Osgoode Hall Law Journal,* **16**, 321–336.

Saslove, H. and Yarmey, A.D. (1980). Long-term auditory memory: Speaker identification. *Journal of Applied Psychology,* **65**, 111–116.

Sobel, N. (1972). *Eyewitness Identification*. New York: Boardman. Supplement added, 1979.

Wall, P.M. (1965). *Eyewitness Identification in Criminal Cases*. Springfield, Ill.: Charles C. Thomas.

Wells, G.L. (1980). Eyewitness behaviour: The Alberta Conference. *Law and Human Behavior,* **4**, 237–242.

Yarmey, A.D. (1979). *The Psychology of Eyewitness Testimony*. New York: Free Press.

Yarmey, A.D. and Kent, J. (1980). Eyewitness identification by elderly and young adults. *Law and Human Behavior,* **4**, 359–371.

Yerkes, R.M. and Dodson, J.D. (1908). The relation of strength of stimulus to rapidity of habit-formation. *Journal of Comparative and Neurological Psychology*, **18**, 459–482.

Evaluating Witness Evidence
Edited by S.M.A. Lloyd-Bostock and B.R. Clifford
© 1983 John Wiley & Sons Ltd.

Chapter 3

How do People Infer the Accuracy of Eyewitness Memory? Studies of Performance and a Metamemory Analysis

Gary L. Wells and R.C.L. Lindsay

Problems inherent in eyewitnesses' accounts of events received serious scientific documentation in the 1970s (see Clifford and Bull, 1978; Loftus, 1979; Yarmey, 1979). At the end of the decade the first conference was held that was devoted solely to the psychology of eyewitness testimony (Wells, 1980) and the experimental literature of recent years has shown its promising forensic relevance.

Developing the experimental literature on eyewitness testimony, however, seems to require a concurrent development dealing with people's naive understanding of eyewitness testimony. It seems that each step we make in documenting some eyewitness problem poses a counterpart question of whether or not people in general (and jurors in particular) have an intuitive understanding of the problem. The work of Yarmey, elsewhere in this volume, represents an approach to this issue by posing questions to people regarding their beliefs about certain 'effects' that have been discovered in eyewitness experiments.

The question of how adequately the juror can assess the credibility of eyewitness testimony is an important one since it is the juror or some other intuitive trier-of-fact who runs the risk of the ultimate error, namely believing an inaccurate eyewitness account or disbelieving an accurate eyewitness account. Does the lay person understand the problems of eyewitness memory? Many judges seem to think so as it is common for expert testimony on eyewitness matters to be prohibited by a judge on grounds that the problem of eyewitness memory is something that is intuitively appreciated by the jurors. Data reviewed in this chapter call this assumption into question.

Because psychologists are increasingly being called upon to give expert testimony in court on eyewitness matters, it is appropriate for us to take serious consideration of how people judge the accuracy of eyewitness memory in our absence. Are people in the roles of jurors making significant errors in the way they treat eyewitness evidence? Can people detect an inaccurate eyewitness? What hypotheses guide their judgments in assigning credibility to eyewitness testimony? Having empirically-based answers to these questions is important for our decisions regarding the structure of expert testimony and our proper role in the justice process (Wells, 1978).

CAN PEOPLE DETECT THE ACCURACY OF EYEWITNESS-IDENTIFICATION TESTIMONY?

This question was first examined experimentally by Wells *et al.* (1979). The paradigm used by Wells *et al.* is also used in several other studies described in this section, so it will be outlined in some detail at this point. The paradigm involves two phases. In Phase 1, the crime-identification phase, a crime is staged for unsuspecting eyewitnesses, usually the theft of a calculator or video game. The eyewitnesses, usually undergraduates, arrive at a room where they believe they are to take a personality test. Upon arrival, another person (actually a confederate of the experimenter) is seen in the room suspiciously removing a valuable object, hiding it in his/her coat and quickly exiting the room. The experimenter enters the room within a few minutes, discovers that the object is missing, enquires about its absence, and gets a statement from the subject that someone took it. (Sometimes the subject-witness reports that someone 'stole' the object, sometimes the subject-witness simply says it was 'taken'.) The experimenter then informs the subject-witness that the theft was staged, and that we are interested in whether the witness can identify the thief from a lineup. This is followed by a lineup (picture array) containing six persons. The eyewitness is always informed that the thief may or may not be present in the lineup.

After the attempted identification, Phase 2 begins. Phase 2, the cross-examination-juror reaction phase, takes the eyewitness to a different location (mock courtroom) where he or she is seated at a witness stand, sworn in, and cross-examined. The cross-examination is videotaped with a high-quality colour system and subsequently shown to subject-jurors. The cross-examination is a fixed set of questions delivered by someone who is blind to the accuracy or inaccuracy of the eyewitness's identification and blind to the witnessing conditions. In a typical study, there are 22–27 questions that include such items as 'what did you see?' 'what was the thief wearing?' 'describe the thief' 'how good a view did you get of the thief?' 'how certain are you that you have identified the true thief versus an innocent person?' The final part of Phase 2 is the subject-jurors' viewing of the cross-examination. The subject-jurors are told that their role is similar to that of a juror, but their specific task is one of deciding whether the witness had identified the actual thief (hereafter referred to as 'belief of the witness') or had identified an innocent person ('disbelief of the witness'). The subject-jurors might also be asked to make other evaluations of the eyewitness (e.g. estimating the eyewitness's confidence).

The ideal outcome from this two-phase paradigm would be for subject-jurors to believe the eyewitnesses who had made accurate identifications of the thief and disbelieve eyewitnesses who had made false identifications. At this point there are four published studies using the paradigm. The next four paragraphs briefly summarize these studies.

Wells, Lindsay, and Ferguson (1979)

This was the first use of the paradigm. There were 127 eyewitnesses to individually-staged thefts, 74 made accurate identifications of the thief, 26 made false identifications, and 27 made no identification. Forty-two eyewitnesses were cross-examined (18 who made false identifications and 24 who made accurate identifications). Subject-jurors in groups of four or five (total=201) viewed the cross-examinations and indicated whether they believed the eyewitness had identified the actual offender or had made a false identification. The results showed that eyewitnesses were believed by 79.5% of the subject-jurors and this was true regardless of the eyewitnesses' actual accuracy. In other words, subject-jurors were as likely to believe an eyewitness who made a false identification as they were to believe an eyewitness who had in fact identified the actual offender. Finally, subject-jurors were asked to estimate the confidence of the eyewitness. Confidence ascribed to eyewitnesses was unrelated to the eyewitnesses' accuracy, but was highly correlated ($r=.71$, $p < .01$) with the subject-jurors' belief of the eyewitnesses. In summary, subject-jurors were unable to detect the difference between accurate and inaccurate eyewitness identification testimony. It is also of particular importance to note that the confidence exuded by the eyewitnesses under cross-examination bore no relationship to the eyewitnesses' accuracy, but was highly related to whether or not the subject-jurors believed the witnesses.

Lindsay, Wells, and Rumpel, 1981

Thefts were staged 108 times for as many unsuspecting eyewitnesses. This time, however, there were three different theft conditions. Thefts were staged under conditions designed to yield low (33%), moderate (50%), or high (74%) proportions of accurate identifications. (Each of these percentages is statistically different from the others at $p < .01$). The rationale behind this change (i.e. three theft conditions rather than one) is that jurors may not be able to distinguish between accurate and inaccurate witnesses to a *given* crime, but may be able to detect the likelihood of witness accuracy *across* crimes. The differences between the three theft conditions had to do with how good a look the criminal allowed the eyewitness to get of him. The manipulation of crime conditions was carefully pilot tested so that the likelihood of a false identification was greatly discrepant across crimes. In fact, the low-accuracy crime yielded a likelihood of false-identification that was over two and one-half times that found in the high-accuracy condition. A total of 48 witnesses were cross-examined (8 accurate and 8 false identification eyewitnesses from each of the three crime conditions) and subject-jurors ($n=96$) viewed cross-examinations and made judgments of the eyewitnesses' accuracy. The results replicated the Wells *et al.* (1979) study within crimes. Specifically, subject-jurors were as likely to believe an inaccurate witness as they were to believe an accurate witness. Across crime conditions, however, the results were a bit more encouraging. Subject-jurors were most likely to believe witnesses in the high-accuracy conditions (77% belief), less likely in the moderate-accuracy conditions (66% belief), and least likely in the low-accuracy conditions (62% belief). (The trend was statistically significant at $p < .01$) Note, however, that each of these rates of juror belief is above the actual rate of eyewitness accuracy. Thus, we could conclude that subject-jurors did take the witnessing conditions into account, but they tended to over-believe eyewitnesses. Over-belief was especially dominant in the low-accuracy conditions where the witnessing conditions were actually quite poor. Finally, the jurors continued to exhibit a pattern of belief that was highly correlated with witnesses' confidence, yet confidence attributed to the witness was unrelated to witness accuracy.

Wells, Ferguson, and Lindsay (1981)

Thefts were staged 80 times for an equal number of eyewitnesses who then attempted identifications from a six person picture array that either included the thief or did not. Half of the eyewitnesses were then 'briefed' in a manner akin to the briefing an attorney might give his or her witness. Specifically, the briefed witnesses were warned of the impending cross-examination, given some indication of the questions that might be asked, and told that the cross-examiner is likely to probe for inconsistencies in their memory for what occurred. The other half of the witnesses knew that they were to be cross-examined, but were not further briefed. Twenty accurate-identification witnesses (half of whom were briefed) and 18 false-identification witnesses (half of whom were briefed) were then cross-examined. Films of the cross-examinations were presented to subject-jurors (total $n=152$) in groups of four along with some weak circumstantial evidence. Subject-jurors made individual judgments regarding whether they thought the eyewitness had identified the true culprit from the lineup and then deliberated as a group regarding their judgments of guilt or innocence. Finally, each subject-juror estimated the confidence of the eyewitness that he or she viewed. The results showed that: (a) briefed eyewitnesses were judged more confident than non-briefed eye-witnesses; (b) there was a small, but statistically significant confidence–accuracy correlation for non-briefed eyewitnesses, but briefed eyewitnesses showed no relationship; and (c) greater belief was accorded testimony from briefed eyewitnesses than from non-briefed eyewitnesses and the percentages of guilty votes followed the same pattern. Once again, there was no ability of subject-jurors to detect the accuracy of the eyewitnesses and confidence was a principal determinant of the jurors' judgments of belief in testimony within and across conditions. This study shows that confidence can be determined by things unrelated to accuracy (i.e. holding constant the level of accuracy, confidence can be inflated via simple interventions). It also shows that the confidence of an eyewitness is more than just a correlate of the extent to which the witness is believed by subject-jurors; manipulation of the witnesses' expressed confidence increased subject-jurors' reliance on their testimony.

Wells, Lindsay, and Tousignant, 1980

The previously described studies by Wells et al. (1979), Lindsay et al. (1981), and Wells et al. (1981) corroborated the common-sense assumption that people's tendencies to believe an eyewitness's testimony are strongly related to the confidence of the eyewitness. Yet, these studies also demonstrated that the confidence of an eyewitness is, practially speaking, useless as a cue to the eyewitness's accuracy. Wells et al. (1980) conducted a replication of the Lindsay et al. study, this time telling half of the subject-jurors to ignore the confidence of the eyewitness as it has not proven to be a reliable indicator of eyewitness accuracy. In every other respect the study was identical to the Lindsay et al. study; that is, there were three witnessing conditions (low, moderate, high) and eight accurate and eight false-identification witnesses were cross-examined in each witnessing condition. The results for those subject-jurors who were *not* told to ignore confidence (control subjects) replicated the results of Lindsay et al. (i.e. no ability of subject-jurors to distinguish between accurate and false-identification witnesses, tendencies to over-believe eyewitnesses under poor witnessing conditions and some adjustment in belief rates according to the witnessing conditions). It was hoped that the subject-jurors who were told to ignore confidence would fare better. In fact, however, these subject-jurors also showed no ability to distinguish between accurate- and false-identification eyewitnesses nor did they fare better in taking witnessing conditions into account. They did, however, greatly reduce their belief in the eyewitnesses' testimony. The average rate of juror belief was 40.5% with advice to ignore confidence whereas the control groups' average rate of belief was 61.5% ($p < .05$). Furthermore, the advice to ignore eyewitness confidence was successful in that the high-confidence eyewitnesses were no more likely to be believed than were the low-confidence eyewitnesses, in remarkable contrast to the control groups. From this study we might conclude that the strategy of using eyewitness confidence to infer eyewitness accuracy is not a *fait accompli*. At the same time, simply removing the subject-jurors' reliance on eyewitness confidence may not make them better judges of eyewitness accuracy.

WHAT MAKES A CREDIBLE EYEWITNESS? A METAMEMORY ANALYSIS

The previous section dealt with the question of whether or not people can discern the accuracy of an eyewitness's lineup identification from the testimony of the eyewitness. In that research we learned that the subject-juror is unlikely to perform very well. We also learned something about the process of inference — specifically, people will rely heavily on eyewitness confidence to infer the credibility of eyewitness memory.

Nevertheless, there are eyewitnesses who are quite confident, and perceived as such by subject-jurors, yet not believed. Similarly, there are eyewitnesses who are not very confident and yet are believed. Clearly there are other factors that affect the subject-jurors' perceptions of the credibility of an eyewitness. It seems reasonable to assume that people have hypotheses, suppositions, and perhaps even theories of memory that they use when their task is to judge the accuracy of another person's memory. We might call this 'intuitive memory theory' although there is some precedent for considering the label 'meta-memory'. Metamemory refers to 'the individual's knowledge of and awareness of memory, or of anything pertinent to information storage and retrieval' (Flavell and Wellman, 1977, p. 4). Although there is some empirical research in metamemory, it has been almost exclusively devoted to the question of how young children develop concepts regarding their own memory. While developmental metamemory research is related to the current concern, it is somewhat removed from the question of how people infer the accuracy of someone else's memory.

As for the question of how the person on the street comes to rely on or discount someone else's memory, we have little in the way of theoretical or empirical analyses. In some ways this seems surprising. Social psychologists, for example, have spent a great deal of research effort on other areas of social cognition — most notably people's intuitive theories of causality (i.e. attribution theory — see, for example, Kelley, 1967) and people's intuitive theories of personality (see, for example, Bruner and Taguiri, 1954).

The current analysis of intuitive memory theory could be considered part of a larger picture emerging in social psychology on the layperson-as-psychologist. In fact, there is nothing peculiar in this metamemory analysis that would make it pertain only to eyewitnesses and jurors. The analysis is more general than the courtroom setting, although the examples given herein pertain to that setting.

There are three sources of evidence that served as the foundation for the current analysis. First, there is the experimental work and results reviewed in the previous section. Second, there is some unpublished work, conducted in our laboratories, wherein subjects viewed cross-examinations of eyewitnesses with instructions to 'think aloud' (as in Newell and Simon, 1972). These sessions were tape recorded and reviewed for recurring themes regarding the cues that people use and the processes they follow in judging the accuracy of eyewitnesses' memories. Finally, use was made of any relevant developmental metamemory research. None of these sources of evidence is perfect or ideal. Indeed, the current theoretical analysis necessarily outstrips the available data. Yet, it seems a reasonable starting point and a useful reference for approaching future empirical tests of people's intuitive theories of memory, whether these people are subject-jurors assessing eyewitnesses' memory or whether it be some extra-legal situation.

Three types of information

It might be argued that the intuitive theories people hold about memory credibility are so sophisticated and complex or, at the other extreme, so unsystematic and random that it is impossible to capture them in a model. It seems more likely that the truth lies between these extremes. In fact, it seems that most of the process revolves around the perceiver's use of three types of information as shown in Table 3.1. Although these three types of information are addressed in a particular order here, it should be noted that they may be encountered in any order by the memory judge. In fact, the order in which these types of information are encountered could be a variable of importance for the memory judge. It should also be noted that in a given setting the memory judge might not have all three types of information. Finally, it should be explicitly stated that this analysis does not pertain to how people

Table 3.1 Three types of information used by people to infer the accuracy of another person's memory

---

I.   *CONDITIONAL INFORMATION*: e.g. length of time the person was exposed to stimulus, lighting conditions at time of exposure, previous familiarity with stimulus, complexity of stimulus, length of time between exposure to stimulus and memory test.
    A. Processing influenced by self-based judgments (e.g. would I have remembered 'X' under those conditions?)
    B. Sample-based, scientific reference taken into account when such information is available.

II.   *INTRA- AND INTERSUBJECTIVE AGREEMENT INFORMATION*
    A. Intrasubjective — does memorial report show inconsistencies over time or modalities?
    B. Intersubjective — does memorial account show inconsistencies across persons?

III.   *RESPONSE-BIAS INFORMATION*
    A. Confidence in current memorial account.
    B. Previous free-admissions of memory failure.

---

evaluate the memorial recounting of someone who may be motivated *intentionally* to distort his or her reported memory. The model would hardly apply, for example, to the testimony of a mother whose memorial recounting serves to exonerate her son.

Conditional information

One type of information that people use in judging the accuracy of another person's memory is *conditional* information. The memory judge will certainly take account of the witnessing conditions (e.g. length of time the person was exposed to the stimulus, the lighting conditions, etc.). The Lindsay *et al*. (1981) study showed that subject-jurors are not impervious to such factors. People may also take into account such conditional information as the length of time between exposure to a stimulus and the recall or recognition test as well as the conditions of testing. The list of possible conditionals that people take into account is a large one indeed and we are not willing to speculate on the nature of such a list at this time. In fact, we know little about this list. Regardless of this limitation, however, it seems that the *process* by which people use conditional information revolves around 'self-based judgments'. Specifically, the memory judge seems to ask the question, 'would I have remembered that under those conditions?'

There are two lines of evidence suggesting that conditional information is processed in terms of self-based judgments. First, research in metamemory shows that young children predict each other's ability to recall at about the same mean level of accuracy as they do their own, with the two scores also being positively correlated within individual subjects (Markman, 1973). This is not unusual in other areas of prediction as well (e.g. see Ross *et al*., 1977). A second line of evidence implicating the self-based process in inferring the accuracy of another's memory comes from the 'thinking aloud' studies referred to earlier. A recurring style in the phraseology of subjects is typified by the statements 'I don't think I would have remembered that' or 'I could have recognized someone under those conditions'. This self-based referencing was quite pervasive and seems to reflect a type of processing that relies heavily on one's previous encounters with stimuli and situations.

Although the processing of conditional information is heavily biased toward self-referencing, this does not mean that people will ignore other types of referencing. For example, when information is explicitly provided from a credible source of the form 'people have been shown to have poor recall under condition x, but not under condition y', we can expect the memory judge to take that information into account. In other words, the self-reference process is not totally pervasive; people are receptive to sample-based information. Sample-based information or expert opinions might not be optimally utilized when people judge memory, but people are not impervious to using such information at some level (Loftus, 1980). When people are given convincing data regarding how memory operates under certain conditions, they might show significant shifts in their interpretation of those conditions and perhaps even abandon the self-based strategy and opt for the more scientific base-rate information. The assertion that people will use normative data to predict the accuracy of memory is also consistent with Yussen and Levy's (1975) meta-memory studies.

One of the more interesting facets of conditional information is that it is often available only through interrogation of the very person whose memory is being called into question. This is a situation that might not be fully appreciated by the memory judge. For example, an eyewitness may give testimony saying that the crime took approximately 2 minutes and that he, therefore, had an adequate amount of time to view the criminal's face. The memory judge might consider the 2 minutes sufficient grounds to believe that the eyewitness could not be mistaken. What the memory judge has overlooked, however, is that the conditional information might itself be in error. In fact, it is a well-documented finding that people consistently overestimate the duration of such events (e.g. Marshall, 1969; Schiffman and Bobko, 1974).

Intra- and intersubjective agreement information.

Few single events have as much discrediting effect as does lack of intra-subjective agreement in the communication of a memory. Intrasubjective disagreement, defined here as the lack of consistency in what one reports as his/her memory of an event, signals to the memory judge that the memorial record of this individual is ridden with imperfection. It is unlikely that the effect is limited only to that item or items on which there is inconsistency. Instead, it seems to produce a more general discreditation of the person, implying imperfection in his or her entire memory for an event. Data from cross-examinations of eyewitnesses, for example, show that an eyewitness whose report changes on some trivial detail (e.g. reporting that a stolen calculator had a carrying case, then later reporting that no case existed) is judged less likely to have accurately identified the thief from a lineup (Wells and Leippe, 1981). The concept of intrasubjective agreement is an obvious component of people's intuitive theories of memory. Whether people too readily discount others' memories on the basis of trivial intrasubjective disagreements is not known at this time. Alternatively, we might question whether or not high levels of intrasubjective agreement by a witness evoke too much confidence in the witness's memory.

Intersubjective agreement refers to the consistency of memorial accounts between two or more witnesses. There is little doubt that it is appropriate to discount the memorial account of someone whose recall fails to match the recall of another person. Which person's account will be discounted the most depends, of course, on other factors such as the conditional information applying to the individual witnesses. If conditional information is favourable to memory for one witness (e.g. good viewing conditions) more than the other, then it is the latter whose memory is most discounted.

For the most part we can consider this use of intersubjective-agreement information to be a rational process of inference on the part of the memory judge. However, there is also the possibility that the memory judge will misinterpret intersubjective agreement by failing to consider that memory errors are not necessarily independent processes. Two witnesses who agree that a crime event spanned a 15–20 minute time frame, for example, may be subject to the same error of overestimating the duration of events. In fact, this overestimation error is more likely to receive intersubjective agreement than it is to receive intersubjective disagreement (Schiffman and Bobko, 1974).

There are a number of reasons why intersubjective agreement may be misleading, such as the one mentioned in the previous paragraph. Another situation in which we could expect errors in memory to be correlated across individuals is when two or more eyewitnesses use the same lineup to make an identification. Under these conditions any lineup biases against the defendant (see Wells *et al.*, 1979) will simply replicate themselves across eyewitnesses, thereby producing spurious high intersubjective agreement. Even more obvious is the relatively common problem of verbal interaction among eye-witnesses prior to testimony. Any failure on the part of the memory judge to note and take account of pre-trial eyewitness interactions is certain to create problems in interpreting the nature of intersubjective agreement.

One kind of intersubjective disagreement to which subject-jurors seem sensitive was explored in a study by Wells and Leippe (1981). Eyewitnesses to staged crimes were cross-examined and asked a series of questions regarding trivial, peripheral details about the crime scene (e.g. how many pictures were on the walls in the room where the theft occurred?). A mistake on any of these times was noted by the cross-examiner and documented by photographs of the scene of the crime. Those eyewitnesses who made many errors on these peripheral details were readily discounted by subject-jurors with regard to the witnesses' lineup identification. Note, however, that it was not the witnesses' memories for the criminal that were shown in error, but instead it was the witnesses' memories for *peripheral* matters. In fact, the witnesses who erred on the peripheral details were *less* likely to make a false identification in the lineup whereas subject-jurors operated as if the opposite were true. If we conceive of the camera as another subject (albeit inanimate), we might consider this a case where intersubjective disagreement (between camera and witness) is resolved against the witness. In itself this resolution is rational, but can lead to problems to the extent that it produces a general discrediting of the witness's memory. Perhaps the basic problem here is that the memory judge conceives of human perception as always being holistic (e.g. Navon and Gopher, 1979), whereas limited processing capacity (Kahneman, 1973) may produce negative correlations between performance on central and peripheral tasks (Hagen *et al.*, 1970).

Response-bias information

It has already been noted that confidence in reporting a memory is a primary predictor of whether the memory report will be believed (e.g. Lindsay *et al.*, 1981; Wells *et al.*, 1979). A recent study shows that this confidence-credibility effect is true of both measured and manipulated levels of witness confidence (Wells *et al.*, 1981). The term 'confidence', however, might not capture the broader nature of the phenomenon being observed. Although the confidence–credibility effect is real, confidence might simply be a way in which the memory judge discerns the existence of a response bias. In that sense, the confidence–credibility effect might best be construed as one example of response-bias information.

In the context of the current metamemory analysis response bias refers to the tendency of a person to report having remembered something regardless of the strength of the memory trace. This is analogous to the concept of response bias in Signal Detection Theory (see Editors' Note, page   ) wherein there may be a tendency for a person generally to report detecting a signal (low criterion for 'yes' response) or generally report not detecting a signal (high criterion for 'yes' response). In eyewitness identifications from a lineup, for example, some witnesses have a response bias to choose some lineup member and do so in spite of low certainty. Other witnesses, whose response bias is not to identify someone from a lineup, may be equal or higher in confidence that a particular lineup member is guilty, but do not choose because of their 'conservative' bias.

Lay judges of memory might not have a sophisticated understanding of response bias, but they act as though they understand the concept at some level. For example, an analysis of videotapes of eyewitness testimony (from Wells and Leippe, 1981) shows that witnesses who freely admit to not remembering something are judged more credible on subsequent items than are those who never make such admissions. In other words, greater credibility is accorded to a person's memorial account if he or she previously made a *free admission of memory failure* on some other memory item. An individual's free admission of memory failure seems to communicate to the memory judge that this person is not prone to fabricate a response (i.e. he or she gives no appearance of a bias to respond in the affirmative to a memory probe).

Similarly, when an individual expresses high confidence in his or her memory report it seems to tell the memory judge that the memory trace exceeds a high criterion. Low expressed confidence, however, tells the memory judge that the memory might not have been reported had a higher criterion been applied and, therefore, there may be a response bias to report a memory *in spite* of its weak trace.

A close analysis of the confidence-credibility effect reveals an interesting anomaly. Specifically, eyewitnesses who consistently show high confidence on *every* probe of their memory (i.e. every cross-examination question) are not believed. Consistent high confidence apparently suggests to the memory judge that the witness has a bias to respond with high confidence and, therefore, confidence is a non-discriminator for that witness. For example, during jury deliberations in the Wells *et al.* (1981) study, several subject-jurors openly questioned the testimony of witnesses who claimed to be sure of every detail because the witnesses were 'too sure' of themselves.

Expressed confidence in one's memorial report, or lack thereof, is not always communicated *directly* to the memory judge. For example, it is rare for a witness to say during cross-examination 'I'm absolutely certain . . .' or 'I am reasonably confident . . .' unless directly asked about his or her certainty or confidence. In fact, it is instructive to note that whether or not a witness explicitly states his or her confidence under cross-examination seems to have little or no effect on the correlation between the witness's private self-rating of confidence and the lay memory judge's rating of the witness's confidence (correlation ranges between +.6 and +.7).

Confidence is communicated in many ways, through both verbal and non-verbal means. It is always difficult to get an empirical handle on how people communicate a global concept such as confidence. Nevertheless, judging from videotapes of eyewitness testimony and examining how confident the witnesses were judged to be, it seems that one of the most consistent factors is the 'verbal qualifiers' people use in reporting a memory. Among the verbal qualifiers it is possible to discern an underlying concept that might be labelled 'constructive invocation'. Examples of constructive invocation as qualifiers include 'I think . . .', 'It must have been . . .', 'I guess . . .'. When a witness uses one of these qualifiers in response to a memory question it is greeted with considerable scepticism by the memory judge and the memorial report is judged to be lacking certainty. Constructive invocation refers to the fact that the witness is appealing to constructive or reconstructive memory. A constructive invocation (e.g. 'I think he had a hat . . . yes, he had a blue hat') signals to the memory judge that the memorial reporter is in a state of reconstructive memory. The lay judge of memory need not read Bartlett (1932) to appreciate the fact that many reports of memory are reconstructed products. Once again, the use of constructive invocation indicates that the memory reporter has a response bias — a bias towards giving an answer whether it is truly remembered or not!

Other sources of information?

There are many possible ways to characterize how people ascribe credibility to another person's memorial account. The metamemory analysis presented in the previous section characterized the process as one wherein the memory judge considers conditional information, intra- and intersubjective agreement, and response-bias information. It is possible to argue that the tripartite model fails to give due consideration to such factors as the physical attractiveness of the person communicating the memory (as in Garcia and Griffitt, 1978) or the sex of the witness (as in Taynor and Deaux, 1973). It may turn out that these are important factors. However, it seems likely that they achieve influence via the three informational factors presented in the previous section. Consider, for example, the variable of sex of witness. A sample of the cross-examinations in the studies by Wells et al. (1979) and Lindsay et al. (1981), for example, reveal that a male's eyewitness accounts are more likely to be believed than those of a female. However, it is also the case that females are more likely to exhibit constructive invocation as defined earlier and are thereby judged to be less confident.

Thus, certain variables that influence eyewitness credibility are not explicitly listed in the metamemory analysis because they are relegated to the role of epiphenomena. This is not to say that such variables are unimportant.

Conclusions

A juror's opinion regarding whether or not an eyewitness properly identified the defendant or identified an innocent person can critically decide the juror's vote. Often the issue of identification accuracy is sufficient to decide the case in that if a witness's memory is correct then the defendant is undoubtedly guilty. Eyewitness testimony is considered direct evidence rather than circumstantial evidence. Therefore, the need to know how people make judgments of eyewitness accuracy is of obvious importance. Data from recent experiments suggest that the task of inferring the accuracy of eyewitnesses' memories is made difficult by the eyewitnesses' own lack of awareness that their memories are in error (i.e. lack of an appreciable confidence–accuracy correlation).

An attempt was made in this chapter to build a metamemory analysis of how people infer the accuracy of another person's memory. The analysis is far from being perfect or complete. However, it may represent a starting point for understanding the way people judge eyewitness evidence. Ultimately, a good theory of how people infer the accuracy of another's memorial account will serve three functions: (a) it will provide a basis for our judgments of how best to present expert testimony in courts regarding eyewitness memory; (b) it can guide hypothesis-testing research which compares and contrasts the lay juror's hypotheses with empirical results regarding eyewitness matters; and (c) it might represent a useful level of analysis for examining perceptions of others' memories in extra-legal situations where matters of memory credibility may have significant social implications. To the extent that we understand the lay person's conceptions of memory, we may have a better context for studying the psychology of eyewitness accounts.

EDITOR'S NOTE

While Signal Detection Theory (SDT) originated in electrical engineering and statistical decision theory, where 'signal', 'noise' and 'signal to noise ratio' had precise definition, psychologists have adapted and modified these concepts. Thus in memory research for example, 'signal' refers to the item, stimulus or person the experimental subject is asked to identify in 'noise', now defined as the context of stimulation, that may be produced internally, as by a weak memory trace, or externally, as in the present case, by employing highly similar foils in a recognition set. In SDT, four conditions may pertain: First, the signal (or target) is present and correctly detected by the witness (HIT); second, while the signal is again present the witness fails to detect it (MISS); third, the target is not present and is correctly indicated to be absent by the witness (CORRECT REJECTION). The fourth possibility is that the target is again absent but this time the witness incorrectly indicates that it is present (FALSE POSITIVE). By mathematical formulation these four types of response can be used to compute d' (a measure of discriminative sensitivity) and β (a measure of bias or the subject's lax or conservative response criterion). The chief value of SDT is that it indicates clearly that a subject's response criterion for making a detection (identification) is a function of *both* signal magnitude (memory strength) *and* such things as the expectation of target presence and outcome likelihoods, that is, the witness's response bias.

REFERENCES

Bartlett, F.C. (1932). *Remembering*. London: Cambridge University Press.

Bruner, J.S. and Taguiri, R. (1954). Person perception. In G. Lindsay (ed.), *Handbook of Social Psychology* (Vol. 2) Reading Mass.: Addison-Wesley.

Clifford, B.R. and Bull, R. (1978). *The Psychology of Person Identification*. London: Routledge and Kegan Paul.

Flavell, J.H. and Wellman, H.M. (1977). Metamemory. In R.V. Kail and J.W. Hagen (eds), *Perspectives on the Development of Memory and Cognition*. Hillsdale, NJ.: L. Erlbaum Assoc.

Garcia, L.T. and Griffitt, W. (1978). Impact of testimonial evidence as a function of witness characteristics. *Bulletin of the Psychonomic Society*, **11**, 37–40.

Hagen, J.W., Meacham, J.A. and Mesibov, G. (1970). Verbal labelling, rehearsal, and short-term memory. *Cognitive Psychology*, **1**, 47–58.

Kahneman, D. (1973). *Attention and Effort*. Englewood Cliffs, NJ: Erlbaum Assoc.

Kelley, H.H. (1967). Attribution theory in social psychology. In D. Levine (ed.), *Nebraska Symposium on Motivation*. Lincoln: University of Nebraska Press.

Lindsay, R.C.L., Wells, G.L. and Rumpel, C. (1981). Can people detect eyewitness identification accuracy within and between situations? *Journal of Applied Psychology*, **66**, 79–89.

Loftus, E.F. (1979). *Eyewitness testimony*. Cambridge, Mass.: Harvard University Press.

Loftus, E.F. (1980). Impact of expert psychological testimony on the unreliability of eyewitness identification. *Journal of Applied Psychology*, **65**, 9–15.

Markman, E. (1973). Factors affecting the young child's ability to monitor his memory. Unpublished doctoral dissertation, University of Pennsylvania.

Marshall, J. (1969). The evidence: Do we see and hear what it is? Or do our senses lie? *Psychology Today*, February, 48–52.

Navon, D. and Gopher, D. (1979). On the economy of the human processing system. *Psychological Review*, **86**, 214–255.

Newell, A. and Simon, H.A. (1972). *Human Problem Solving*. Englewood Cliffs, NJ: Prentice Hall.

Ross, L., Greene, D. and House, P. (1977). The 'false consensus effect': An egocentric bias in social perception and attribution processes. *Journal of Experimental Social Psychology*, **13**, 279–301.

Schiffman, H.R. and Bobko, D.J. (1974). Effects of stimulus complexity on the perception of brief temporal intervals. *Journal of Experimental Psychology*, **103**, 156–159

Taynor, J. and Deaux, K. (1973). When women are more deserving than men: Equity, attribution, and perceived sex differences. *Journal of Personality and Social Psychology*, **28**, 360–367.

Wells, G.L. (1978). Applied eyewitness testimony research: System variables and estimator variables. *Journal of Personality and Social Psychology*, **36**, 1546–1557.

Wells, G.L. (1980). Eyewitness testimony: The Alberta Conference. *Law and Human Behavior*, **4**, 237–242.

Wells, G.L., Ferguson, T.J., and Lindsay, R.C.L. (1981). The tractability of eyewitness confidence and its implications for triers of fact. *Journal of Applied Psychology*, **66**, 688–696.

Wells, G.L., Leippe, M.R., and Ostrom, T.M. (1979). Guidelines for empirically assessing the fairness of a line up. *Law and Human Behavior*, **3**, 285–293.

Wells, G.L. and Leippe, M.R. (1981). How do people infer the accuracy of eyewitness identifications? Memory for peripheral detail can be misleading. *Journal of Applied Psychology*, **66**, 682–687.

Wells, G.., Lindsay, R.C.L., and Ferguson, T.J. (1979). Accuracy, confidence, and juror perceptions in eyewitness identification. *Journal of Applied Psychology*, **64**, 440–448.

Wells, G.L., Lindsay, R.C.L., and Tousignant, J.P. (1980). Effects of expert psychological advice on human performance in judging the validity of eyewitness testimony. *Law and Human Behavior*, **4**, 275–286.

Yarmey, A.D. (1979). *The Psychology of Eyewitness Testimony*. New York: Free Press.

Yussen, S.R. and Levy, V.M., Jr. (1975). Developmental changes in predicting one's own span of short-term memory. *Journal of Experimental Child Psychology*, **19**, 502–508.

Evaluating Witness Evidence
Edited by S.M.A. Lloyd-Bostock and B.R. Clifford
© 1983 John Wiley & Sons Ltd.

Chapter 4

Eyewitness Testimony and the Discrediting Effect

David M. Saunders, Neil Vidmar, and Erin C. Hewitt

Members of the legal profession (e.g. Starkman, 1979; Woocher, 1977; see also *United States* v. *Telfaire*, 1972; *United States* v. *Wade*, 1967) and social scientists (e.g. Lezak, 1973; Loftus, 1979) generally agree that testimony from an eyewitness may be inherently unreliable. A great deal of research designed to investigate the numerous factors which have the potential to reduce the accuracy of an eyewitness's report was conducted throughout the 1970s (for excellent reviews see Buckhout, 1976; Loftus, 1979; Yarmey, 1979) and, as the papers in this current volume indicate, interest in the topic continues. Such research has potential applicability to the legal system and can support or contradict the legal folklore surrounding eyewitness testimony. Woocher (1977) compactly summarized the view of many legal professionals when he stated:

> . . . most juries, and even some judges, are unaware of the sources of error in eyewitness testimony and consequently place undue faith in its veracity . . . For the layperson, visual identification of the defendant by the victim or the witness often provides the most persuasive evidence, which cannot be overcome by contrary evidence supporting the accused.
>
> (p. 970, footnotes omitted)

While the documentation of factors which may affect the perception, memory, and recall of an eyewitness is an excellent topic for basic research, the direct application of these findings to the courtroom is another matter. As part of his famous critique of Munsterberg (1908) the distinguished legal scholar John Wigmore noted that the critical aspect of eyewitness testimony was its effect on jury verdicts: 'The question . . . [is] whether the alleged percentages of testimonial error . . . do really, in trials, produce misleading results in verdicts' (1909, p. 426). That is, *if* juries can distinguish 'good' from 'poor' eyewitness testimony, then the degree of unreliability in eyewitnesses' reports would have few practical consequences. However, the number of studies addressed to the issue of how juries deal with testimony from an eyewitness is quite small.

Wells *et al*. (1979) used a 'staged incident' paradigm to investigate the problem. Subjects were exposed to an incident in which they were witnesses to a staged crime. These witnesses were then questioned concerning what they saw, and a group of simulating jurors rated the witnesses in terms of their confidence and accuracy. Wells *et al*. found that the jurors tended to believe witnesses almost 80% of the time and that belief in a witness was not correlated with the witness's actual accuracy. Wells *et al*. suggested that one possible reason is that jurors may have responded to the witnesses' expressed confidence in the identification, a characteristic which was not related to accuracy. Using another approach, Loftus (1979, Ch. 9) conducted a survey study which found that citizens were correct only about 50% of the time regarding some important assumptions about eyewitness behaviour.

While this research by Wells *et al*. and Loftus is interesting and raises questions about juror competence, it does not directly address the question of how juries deal with testimony from an eyewitness and whether their handling of the evidence adversely affects verdicts. Loftus (1974) approached the problem more directly by use of a juror simulation study. In her experiment subjects were asked to render a verdict in a robbery-murder case in which the evidence consisted of either: (a) circumstantial evidence; (b) circumstantial evidence and eyewitness testimony; or (c) circumstantial evidence and eyewitness testimony that was subsequently discredited. Loftus found that jurors in the discredited and not discredited eyewitness conditions rendered significantly more guilty verdicts than jurors in the no eyewitness control condition. The results of her experiment may be interpreted as indicating that jurors may be so convinced by an eyewitness's report that they will persist in believing the testimony, even under circumstances where they should not. This 'discrediting failure effect' may be characteristic of a tendency on the part of jurors to be over-credulous of eyewitness reports.

Our own initial interest concerning the topic of eyewitnesses was in response to the discrediting failure effect reported by Loftus (1974). We were intrigued not only by the seeming lack of ability of jurors to evaluate the discredited eyewitness testimony in a rational manner, but also by the broader implications of Loftus's results. That is, the results of the Loftus study would appear to be a substantial piece of evidence supporting the notion that juries are not very competent triers of fact, at least where eyewitnesses are concerned (for arguments on both sides of the jury competence issue see Kalven and Zeisel, 1966; Simon, 1967).

At the time of our initial interest, no study had been reported which had further examined the limits of juror competence in this area. Recently, however, a number of other researchers have investigated further the discrediting failure phenomenon. Cavoukian (1980), using Loftus's case materials, basically replicated the earlier findings, although the absolute conviction levels in the replication were substantially lower than in the original experiment. Cavoukian also conducted a second experiment that used a different set of stimulus materials. The case contained circumstantial evidence against the defendant plus one of three 'key witness' factors: a civilian eye-witness, a ballistics expert, or a handwriting expert. Crossed with the 'key witness' factor was another factor, whether the witness was discredited or not discredited. A control condition involving circumstantial evidence but no 'key witness' was also included. Cavoukian found that the discrediting information reduced the proportion of guilty verdicts in the ballistics and handwriting expert conditions, but the proportion of guilty verdicts was not reduced in the civilian eyewitness condition. She interpreted this result as suggesting that there is something especially persuasive about eyewitness testimony.

On the other hand, there are also research findings which do not support the assumption that jurors are, as a rule, heavily influenced by eyewitness identifications. Myers (1979) conducted a field study which analysed pro-secutors' records of felony cases that went to a jury trial. One of her conclusions was that juries assigned little weight to evidence from eyewitnesses, at least in her sample of 201 cases. Myers's findings, incidentally, are consistent with Kalven and Zeisel's (1966) conclusion that juries are generally competent. While Kalven and Zeisel did not specifically focus on eyewitness identification, it is noteworthy that in their analyses of instances of judge–jury disagreement the problem of the jury being overly credulous of eyewitnesses was not significant enough even to be mentioned.

Of particular significance, however, is the fact that several attempts at conceptual replication of Loftus's (1974) original findings have failed. Hatvany and Strack (1981) found that the verdicts of simulating jurors in a discredited eyewitness condition were significantly different from those of simulating jurors in a not-discredited condition and not significantly different from those in a no eyewitness control condition. There are conceptual problems with Hatvany and Strack's study in that the 'discrediting' manipulation was effected by having the witness herself recant her identification, a situation considerably different from Loftus's manipulation, which involved discrediting by the defence attorney. However, two attempts by Weinberg and Baron (in press) also failed to support Loftus's results, and that research raises more serious concerns about the robustness of the discrediting failure effect. While Weinberg and Baron's (in press) first experiment was an attempt conceptually to re-create the Loftus experiment from her published summary of the study, in their second experiment the authors utilized Loftus's original stimulus materials. In comparison with Loftus and the replication by Cavoukian, Weinberg and Baron found *no* support for the hypothesis that simulating jurors' verdicts are influenced nearly equally by discredited and non-discredited eyewitness testimony (see Table 4.1).

In summary, the body of empirical research bearing on the discrediting

Table 4.1 Proportion of guilty verdicts from four experiments using the Loftus (1974) stimulus materials

Study	Eyewitness (%)	Discredited eyewitness (%)	Circumstantial evidence only (%)
Loftus (1974)	72	68	18
Cavoukian (1980)	35	30	0
Weinberg and Baron (in press)			
Experiment 1	57	23	32
Experiment 2	53	29	N/A

failure effect is contradictory and ambiguous. This fact, in and of itself, calls for additional research. The issue takes on additional importance, however, in light of the fact that the original Loftus (1974) findings are usually cited as leading evidence for the more general hypothesis that jurors are overly credulous of eyewitness evidence. Recently, several studies have been directed toward discovering whether expert testimony by a psychologist might cause jurors to view eyewitness identification evidence with more critical attitudes (Hosch, 1980; Hosch et al. 1980; Loftus, 1980; Wells et al. 1980). Explicitly or implicitly these studies assume that jurors are over-credulous of eyewitness reports and proceed to test the effectiveness of an ameliorative procedural device, namely expert psychological testimony. Such studies have obvious policy implications but, as our review indicates, the assumption of juror credulity which underlies them, has inconsistent empirical support.

The remainder of this chapter is divided into three main sections. In the first section, two attempts to replicate and extend the Loftus and Cavoukian findings are reported. The attempts failed. The following section reports a third experiment with somewhat greater structural and conceptual verisimilitude (see Vidmar, 1979) than those utilized by Loftus and Cavoukian. It yielded some equivocal support for the hypothesis about juror credulity in the instance of discrediting and suggests *how* eyewitness identification, discredited or not, may affect jury verdicts. The final section offers a critique of the literature as it exists at present and outlines the parameters that must be considered in experiments investigating how jurors' verdicts are affected by eyewitness evidence.

REPLICATION ATTEMPTS

Experiment 1

The first replication attempt involved the stimulus materials utilized by Loftus (1974). However, a number of additional conditions were added to the three (eyewitness, discredited eyewitness, control) from the Loftus experiment. First, examination of the stimulus materials revealed a potential confounding element in the case (a confounding also detected by Weinberg and Baron, in press). Specifically, in the Loftus experiment the eyewitness in the not discredited condition was portrayed as identifying the accused, but he did not mention seeing the accused's face; in the discredited eyewitness condition, however, the eyewitness not only repeated his identification after being discredited but also stressed that he had seen the accused's face. Thus, while the results obtained by Loftus (1974) and in the subsequent replication by Cavoukian (1980) could be due to the fact that the discrediting was ineffective, they could also be ascribed to the additional information concerning the recognition of the accused's face, or to the influence of both factors. Experiment 1 addressed this issue by including identification of the accused's face as an experimental factor.

Second, the Loftus stimulus case lacked an element that might be present in a real trial, namely judicial instructions regarding the fallibility of eyewitness identification. When the primary evidence against an accused is an eyewitness identification, judges may admonish the jury about its potential unreliability. The use or non-use of judicial admonitions and their precise form vary from country to country and jurisdiction to jurisdiction, and depend on the nature of the case (see Cavoukian, 1980, for an excellent review). Nevertheless, such instructions are one of the recommended procedural devices to ameliorate jurors' credulity of eyewitnesses (see, e.g. *United States* v. *Telfaire*, 1972; *R.* v. *Spatola*, 1970 (Canada); *People* v. *Casey*, 1963 (Ireland)). A judicial admonition might well lessen eyewitness effects, especially in a discredited witness condition. Hence, a judicial admonition factor was added to the experiment.

In sum, the design of Experiment 1 was a 2 (eyewitness discredited or not) ×2 (face mentioned or not) × 2 (judicial instructions or not) factorial plus an additional control condition that had no eyewitness and contained only circumstantial evidence. The main hypotheses were as follows: (a) the three cells identical to the original Loftus experiment would yield a pattern of results similar to her findings; (b) the absence of mention of the accused's face would lower the number of guilty verdicts; and (c) judicial cautioning instructions would lower the percentage of guilty verdicts but have a stronger effect on the discredited in comparison to the not discredited eyewitness conditions.

Method

Subjects. Two hundred and forty-five introductory psychology students, participating in order to fulfil a course requirement, were randomly assigned to one of the nine conditions.

Stimulus materials. The stimulus materials were from Loftus (1974). Briefly, the materials portrayed a crime in which a double murder was committed during a robbery. There was some circumstantial evidence against the accused and in the appropriate conditions testimony from an eyewitness was included. The identification of the accused's face was systematically varied across conditions. The special judicial instructions were an abstraction of the Casey (1963) charge (for discussion, see Cavoukian, 1980) and were as follows:

> The judge, in his charge to the jury explained that it was dangerous to convict *solely* on the basis of uncorroborated evidence of one identification witness as this type of evidence is potentially unreliable. The judge further stated that this did not mean that the eyewitness was dishonest, but that the jury should carefully examine the eyewitness evidence in light of all the circumstances before reaching their verdict.

Procedure. After participation in another unrelated experiment subjects were randomly assigned to one of the conditions. Subjects were asked to read one version of the stimulus case and were instructed to render a verdict. They worked individually in groups of 15 to 20 and within each group all nine conditions were represented. After rendering their verdicts subjects were debriefed and thanked for their participation.

Results and discussion

The factor involving identification of the accused's face did not yield significant differences, so the data were collapsed across this factor. A factorial analysis of variance (ANOVA) with the eyewitness and judicial instructions factors revealed a significant main effect for eyewitness discrediting, $F(1,213) = 6.89$, $p < .01$, for the dichotomous verdict measure (Lunney, 1970). Tests of means[1] revealed that subjects exposed to a discredited eyewitness rendered significantly ($p < .05$) fewer guilty verdicts than subjects exposed to a not-discredited eyewitness (see Table 4.2). This effect was obtained regardless of judicial instructions. The proportion of guilty verdicts rendered in the no-eyewitness control condition was not significantly different from those of any of the experimental conditions.[2]

Thus, the results of Experiment 1 indicate a failure to replicate Loftus's finding that mock jurors believed discredited eyewitness testimony. Interpretation of the main effect for discrediting should be done with caution, however, as the experimental conditions did not differ significantly from the control group. The results of Experiment 1 tend to support Weinberg and Baron's (in press) findings that suggested that eyewitness discrediting information was effective. As Experiment 1 did not support the discrediting failure

Table 4.2 Percentage of guilty verdicts rendered in experiment 1

	Eyewitness (%)	Discredited eyewitness (%)	Circumstantial evidence only (%)
Judicial instructions absent	45	35	
	(55)*	(54)	
			36
			(28)
Judicial instructions present	48	24	
	(54)	(54)	

* Numbers in parentheses indicate the number of subjects per cell.

effect, a proper comparison of the predictions concerning judicial instructions could not be made.

Experiment 2

The failure to replicate the Loftus results led to an attempt to replicate part of Cavoukian's (1980) second experiment, which used different stimulus case materials. As described above, Cavoukian used the same general paradigm as Loftus (1974) but extended it by varying the type of 'key witness'. Conceptually replicating Loftus's results, Cavoukian found that discrediting information had a negligible effect in the eyewitness condition; in contrast, discrediting did have an effect in the ballistics and handwriting expert conditions. As in the Loftus study, however, Cavoukian's experiment did not include the potentially important element of judicial cautionary instructions to the jury.

Experiment 2 used Cavoukian's stimulus materials, although the handwriting expert conditions were omitted to conserve resources. As in our first experiment a judicial instructions factor was crossed with the other factors. In summary the design of Experiment 2 was a 2 (eyewitness or ballistics expert) × 2 (testimony discredited or not) × 2 (judicial instructions or not) factorial plus an additional control condition containing circumstantial evidence but no testimony from a key witness. It was hypothesized that the conditions with no judicial instructions would yield a pattern of results similar to those obtained by Cavoukian, and that the judicial instructions would reduce the number of guilty verdicts but have stronger effects in the discredited conditions.

Method

Subjects. Two hundred and ten introductory psychology students, participating in order to fulfil a course requirement, were randomly assigned to one of the nine conditions.

Stimulus materials. The stimulus materials were from Cavoukian (1980, Experiment 2). Briefly, the materials portrayed a case of armed robbery and attempted murder. There was some circumstantial evidence against the accused and, where appropriate, testimony from either an eyewitness or a ballistics expert.

In the key witness discredited conditions, testimony from either the eyewitness or ballistics expert was subsequently discredited. The eyewitness was discredited by establishing that he was short sighted and had not been wearing his glasses when he saw the robber. It was determined that the eyewitness had only a '70% chance' of identifying the accused. The ballistics expert was discredited by the introduction of evidence that indicated that ballistics analyses were accurate 70% of the time. While the 'evidence' indicating only 70% accuracy for both the eyewitness and the ballistics expert is clearly artificial, Cavoukian included the respective accuracy levels in order to 'psychologically equate' the discrediting in both conditions.

Procedure. The procedure for this experiment was the same as that described above for Experiment 1.

Results and discussion

A factorial ANOVA with key witness, discrediting information and judicial instructions as factors revealed a significant two factor interaction between key witness and judicial instructions, $F(1,178) = 3.97$, $p < .05$, on the dichotomous verdicts. Subjects from the ballistics expert–no judicial instructions conditions rendered significantly more guilty verdicts (87%) than did jurors from the ballistics expert–judicial instructions conditions (65%), $t(\infty) = 2.38$, $p < .05$, the eyewitness–no judicial instructions conditions (68%), $t(\infty) = 2.05$, $p < .05$, and from the eyewitness–judicial instructions conditions (72%), $t(\infty) = 1.67$, $p < .10$ (see Table 4.3). No other main effects or interactions were significant. The proportion of guilty verdicts found in the no key witness control condition (88%) was not significantly different from those rendered in the experimental conditions. Interpretations of the differences found between the experimental groups are completely qualified by the high proportion of guilty verdicts rendered by the no key witness control condition subjects.

In summary, the results of our first experiment failed to support the discrediting failure effect; the results of the second experiment failed to replicate

Cavoukian (1980). It is not clear why some researchers find support for the discrediting failure effect (e.g. Loftus, Cavoukian) while others (e.g. Weinberg and Baron, the current authors) do not support it, even in experiments where exactly the same stimulus materials are used. It may be speculated that different subject populations, minor procedural differences, experimenter effects, Type II errors (Loftus, Cavoukian) or Type I errors (Weinberg and Baron, the current research)[3] may be causes of the discrepant pattern of results found to date.

A CONCEPTUAL REPLICATION ATTEMPT

The failures of Experiments 1 and 2 to replicate earlier results do not demonstrate that the discrediting failure effect is false, only that it is not so robust as some of the literature has implied. After all, Loftus and Cavoukian did support the hypothesis in three separate experiments. Therefore, we undertook a third experiment. One of its goals was to attempt to determine how

Table 4.3 Percentage of guilty verdicts rendered in experiment 2 and Cavoukian (1980)

Study	Eyewitness (%)	Ballistics expert (%)	No key witness control (%)
No Judicial instructions			
Not discredited witness	70 (23)*	91 (23)	
Discredited witness	67 (24)	83 (23)	
			88 (24)
Judicial instructions			
Not discredited witness	78 (23)	64 (22)	
Discredited witness	67 (24)	67 (24)	
Cavoukian (1980)			
Not discredited witness	70	60	
			25
Discredited witness	80	35	

* Numbers in parentheses indicate the number of subjects per cell.

simulating jurors deal with eyewitness evidence and discrediting information during jury deliberations. A second goal of the experiment was to increase structural and conceptual verisimilitude over that provided in the Loftus and Cavoukian experiments. Even if the results of the two experiments reported above had been supportive of the discrediting failure effect, serious questions about external validity would remain. Among criticisms that could be levelled are the following. The experiments focused on the decisions of individual jurors whereas actual verdicts are rendered after group deliberations among jurors, all of whom have heard the evidence and who apply their joint 'common understanding' to the problem. The stimulus tasks were brief paper and pencil tasks whereas juries are exposed to longer, more complex oral (and visual) evidence. Relatedly, in both the Loftus and Cavoukian experiments the identification evidence constituted a very high proportion of the stimulus presentation: in actual trials, however, even when eyewitness testimony is the principal piece of evidence, it does not account for such a high percentage of the trial time. Thus, one may speculate that the discrediting failure effect, when found in these simulation experiments, may be due in part to the salience of the eyewitness testimony. Also, the Loftus stimulus materials failed to include closing judicial instructions stressing the reasonable doubt standard, a factor which might itself cause jurors to treat the evidence more cautiously. Of course, any simulation experiment can be criticized on additional grounds, such as that the jurors are making only hypothetical decisions, but the above factors would seem to have an especially important bearing on the external validity of an experiment.

Experiment 3, therefore, attempted to create a more approximate analogue of the courtroom process. The stimulus case was written to portray the adversary process, with opening and closing arguments by prosecution and defence and with witnesses being questioned in both direct examination and cross-examination. The materials also contained judicial instructions regarding the standard of reasonable doubt. While the testimony of the eyewitness was still the key element, the evidence also involved a substantial amount of circumstantial evidence that could be weighed in conjunction with the eye-witness testimony. Finally, the case was presented to groups of jurors who listened to the case via audiotape and who then deliberated and rendered a unanimous verdict. Because the deliberations were recorded the jury inter-action process could be studied to determine how the jurors discussed the evidence.

The content of the stimulus case for Experiment 3 involved a man breaking into a private home and stealing $280. While he was still in the home the owner returned and the thief fled. For the three experimental conditions the owner/eyewitness saw the thief climbing over the fence at the end of her backyard. In the eyewitness not discredited condition the eyewitness was portrayed as having no impairment of distance vision. In the eyewitness partially discredited condition as having 20/60 vision and in the eyewitness totally discredited condition the eyewitness had 20/400 vision. For the three experimental conditions the eyewitness was described as not wearing her glasses when she observed the thief running from the yard. A control condition consisting of circumstantial evidence but no testimony from an eyewitness was also included.

Method

Subjects. One hundred and sixty-seven introductory psychology students participated in the study in order partially to fulfil a course requirement. Three groups that failed to reach a unanimous verdict were removed from all analyses; 40 groups remained with 10 groups randomly assigned to each of the 4 conditions.

Procedure. Subjects were randomly assigned to mock jury groups of three to five members each. The only proviso regarding subject assignment was to have members of each gender in each jury whenever possible.

The experiment was conducted with one to five groups at a time. Groups of subjects were assigned randomly to juries and were taken to private rooms where they listened to one version of the stimulus case. After hearing the case each group was instructed to deliberate as a jury and to reach a unanimous verdict. Their deliberations were tape recorded. After rendering verdicts jurors from all groups completed individual questionnaires concerning the case. Subjects were then completely debriefed and thanked for their participation.

Dependent measures. There were three categories of dependent measures.
1. Group measures: Three unanimous measures of the group verdicts were collected: (a) a dichotomous verdict; (b) a rating of the degree of the accused's guilt (0 = not guilty to 10 = guilty); and, (c) a rating of confidence as to whether the accused actually committed the crime (0 = not at all confident he did to 10 = completely confident he committed the crime).
2. Individual measures: For both the accused's and eyewitness's testimony ratings of believability, accurateness, reliability, and honesty (all 9 point scales summed into one evaluative index for each witness) were collected from each juror.[4] The evaluation of the eyewitness's testimony was used to evaluate the success of the discrediting manipulation.
3. Jury deliberation measures: Two independent raters, blind to experimental condition, listened to each group's deliberation and coded the discussion of the eyewitness's testimony and the circumstantial evidence. Statements were coded a +1 if they were judged to be evaluating a single

piece of evidence as indicating the accused's guilt or a −1 if they were judged to be used to indicate the accused's innocence. For instance, the statement 'The money found in the accused's car was about the same as what was stolen and seems suspicious' would be coded a +1 while the statement 'The money found in the car proves nothing; anyone can keep money in their car' would be coded a −1. For each individual piece of evidence discussed the dependent measure was the number of statements indicating the accused's guilt divided by the total number of statements made by the jurors regarding that evidence. As the interjudge reliabilities were high for all measures (all r's (40) > .95, all p's < .001) the mean of the two judges' ratings was used in all analyses of the group discussions.

Results and discussion

Manipulation check. The individual jurors' combined ratings of the eyewitness's testimony were analysed by a hierarchical ANOVA in which jury group was nested in eyewitness condition. This analysis revealed a significant main effect for eyewitness condition, $F(2,27)$ = 5.13, p < .02. Jurors in the eyewitness not discredited condition (M = 10.3) rated the eyewitness's testimony significantly (p's < .01) more positively than did jurors from either the eyewitness partially discredited (M = 15.2) or eyewitness totally discredited (M = 14.4) conditions. This lower evaluation of the eyewitness in the two eyewitness discredited conditions is evidence that the discrediting manipulation was successful.

The overall ANOVA on the ratings of the eyewitness's testimony also revealed a significant main effect for jury group, F (27, 87) = 2.17, p < .01. Tests of simple main effects revealed that there was a significant variability in the ratings of the eyewitness's testimony across the partially discredited, F (9, 87) = 2.28, p < .05, and totally discredited, $F(9, 87)$ = 3.05, p < .01, eyewitness conditions while the groups in the eyewitness not discredited condition did not differ significantly, $F(9, 87)$ = 1.38, n.s. This appears to indicate that the discrediting manipulations were differentially effective across groups in both conditions where the eyewitness was discredited.

Group measures. A one way ANOVA of the dichotomous verdict revealed a significant main effect for eyewitness condition, $F(3, 36)$ = 11.76, p < .001. Groups from the eyewitness not discredited (90%), the eyewitness partially discredited (50%), and the eyewitness totally discredited (80%) conditions all rendered significantly more (p's < .05) guilty verdicts than did groups in the no eyewitness control condition (0%). Juries from the three eyewitness conditions did not significantly differ from each other in the proportion of guilty verdicts found. The results of the other two group measures, the ratings of the degree of the accused's guilt and whether he actually committed the crime, followed exactly the same pattern as the dichotomous verdicts, F's $(3, 36) = 29.73$ and 15.93, p's $< .001$, respectively.

Thus, the pattern of verdicts found in this experiment is consistent with the Loftus (1974) results and supports the discrediting failure effect. The rest of the experiment was aimed at examining the manner in which the juries dealt with the eyewitness evidence.

Group deliberation measures. One method of examining *how* the juries deal with the eyewitness's testimony is to analyse their deliberations. Analysis of the three eyewitness conditions' jury deliberations concerning the eyewitness's testimony revealed a significant main effect for eyewitness condition, $F(2, 22) = 3.84$, $p < .05$, on the proportion of 'guilt indicated' statements concerning the eyewitness's testimony.[5] Juries in the eyewitness not discredited condition $(M = .80)$ evaluated the eyewitness's testimony as indicating the accused's guilt significantly more often than did juries in the eyewitness partially discredited, $M = .40$, $p < .02$, or the eyewitness totally discredited, $M = .67$, $p < .10$ conditions (see Table 4.4). Thus, jury groups in the two discredited conditions tended to be less accepting of the eyewitness's testimony than were groups in the eyewitness not discredited condition.

Table 4.4   Jury groups' oral evaluations of the evidence in experiment 3[†]

Evidence	Condition			
	No eyewitness	Eyewitness	Eyewitness partially discredited	Eyewitness totally discredited
Eyewitness testimony	N/A	.80 a‡	.40 b	.67 ab
Money	.49 a	.91 b	.89 b	.89 b
Scraped hand	.47 a	.85 b	.82 b	.88 b

† Table values are the mean number of jury statements about each piece of evidence that are used to indicate the accused's guilt divided by the total number of statements about that evidence.

‡ Means within the same row with the same subscript do not differ significantly at the .05 level.

Another way of investigating the impact of eyewitness testimony is to examine how the other evidence in the case is evaluated in light of the eyewitness's report. One piece of circumstantial evidence in the case which was common to all four conditions was a sum of money found in the accused's automobile when he was arrested. An ANOVA of the evaluation of this evidence revealed a significant main effect for condition, $F(3, 28) = 9.28$, $p < .001$. Juries in the no eyewitness control condition were not overly impressed by this piece of evidence as about half $(M = .49)$ of the statements evaluating it were positive and half were negative. On the other hand, juries from the eyewitness not discredited ($M = .91$), eyewitness partially discredited ($M = .89$), and the eyewitness totally discredited ($M = .89$) conditions all evaluated this evidence as significantly more indicative of guilt than did the control group jurors (p's $< .001$). Discussions of the other pieces of circumstantial evidence, such as the accused's scraped hand, followed similar patterns (see Table 4.4).[6]

In summary, examination of the juries' deliberations revealed that juries in the discredited eyewitness conditions were less impressed by the eyewitness's testimony than were juries exposed to the eyewitness who was not discredited. However, juries from all three conditions where an eyewitness testified were more impressed by the circumstantial evidence than were juries in the control condition which contained no testimony from an eyewitness.

Individual measures. Further evidence of how eyewitness testimony may affect the evaluation of other evidence in a trial may be found by examining the individual jurors' evaluations of the accused's testimony. A hierarchical ANOVA, with jury group nested within experimental conditions, revealed a significant main effect for eyewitness condition, $F(3, 36) = 26.75, p < .001$, on the evaluative index measure of the accused's testimony. The jury group main effect was not significant, $F(36, 114) = 1.32$, n.s. Jurors in the no eyewitness control condition ($M = 15.9$) rated the accused's testimony significantly (p's $< .001$) more positively than did jurors from the eyewitness not discredited ($M = 28.0$), eyewitness partially discredited ($M = 23.9$), and eyewitness totally discredited ($M = 26.6$) conditions. Further, jurors in the eyewitness not discredited condition evaluated the accused's testimony significantly more negatively than jurors in the eyewitness partially discredited ($p < .001$) and the eyewitness totally discredited ($p < .10$) conditions.

In summary, analyses of both the groups' deliberations and the individual subjects' ratings of testimony offer converging evidence regarding the potential effects of eyewitness testimony. It appears that testimony from an eyewitness, whether it is subsequently discredited or not, may systematically affect the evaluations of the other evidence and testimony in a trial. Specifically, jurors in the three eyewitness conditions tended to be more accepting of the circum-stantial evidence and more critical of the defendant's testimony than were jurors in the control condition. It is important to note that the increase in the weight assigned to the other evidence in the trial occurred in both the dis-credited and in the not discredited eyewitness conditions. Thus, it is possible that eyewitness reports may affect juries' verdicts because they change the context in which the other evidence in the trial is evaluated. It appears that this reweighting of the circumstantial evidence, and not the belief in *what* the eyewitness was reporting, may account for the verdicts rendered by the juries in the discredited eyewitness conditions. Juries in the not discredited eyewitness condition appear to have been influenced by both the information in the testimony and the reweighting of the other evidence caused by the eyewitness's testimony.

One potential implication on this finding is that the effects of eyewitness testimony may be more difficult to counteract than previous authors have considered. Methods aimed at increasing the jurors' scepticism regarding an eyewitness's testimony may cause the eyewitness to be discounted, but the evaluation of the other evidence in the trial may remain at an inappropriate level.

CONCLUSIONS AND RESEARCH PROSPECTUS

In this concluding section we will first address our attention to the discrediting failure hypothesis; we then expand our discussion to make a critique of other research bearing on the more general issue of whether jurors give too much weight to eyewitness evidence.

The discrediting failure hypothesis

The empirical results reported in this chapter are contradictory, but they mirror prior research findings about the discrediting failure effect. The results of the first two experiments, viewed in conjunction with the two experiments reported by Weinberg and Baron (in press), raise serious questions about the robustness of the effect first reported by Loftus (1974). On the other hand the results of our third experiment, while not without qualification, yield some support for the discrediting failure effect and, more important, suggest potential cognitive mechanisms by which the effect may be produced.

The question naturally arises, where do we go from here? One may be tempted to search for explanations of the replication failure in terms of subtle methodological differences, subject population differences, or experimental demand characteristics. But, such an approach begs the more important issue, namely the robustness of the discrediting failure effect. A more beneficial approach is to start from the beginning and reconceptualize the issues surrounding the controversy about the effects of eyewitness testimony on jury decisions. We anticipate future research occurring on two levels: (1) research examining the dimensions which relate to the discrediting failure hypothesis; and (2) conceptualizations and research devoted to the broader issue of the potentially deleterious effect of eyewitness evidence, or what might be entitled the 'juror credulity hypothesis'.

Research on the discrediting failure effect clearly requires more sophisticated theoretical and analytical underpinnings than, heretofore, have been considered. Until this point the research has asked, does discredited eyewitness testimony have an undue impact on jurors? The proper question would seem to be the following: Under what conditions and how does it have an undue impact on the jury? The first step in building such a theoretical base is to define the parameters and dimensions related to the first part of the question. The major parameters associated with the theoretical base can be subsumed under three categories of variables which we can label as legal variables, process variables, and eyewitness variables.

The legal variables here are those associated with the basic legal structure of the case. The type of crime is one important consideration, and although we know nothing about the relative impact of the eyewitness on the jury, Kalven and Zeisel's (1966, pp. 142–143) research indicates that the probability of an eyewitness being called depends upon the type of crime. A second and extremely crucial consideration is the degree to which the eyewitness forms a part of the prosecution's case. The importance of the identification can range along a continuum defined at one end by instances in which the prosecution's case hinges entirely around a single eyewitness and at the other end by instances in which the eyewitness testimony is supplemented by substantial amounts of circumstantial evidence or the testimony of other witnesses. The Loftus stimulus case was close to the 'eyewitness only' end of the continuum, the Cavoukian case was slightly less extreme and our own stimulus case was slightly further from the end still. Discussion of the issue of eyewitness unreliability has been directed primarily towards cases falling towards the 'eyewitness only' end of the continuum, though this fact has not been adequately articulated in the psychological research literature. But it is an important point. The number of actual cases falling at the extreme end is probably low (field surveys could provide data on this). In most cases there is some additional circumstantial or other evidence and the results of Experiment 3 indicate that this other evidence is evaluated in the context of the eyewitness testimony. It is therefore important to know where along this continuum eyewitness unreliability becomes a crucial factor. The construction of cases for simulation experiments must take this dimension into account in investigating the discrediting failure effect.

The process variables include the mode by which the eyewitness is discredited. In the Loftus (1974) case the evidence contradicting the witness was presented as a summary of the defence attorney's case: 'Counsel for the defence showed that this witness had not been wearing his glasses on the day of the robbery, and since his vision was poorer than 20/400, he could not have seen the face of the robber from where he stood.' Aside from the issue of whether a summary sentence adequately represents the stimulus richness of a real trial, there is the additional issue of the credibility of the discrediting since the simulating jurors might rightfully have treated evidence emanating from the defence attorney as suspect. Cavoukian's (1980) stimulus case presented more detail about the discrediting than Loftus's. The materials in our third experiment, again involving absence of glasses and 20/400 vision, were even more detailed, and contained a contradictory statement by the witness herself during cross-examination (see Saunders, 1981, Appendix A). In the Hatvany and Strack (1981) study the witness was not only discredited, she admitted her error and retracted her testimony. Thus, the discrediting manipulations may be seen to run from Loftus's very weak manipulation to Hatvany and Strack's manipulation that was so strong that one could expect the testimony not to have much impact on jury decision-making.

These examples only touch upon some of the ways in which testimony can be discredited. In a real trial, for example, an optometrist might be called to testify about faulty vision, there may be additional eyewitnesses who contradict the key eyewitness or the defendant may produce his own witnesses to support his alibi and whose testimony, if believed, *ipso loquitor* discredits the eyewitness. These various forms of discrediting may have different effects on the evaluation of the eyewitness testimony or upon the evaluation of other pieces of evidence. Needless to say, the balance of the quantity and quality of evidence presented by the eyewitness compared with that produced in the discrediting process should be the crucial factor in determination of an eyewitness effect.

The third category of variables involves those associated with the witnesses themselves. These include such characteristics as the witness's appearance of confidence, competence, consistency, and style of presentation. Wells *et al.* (1979) have begun to investigate the confidence dimension. Lind and O'Barr (1979) have shown in a slightly different context that style of delivery also affects juror judgments. These individual characteristics will also interact with the discrediting process variables, although in ways that we cannot as yet predict.

In addition to the question of if and when discredited eyewitness identification has undue impact, it is important to begin to specify how it has this impact. Loftus's (1974) original experiment did not attempt to define the underlying process by which discrediting was assumed to be ineffective, but Cavoukian (1980), set forth the hypothesis that the initial eyewitness identification of the defendant helps to create an impression or stereotype of the defendant as a criminal. Even when the testimony that led to the stereotype is discredited, the stereotype persists and ultimately moves the jurors towards a verdict of guilty. Cavoukian's research provides two streams of indirect evidence which combine to support her hypothesis. First, when evidence by other experts, such as a handwriting or ballistics expert, was discredited jurors moved away from verdicts of guilty. Second, in another experiment she found that eyewitness identification, discredited or not, caused subjects to ascribe more criminal traits to the defendant on a 'criminal stereotype' scale whereas the testimony of other experts, discredited or not, did not lead to more ascription of such traits than a control condition with no witnesses. These data suggest there is something unique about eyewitness identification, such that it tends to create a stereotype.

Hatvany and Strack (1981) proposed a perseverance hypothesis not dissimilar to the Cavoukian hypothesis except that the criminal stereotype was not specifically posited. Those authors drew upon person perception literature suggesting that after receiving initial information about another person we tend to generate explanations or causal scenarios that form the basis of an impression. Other data suggest that even when the initial information that led to the impression is subsequently undermined the impression will persist. Hence, the initial identification of an accused causes jurors to develop an impression of guilt, but the subsequent discrediting of that information fails to change the impression. Though Hatvany and Strack did not get a perseverance effect, their hypothesis remains a viable one. The analysis of the jury deliberations in our own third experiment leads to a somewhat different hypothesis. Specifically, it suggests that the original eyewitness identification enhances the weight given to other pieces of information that could be construed as pointing to the defendant's guilt. Even if the discrediting of the eyewitness is effective, the changed weight of the other information will remain and ultimately tip the decision towards guilt. None of these three proposed hypotheses is necessarily contradictory of the others and they all begin to suggest why discrediting might be ineffective — if it is.

The juror credulity hypothesis

While the more sophisticated conceptual approach outlined above should lead to a better understanding of the discrediting process, it is important to place the discrediting failure hypothesis in context. In fact it bears on only one aspect of the issue of whether jurors are over-believing of eyewitness evidence. There is a danger that by focusing on discrediting we will lose sight of this broader issue. Even if discrediting were ultimately shown to be effective in cancelling eyewitness testimony (i.e. the discrediting failure hypothesis was rejected), critics could still argue that jurors are too credulous of eyewitness evidence because they lack information about psychological sources of error in witnesses or because they focus on the wrong characteristics as indicants of witness accuracy.

The 'staged incident' paradigm, as exemplified by the work of Wells and his associates (Wells et al., 1979; Wells et al., 1980), is probably a more profitable approach to understanding the issue of juror credulity. Briefly, this approach involves exposing witnesses to a staged crime and then examining how other subjects ('evaluators' or mock jurors) evaluate the eyewitnesses' reports. As noted earlier, one important finding from this research is that simulating jurors apparently place substantial weight upon the confidence of the eyewitness even though confidence appears to be unrelated to accuracy (see Deffenbacher, 1980; Wells et al., 1979).

There is, however, a problem in applying existing research from the staged incident paradigm to the juror credulity hypothesis. First, Wells and his colleagues have focused on the eyewitness independent of other trial evidence in an attempt to obtain 'a "pure" measure of how well people can judge the validity of eyewitness accounts. . .' (Wells et al., 1980, p. 277). Second, and relatedly, they have focused on evaluations of the witness rather than on verdicts. As already noted, over 70 years ago Wigmore (1909) stressed the importance of considering the relation between the totality of evidence and jury verdicts. The early research by Marston (1924), while not without methodological problems as viewed by today's standards, helps to illustrate Wigmore's point. Marston used a staged incident paradigm and found that individual eyewitnesses were often inaccurate. He also found, however, that triers of fact who read the witnesses' accounts were able to re-create the original incident with greater accuracy than the witnesses themselves. The results of our Experiment 3 indicate the importance of the totality of evidence in another way, namely that the presence of eyewitness evidence influences the weight given to other evidence. As with research using the discrediting paradigm, the staged incident paradigm would do well to examine the verdicts of deliberating juries (see, e.g. Hosch et al. 1980; Loftus, 1980), not only because it increases the external validity of the research, but also because analysis of group deliberations provides a means of determining how both individuals and the group utilize the evidence. In brief, the staged incident paradigm has considerable potential to shed light on the juror credulity hypothesis, but no clear picture will emerge until it is used to study the verdict-making process.[7]

Two additional points about research on the juror credulity hypothesis deserve to be made. The first is that while we have centred our attention on simulation research it is not the only way to study the problem. On the whole social psychologists interested in the jury have demonstrated little ingenuity in using field research methods and, indeed, often appear reluctant to study the problem in situ (see Ebbesen and Konecni, 1975; Vidmar, 1979 for discussions). The methodological difficulties, however, are not insurmountable, and the information gain is potentially great. Myers (1979), for example, studied prosecutors' notes as a way of shedding insight on jury performance in 201 felony cases that went to trial. She concluded that juries assigned little weight to evidence from eyewitnesses. Eyewitness evidence was not a major focus of her study but her results suggest that archival records may be a promising way of investigating such issues as the juror credulity hypothesis. Kalven and Zeisel (1966) also devoted little attention to the problem of the eyewitness (see pp. 137–138 and 142–143) but their approach could also be utilized. As it is, their data indicate that, aside from the complainant, eyewitnesses appear in 31% of all trials, that the eyewitness is much more likely to be called by the prosecution than the defence; and that the likelihood of an eyewitness being called varies with the type of crime. Their data also suggest something about eyewitness impact. For example, there was no relationship between eyewitnesses appearing, and judges' estimates of the overall strength of the evidence against the defendant. Field studies of the eyewitness at trial, we suggest, can tell us much about the impact of eyewitness testimony on jurors.

The second point concerns the selection of variables to be investigated, and subtle biases in the selection process (see Vidmar, 1979). There has been a tendency for research psychologists to take as given that jurors are too credulous and to proceed to investigate procedural remedies, such as expert psychological testimony (e.g. Hosch *et al.*, 1980; Loftus, 1980; Wells *et al.*, 1980). But even if research confirms that jurors are indeed over-credulous of eyewitness testimony, it is worth noting that none of these studies has included as an experimental condition the more conservative remedy, namely judicial cautionary instructions such as those given approbation in *US* v. *Telfaire* (1972). Such instructions may suffice to correct juror credulity without resorting to expert psychological testimony (for an opposing opinion, see Woocher, 1977). Research designs, therefore, should incorporate judicial instructions as a factor: the effectiveness of such instructions provides an appropriate standard against which to evaluate the benefits of expert psychological testimony.

Summary

It is the authors' position that the importance of research on eyewitness identification depends upon the demonstration that it has an adverse effect on jury verdicts. A review of the studies addressing the 'discrediting failure' effect indicates inconsistent support for this hypothesis. It was noted, however, that the discrediting failure effect is only one small portion of the broader juror credulity hypothesis. A number of suggestions and guidelines for future research concerning jury evaluations of eyewitness testimony were made. The possibility that jurors may be over-credulous of eyewitness evidence remains an important problem that deserves concentrated research attention.

NOTES

This research was supported, in part, by a Social Science and Humanities Research Council of Canada grant to the second author. The authors would like to thank William Fisher, Tory Higgins, Richard Sorrentino, and Jim Olson for their helpful comments regarding many aspects of this research. Portions of this chapter were presented at the Midwestern Psychological Association meeting, Detroit, April 1981, and the Canadian Psychological Association meeting, Toronto, June 1981.

1.   All tests of means reported in this chapter are two-tailed t-tests based on the within cell error term of the appropriate ANOVA (Carmer and Swanson, 1973).

2. Comparisons of the control groups and experimental groups in experiments one and two were done with a procedure recommended by Himmelfarb (1975).
3. (Editor's note) A Type I error has occurred when a false research hypothesis is accepted as true, and a Type II error has occurred when a true research hypothesis is rejected as false.
4. Clearly, ratings of the eyewitness's testimony were not collected from the no eyewitness control condition subjects. All analyses of the ratings of the eyewitness are across the three experimental conditions only.
5. The degrees of freedom in the analysis of the group discussion measures vary as only data from groups which discussed a given piece of evidence were included in the analyses. Most of the instances of not discussing a piece of evidence were due to groups reaching a rapid verdict in the case. Chi-square analyses indicated that these 'immediate verdict' groups were randomly distributed over conditions.
6. A more complete discussion of these results may be found in Saunders (1981). One further point concerning the stimulus case deserves mention. The eyewitness in the three eyewitness conditions described the clothes that the thief was wearing (blue jeans and a black coat), while this information was not available to the juries in the no eyewitness control condition. While it is possible that this additional piece of circumstantial evidence could account for any differences between experimental and control conditions, it is unlikely as this clothing is fairly common (a point made by many juries in their deliberations). It is possible, however, that this additional 'evidence' could account for the increased weight assigned to the other circumstantial evidence in the case.
7. In their latest study using the staged incident paradigm, Wells and his associates (Wells et al., in press) have begun to address these issues.

REFERENCES

Buckhout, R. (1976). Psychology and eyewitness identification. *Law and Psychology Review*, **2**, 75–91.

Carmer, S.G. and Swanson, M.R. (1973). An evaluation of ten pairwise multiple comparison procedures by Monte Carlo methods. *Journal of the American Statistical Association*, **68**, 66–74.

Cavoukian, A. (1980). *The influence of eyewitness identification evidence*. Unpublished doctoral dissertation, University of Toronto.

Deffenbacher, K.A. (1980). Eyewitness accuracy and confidence: Can we infer anything about their relationship? *Law and Human Behavior, 4*, 243–260.

Ebbesen, E.B. and Konecni, V.J. (1975). Decision making and information integration in the courts: The setting of bail. *Journal of Personality and Social Psychology*, **32**, 805–821.

Hatvany, N. and Strack, F. (1981). The impact of a discredited key witness. *Journal of Applied Social Psychology*, **10**, 490–509.

Himmelfarb, S. (1975). What to do when the control group doesn't fit into the factorial design? *Psychological Bulletin*, **82**, 363–368.

Hosch, H.M. (1980). Commentary: A comparison of three studies of the influence of export testimony on jurors. *Law and Human Behavior*, **4**, 297–302.

Hosch, H.M., Beck, E.L., and McIntyre, P. (1980). Influence of expert testimony regarding eyewitness accuracy on jury decisions. *Law and Human Behavior*, **4**, 287–296.

Kalven, H., Jr. and Zeisel, H. (1966). *The American Jury*. Chicago: University of Chicago Press.

Lezak, M.D. (1973). Some psychological limitations on witness reliability. *Wayne Law Review*, **20**, 117–133.

Lind, E.A. and O'Barr, W.M. (1979). The social significance of speech in the courtroom. In H. Giles and R.N. St. Clair (eds), *Language and Social Psychology*. Oxford: Basil Blackwell.

Loftus, E.F. (1974). The incredible eyewitness. *Psychology Today*, **8**(7), 116–119.

Loftus, E.F. (1975). Leading questions and the eyewitness report. *Cognitive Psychology*, **7**, 560–572.

Loftus, E.F. (1979). *Eyewitness Testimony*. Cambridge, Mass.: Harvard University Press.

Loftus, E.F. (1980). Impact of expert psychological testimony on the unreliability of eyewitness identifications. *Journal of Applied Psychology*, **65**, 9–15.

Lunney, G.H. (1970) Using analysis of variance with a dichotomous dependent variable: An empirical study. *Journal of Educational Measurement*, **7**, 263–269.

Marston, W.H. (1924). Studies in testimony. *Journal of Criminal Law and Criminology*, **15**, 5–32.

Munsterberg, H. (1908). *On the Witness Stand*. New York: Doubleday.

Myers, M.A. (1979). Rule departures and making the law: Juries and their verdicts. *Law and Society Review*, **13**, 781–797.

People v. *Casey*. No. 2, (1963) I.R. 33, apld.

Regina v. *Spatola*. (1970), 10 C.R.N.S. 153.

Saunders, D.M. (1981). *Discredited eyewitness evidence and jury deliberations*. Unpublished master's thesis. University of Western Ontario.

Simon, R.J. (1967). *The Jury and the Defence of Insanity*. Toronto: Little Brown.

Starkman, D. (1979). The use of eyewitness identification in criminal trials. *Criminal Law Quarterly*, **21**, 361–386.

United States v. *Telfaire*. (1972). 469 F. 2d 552.

United States v. *Wade*. (1967). 388 U.S. 218.

Vidmar, N. (1979). The other issues in jury simulation research: A commentary with particular reference to defendant character studies. *Law and Human Behavior*, **3**, 95–106.

Weinberg, H.I. and Baron, R.S. The discredible eyewitness. *Personality and Social Psychology Bulletin*, in press.

Wells, G.L., Ferguson, T.J., and Lindsay, R.C.L. The tractability of eyewitness confidence and its implications for triers of fact. *Journal of Applied Psychology*, in press.

Wells, G.L., Lindsay, R.C.L. and Ferguson, T.J. (1979). Accuracy, confidence, and juror perceptions in eyewitness identifications. *Journal of Applied Psychology*, **64**, 440–448.

Wells, G.L.. Lindsay, R.C.L., and Tousignant, J.P. (1980). Effects of expert psychological advice on human performance in judging the validity of eyewitness testimony. *Law and Human Behavior*, **4**, 275–285.

Wigmore, J.H. (1909). Professor Munsterberg and the psychology of evidence. *Illinois Law Review*, **3**, 399–445.

Woocher, F.D. (1977). Did your eyes deceive you? Expert psychological testimony on the unreliability of eyewitness identification. *Stanford Law Review*, **29**, 969–1030.

Yarmey, A.D. (1979). *The Psychology of Eyewitness Testimony*. New York: Free Press.

PART II

TECHNIQUES OF MAXIMIZING AND EVALUATING THE RELIABILITY OF EVIDENCE

Evaluating Witness Evidence
Edited by S.M.A. Lloyd-Bostock and B.R. Clifford
© 1983 John Wiley & Sons Ltd.

Chapter 5

Measuring the Fairness of Eyewitness Identification Lineups

Roy. S. Malpass and Patricia G. Devine

Fairness in lineup construction is important to both legal scholars and psychological researchers. However, even the best, most focused and most ambitious of the legal literature provides only very general guidelines for the physical construction of lineups and provides no measurement criterion against which the success of the attempt to construct a fair lineup can be evaluated. (Brooks, 1980; Devlin, 1976; LaSota and Bromley, 1974; Sobel, 1972; Wall, 1965). Psychological research has, with few exceptions, glossed over the issue. Wells *et al.* (1979) assess the fairness issue in the following terms: 'Current courtroom discussions of lineup fairness are subjective and confusing, with no empirical or scientific base. Law enforcement officials have not been provided with specific criteria by which they can assess their own procedures, and the logical issue of a fair lineup is often phrased in confusing, ill-defined verbal statements.' (p. 291) Guidelines for the conduct of eyewitness identifications focus primarily on reducing the *suggestiveness* of the identification situation (Sobel, 1972). Suggestiveness refers to any attribute of lineup procedure or lineup structure that implies to the witness that the lineup contains the offender or that a particular individual is the suspect.[1] Preventing suggestiveness which arises from lineup structure generally focuses on avoiding distinctiveness in the suspect's appearance which would indicate his identity to a witness. Authorities generally recommend that lineup participants should be of the same sex and race, of approximately the same age, height, and build, have similar hair length and colour, and be similar in general demeanour and position in life.

The British Home Office Circular No. 9/1969 (reproduced in Devlin, 1976, pp. 158–161) states that 'Identification parades should be fair and should be seen to be fair. Every precaution should be taken to see that they are, and, in particular, to exclude any suspicion of unfairness or risk of erroneous identification through witnesses' attention being directed specially to the suspected person instead of equally to all persons paraded.' The revised edition (Home Office Circular, No. 109/1978) reaffirms this guidance. Methods for accomplishing these tasks and for assuring fairness are left unspecified, however. Because satisfactory means for measuring the fairness of the physical construction of lineups are not generally available, lineup construction and its evaluation often appear to be haphazard and the research literature in eyewitness identification contains many studies of questionable comparability. While it is difficult to estimate the frequency with which inadequate lineups are used in practice, clear documentation of some instances is available (Ellison and Buckhout, 1981; Biederman, 1980).

Although there is a small literature on the measurement of lineup fairness (Doob and Kirshenbaum, 1973; Malpass, 1981; Wells *et al*. 1979) a suitable conceptualization of fairness has not emerged, and the degree to which available measures respond to variations in the physical construction of lineups has not yet been investigated. Relating the fairness of lineups to their physical construction would aid in both their construction and evaluation. The validity of eyewitness testimony cannot be accepted without either assuming or demonstrating that the identification was fairly made, and the lack of acceptable measurement techniques renders imprecise both eyewitness evidence and its criticism. If the police knew what criteria would be applied to the evaluation of eyewitness evidence and if the relationship between fairness and the physical aspects of lineup construction were known, routine construction of fair lineups could be achieved. In addition, jurors would be aided in estimating the probative value of eyewitness testimony if they were presented with objective information of the fairness of lineup construction. The same information might also be useful in the plea bargaining process.

While lineup fairness is a substantive problem in the criminal justice system, it is a methodological issue in eyewitness identification research. The criteria used by eyewitness researchers for lineup construction are certainly no more rigorous, nor more consistently applied, than those suggested in the legal literature. For example, Buckhout *et al*. (1974) selected lineup members (foils) 'on the basis of their resemblance to the suspect' (p. 9); Egan *et al*. (1977) chose confederates 'to look alike: all were similar in height, body build and hair colour' (p. 201); Gorenstein and Ellsworth (1980) chose foils 'who in the experimenter's eyes, bore some resemblance to one another' (p. 619); and Malpass and Devine (1981) chose foils 'similar in height, body build and hair colour and style' (p. 484). This variability and lack of explicitness in lineup construction procedures underscores the need for objective measures of lineup fairness. As matters stand we cannot reliably attribute differences in identification rates between studies to the effect of different conditions or manipulations. As Wells (1978) points out, the differences may be an artefact of the method of lineup construction leading to variations in the relative distinctiveness of the 'offender' in comparison with the foils. The lack of standards of lineup construction and the absence of means of measuring lineup fairness raise the question of the replicability of results from eyewitness studies. With no metric for assessing lineup fairness the usefulness of findings from this research area for the criminal justice system is somewhat limited. Thus the quantification of lineup fairness is an important research problem as well as an important substantive problem for law enforcement personnel.

A few studies in the eyewitness identification literature have attempted to deal with the measurement of lineup fairness using conventional statistical techniques. At this level of analysis, fairness can be defined as the failure of the identifications made to depart significantly from chance expectation. For example, the distribution of choices across all lineup members made by a suitably large group of 'witnesses' can be tested for departure from chance expectation by tests such as chi-squared (Malpass and Devine, 1981) or alternatively, the proportion of 'witnesses' choosing the suspect can be tested for its departure from chance expectation by statistical tests on proportions (Doob and Kirshenbaum, 1973). Recently, others have attempted to develop tests of lineup fairness specific to the identification context (Wells *et al.* 1979; Malpass, 1981). These measurements of lineup fairness will be described below. However it is important to note that their use has only been as a *post hoc* report on the fairness of lineup construction. These measures have not yet been related to processes for constructing fair lineups.

LINEUP FAIRNESS AND SUSPECT-FOIL SIMILARITY

A major difficulty with the evaluation of lineup fairness in the criminal justice system and in psychological research is the lack of a clear or comprehensive conceptual definition of lineup fairness. Yet the conditions that are believed to lead to unfairness seem to be well known and established. We will begin with a brief view of these conditions and develop from them a more differentiated conceptualization of 'fairness'. It will be useful to begin by contrasting lineups with simpler forms of identification procedures which illustrate the problems of identification in extreme ways. According to Devlin (1976) lineups originated in response to judicial criticism of more crude and suggestive methods of identification, particularly the *showup* (or confrontation). A showup presents the suspect singly to a witness who must say that the suspect is the offender, or that the suspect is not the offender, or that he/she cannot make a determination. Showups are unfair because they suggest directly who is the police suspect. The cooperative or compliant witness who feels constrained to identify someone has only the one alternative from which to choose. Although lineups suggest to the witness that the police suspect is among those in the lineup it is not necessarily apparent which lineup member is the police suspect. A lineup is in principle more fair than a showup because it distributes the probability of identification of an innocent suspect across the lineup foils, reducing the risk of an identification error. This probability is a decreasing function of the number of individuals in the lineup: $1/N$ where N = the number of persons in the lineup (the lineup's nominal size). The absolute level of this probability that is acceptable is not precisely defined, but appears to vary between .167 (when there are six lineup members, a minimum size often suggested in the United States) and .10 (when there are 10 lineup members, a figure frequently mentioned).

A major point shared by all the guidelines we have reviewed for the construction of fair lineups is that the foils should be selected so as to be similar in appearance to the suspect. Wall (1965) points out that this obvious point 'is emphasized whenever proper lineup procedures are discussed' (p. 53), and cites Rolph's contention that for a lineup to test fairly and adequately the witness's ability to discriminate the offender from other lineup participants, the witness 'must never be directed to the suspected person in particular instead of indifferently to all the people paraded' (pp. 40–41). Shepherd *et al.* (1980) point out that to serve this function most rules of lineup construction demand that other lineup members be similar in appearance to the suspect on the dimensions of similarity previously mentioned (e.g. sex, race, height, etc.). For the suspect to be distinctive suggests to witnesses the identity of the police suspect and is therefore suggestive and unfair. The reasoning behind requiring similarity of lineup participants appears to be that witnesses to criminal events possess information about the unique and individual appearance of the offender and that they will therefore be able to distinguish between the offender (should he/she be present in the lineup) and others who possess the same general characteristics but whose individual appearance is not identical. Thus similarity of lineup members serves primarily to protect innocent suspects, and not to hinder the identification of the guilty.

TWO ASPECTS OF FAIRNESS: SIZE AND BIAS

Two distinct principles of lineup fairness are embedded in this discussion, and the legal considerations on which it is based: (1) that lineups should be of sufficient size that the probability of a chance identification of an innocent suspect is low — that the potential for errors is distributed across a number of persons; and (2) that the suspect must not be distinctive in comparison with the foils. These two principles focus on different aspects of lineup fairness, and a lineup is fair only if it satisfies both of them. We will refer to the first of these as lineup *size*, and the second as lineup *bias*. The size and bias aspects of lineup fairness refer to quite different levels of analysis of the lineup. The size question considers the lineup as an aggregate, whereas the bias question considers only the suspect while ignoring any variations that exist among the foils. Both size and bias are affected by the relative probabilities of lineup members being identified as the offender in the absence of the unique information about the offender's identity possessed by an eyewitness. Both are based on the similarity of the lineup foils to the suspect and to each other. The question of a lineup's *size* focuses on whether one or more members of the lineup are identified sufficiently less than expected so that they can be considered implausible foils, thereby reducing the number of people actually in the lineup, and increasing the absolute level of risk of having the suspect erroneously identified. The question of *bias* focuses on whether the suspect is identified sufficiently more or less than expected so that the lineup should be considered biased towards or away from the identification of the suspect.

While the size and bias attributes of a lineup are conceptually distinct they will be empiricially related because they both result from departures of identification probabilities from expectation in a situation where the choice probabilities of the various members of the lineup are not independent of each other. If the identification frequencies that are not drawn by an implausible foil are drawn instead by the suspect, then the resulting decrease in lineup size will also be reflected in an increase in bias towards the suspect. If these same frequencies instead are distributed only among the remaining foils, the reduction in size will not be reflected in bias. Likewise, if an increase in preference for the suspect (bias) is present, the degree to which a corresponding reduction in size will also occur depends on whether these identifications were drawn equally from all the foils, or whether they came disproportionately from one or more foils.

Lineup size

The idea of constructing lineups of sufficient size is basic to all conceptions of the lineup we have read and is basic to the various guidelines suggested. Increasing the nominal size of an identification procedure from one (a showup) to some suitably large number is a strategy for reducing the risk of a false identification, and preserving the fairness of the identification in the face of the problems of suggestiveness inherent in any identification situation. To work as a strategy for attaining greater fairness, however, the lineup foils must be plausible alternatives to the suspect and therefore must be generally similar in their appearance and generally similar in appearance to the suspect (Wells *et al*., 1979). There can be many different patterns of departure from a homogeneous state of similarity among lineup members, and different patterns affect the fairness of the lineup in different ways (Malpass, 1981). Consider, for example, a lineup containing a suspect and nine foils, four of whom are not sufficiently similar to the suspect (or to the description of the offender) to be plausible choice alternatives (see Lineup 1, Table 5.1). This lineup would contain one cluster of six plausible alternatives (including the suspect) and four implausible alternatives. One could argue that these four might as well not be included in the lineup (Malpass 1981; Wells *et al*., 1979) and the lineup's size should be considered six instead of the nominal size of ten. Following this line of reasoning, the consequence of the dissimilarity of these four foils in comparison with the remaining members of the lineup would be for the size of the lineup to be reduced from its nominal size. As a consequence, the absolute size of the probability of a false identification may increase, reducing the lineup's fairness. Consider also a lineup in which the nine foils are similar with respect to each other, but are not highly similar to the suspect who, in addition, fits the description of the offender better than do the foils. In this case the most plausible lineup alternative is the suspect — who stands essentially alone. A lineup of this kind would be radically smaller than its nominal size, to the extent that it is essentially a showup, with the suspect the only plausible alternative. These examples help to define an important dimension of lineup fairness where fairness is a direct function of the degree to which the lineup departs from its nominal size, and in which the dissimilarity among lineup members is an important determinant.

Lineup bias

Another form of unfairness results when a suspect has a greater or less likelihood of being chosen than is expected by chance, based on the nominal size of the lineup. Some degree of bias is almost inevitable, in practice, and the extent of bias to be regarded as tolerable is a separate issue, discussed below. While the problem of lineup size focuses on the possibility that one or more of the foils will be identified with a probability less than expectation, the problem of bias focuses only on whether the identification of the suspect departs from expectation. If the suspect has an identification probability greater than expectation the lineup is biased towards the suspect; if the suspect has an identification probability less than expectation the lineup is biased away from the suspect. Thus in a lineup of two members the probability that each is chosen may be equal (as expected), and therefore fair in the bias sense, yet the lineup is too small to be considered fair in the size sense because the absolute level of the probability of an identification of an innocent suspect is too high (.50). Conversely, a lineup may contain nine acceptable foils, and yet be biased. Lineups 2 and 3 in Table 5.1. illustrate this possibility. Chance expectation is that each lineup member will be chosen as the offender with a probability of $1/N = .10$, and a departure from this value would indicate a bias towards or away from the suspect. The bias might have its source in a number of attributes of lineup structure or the identification process. If each foil has an identification probability of .09 (or if the foils have an *average* probability of identification of .09, as in Lineup 3, Table 5.1) and the suspect is identified with a probability of .19,

Table 5.1   Identification probabilities of suspect and foils in hypothetical lineups

Lineup	Suspect	1	2	3	4	5	6	7	8	9	TOTAL
1	.167	.167	.167	.167	.167	.167	00	00	00	00	1.00
2	.19	.09	.09	.09	.09	.09	.09	.09	.09	.09	1.00
3	.19	.085	.092	.086	.087	.094	.108	.086	.087	.085	1.00

the rate of identification of the suspect will be biased while the rate of identification of the foils will be at least as high as 85% of expectation. Assuming that 85% of expectation is an appropriate criterion for the acceptability of foils, these examples illustrate that a distribution of identification probabilities may be fair from a size point of view while the lineup may none the less be biased with respect to the suspect.

To summarize: there are two conceptually distinct aspects of lineup fairness: the lineup's *size* and the presence of *bias* towards or away from the suspect. A lineup is less than fair in the *bias* sense if the suspect is identified with a probability meaningfully greater or lesser than expected by chance. It is unfair in the *size* sense if the number of plausible choice alternatives in the lineup is less than the lineup's nominal size. The lineup's nominal size is in turn based on an *a priori* decision as to an appropriate level of risk to which innocent suspects may be exposed.

OBTAINING EMPIRICAL EVIDENCE ON THE SIMILARITY–FAIRNESS RELATIONSHIP

The notion that variations in the distribution of similarity among lineup members affect the lineup's fairness is a theoretical statement requiring validation. Studying the empirical relationship between lineup construction and witnesses' judgments requires independent measurements of these variables, obtained from samples of witnesses. Witnesses to crimes are usually scarce however, and cannot be used in methodological investigations of lineups that will later be used to test their judgment. In addition, the responses of real witnesses cannot be used to evaluate the fairness of the lineups which they observe, because their choices are a function of a number of independent sources of influence, including the information the witness has about the unique physical appearance of the offender, suggestiveness in the physical construction of the lineup, or suggestiveness in the procedures of the identification. There is no independent way to assess objectively the amount or quality of the information possessed by witnesses. Therefore, when a real witness identifies the police suspect from a lineup we cannot determine after the fact which of these sources was influential in the witness's decision, or how they were weighted. If the witness's identification is to be informative about the guilt or innocence of the suspect it should be based only on the witness's information of the offender's unique identity. Therefore, suggestiveness in lineup construction and procedure must be eliminated prior to the witness's judgment. Analogously, in order to show that a lineup is fair (not suggestive) from the point of view of its physical construction, both procedural suggestiveness and the presence of information about the unique identity of the offender must be absent when investigation of its fairness is being made. Demonstrations of the structural fairness of a lineup, therefore, cannot be based on the choices of real witnesses, who have information about the offenders' identity.

Doob and Kirshenbaum (1973) suggested that persons who had not actually witnessed an offence, i.e. mock witnesses, be given a description of the offender (as obtained from actual witnesses), be shown the actual lineup (or a photograph of it), and be asked to identify the offender from the lineup on the basis of the general description of the offender/suspect and whatever other information they find in the structure and procedure of the lineup. If the lineup is fair, all lineup participants should seem approximately equally plausible to mock witnesses and none should be preferred over the others. Real witnesses, however, who possess information about the unique physical appearance of the offender, should be able to identify him/her from among the (similar/plausible) foils if he/she is, in fact, present.

The use of mock witnesses also provides a means of quantifying the likelihood of the various members of a lineup being identified. With 100 mock witnesses, for example, one can obtain estimates of identification probabilities and evaluate the lineup's fairness. A reduction in the size of a lineup from its nominal size would be apparent in the pattern of mock witness identifications as a substantially lower than expected identification rated for one or more foils. Bias would be apparent as either a higher or lower than expected rate of identification of the suspect in a lineup containing a full complement of acceptable foils.

The major purpose of the research reported here is to explore the relationship between lineup construction and the two dimensions of lineup fairness: size and bias. The first step in the investigation of this relationship is to determine whether or not measures of lineup fairness do in fact respond to manipulations in the antecedent conditions that are theoretically viewed as responsible for variations in fairness: the similarity of the lineup members to each other and the suspect. The strategy we have pursued is to construct experimentally lineups that systematically vary in the degree of similarity between the 'suspect' and the lineup foils, to ask mock witnesses to choose the offender from a photographic lineup, and then to apply various measures of lineup fairness to the resulting distribution of mock witness choices for each lineup.

Method

Overview

Four photographic lineups were constructed, of varying similarity of the foils to the suspect. Mock witnesses were given a description of the offender, and were then asked to view one of the four lineups and identify him. Seven measures of the fairness of lineup construction were calculated on the basis of the mock witness's choices, and the four photographic lineups were compared on the basis of these measures.

Construction of photo lineups

Full length photographs of college age white males were taken standing before a white wall, facing the camera with feet apart (approximately 6 inches), one hand holding in full the other wrist, with a neutral gaze fixed on a position about 12 inches above the camera. Each person wore jeans, a white T-shirt and sneakers or running shoes, in order to keep a relatively constant background against which six dimensions of physical appearance were systematically varied. Consistency of dress is a commonly recommended attribute of lineups (Devlin, 1976; LaSota and Bromley, 1974; Sobel, 1972; Wall, 1965). These photographs were made into $5'' \times 7''$ colour prints, from which photo lineups were constructed. The individuals photographed were chosen because of their composite position on the following set of six dimensions.

Dimension	Level 1	Level 2	Level 3
Hair colour:	blonde	brown	black
Hair length:	short	medium	long
Hair style:	straight	wavy	curly
Height:	short	medium	tall
Build:	thin	medium	husky
Eye colour:	light	dark	

The boundaries of these categories as judged in photographs are not sharp, so a set of approximately 20 judges rated each photograph on each of these six dimensions, choosing which of the descriptors best characterized the person photographed. The average score across judges was the value of each photograph on each dimension. Each photograph was then given a discrepancy score, which was obtained in the following way. The 'offender/suspect'[2] was described as a young male, characterized by the Level 2 descriptors given above. His composite score was therefore 12.0 (the level of each dimension, summed across the six dimensions). The composite score of each of the photographs was obtained in the same way, summing the mean ratings given by the judges to each photograph across the dimensions. The absolute difference of this score from the suspect's score of 12.0 is then obtained. This is the photograph's discrepancy score which represents variations in similarity between the description of the suspect and the description of the foils as noted by the panel of judges. Since the most any photograph can differ from the suspect's description on any dimension is 1.0, the maximum discrepancy score that a photograph can obtain is 6.0 (1.0 summed across six dimensions). By selecting individual photographs with particular discrepancy scores, lineups can be constructed which have a range of composite similarities between the lineup foils and the suspect. Composite suspect–foil discrepancy for a lineup can be characterized by summing the individual discrepancies from the offender across foils. The lineups used in the present study contained a photograph of the suspect and each of five foils. An attempt was made to keep all foils in a given lineup approximately equally discrepant from the suspect. The dimensions on which the foils differed were systematically varied, however, so as not to be the same across the foils. For example, in Lineup D (Table 5.2) all lineup foils had a discrepancy level of at least 4.0, but the dimensions on which they were discrepant were not constant across the foils. The other lineups were constructed in a similar fashion. The lineups then, can potentially have discrepancy values ranging from 0.0 (where all foils fit the suspect's description) to 30.0 (where five foils differ from the suspect on six dimensions). Four lineups (A–D) were constructed with the suspect–foil discrepancy values indicated in Table 5.2. With lineups varying in discrepancy levels we examined the relationship between discrepancy level and lineup fairness with respect to both size and bias.

Mock witness identifications

Two hundred and forty mock witnesses, drawn from classes in the behavioural science disciplines were asked to make identifications. Some of the mock witnesses received course-credit for their participation. Each made the identification individually.

Mock witnesses were greeted individually, and given an informed consent document that described the study. They were then asked to read a two page summary of a breaking and entering incident which included the offender's description twice — once at approximately the midpoint of the summary and once at the end. Within a few minutes of having read the summary, mock witnesses were shown a photographic lineup which was displayed on a wooden easel, elevated about 45 degrees from the table on which the easel rested. The photographs were displayed behind a black matte-board frame which covered the borders between the photographic prints. Between each print the frame contained two white lines parallel to the base of the easel which served as height category boundaries.[3] This display was illuminated by four 15-watt Cool-White fluorescent tubes, placed immediately above the easel. After the mock witness was seated in front of the easel a cover placed over the display was removed and the witness was asked to identify the offender. Witnesses were allowed as much time as necessary without prodding from the experimenters. Immediately after their choice, mock witnesses were asked to note which, if any, of the persons in the lineup they knew personally. Witnesses rated each lineup participant on each of the six dimensions, completed a brief questionnaire, were thanked and then dismissed. Six different versions of each lineup were constructed so that across mock witnesses the suspect appeared in each of the six lineup positions (from left to right) approximately equally often.

Measures of lineup fairness

Seven measures of lineup fairness are presented below which are either standard statistical techniques which have previously been applied in eye-witness identification studies; or measures which have been designed specifically for evaluating lineup fairness. The mock witness data were evaluated on each of these measures. The first two focus on the distribution of choices across the members of the lineup. The second two focus specifically on the degree to which the lineup contains fewer plausible choice alternatives than its nominal size; and the last three focus on the degree to which the lineup is biased towards or away from the suspect. All involve comparison of the rates at which lineup members were chosen with the chance rates which could be expected if all members were equally plausible. However, each measure looks at a slightly different aspect of fairness, and the measures differ in the way in which information about the lineup is used or expressed.

Distribution of choices across members of the lineup
1. The chi-squared test: this evaluates whether the distribution of mock witness choices across the members of the lineup departs significantly from chance expectation.
2. The cumulative distribution of observed choice frequencies, expressed in units of expected frequency: this is less a measure and more a graphic expression of the departure of the observed choice distribution from chance expectation.

Lineup size
3. The number of mock witnesses identifying each individual, expressed as a proportion of expectation. This is an indication of the degree to which a lineup member is a plausible choice alternative. An acceptable foil could then be defined by choosing a cut-off point, such as a member who is chosen with a frequency that is at least 90% (or 75%, or 50%, etc.) of expectation. The number of foils whose choice frequency surpasses such a criterion is the number of plausible foils in the lineup. The difference between this number and the lineup's nominal size is the degree of reduction from nominal size.
4. The effective size of the lineup (Malpass, 1981): this is an alternative

measure of the lineup's departure from its nominal size but one which does not involve selection of members who meet a certain criterion and discounting those who do not. To obtain the effective size of a lineup the choice frequencies of those lineup members who are chosen less than expected are subtracted from chance expectation, these differences summed, divided by the frequency expected by chance, and the resulting figure subtracted from the lineup's nominal size. This procedure adjusts the nominal size of the lineup by subtracting from it the degree to which lineup members are chosen less than chance expectation.

Lineup bias
5.   The difference between the proportion of mock-witness identifications of the suspect expected by chance and the proportion observed. This is one indicator of bias towards or away from the suspect. Bias would exist if there were a statistically significant difference between the observed and the expected identification proportions, tested by the 'z-test' for proportions, using conventional statistical criteria.
6.   The defendent bias measure proposed by Malpass (1981): this is an alternative to (5) above, in which the lineup's effective size rather than its nominal size is used for calculating the adjusted expected proportion of identifications of the suspect (E_a).
7.   The lineup's functional size (Wells *et al*. 1979): this is the total number of mock witnesses divided by the number of mock witnesses identifying the suspect (the reciprocal transformation of the proportion of mock witnesses identifying the suspect). A lineup is biased towards the suspect if the functional size is smaller than the nominal size, and is biased away from the suspect if the functional size is larger than the nominal size.

Results

Identification proportions

The identification proportions obtained for each of the four lineups are shown in Table 5.2 for the suspect and each of the five foils. In each case the proportion of correct identifications expected by chance is .167.

Fairness measures

The identification proportions in Table 5.2 are the raw data to which the seven measures are applied. The results are shown in Table 5.3 and Figure 5.1. All four lineups are unfair in that they depart significantly from chance expectation when tested by chi-squared. This departure is shown graphically in Figure 5.1. All four lineups depart considerably from their nominal size (six members)

Table 5.2 Identification proportions for four photographic lineups of varying suspect-foil discrepancy

Lineup	Suspect foil discrepancy	Number of mock witnesses	Suspect	Identification proportions Foils				
				1	2	3	4	5
A	8.45	67	.119	.373	.358	.060	.045	.045
B	10.06	66	.197	.576	.076	.076	.061	.015
C	16.98	68	.794	.118	.044	.029	.015	.000
D	23.78	39	.846	.026	.026	.103	.000	.000

(Expected proportion = .167)

according to the effective size index and according to three *a priori* criteria of foil acceptability: that to be acceptable a foil's proportion of mock witness identifications must exceed 50% (or 75%, or 90%) of its chance expectation. The rank ordering of the lineup's fairness, according to these lineup size criteria is approximately the same as the lineup's suspect-foil discrepancy levels. The

Table 5.3 Seven fairness indicators applied to four mock witness lineups

Fairness indicator	Lineup			
	A	B	C	D
	Distributional Indicators			
1. Chi²	49.47**	86.73**	196.23**	184.31**
2. Cumulative	See Figure 1			
3. Number of lineup members exceeding criterion:				
$.90 \times E$	2	2	1	1
$.75 \times E$	2	2	1	1
$.50 \times E$	3	2	2	2
4. Effective size	3.61	3.37	2.03	1.62
	Bias Indicators			
5. 0 − E	−.48	.03	.627	.679
z-test for proportions	−1.05ns	.65ns	13.86**	11.36**
6. Defendant bias (O − Ea)	−.158	−.100	−.301	.229
Ea	.277	.297	.493	.617
z-test for proportions	2.98*	1.78ns	4.96**	2.94*
7. Functional size	8.38	5.08	1.26	1.18

*p < .01
**p < .001

three bias measures show a slightly different result. The comparison of obtained and expected proportions of suspect identifications show that Lineups C
and D yield significantly more identifications of the suspect than expected by
chance, while Lineups A and B do not differ significantly, given the present
sample size. When the calculation of chance expectation is based on the
lineup's effective size (rather than its nominal size) only Lineup B fails to differ
from chance expectation: Lineups C and D are shown to be biased towards the
suspect while Lineup A is biased away from the suspect. This is reflected in the
functional size index as well, which shows very small numerical results for
Lineups C and D, indicating that they are biased towards the suspect. For
Lineup B the index is very close to the lineup's nominal size, and for Lineup A
the index is larger than nominal size, indicating a bias away from the suspect.

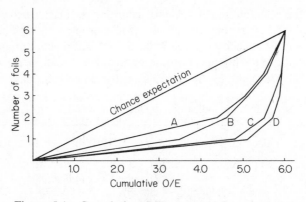

Figure 5.1   Cumulative O/E, summed from largest to
smallest, for lineups A through D

Discussion

The results indicate that the relationship between the physical construction of
the lineup and its resulting fairness takes the form suggested in the literature:
decreasing the similarity of the lineup foils to the suspect leads to decreasing
fairness of the lineup. All of the measures that consider the distribution of
choices across lineup participants (or the 'size' of the lineup) indicate that as the
foils become less similar to the suspect the number of plausible foils decreases.
The dissimilarity level of Lineup D, for example, is so extreme that the suspect
is the only plausible choice even for witnesses who have not previously seen the
offender and have been provided with only his general description. This lineup
is essentially a showup. The three fairness measures primarily concerned with
bias (choices of the suspect) indicate that some of the lineups are unfair in the
sense of bias toward the suspect on all three measures. Lineup A shows
substantial bias away from the suspect on two of the three measures while

Lineup B is shown to be unbiased on two of the three measures, when conventional statistical criteria are used to define the boundary between biased and unbiased.

The results also reveal some ambiguities in the evaluation of lineup fairness. For example, lineup B would be considered unfair in the size sense, but could be considered fair in the bias sense. Both the defence and the prosecution could find support for their cases. The defence could propose that the lineup is unfair because it contains only two or three plausible choices (depending on which criterion of acceptability is used), which is too few to offer sufficient protection to a potentially innocent suspect. The prosecutor could point out that even though there are only two or three plausible choices, the lineup is not biased toward the suspect and therefore presents no real problem. The question that would have to be resolved by jurors is whether or not a lineup is fair which has a nominal size of six with only two or three plausible alternatives but with no systematic bias towards the suspect.

It appears confusing for different measures to have contrasting implications for a lineup's fairness. We might be able to ignore this problem and opt to consider only one or the other aspect of fairness were it not for the fact that the size and bias aspects of fairness arise from two conceptually distinct principles of lineup construction found in the legal literature. To remove the ambiguity of a finding of bias in a lineup, and to unconfound the size and distinctiveness interpretations of bias, lineups should be shown to have a full complement of plausible foils before being examined for bias. In any case, it seems clear that lineups may be unfair in at least two ways, and that these are related, both being affected by some (but not all) of the same departures of lineup probabilities from what might be called a state of perfect fairness where all members of the lineup are equally likely to be chosen by persons without information about the unique physical appearance of the actual offender.

A particularly difficult problem for the interpretation of evidence on lineup fairness is the following. Consider again Lineup 1 in Table 5.1. While there are 10 individuals present, only 6 are plausible choice alternatives. The lineup may be considered unfair on size grounds, which may result in bias towards the suspect, in that he is identified with a probability of .167 instead of .10. However, if one accepts the suggestion put forth by Malpass (1981) that the chance expectation be recalculated based on the number of plausible lineup alternatives actually present, this lineup shows exactly the identification rate expected by the new, adjusted chance figure. Two practical issues are raised here. The first is whether a lineup that is shown to have fewer plausible choice alternatives than its nominal size can be accepted as fair. If so, how much of a departure from nominal size is acceptable, and is there a lower limit? Questions such as these will ultimately be decided in the legal process. However, our own opinion is that lineups should be constructed so as to contain a number of plausible choice alternatives equal to the lineup's nominal size. To do otherwise introduces questions that are difficult to resolve. The second issue arising from the above discussion provides an example.

The second issue is whether measures of bias should be based on chance expectations which have been recalculated on the basis of evidence that there are fewer plausible choice alternatives than nominal size. Wells *et al.* (1979) argue that 'bad foils are functionally not there' and conclude that they are therefore functionally irrelevant to the evaluation of lineup size. Malpass (1981) suggests that before bias measures are calculated chance expectation should be adjusted to reflect the fact that some foils are less than fully plausible choice alternatives by virtue of their low probability of identification by mock witnesses. He suggests that such foils 'should not be accorded the equality with other lineup members implicit in determining chance expectation by 1/*nominal size*.' These positions imply both that these foils can be considered absent from the lineup and that they play no role in witnesses' decision processes. There are three problems with this approach. First, criteria for dropping a foil must be settled upon. A judgment must be made about the point of identification probability at which a lineup member should be considered so implausible that he/she will be eliminated from the lineup for purposes of calculating an adjusted chance expectation. Second, there is a statistical issue involved. Any estimate based on a sample of cases (as with the use of mock witnesses) has associated with it a degree of error, and this is true of the estimate that a lineup alternative has so low an identification probability that it will be ignored in further calculations. Consequently, when this estimate is used as the basis for recalculating chance expectation, the resulting adjusted chance expectation will itself have an associated error, which affects the statistical evaluation of bias. This is a simple enough matter to cope with statistically, but it has some disadvantages for application in the eyewitness lineup area, for reasons which we will discuss briefly below. Third, even though adjusting chance expectation may be reasonable from a statistical perspective it may not be psychologically defensible. The fact remains that the foils, plausible or not, are present in the lineup. That a foil is chosen infrequently is not necessarily evidence that it plays an insignificant role in the witness's decision-making process. To ignore infrequently chosen foils in the evaluation of lineup bias implies that we have specific knowledge of how witnesses approach the identification task, what information they seek, how they integrate that information, how *they* eliminate foils from consideration and how they make a final judgment. This level of sophistication and specificity seems beyond our present knowledge or at least our ability to apply our knowledge to this problem. Recalculating chance expectation may turn out to be psychologically defensible, but its defensibility should be documented before we proceed to use it in applied settings. While it may be an interesting approach in eyewitness research, its applicability in the real world, where the costs of errors may be high, should be viewed conservatively.

Other important questions remain. Are some of the measures better than others? How should we choose? What are the boundaries of fairness for any given measure? How unfair must a lineup be before the information obtained from it (from eyewitness testimony) is of little probative value? Who should make such decisions?

Choosing a fairness measure

We suggest three related criteria for choosing among fairness measures. The first is that the measure be understandable to laymen. The second is that the measure be close to the 'raw data', with few numerical transformations or manipulations and that it should depend on a minimum of statistical assumptions. Third, the measure should not have embedded in it value judgments or decisions that are not open to inspection and understanding by laymen (e.g. sample size, confidence interval size, chance probability levels, etc.). These latter issues are discussed by Wells *et al.* (1979). The further a fairness measure is from the raw data and the more assumptions that are required, the more confusing and less useful it becomes in the applied setting of identification processes in the criminal justice system: it will be less easily employed by law enforcement personnel and less well comprehended by jurors who need to evaluate the probative value of identification testimony obtained from lineups. Measures which are heavily dependent on statistical assumptions seem unsatisfactory because the assumptions are not readily evident to the layperson. The methods offered by Wells *et al.* (1979) and Malpass (1981) involve transformations or interpretation which may obscure their intended meaning. Of the measures considered here, the most straightforward, accessible, and least value laden are those which define both bias and the acceptability of a foil directly in terms of the degree to which the obtained probability of identification departs from chance expectation. We therefore suggest that the number of lineup members identified with some minimum percentage of expectation is a suitable measure of lineup size (the third size measure we presented). The same approach can be used to evaluate whether there is bias present towards or away from the suspect. If the suspect is identified with 90% (or 80%, or 75%) of chance expectation the lineup might be said to be biased away from the suspect, and, if the suspect is identified with 110% (or 120% or 125%) of chance expectation the lineup might be said to be biased towards the suspect. This establishes a plus or minus 10% (20%, 25%) interval around chance expectation, and if the empirical estimate of the identification probability of the suspect falls outside this interval the lineup may be considered to be biased. Similarly if the identification percentages of a foil fall below the lower limit of the interval, the foil is considered unacceptable.[4] For the layman this approach and its interpretation is straightforward and does not suggest meaning beyond its operationalization. Furthermore it makes clear the nature and the locus of the value judgments needed.

Values and technical judgments

As we have attempted to develop recommendations for the construction and evaluation of lineups we have become increasingly aware of the distinction between technical judgments and value judgments. While technical experts, such as experimental psychologists, can provide valuable information, identify value judgments to be considered, and advise on the implications of value judgments and other decisions in the legal process, we believe that value judgments are properly made by others within the legal system. In the context of the lineup fairness problem we believe our role is to develop measures of fairness that are highly accessible to jurors, lawyers, and judges and to reveal the locus of necessary value judgments. This allies us with a stance on the role of science in society which leaves value judgments for public (perhaps political) debate and reserves the application of technical expertise to technical issues and their implications for values. A particularly clear demonstration and discussion of this stance is provided by Hammond and Adelman (1976) who show how a utilitarian decision-making approach to public policy can structure the process so as to clarify the locus of technical and value decisions and clarify the division of labour appropriate to carrying through public decision-making where technical issues are involved. Wells *et al.* (1979) take a similar stance in their discussion of lineup fairness. This appears to be the only fruitful stance if technical information is to be imported into the legal system, since the law has very clear ideas and customs concerning who makes what kinds of decisions, and it seems neither likely nor reasonable that it should give over decision-making prerogatives to technical experts. Thus whether a 10%, 20%, 25% or greater departure from chance expectation is to be considered evidence of lineup fairness in either the size or bias sense is a value judgment that must be made within the legal system, as is the determination of the absolute level of risk of false identification to which innocent suspects should be exposed. Such value judgments should not be concealed within the advice contributed by technical consultants such as experimental psychologists.

A final problem

The implications of this discussion for the evaluation of evidence obtained through the use of lineups provide both prosecution and defence with a number of interesting avenues of enquiry through the use of the mock witness paradigm. A problem in the application of the mock witness paradigm to the process of the initial lineup construction is that the probability of identification of a given lineup member is not independent of the identification probabilities of the other lineup members. Therefore a foil that is acceptable given a particular set of other lineup members may not be acceptable if one or more of the others were dropped because of their implausibility. We can imagine attempting to construct a lineup, gathering mock witness data, eliminating a foil, replacing it and finding that things again do not look quite right, gathering more data, eliminating another foil, etc., through many iterations of the process. This would be an expensive and frustrating process, unlikely to be repeated voluntarily. This problem emphasizes the importance of relating the fairness of lineups to the physical construction of the lineup: the suspect–foil similarity. Providing that the relationship between suspect–foil similarity is a strong one, police can routinely construct fair lineups by careful attention to the physical features of the suspect and those individuals they intend to use as foils, without recourse to mock witness data. The problem is to know in advance the importance of various physical attributes, especially those which do not have simple physical referents, such as attractiveness (Doob and Kirshenbaum, 1973). This is an area in which experimental psychologists can continue to make a contribution both to due process and to the effectiveness of investigation.

Summary and recommendations

Two principles of lineup fairness were identified: (1) that lineups should be of sufficient size that the probability of a chance identification of an innocent suspect is low — that the potential for errors is distributed across a number of persons; and (2) that the suspect must not be distinctive in comparison with the foils. The seven measures of lineup fairness discussed fall into groups corresponding to these two principles: four of the measures are concerned with the distribution of identification probabilities across the members of the lineup and address the question of the number of acceptable foils present, while the remaining three measures focus on the presence of bias towards or away from the suspect. The data indicate that the fairness of lineups in both the size and bias senses depends on the physical similarity of the lineup foils to the suspect, and that the relationship is monotonic.

Discussion of problems in the application of the measurement techniques studied leads to the following recommendations for their use:

1. The measurement of the size of a lineup should be accomplished by counting the number of lineup members who have an identification probability greater than a specified percentage of chance expectation. The specific percentage should be argued and decided within the criminal justice system.

2. The measurement of bias towards or away from the suspect should be accomplished by observing whether the suspect's identification probability falls outside of an interval established around chance expectation whose boundaries extend to a specified percentage below and above chance expectation. Again, the specific percentage is a matter to be argued and decided within the criminal justice system. These first two recommend-

ations are based on criteria for selection of fairness measurements which emphasize that these measures be easily understood and used by laymen, that they be based on few measurement and statistical assumptions, and that they make explicit the value judgments involved in their use.

3. It is not meaningful to examine the bias present towards or away from the suspect before it is assured that the remaining members of the lineup are plausible choice alternatives to the suspect since the presence of implausible foils will affect measures of bias. Thus fairness in the *size* sense must be assured before fairness in the sense of *bias* towards or away from the suspect.

4. The police should construct lineups in which the physical similarity between the suspect and the lineup foils is very high. This is based on the finding that moderately small degrees of suspect–foil dissimilarity lead to unfairness.

5 Criticism of identification evidence obtained in lineups or photo arrays by the defence should examine both the suspect–foil similarity present in the lineup and the identification probabilities of the lineup members based on mock witness choices.

With the availability of fairness measures reflecting the conceptions of fairness found in the legal literature and with the indications of a strong relationship between suspect–foil similarity and fairness, the construction of fair lineups should be routine and the criticism of unfair lineups should be highly focused and effective. Research studies will be able to report on the fairness of their lineups, and higher levels of comparability across studies can be attained.

NOTES

The preparation of this article was facilitated by a Faculty Research Fellowship and Grant-in-Aid from the Research Foundation of the State University of New York to R.S. Malpass. We would like to thank Cathy Fleischman and Paul Pekar for their assistance in collecting the data reported here. Correspondence concerning this article should be addressed to R.S. Malpass, Behavioural Science Program, State University of New York College of Arts & Science, Plattsburgh, NY 12901 USA. Patricia G. Devine is currently in the Department of Psychology, Ohio State University, Columbus, Ohio.

1. Procedural matters include such things as preidentification viewing of the suspect by witnesses, comments made by investigating officers and the instructions given the eyewitness, the behaviour of the investigating officers and the lineup members (during a corporeal lineup), the gross aspects of similarity of the photographs used in photographic lineups — their quality, whether all are identifiable as being from police files — and others.

2. In experimental investigations, unlike the real world, the identity of the 'offender' is known. In the present study the offender and the suspect are the same. We will refer to this individual as the suspect since in real criminal investigations we can only work with suspects.

3. Height markers were used to constrain variation in height judgments in both the initial ratings of the photographs and in the mock witness judgments. While other

dimensions seem to carry greater intersubjective agreement about the absolute meanings of the terms (e.g. short, black and wavy hair; thin, v. medium or husky build) judges and witnesses can see only relative height, and the terms short, medium, and tall have little absolute meaning without reference marks of some kind.

4. While we suggest that statistical issues be ignored with respect to the 'percent of expectation' criteria, and that any estimate of identification probability falling outside the interval established be excluded, no quantitative estimate can totally escape statistical treatment or implications. The statistical meaning of our suggestion is (approximately) that an empirical estimate of the identification probability of a lineup member will be considered inside the *a priori* interval only if at least 50% of the estimate's sampling distribution falls within the interval — that is, only if the sample estimate has a .5 or greater probability of having been sampled from a population of values whose true mean is a value within the *a priori* interval. The qualification that this is an approximation results from the fact that as probability values approach the extremes of 0 or 1.0 their sampling distributions become skewed. The problem with conventional statistical criteria is not that they are arbitrary, but that they involve many metric and distributional assumptions, and are far removed from the concrete issues of what is fair and what is unfair. Whether the issue is the size of a confidence interval, the size of a sample of mock witnesses or the relatively more absolute question of how much more frequently must a defendant be identified than chance expectation, the closer the answer is to substantive value judgments made by a constituency that is theoretically/philosophically entrusted with such decisions, the better off the process will be.

REFERENCES

Biederman, I. (1980). *A Non-obvious factor in assessing the fairness of a lineup*. Buffalo, NY: Department of Psychology, State University of New York at Buffalo.

Brooks, N. (1980). *Guidelines for the conduct of pre-trial eyewitness procedures. A study paper prepared for the Law Reform Commission of Canada*. Osgoode Hall Law School, York University, Downview, Ontario, Canada M3J 1R5.

Buckhout, R., Alper, A., Chern, S., Silverberg, G., and Slomovits, M. (1974). Determinants of eyewitness performance on a lineup. *Bulletin of the Psychonomic Society*, **4**, 191–92.

Devlin, Honorable Lord Patrick (chair) (1976). Report to the Secretary of State for the Home Department of the Departmental Committee on Evidence of Identification in Criminal Cases. London: HMSO.

Doob, A.N. and Kirshenbaum, H.M. (1973). Bias in police lineups — partial remembering. *Journal of Police Science and Administration*, **1**, 287–293.

Egan, D., Pittner, M., and Goldstein, A.G. (1977). Eyewitness identification — photographs vs. live models. *Law and Human Behavior*, **1**, 199–206.

Ellison, K.W. and Buckhout, R. (1981). *Psychology and Criminal Justice*. New York: Harper & Row.

Gorenstein, G.W. and Ellsworth, P.C. (1980). Effect of choosing an incorrect photograph on a later identification by an eyewitness. *Journal of Applied Psychology*. **65**, 616–622.

Hammond, K.R. and Adelman, L. (1976). Science, values & human judgment. *Science*, **194**, 389–396.

La Sota, J.A., Jr. and Bromley, G.W. (1974). *Model Rules: Eyewitness Identification*. Tempe, Arizona: College of Law, Arizona State University.

Malpass, R.S. (1981). Effective size and defendant bias in eyewitness identification lineups. *Law and Human Behavior*, **5**, 299–309.

Malpass, R.S. and Devine, P.G. (1981). Eyewitness identification: Lineup instructions and the absence of the offender. *Journal of Applied Psychology*.

Shepherd, J.W., Davies, G.M., and Ellis, H.D. (1980). *Identification after delay*. (Final report for Grant RES 522/4/1) Aberdeen, Scotland: Department of Psychology, University of Aberdeen.

Sobel, N.R. (1972). *Eyewitness Identification: Legal and Practical Problems*. New York: Clark Boardman.

Wall, P. (1965). *Eyewitness Identification in Criminal Cases*. Springfield, Ill.: Charles C. Thomas.

Wells, G.L. (1978). Applied eyewitness-testimony research: system variables and estimator variables. *Journal of Personality and Social Psychology*, **36**, 1546–1557.

Wells, G.L., Leippe, M.R. and Ostrom, T.M. (1979). Guidelines for empirically assessing the fairness of a lineup. *Law and Human Behavior*, **3**, 285–293.

Chapter 6

Forensic Face Recall: the Role of Visual and Verbal Information

Graham M. Davies

Richard Whitmore's pictorial survey of Victorian crime (1978) contains a striking illustration of a 'wanted' notice, culled from the *Police Gazette* of 1888. It shows an artist's impression of a villain and, beneath, a description of his height, dress, habits, distinguishing marks, and facial appearance. Change the dated sketch for a contemporary 'Photofit' or 'Identi-kit' likeness and this notice would slip into any of today's newspapers without comment. Clearly, the police in Britain, as elsewhere, have sustained and stable beliefs about the appropriate balance of verbal and pictorial information in publicizing the details of a suspect.

But how well founded are these intuitions from the standpoint of contemporary research in forensic and cognitive psychology? The police place value upon constructing a visual impression of the suspect's face, both during the interrogation of the witness and in the later diffusion of information to fellow officers and the public. Does the pictorial mode provide a unique and effective channel for communicating such information? Or can a verbal description function equally efficiently? Or does the answer lie in some calculated mix of the two? In this chapter it is hoped to provide some answers to these questions, by reference both to research concerned specifically with face memory and to investigations of the more general properties of the verbal and pictorial modes.

The chapter begins by surveying briefly the principal methods used by the police for representing the facial appearance of a suspect. Field and laboratory research on the relative effectiveness of these systems in action is then surveyed. The main emphasis will be upon those studies which permit a comparison to be made between results from verbal and pictorial methods. Certain deficiencies in existing pictorial methods which are revealed by this survey will then be discussed and a provisional balance sheet drawn up regarding the relative value of the rival mediums in police identification procedures.

POLICE IDENTIFICATION SYSTEMS

The systems used by the police for presenting facial information are rarely exclusively verbal or pictorial in their mode of operation. For convenience of review, the systems have been divided into 'verbal' and 'pictorial', but such procedures often rely upon a subtle interplay between verbal and non-verbal processes in the generation phase. An additional caveat concerns the emphasis upon facial appearance. While composite systems like Photofit and Identi-kit concentrate purely upon the face, verbal descriptions present information on non-facial aspects of the suspect as well. However, for the purpose of comparing the systems, priority is given here to information about the common element, the representation of facial characteristics.

Verbal descriptions

It is the common experience of police procedure that the spontaneous verbal descriptions provided by witnesses tend to be vague, general, and incomplete (Rolph, 1957). For this reason, a number of techniques have evolved, aimed at eliciting more systematic and comprehensive information on the suspect's appearance.

At their simplest, they take the form of a *Cued Description*; simply a list of headings referring to different features or attributes on which the witness is invited to comment. A more elaborate variant is the *Prompted Description*; here the list of features is supplemented by a number of adjectives which the witness may draw upon. There are numerous versions of this system in use in different regional police forces in the UK. The Scottish variant refers to 14 facial dimensions: complexion, face shape, hair, forehead, eyebrows, eyes, nose, mouth, lips, teeth, chin, ears and headshape as well as marks and mannerisms. For 'mouth', for instance, the witness is offered 'large, small, habitually open, closed-shut'; for ears: 'large, small, protruding, cauliflower, lobeless, large lobes, pierced' and so on. The use of such procedures in obtaining descriptions is not mandatory, but Lord Devlin in his Report (1976) recommended that they should be used as a matter of course in interviewing witnesses.

The difficulty with a purely verbal approach is that the witness may lack the vocabulary effectively to describe a face. For this reason pictures may be used to illustrate descriptions, as in *Portrait Parlé*. This method was invented in 1886 by Alphonse Bertillon, the renowned French criminologist (Thorwald, 1965) and continues to be employed today. Allison (1973) describes a variant in use with the American Army. The dimensions of the face covered are virtually the same as for prompted descriptions but each qualifier is accompanied by a small illustration. Thus, 'head shape' is linked to a series of pictures showing 'round'; 'flat in back'; 'flat on top'; 'egg shaped'; 'high on crown'; and 'bulging at back'.

While Bertillon's original classification arose from a systematic study of faces in the criminal archives (Rhodes, 1956), current descriptive systems appear to be based upon custom and precedent rather than upon serious scientific research. Most police identification files attempt some form of cross-indexing between verbal descriptions from witnesses and criminal records, but this is not normally done on the basis of facial features, unless a deformity is involved. Little or nothing is known about the reliability and consistency of the various descriptive systems in regular police use.

Visual impressions

As has been noted, the use of artists to produce a visual impression of a suspect has a long history in police methods. However, the successful police *sketch artist* must possess skills which go beyond mere artistic talent: he must be able to draw from descriptions and if necessary, ask the right questions which will bring out relevant detail from the witness (Garcia and Pike, 1977). While most British police forces will call upon artists on special occasions, only one force, Lancashire Constabulary, relies exclusively upon them.

In the United States, the FBI have developed an ingenious method for maximizing the use of a scarce resource. The sketch artists are located in Washington DC and keep in touch with the interviewing officers in the field by telephone. The field officer is equipped with a large collection of sample photographs of faces. The witness is encouraged to select those photographs which contain features similar to the suspect. Picture references and a full description are passed back to the artist who in turn relays a sketch to the agent in the field, using 'facsimile transmission' equipment. This can then be shown to the witness and progressively modified in much the same way as if artist and witness were in the same room. Such an elaborate system is beyond the budget and operational requirements of most forces; for them, the alternative to the artist is the face composite kit, of which the best known are Identi-kit and Photofit.

Identi-kit

This was the invention of Hugh McDonald; introduced in the United States in 1959 it came to the United Kingdom 2 years later (Sondern, 1964; Jackson, 1967). Identi-kit consists of some 568 transparent acetate sheets portraying drawings of varieties of the following features: chin, eyebrows, eyes, hair, lips and nose. The recommended method for using the system is for the witness to furnish a cued description which the Identi-kit's operator then uses as a basis for constructing a first composite. This is done by superimposing relevant features in a special frame. The completed 'face' is then shown to the witness who suggests alterations which the operator accomplishes by exchanging features until a satisfactory likeness emerges (McDonald, 1960). In addition to facial features, accessories such as age lines, glasses, moustaches, and scars are available to produce a more life-like appearance. All elements in the kit are coded for ease of transmission and filing. The original Identi-kit has now been superseded by Identi-kit II, which retains the same principle of construction but uses photographs rather than line drawings as the medium of representation.

Identi-kit's main rival in Europe is *Photofit* which was conceived and invented quite independently by Jacques Penry (Penry, 1970; Simpson, 1955). Photofit made its appearance in 1970. Like Identi-kit, Photofit uses a coded range of basic features: forehead/hair, eyes, nose, mouth, and chin. However, these features are all photographs printed on thin card which are assembled, jig-saw fashion, in a special frame. There is no one recommended method of construction, but most operators use the system like Identi-kit; first securing a description and then assembling a composite, which can be corrected according to the witness's instructions. Features in the kit may be amended or altered by the use of black or white wax pencils. It is again possible to elaborate the basic image through the provision of a hat, glasses, moustache or beard. One important difference from Identi-kit is that Photofit has the facility to capitalize more readily upon visual *recognition* as opposed to verbal *recall*. Photofit contains a 'Visual Index', a collection of miniature pictures of all the features in the kit and a chart of basic face shapes which the witness is encouraged to consult.

Advocates of both Identi-kit and Photofit recommend that the classification for feature components in the kit be cross-indexed with criminal records to allow a sample of persons to be identified who resemble a given composite. McDonald (1960) describes the IDMO system (Identification and Method of Operation) which uses height, hairstyle, chin, and lips as its major classificatory dimensions. While occasional successes have been reported for IDMO (e.g. Owens, 1970), its use does not appear to be widespread; parallel systems for Photofit have not gone beyond the experimental stage.

An attempt was made by Interpol to introduce a uniform composite system for all police forces, but like so many attempts at international standardization this ended in failure (Jackson, 1967) and there is now a proliferation of rival systems world-wide. However, such systems, like the French *Robot Photo*, the American *MIMIC*, and the Japanese *Minolta Photomontage Synthesizer* are essentially variations on a theme. They differ from Photofit and Identi-kit in the division of the face and range of features but not in their basic rationale (see Allison, 1973 and Davies, 1981, for reviews).

THE TECHNIQUES IN ACTION: FIELD AND LABORATORY EXPERIENCE

The foregoing discussion has concentrated upon those systems on whose effectiveness some information has been gathered under operational and laboratory conditions. There is now a number of laboratory studies on the effectiveness of pictorial and verbal systems of identification. This survey concentrates on the relative success of visual and verbal procedures for transmitting likeness information and examines the influence of three variables (delay, sex, and race), which have been shown to influence recognition (Ellis, 1975).

Verbal descriptions

Field experience

Still the only field study on the value of verbal descriptions appears to be that of Kuehn (1974), who studied the information supplied by witnesses in a series of 100 cases of violent crime reported to the Seattle Police Department. Descriptions covered non-facial as well as facial information and were limited to nine basic items of information: the race, sex, age, height, weight, build, complexion, hair, and eye colour of the assailant. Kuehn found that most victims were able to supply information on six or more of these items. More information was supplied by men than by women; by victims of robbery than those subjected to assault; by white victims than blacks; and for crimes committed during the day or night compared to those in twilight. Kuehn's survey was confined solely to completeness and nothing is known of the absolute accuracy of the facial or non-facial information elicited from the victims.

Laboratory studies

While there have been numerous studies of the accuracy of testimony regarding general appearance, there have been relatively few which have concentrated wholly or mainly on the face. The majority of the latter have been done at Aberdeen University. In general, there has been no attempt at a 'real-life incident': emphasis has been upon the absolute accuracy of information transmission under ideal conditions. Thus, in the light of Kuehn's findings, the figures quoted should be looked upon as an upper rather than a lower limit.

Two studies examined the number of pieces of information witnesses are capable of recalling about the facial appearance of a target seen briefly immediately prior to recall. Shepherd *et al.* (1978a) reported an average of 7.5 descriptors, and Ellis *et al.* (1980), 9.4 for undergraduate subjects describing an unknown face. Acquaintance did not appear to lead to more elaborate descriptions: Shepherd *et al.* quote an average of 5.7 items for university personnel describing colleagues from memory. These estimates agree surprisingly well with the operational figures reported by Kuehn and the estimates of recall of information from police briefings reported by Bull and Reid (1975). They are also in accord with the idea that there is a certain stability in the number of separate units of information retrievable from memory on a given occasion (Broadbent, 1971; Mandler, 1967).

As regards the priority accorded to the different features of the face there appears to be a reasonably high concordance across faces and conditions. Ellis *et al.* (1980) compared the relative frequency of mention of different parts of the face in two experiments, one involving recall after delays of up to a week and the second, free description in the presence of a photograph. Order of saliency was highly correlated in the two experiments with hair emerging as the dominant cue, followed by eyes and nose, general facial structure, eyebrows, chin, lips and mouth. Cheeks, forehead, and complexion were rarely spontaneously mentioned; it is notable that complexion figures prominently in standard police prompted recall forms.

The effectiveness of verbal descriptions for retrieving a target face from a file was explored in a series of studies reported by Goldstein *et al.* (1971). They employed a population of 255 white male faces whose features were rated for size and shape, and these characteristics were entered into a computerized file. Goldstein *et al.* examined the relative effectiveness of various search routines for locating a target face within the computer file on the basis of a description provided by a witness. Descriptions were generated by the witness from a photograph of the target to which he could refer at all times. The most successful method involved the preliminary isolation of a subsample identified on the basis of extremity of feature. This was followed by a search routine controlled by the computer which located the dimensions which most readily discriminated between members of the subsample and requested the relevant information from the witness. This procedure culminated in a listing of faces in order of likelihood; the target topped the list on 67% of occasions and was in the upper 4% of the list on 99% of trials. Goldstein *et al.*'s system clearly shows the effectiveness of verbal information and provides support for those police systems which are indexed on the basis of extreme features. However, it is important to emphasize that all descriptions were secured with the face in front of the witness subject; as has been noted, subjects' spontaneous recall is limited in extent and not drawn uniformly from all areas of the face as Goldstein *et al.*'s system requires.

What of the accuracy of descriptions from memory? The length and the elaboration of descriptions have not always been significantly related to their efficiency as an aid for identifying the individual concerned (Shepherd *et al.*, 1978a). In this study, judges familiar with the appearance of eight targets were required to assign descriptions of their faces to the persons concerned: overall accuracy on this straightforward task was only 47%, a figure which was reduced to 39% when judges were used who did not know the targets. Interestingly, the pattern of error was systematic and very similar for judges who were familiar and unfamiliar with the targets, suggesting that the two groups accorded priority to the same range of cues.

In addition to face descriptions, Shepherd *et al.* (1978a) also examined the value of rating scales and the use of non-physical attributional judgments as aids to identification (i.e. comments on the supposed intelligence or character of the target). They reported that a series of eight rating scales covering features which proved particularly salient in free-descriptions experiments were as effective as free descriptions in enabling others to identify target individuals. The addition of the attributional information had no facilitating effect upon subsequent identification over and above the physical description.

Goulding (1971) contrasted the effectiveness of free and cued descriptions for conveying likeness information. Police officers acting as judges attempted to assign such descriptions to a series of target faces. On this criterion, free descriptions were significantly superior to cued descriptions. Goulding attributed this result to the greater range of attributes mentioned in the free descriptions and the readiness of his student describers to draw upon structural and relational information. He speculated that a less articulate group might benefit more from the use of cues, though, clearly, the choice of cues would be critical.

In all the studies reviewed so far descriptions were made either in the presence of the target or immediately afterwards. Ellis *et al.* (1980) examined the effect of delay on communication accuracy and on completeness of description. Witnesses were questioned about the appearance of a male target, 1 hour, 1 day, and 1 week following initial exposure. The effectiveness of the descriptions was assessed by a forced-choice discrimination task in which judges assigned descriptions to faces. Description effectiveness declined steadily over time on this task as did the completeness of the descriptions that subjects furnished of the targets.

Sex of witness or target has been included as a factor in a number of studies. No effects upon identification accuracy or completeness were found for the sex of witness in the studies of Shepherd *et al.* (1978a), Ellis *et al.* (1980) or Goulding (1971). All these studies, however, used only male targets. Manipulation of the sex of the target had no effect on the nature of the descriptions elicited in a study by Ellis *et al.* (1975a), but no data were collected on identification accuracy. These negative results need to be treated with caution in view of the sex effects noted by Kuehn in field studies. This may be one area where the use of a non-emotive context provides a poor guide to the performance of male and female witnesses in criminal cases, particularly those involving violence (cf. Clifford and Scott, 1978).

To this author's knowledge, no study has examined the relative accuracy or effectiveness of verbal descriptions provided by Negro and Caucasian subjects. Ellis *et al.* (1975a) examined the content and completeness of descriptions of a sample of black and Caucasian faces provided by Kenyan and Scots subjects. Contrary to the findings of Kuehn, black subjects provided more elaborate descriptions than whites. They also showed some interesting departures from the well-established order of precedence in mention of different features. Black subjects were more likely to mention the chin, ears, and all aspects of the eyes except iris colour. Interestingly, the failure of black subjects to mention eye colour was also reported by Kuehn among his American negro eye-witnesses. Ellis *et al.* attribute these differences in rates of description to differences in pattern of attention, which in turn reflect those aspects of the face which are critical for discrimination among fellow race members.

Clearly, research into the effectiveness of verbal descriptions of faces, as such, is at an early stage and more work is required, particularly analyses of data derived from actual police investigations and studies within an 'incident' methodology: pilot work suggests that the face area is accorded low priority in free descriptions following casual encounters, particularly when there is no direct social interaction (Malbon, 1981). As regards the parallels with face recognition studies, experiments to date suggest verbal recall is sensitive to delay and race effects, but no consistent differences emerge with regard to sex, though females may show a greater propensity for spontaneous atrributional judgments (Baker, 1967). Whatever data are available suggest that witnesses can communicate the identity of another by verbal means, particularly if that person possesses extreme features, though there appears to be a relatively low upper limit on the number of descriptors spontaneously proffered. As in more general work on testimony (Marshall *et al.*, 1972), it has yet to be demonstrated that the use of cued or prompted recall actually amplifies this nugget of useful, useable information. But are pictorial representations any more effective?

Visual impressions

Field experience

As with verbal descriptions, systematic studies of the operational effectiveness of visual identification systems are rare and, when available, plagued with interpretative problems. The composite or sketch is but one element in the evidence which may lead to a conviction; the presence of a visual represent-ation may have been critical, irrelevant, or even counter-productive to the arrest. Whether a visual representation is made at all is normally within the discretion of the officers investigating the case, who vary widely in their enthusiasm for the technique (Darnbrough, 1977); there will be occasions when this method should have been invoked but was not; and others where the reverse is true. Such criticisms should be borne in mind in interpreting such studies as that mentioned by Sondern (1964) on Identi-kit. He reported a 14% clear-up rate for a series of 123 cases in California in which the kit had been employed. Again, Venner (1969), in an early study on Identi-kit effectiveness, quoted detectives as claiming that it had played 'an important role' in 5–10% of cases.

Even this fragmentary information is unavailable for artists' impressions: one can only note the yawning gap between Allison's (1973) claim that 'many cases have been brought to a successful conclusion by this method', and Penry's (1975) assertion that 'there is no record at the Yard of anyone being apprehended as a result of an artist's impression'.

The most comprehensive survey to date was probably the Home Office survey on Photofit reported by Darnbrough (1977) (see also Clifford and Bull, 1978). This suggested that the typical police authority produced Photofits for around 80 cases a year. Operators were rarely full-time, but made composites as part of a range of duties; they could be civilian or uniformed personnel, and the majority had received no formal training. Most Photofit interviews were made within 3 days of the crime but a significant minority (36%) occurred a week or more following the incident. Operators adopted one of two strategies in construction. The majority opted for 'face frame first': forehead/hair and chin sections followed by eyes, nose, and mouth, but some preferred the 'down-through' method: forehead/hair, eyes, nose, mouth, and chin. The majority of all Photofits required pencilled amendments to produce a likeness satisfactory to the witness.

A follow-up on a series of 728 cases over a 2 month period revealed a clear-up rate of 19% of which the investigating officers estimated that some 25%, or 5% of the total sample, had been greatly assisted by the availability of a Photofit likeness. This rather low figure needs to be treated with caution, given the short follow-up period. Further, as Laughery and Fowler (1980) point out, in emphasizing the effectiveness of composites in positively identifying the guilty, one may be overlooking their value in eliminating innocent suspects from a case.

Laboratory studies

Much of the laboratory research on visual impressions is derived from experiments on Photofit at Aberdeen University and a comparative study of sketch artists and Identi-kit by Laughery and his colleagues at the University of Houston (see Davies, 1981, for a detailed survey).

Both groups have examined the absolute effectiveness of the various techniques in communicating identity information under optimal conditions. As part of an initial study of Photofit, Ellis et al. (1975b) asked subjects to work with the operator to produce composites of three male faces which were seen as photographs. Reconstruction followed immediately after the presentation of each face which was seen for 10 seconds. The resulting composites were then given to panels of judges who attempted to identify the faces concerned in an array of 36 alternatives. First-time identification accuracy averaged 1 in 8 or 12.5% which was raised to 1 in 4 (25%) when second and third choices were taken into account. Subjects were free to choose their own order of construction and opted overwhelmingly for the 'down-through' strategy, starting with the forehead and ending with the chin. In this study, witness subjects were allowed only a brief look at the target and pencil work, a feature of most police composites, was rarely employed. Given these conditions, such percentage accuracy figures probably constitute the lower bound for Photofit accuracy.

Ellis *et al*. (1978a) contrasted the accuracy of Photofit likenesses produced in the presence of the target with those made immediately after observation. Contrary to expectation, there was no difference in rated likeness under the two conditions. In a further experiment, Photofit was compared with a condition in which witness subjects made their own drawings of the faces concerned. Faces drawn in the presence of the target were rated by judges as more accurate than those completed in its absence. Once again, Photofit failed to show a presence/absence effect and composites made in the presence of the target were rated significantly poorer likenesses than the witnesses' own drawings.

The insensitivity of Photofit to the effects of delay also emerged from a study by Davies *et al*. (1978a) where in one experiment an interval of a week separated the first and second composites, and in a second experiment, 3 weeks intervened between production of composites. No measurable difference in quality of the picture could be found in the composites made at the two time intervals. However, separate groups of subjects were involved in each experiment who also attempted to recognize the target in a mugshot sequence. On this latter measure, recognition declined significantly. Thus a genuine decline in memory strength appeared to have occurred which was not registered and transmitted successfully by the Photofit likeness.

Evidence of the insensitivity of composite systems is not confined to Photofit, as the work of Laughery and his colleagues on Identi-kit makes plain. In a study reported by Laughery and Fowler (1980), witness subjects conversed with a male target for 8 minutes prior to constructing a likeness, either with the Identi-kit, or with the help of a sketch artist. Subsequently, artist and Identi-kit operator made a second likeness working in the presence of the target. Irrespective of method, subjects spent more time on upper features (hair, eyes) than lower (mouth, chin). As in an earlier pilot study reported by Harmon (1973), sketch artists' drawings made with the target present were rated better likenesses than those made on the basis of the witnesses' memory. However, the same contrast was not significant for Identi-kit: as in the studies of Ellis *et al*. on Photofit, the presence of the target did not improve the quality of likeness.

In a subsequent study, Laughery and Smith (1978) examined the value of composites and sketches which had received high or low ratings, as aids to identifying the target face in a mugshot file. Sketches were a consistently better guide than Identi-kit. On a lax criterion (any target face which achieved a rating of 'possibly yes' or better), highly rated sketches were identified 71% of the time, while similarly rated Identi-kits were recognized on 51% of occasions. However, such accuracy was accompanied by very high false alarm rates of

19% in each instance. Composites receiving low ratings failed to be recognized at above chance level, but low rated sketches exceeded chance.

Both the Aberdeen and Houston groups have investigated the influence of the sex of the observer and target upon likeness accuracy. Working with Photofit, Ellis *et al.* (1977) had male and female witnesses construct likenesses of male and female targets, from coloured photographs. No ascertainable differences emerged in the quality of composites produced by the two sexes, nor were there any obvious differences in order of precedence in choice of features from the kit. Similar negative findings emerged from studies involving the sketch artist and Identi-kit methods. Laughery and Fowler (1980) could find no difference between male and female subjects in the quality of image produced for their male targets. In another study described by Laughery *et al.* (1977), male and female subjects used the rival systems to construct a likeness of a female target. Once again, sketches received better ratings than the composites and the drawings made by the operators from life were better than those obtained through subjects providing descriptions from memory. No comparable difference was noted for the Identi-kit. Construction times showed the same preponderance of effort directed towards upper features with the eyes on this occasion receiving most attention.

The effects of race of target have also been investigated. Ellis *et al.* (1979a) used photographs of both Caucasian and Negro males in a Photofit study in which witnesses made constructions immediately after a 15 second exposure to the target. White judges were able to discriminate almost twice as effectively between likenesses of white targets than between likenesses of black targets. The study also employed both white and coloured witness subjects. White witnesses produced more recognizable composites than blacks when working with white targets but no difference emerged with black targets. The failure of the black witnesses to show a compensating superiority on the black targets was attributed to the limited range of appropriate features available in the kit, an interpretation compatible with the lower overall discriminability of the black composites.

Laughery *et al.* (1977) working with sketch artists and the Identi-kit also found an overall superiority in likeness for images of Caucasian, as opposed to Negro targets. Informal comparisons by the authors failed to reveal any 'own race' encoder effects though there was an interesting change in the allocation of time across different features. Subjects spent proportionately more time on the eyes and the mouth and lips region and less on the hair with Negro targets (cf. the results of Ellis *et al.*, 1975a on descriptor precedence).

As part of the same project, the Houston group also investigated the effectiveness of Identi-kit and sketch likenesses in locating the target in a simulated criminal record file. A computer was programmed to extract measurements between fixed points on the facial images which then formed the basis of an automated search. The resolving power of this procedure was disappointingly low, though the findings for sketches were consistently better than chance (see Laughery et al., 1981).

Taken together, these results obtained under experimental conditions, suggest that the quality of images achieved by commercial composite systems is generally quite coarse. Both Photofit and Identi-kit appear to be surprisingly insensitive to the presence or absence of the target face during production. Such a result could be attributed to some unique resistance of the visual trace to decay processes, but this seems implausible. The drawings of the sketch artists in the study of Laughery and Fowler (1980) and of the subjects themselves in Ellis et al. (1978a) show clear evidence of a decline, a decline which was picked up in the recognition test administered by Davies et al. (1978a). In each instance, however, demonstrable diminution in visual trace strength on one measure was not matched by a measurable fall in composite quality.

It could, of course, be argued that the failure lay not in the systems but in the operators. Such an explanation again seems unlikely. Laughery's operators had attended the official Identi-kit training course and the Aberdeen Photofit operators had been shown to produce likenesses which were a match for those of an experienced police professional (Ellis et al., 1978a). While Laughery et al. (1977) were unable to detect any improvement in their Identi-kit operators over trials, the operator still may play a moderating role in determining the absolute accuracy of the likeness achieved, as recent studies on Photofit appear to demonstrate.

Christie et al. (1981) report a hit-rate for Photofit on an identification task of some 30%, a considerable improvement over that achieved in earlier studies. Further, the operator on that occasion did achieve a significant improvement when working with the face present as opposed to a memory condition. The most plausible explanation for this improvement lies in the quality and experience of the operator concerned, who has some 500 composites to her credit. In a recent study (Milne and Davies — unpublished data), this same operator outperformed a naive one in constructing faces described by witnesses from memory. The skilled operator composites were discriminated better than those produced by the naive operator, irrespective of whether composites were judged with or without the additional of pencilled embellishment to the basic components.

Again all the studies may be criticized for their lack of criminal realism (e.g. Penry, 1975). However while the introduction of an incident methodology would be a useful extension of work in this area, it seems unlikely that the results obtained would show any marked improvement in the quality of likeness produced. In general, as experimental conditions become more realistic, so the accuracy and reliability of a witness's identification performance declines (Clifford, 1978). In the case of Photofit, this is further confounded by the intrusion of attributional judgments into the composites of actual criminals (Shepherd et al., 1978b).

It is difficult to disentangle the failings of the recording equipment from the vagaries of the medium, but there seems little evidence that the pattern of recalled visual impressions is different in kind from verbal descriptions. On one measure or another, there is evidence for race and delay effects and none for sex. Whether the system employed is that of the composite or the drawing, it is clear that the visual medium can transmit useful amounts of information for identity purposes. But how useful is that information relative to a verbal description? And is identity better transmitted in one medium than another? These issues are taken up in the next section.

THE SYSTEMS COMPARED

The foregoing survey suggests a surprising concordance in the range and pattern of information elicited by verbal descriptions and visual illustrations of facial appearance. While the results for the visual medium are influenced by whether sketch artists or composites are employed, both mediums show the influence of delay and race but no ascertainable effect for the sex of the witness. Further, the variety and priority of information extracted from faces also shows a common pattern: for white faces, precedence is accorded to the hair region, closely followed by the eyes with less information being reproduced (verbal) and less time spent (visual) on the lower features. There are indications of a change of pattern with Negro faces: greater attention is paid to the eyes and proportionately less to the hair region. Clearly, there is little indication to date of any unique sensitivity, or even information exclusive to, either the verbal or the visual modality.

But what of the relative accuracy achieved by verbal descriptions and visual impressions? A recently published study by Christie and Ellis (1981) compared the preliminary verbal description elicited from the subject with the final Photofit composite as an aid to identification. Judges were significantly better at identifying target persons on the basis of the preliminary descriptions than they were on the basis of the Photofits. No relationship emerged between the effectiveness of a subject's description and the quality of the Photofit produced. As in other studies (e.g. Laughery and Fowler, 1980) some targets were easier to identify than others. Interestingly, those which were easy to describe were more difficult to model in Photofit and vice versa. However, providing the subject with both description and Photofit failed to increase the overall identification rate, perhaps because judges reported placing greater emphasis upon the verbal component in making identifications.

This is a fascinating result, not least because it is so counter-intuitive: surely a picture is worth 1,000 words? On a theoretical basis, too, it seems surprising. A modality specific encoding model of the kind proposed by Paivio (1971) would imply that a verbal description alone involves two potentially information-wasting transformations; first, when the witness turns his remembered impression into a verbal description (visual to verbal) and, second, when the judge uses that description to guide his identification of the target (verbal to visual). In the case of the Photofit, a visual stimulus is maintained throughout the whole cycle from initial observation to final identification, and recognition performance might therefore be expected to be superior (cf. Standing and Smith, 1975). Yet, the reverse is the case. Consideration of the reasons for this paradoxical finding sheds light not only upon the deficiencies of existing composite systems, but also upon the more general properties of the visual and verbal coding mediums.

Specific v. general information

This writer has argued elsewhere that the picture conveys information on specific examples whereas language is adapted for conveying knowledge of general categories or types (Davies, 1972). This may well be true in an absolute sense, but not when applied to pictorial systems with a limited ensemble size like Photofit. Through the use of modifiers and qualifiers it may be possible to convey a more subtle verbal portrait of an individual than with the restricted pictorial vocabulary of the composite system. There is good evidence from both field and laboratory studies which suggests that composite tools are deficient in the range and representativeness of the features they contain. There are perennial complaints from users of Photofit and Identi-kit of obsolete hair-styles (Venner, 1969; King, 1971) and of a deficiency of youthful features (Darnbrough, 1977). At Aberdeen, Shepherd and Milne have been examining the relative similarity of the components of the standard male Photofit kit using multidimensional scaling techniques. Results to date suggest some redundancy in the selection of features as well as apparent gaps in the range of alternatives on offer.

The restrictions on the range of alternatives may be one of the reasons for the superior likenesses reported by Laughery and Fowler (1980) for sketch artists' impressions compared to composites. The former are able to produce an infinite variation in line, while the latter offer an unsystematic, step-wise approach. One way of achieving the sketch artist's flexibility in a composite system is to use a computer-generated image which has the power to warp, stretch or contract a feature to a client's demands (Gillenson and Chandra-sekaran, 1975). At Aberdeen, preliminary evaluations have been conducted on a prototype computerized composite system developed for the Home Office by the Computer-Aided Design Centre in Cambridge. The flexibility of the system in reproducing different features is impressive, though considerable development is required in order to produce a working system for field use (Christie et al., 1981).

A second aspect of the specificity issue concerns the appropriateness of the medium for representing visual information. Photofit employs a photographic quality of representation and this has also been adopted for the new Identi-kit. There is no doubt that when working from an accurate image, photographic quality is a better guide for identification purposes than even a detailed line drawing (Davies, *et al.*, 1978b). But the problem with a composite is that it is a *proximate* image rather than a *facsimile*. The aim must be to convey salient dimensions accurately while maintaining a certain vagueness regarding specific detail, something for which verbal descriptions and, perhaps, line drawings might well be better adapted (cf. Laughery and Smith, 1978). It is at least debatable, in employing a photographic medium but a restricted range of features, whether contemporary composite systems may be buying the worst of both worlds: an image which is misleading on specific features and vague on general attributes (Venner, 1969). Photofit does convey some types of information accurately (Christie *et al.*, 1981), but perhaps a filtered image (Tieger and Ganz, 1979) or some other combination of shade and line might convey far more.

Recall v. recognition

The failure of composite systems to achieve high standards of accuracy is surprising, given the high levels of competence subjects exhibit at face recognition (Ellis, 1975; Davies, 1978). Part of the reason for this performance gap may lie in the failure of composite systems to capitalize on the witness's recognition abilities: all demand a verbal description prior to construction of the composite. Further, when recognition is encouraged, as in the Photofit system, it is recognition based on isolated fragments of the face which may not elicit good judgments of similarity.

Davies and Christie (1982) investigated this latter problem by asking subjects to rate the similarity of a set of eye and mouth components drawn from the Photofit kit to those same features of a target person seen in a short film. Judgments were made either from memory, or in the presence of a photograph of the target. Further, the Photofit components appeared either in isolation, or in the context of a composite face resembling the target. Results showed an identical pattern for both the eye and mouth comparisons. Judgments of the similarity of the photofit components to the features of the target were comparable for all but one condition: judgments on the features in isolation from memory. The latter condition is, of course, most similar to that actually encountered in police use and it is disturbing that judgments under these conditions should be so wayward.

The fact that placing the features in a facial context restored the reliability of the similarity judgments in the Davies and Christie study supports those theories of face recognition which emphasize holistic processing, rather than the analysis of individual features, as the basis for face recognition (Ellis *et al.*, 1975b; Baddeley, 1979; Woodhead *et al.*, 1979). They suggest that a considerable improvement in visual recall accuracy might be achievable if witnesses were able to work with a complete face rather than with isolated features.

Such an approach was explored in a series of experiments, described by Davies *et al.* (1981), which attempted to operate a standard Photofit kit in a 'whole face' mode. In one study, subjects were provided with an anthropometrically determined 'average' face composed from Photofit components. They were then encouraged to consider how this differed from the target face and to modify it progressively until a satisfactory likeness was achieved. In a second experiment, subjects were offered a variety of different facial 'types' as starting points. Once a given type had been selected, construction proceeded in the orthodox manner. In neither instance was performance any better than when the kit was used in a conventional way. Davies *et al.* attribute this failure to the fact that subjects still had to rely upon access to the Visual Index, with its isolated elements, in choosing alternative features.

The problem of moving directly into a recognition mode, without the need for prior verbal recall or scrutiny of isolated features, has clearly not been solved. Probably only the advent of a computerized system of the kind described by Christie *et al.* (1981) would provide the witness with the necessary flexibility always to view feature alternatives within the context of a total face. However, this seems the only way in which to exploit a witness's recognition capacity and to avoid the constraints of working from verbal recall.

Encoding v. decoding

One note of caution on the relative value of pictorial and verbal identity information concerns the use to which the information is put in police operations. Christie and Ellis's (1981) study may be said to have satisfactorily paralleled the *encoding* of information from witness to operator; it is less clear whether it is relevant to *decoding*: the use of that information by the investigating officer to identify the suspect. Judges had access at all times to the description or composite in making their identifications. Such a procedure could be said to simulate an officer searching criminal records for suspects fitting a description provided by a witness. It is less clear, however, whether it provides a useful parallel with the situation where a police officer memorizes descriptions of current suspects in the hope of apprehending them in the course of his duty.

It has been noted earlier that there seem to be quite modest limits on the amount of descriptive verbal information which can be absorbed by policemen at briefings (Bull and Reid, 1975). The potential for interference and confusion is accelerated when similar information about a number of disparate individuals is provided in the same format (Crouse, 1971). Such a situation might readily arise if, for instance, officers were briefed verbally about the personal details of a gang of IRA bombers. Laboratory studies suggest that pictures or scenes are more readily apprehended and less prone to interference than the corresponding labels or verbal descriptions (Dallet and Wilcox, 1968; Davies, 1969; Kabose and Balsam, 1973; Standing, 1973; cf. Loftus, this volume). These studies have been subject to methodological and procedural criticisms centring upon the comparability of the stimulus material (Goldstein and Chance, 1974; Mandler and Johnson, 1976). While this may qualify any theoretical interpretations of such results, the major practical implication remains, as a study by Anderson and Paulson (1978) illustrates.

Anderson and Paulson compared recognition rates for a series of fictional faces composed from Identi-kit parts with that for verbal descriptions of the same faces. The faces and descriptions were composed so that they varied in the number of shared common features. Irrespective of whether the stimulus was pictorial or verbal, the presence of common features increased recognition errors and decreased response latency. However, the disruptive effect of the shared features was four times as great for the verbal descriptions compared to the pictorial composites. Thus, even when the relative complexity of the material is controlled, pictorial stimuli are superior to verbal stimuli for the speedy apprehension and retention of identity information over time. Composites may not be as well retained as photographs of actual faces (Ellis *et al.*, 1978b), but are likely to be a superior medium for spontaneous recognition compared to descriptions.

CONCLUSIONS

This survey began by posing the question: is the pictorial or the verbal medium better for presenting identity information? As so often, the answer seemed to be more complex than the question. Judged by the available evidence, there is no reason for suggesting that the visual medium is any more sensitive or efficient in conveying identity information than the verbal medium and some evidence that the reverse may be the case.

Within the pictorial medium there is some suggestion that composite systems, in the hands of operators of average ability, produce cruder images than the sketch artist. However, the evidence here is incomplete: there has been no comparison of the artist and Photofit, nor any contrast between the products of Photofit and Identi-kit; nor, indeed, among these and any of the other rival systems. Composite systems are in their infancy and there is no reason for believing that they are inherently inferior to the products of sketch artists. Success will depend on the extent to which they can overcome their present weaknesses in feature selection and presentation, and align their building techniques with the psychological processes involved in facial recognition.

The apparent effectiveness of the verbal description in *encoding* information is but one side of the coin: in operational use, there are reasons for believing that the composite portrait is more readily memorable and less affected by interference than the verbal description, particularly where multiple suspects are involved. There may also be incidental pay-offs to the use of a composite as opposed to purely verbal recall in the enhanced ability of the witness subsequently to recognize the suspect (Mauldin and Laughery, 1981), though the evidence is not entirely unequivocal on this point (Hall, 1977; Davies *et al.*, 1978a).

The current implications of this work suggest a greater respect for, and emphasis upon, accurate verbal descriptions as opposed to visual methods when interrogating witnesses. Clearly, current police description forms are in need of some development with science replacing intuition in the selection of key features and descriptors.

Paradoxically, in the distribution of information to police and public alike, there should be a greater use of pictorial techniques. Given their superior cue potency, there is no reason why the use of illustration should not be extended into those dimensions of height, weight, build, and general appearance traditionally reserved for the verbal medium. What price a 'corpo-fit'?

NOTES

Work described in this paper carried out at Aberdeen University was supported by the Social Science Research Council and the Scientific Research and Development Branch, Home Office. The views expressed are those of the author and do not necessarily represent those of the funding bodies. Thanks are due to Donald Christie, Hadyn Ellis, and John Shepherd for permission to quote from unpublished papers and for much useful discussion.

REFERENCES

Allison, H.C. (1973). *Personal Identification*. Boston: Holbrook Press.
Anderson, J.R. and Paulson, R. (1978). Interference in memory for pictorial information. *Cognitive Psychology*, **10**, 178–202.
Baddeley, A. (1979). Applied cognitive and cognitive applied psychology: The case of face recognition. In L.G. Nilsson (ed.), *Perspectives on Memory Research*. New Jersey: L. Erlbaum.
Baker, E. (1967). *Perceiver variables involved in the recognition of faces*. Unpublished PhD thesis, University of London.
Broadbent, D. (1971). *Decision and Stress*. London: Academic Press.
Bull, R.H.C. and Reid, R.L. (1975). Recall after briefing: Television versus face-to-face presentation. *Journal of Occupational Psychology*, **48**, 73–78.
Christie, D.F.M., Davies, G.M., Shepherd, J.W. and Ellis, H.D. (1981). Evaluating a new computer-based system for face recall. *Law and Human Behavior*, **5**, 209–218.
Christie, D.F.M. and Ellis, H.D. (1981). Photofit constructions versus verbal descriptions of faces. *Journal of Applied Psychology*, **66**, 358–363.
Clifford, B.R. (1978). A critique of eyewitness research. In M.M. Gruneberg, P.E. Morris and R.W. Sykes (eds), *Practical Aspects of Memory* London: Academic Press.
Clifford, B.R. and Bull, R. (1978). *The Psychology of Person Identification*. London: Routledge & Kegan Paul.

Clifford, B.R. and Scott, J. (1978). Individual and situational factors in eye witness testimony. *Journal of Applied Psychology*, **63**, 352–359.

Crouse, J.H. (1971). Retroactive interference in reading prose materials. *Journal of Educational Psychology*, **62**, 39–44.

Dallet, K. and Wilcox, S.G. (1968). Remembering pictures vs. remembering descriptions. *Psychonomic Science*, **11**, 139–140.

Darnbrough, M. (1977). The use of facial reconstruction methods by the police. Paper presented at the Annual Conference of the British Psychological Society, Exeter, Devon.

Davies, G.M. (1969). Recognition memory for pictured and named objects. *Journal of Experimental Child Psychology*, **7**, 448–458.

Davies, G.M. (1972). Qualitative and quantitative changes in the retention of picture stimuli. *Journal of Experimental Child Psychology*, **13**, 382–393.

Davies, G.M. (1978). Face recognition: Issues and theories. In M.M. Gruneberg, P.E. Morris, and R.N. Sykes (eds), *Practical Aspects of Memory*. London: Academic Press.

Davies, G.M. (1981). Face recall systems. In G.M. Davies, H.D. Ellis, and J.W. Shepherd (eds), *Perceiving and Remembering Faces*. London: Academic Press.

Davies, G.M. and Christie, D.F.M. (1982). Face recall: An examination of some factors limiting composite production accuracy. *Journal of Applied Psychology*, **67**, 103–109.

Davies, G.M., Ellis, H.D., and Christie, D.F.M. (1981). Exploring new strategies for facial recall. *Medicine, Science and the Law*, **21** 137–145.

Davies, G.M., Ellis, H.D., and Shepherd, J.W. (1978a). Face identification: The influence of delay upon accuracy of Photofit construction. *Journal of Police Science and Administration*, **6**, 35–42.

Davies, G.M., Ellis, H.D., and Shepherd, J.W. (1978b). Face recognition accuracy as a function of mode of representation. *Journal of Applied Psychology*, **63**, 180–187.

Devlin, Honourable Lord Patrick (1976). Report to the Secretary of State for the Home Department of the Departmental Committee on Evidence of Identification in Criminal Cases. London: Her Majesty's Stationery Office, 1976.

Ellis, H.D. (1975). Recognising faces. *British Journal of Psychology*, **66**, 409–426.

Ellis, H.D., Davies, G.M., and McMurran, M.M. (1979a). Recall of white and black faces by white and black witnesses using the Photofit system. *Human Factors*, **21**, 55–59.

Ellis, H.D., Davies, G.M., and Shepherd, J.W. (1977). *An Investigation of the Photofit System for Recalling Faces*. Final Report to the S.S.R.C. under Grant HR 3123/2.

Ellis, H.D., Davies, G.M., and Shepherd, J.W. (1978a). A critical examination of the Photofit system for recalling faces. *Ergonomics*, **21**, 297–307.

Ellis, H.D., Davies, G.M., and Shepherd, J.W. (1978b). Remembering pictures of real and 'unreal' faces: Some practical and theoretical considerations. *British Journal of Psychology*, **69**, 467–474.

Ellis, H.D., Deregowski, J.B., and Shepherd, J.W. (1975a). Descriptions of white and black faces by white and black subjects. *International Journal of Psychology*, **10**, 119–123.

Ellis, H.D., Shepherd, J.W., and Davies, G.M. (1975b). An investigation of the use of the Photofit technique for recalling faces. *British Journal of Psychology*, **66**, 29–37.

Ellis, H.D., Shepherd, J.W., and Davies, G.M. (1979b). Identification of familiar and unfamiliar faces from internal and external features: Some implications for theories of face recognition. *Perception*, **8**, 431–439.

Ellis, H.D., Shepherd, J.W., and Davies, G.M. (1980). The deterioration of verbal descriptions of faces over different delay intervals. *Journal of Police Science and Administration*, **8**, 101–106.

Garcia, E. and Pike, C.E. *Portraits of Crime*. (1977). New York: Condor Publishing Company.

Gillenson, M.L. and Chandrasekaran, B. (1975). A heuristic strategy for developing human facial images on a CRT. *Pattern Recognition*, **7**, 187–196.

Goldstein, A.G. and Chance, J. (1974). Some factors in picture recognition memory. *Journal of Genetic Psychology*, **90**, 69–85.

Goldstein, A.G., Harmon, L.D. and Lesk, A.B. (1971). Identification of human faces. *Proceedings of the IEEE*, **59**, 748–760.

Goulding, G.J. (1971). Facial description ability. *Police Research Bulletin*, No. 19, 42–44.

Hall, D.F. (1977). Obtaining eyewitness identifications in criminal investigations: Two experiments and some comments on the Zeitgeist in forensic psychology. Presented to the American Psychology-Law Conference, Snowmass, Colorado.

Harmon, L.D. (1973). The recognition of faces. *Scientific American*, **229**, 71–82.

Jackson, R.L. (1967). *Occupied with Crime*. London: Harrap.

Kabose, S.N. and Balsam, P.D. (1973). Differential retroactive inhibition effects with pictures and words. *Bulletin of Psychonomic Society*, **2**, 169–170.

King, D. (1971). The use of Photofit 1970–1971: A progress report. *Police Research Bulletin*, No. 18, 40–44.

Kuehn, L.L. (1974). Looking down a gun barrel: Person perception and violent crime. *Perceptual and Motor Skills*, **39**, 1159–1164.

Laughery, K.R., Duval, G.C. and Fowler, R.H. (1977). *An Analysis of Procedures for Generating Facial Images*. Mug File Project (Report Number UHMUG-2), University of Houston.

Laughery, K.R. and Fowler, R.F. (1980). Sketch artist and Identi-kit procedures for recalling faces. *Journal of Applied Psychology*, **65**, 307–316.

Laughery, K., Rhodes, B., and Batten, G. (1981). Computer-guided recognition and retrieval of facial images. In G.M. Davies, H.D. Ellis, and J.W. Shepherd (eds), *Perceiving and Remembering Faces*. London: Academic Press.

Laughery, K.R. and Smith, V.L. (1978). Suspect identification following exposure to sketches and Identi-Kit composites. *Proceedings of the Human Factors Society 22nd Annual Meeting*, Detroit.

Loftus, E. and Ketcham, K.E. The malleability of eyewitness accounts. This volume.

McDonald, H.C. (1960). *The Identi-Kit manual*. Santa-Anna, California: Townsend Company, (Identi-Kit Division).

Malbon, C. (1981). *Verbal description and identification*. Unpublished B.Sc. thesis, University of Aberdeen.

Mandler, G. (1967). Organisation and Memory. In K.W. Spence and J.T. Spence, (eds), *The Psychology of Learning and Memory*, Vol. 1. New York: Academic Press.

Mandler, J.M. and Johnson, N.S. (1976). Some of the thousand words a picture is worth. *Journal of Experimental Psychology (Human Learning and Memory)*, **2**, 529–540.

Marshall, J., Marquis, K., and Oskamp, S. (1971). Effects of kind of question and atmosphere of interrogation on accuracy and completeness of testimony. *Harvard Law Review*, **84**, 1620–1643.

Mauldin, M.A. and Laughery, K.R. (1981). Composite production effects on subsequent facial recognition. *Journal of Applied Psychology*, **66**, 351–357.

Owens, C. (1977). Identi-Kit enters its second decade — ever growing at home and abroad. *Fingerprint and Identification Magazine*, November, 3–8, 11–17.

Paivio, A. (1971). *Imagery and Verbal Processes*. New York: Holt, Rinehart & Winston.

Penry, J. (1970). Photofit. *Police Journal*, 302–316.

Penry, J. (1975). *Penry Facial Identification Technique*. News Bulletin, 1975–1976 Leeds: John Waddington of Kirkstall Ltd.

Rhodes, H.T.F. (1956). *Alphonse Bertillon: Father of Scientific Detection*. London: Harrap.

Rolph, C.H. (1957). *Personal Identity*. London: Michael Joseph.

Shepherd, J.W., Davies, G.M., and Ellis, H.D. (1978a). How best shall a face be described? In M.M. Gruneberg, P.E. Morris, and R.N. Sykes (eds), *Practical Aspects of Memory*. London: Academic Press.

Shepherd, J.W., Ellis, H.D., McMurran, M., and Davies, G.M. (1978b). Effect of character attribution on Photofit construction of a face. *European Journal of Social Psychology*, **8**, 263–268.

Simpson, A. (1955). Aids to identification. A new method. *Police Journal*, 220–229.

Sondern, F. (1964). The box that catches criminals. *Readers' Digest*, April, 37–44.

Standing, L. (1973). Learning 10,000 pictures. *Quarterly Journal of Experimental Psychology*, **25**, 207–222.

Standing, L. and Smith, P. (1975). Verbal–pictorial transformations in recognition and memory. *Canadian Journal of Psychology*, **29**, 316–326.

Thorwald, J. (1965). *The Marks of Cain*. London: Thames and Hudson.

Tieger, T. and Ganz, L. (1979). Recognition of faces in the presence of two-dimensional sinusoidal masks. *Perception and Psychophysics*, **26**, 163–167.

Venner, B.R.H. (1969). Facial identification techniques. *Police Research Bulletin*, No. 13, 17–20.

Whitmore, R. (1978). *Victorian and Edwardian Crime and Punishment from Old Photographs*. London: Batsford.

Woodhead, M.M., Baddeley, A.D., and Simmonds, D.C.V. (1979). On training people to recognize faces. *Ergonomics*, **22**, 333–343.

Evaluating Witness Evidence
Edited by S.M.A. Lloyd-Bostock and B.R. Clifford
© 1983 John Wiley & Sons Ltd.

Chapter 7

Improving Face Recognition Ability

Alan Baddeley and Muriel Woodhead

Over the last 10 years there has been a considerable interest among psychologists in memory for faces. For the most part this has been concerned with emphasizing the limitations of an eyewitness's ability to recognize a briefly observed face, and the obvious implications of this limitation for the reliability of eyewitness testimony. Such a concern is clearly very important. However avoiding false recognition is not the only problem involved in eyewitness testimony. If it were, then the problem could be avoided by simply ruling out evidence from an eyewitness. Obviously this would be unacceptable since limited though it is, the eyewitness's evidence may be of crucial importance in convicting the guilty. For that reason, it is clearly important to try to improve the quality of testimony in general rather than simply to alert the potential juryman to its limitations. Our own work has been concerned with trying to explore ways in which the performance of a witness recognizing a face might possibly be improved.

Consider the case of the international terrorist, Carlos, who claims to have been involved in both the OPEC hostage incident in Vienna and the Munich Olympic incident when Israeli athletes were kidnapped and shot. His photograph was widely available, yet he apparently was able to move around the world without being picked up by any of the law-enforcing agencies that were looking out for him. This suggests the possibility that, even given a perfectly good photograph of a person, one may still have considerable difficulty recognizing him. Our research is concerned with this problem, and the related question of whether strategies can be taught whereby one may commit a face to memory in such a way that it will subsequently be readily recognized. If this were the case, we might perhaps be able to give general advice to the public on how to maximize the probability of subsequently recognizing a person seen committing a crime.

Our work falls into three sections, the first two being concerned with some possible strategies for improving face recognition, while the third is concerned with some practical implications that developed from our work. The two strategies we explored are based on *two* underlying theories of how faces are perceived. The first emphasizes the fact that faces are made up of a number of

125

features, and follows the suggestion that a face should be analysed into its constituent features and these categorized according to some previously learnt scheme. The second strategy advocates ignoring individual features and concentrating on the personality of the person depicted.

THE FEATURE ANALYSIS STRATEGY

This approach was first suggested by Leonardo da Vinci, who advocated that the human face be analysed into its separate components, each of these then being categorized on the basis of a series of exemplars, some of which are shown in Figure 7.1. Leonardo claimed that this would substantially enhance the user's ability subsequently to recognize a face.

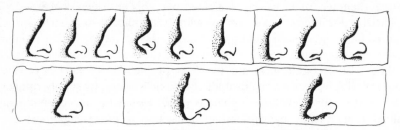

Figure 7.1   Leonardo da Vinci: from the *Treatise on Painting*

A similar approach has been advocated much more recently by Jacques Penry, the deviser of the Photofit system which is discussed elsewhere in this volume (Davies, this volume). Penry makes a persuasive case for this, and was, I understand, almost successful in persuading the Inner London Education Authority to include a teaching package on face recognition in their general curriculum, presumably on the grounds that this would be useful socially, as well as providing a pool of rather better eyewitnesses than at present exists in London.

We were offered the opportunity of evaluating a course that was heavily influenced by Penry's approach to face recognition, and did so using three separate experiments (Woodhead *et al.* 1979). The course was one which lasted for 3 days during which subjects were familiarized with Penry's concept of 'reading' a face by categorizing it along a number of feature dimensions. The course involved practice in face reading, together with various exercises, including that of searching for a given individual in a neighbouring town. It appeared to be carried out with considerable good sense and enthusiasm and we fully expected to see a substantial enhancement in performance when we compared subjects taking the course with groups of comparable subjects who had no such training. In our first experiment we simply presented our subjects with a total of 24 pictures of unfamiliar people, and subsequently re-presented the same faces mixed in with 48 new faces. The faces were shown one at a time and our subjects were required simply to respond as to whether they were 'old' faces which they had previously seen or new and unfamiliar faces. A total of 26 male subjects were tested before the beginning of the course and at the end of the 3 day course. We found no evidence for any enhancement in face recognition as a result of the course, with participants detecting 60% before and 60% after as compared with a similar group who did not take the course and who recognized 59% before and 58% after the 3 day interval.

We went on to conduct two more experiments in which new trainees were this time given sets of photographs of 'wanted' men. They were then exposed to a sequence of 240 single photographs each presented for 10 seconds. Their job was to note and record any target faces that were presented. The results of these two experiments are shown in Table 7.1.

When subjects were searching for a set of four targets, there appeared to be a slight but statistically non-significant tendency for subjects who had taken the course to be somewhat better than the control subjects. However, performance was very high and it seemed possible that a genuine difference may have been masked by a ceiling effect, the tendency for many subjects to be performing almost perfectly even without the course. The second study avoided this by introducing a larger set of targets. This time we did find a significant effect of the course; the subjects taking the course were reliably *worse* than subjects who had not been trained in this way.

Taking our three experiments together then, it does not appear to be the case that inducing subjects to analyse faces into their constituent features is an effective way of enhancing face recognition skills.

Table 7.1   Performance in recognition tests by groups trained in person recognition and by untrained groups

	Number of target faces	Faces in test sets	Groups undergoing training		Untrained groups (same time gap)	
			Before	After	1st test	2nd test
Experiment 2	4	240	81%	87%	80%	81%
			(N = 26)		(N = 26)	
Experiment 3	16	240	61%	57%	52%	66%
			(N = 28)		(N = 28)	

FEATURES VERSUS PERSONALITY

Why should a detailed analysis of faces into component features be so unhelpful? One suggestion is that faces are not perceived as a collection of individual features, but rather as an integrated whole. In looking at people, it is perhaps the way in which the individual features relate to each other that creates the impression of a particular person, and it may well be that attempting to go against this 'natural' way of looking at faces is doomed to be counter-productive.

Another possible reason was suggested by the extensive research on memory for words that was going on at this time. This typically involved presenting subjects with lists of unrelated words which they would subsequently be asked to recall, or to recognize from a larger set. Many experiments have shown that the probability of remembering a word depends crucially on how it is analysed when presented. Consider the word *DOG*. I could present it to a subject and ask him simply whether it was printed in upper or lower case letters. This would subsequently lead to very poor recall. Recall would be somewhat enhanced if I required a rather 'deeper' or more complex classification; does it rhyme with the word *log* for example? However the best recall tends to come if a person is required to process the meaning, for example to answer the question *Is it an animal*? Following on from a range of experiments of this type Craik and Lockhart (1972) proposed the concept of Levels of Processing whereby the probability of recalling or recognizing a word increases as it is processed yet more deeply.

In 1974, Bower and Karlin attempted to apply the Levels of Processing notion to the recognition of faces. They presented their subjects with a sequence of slides, half of male and half of female faces. In one group, the 'shallow' encoders, people were simply required to classify each face as male or female. A second, 'deep' processing group, was required to estimate the intelligence or friendliness of the person depicted. Both groups subsequently attempted to recognize those faces they had seen from a larger set. There was a clear tendency for the subjects who had processed deeply to recognize more faces. On the basis of this result, Bower and Karlin concluded that the concept of Levels of Processing could usefully be applied to face recognition.

While this seemed to be a promising line of development, it could be argued that it did not represent a fair test of the hypothesis. It will typically take only a brief glance to decide whether a person photographed is male or female, whereas deciding whether or not he is intelligent is a much more difficult, indeed perhaps impossible task which is likely to induce the viewer to spend a great deal of time simply looking at the person depicted. Since there is abundant evidence that amount remembered increases directly with amount of time spent learning, this result may have nothing at all to do with depth of processing. Karalyn Patterson and I therefore decided that we would try to arrange a fairer test of the Levels of Processing hypothesis (Patterson and Baddeley, 1977).

We tested two groups of subjects, one of which we induced to use a feature analysis strategy, while the second was induced to analyse the target faces in terms of more semantic personality dimensions. In the features group, subjects categorized faces on the basis of large or small noses, thin or full lips, close or far apart eyes, round or long shape of face, all of which were dimensions taken from those advocated by Penry (1971). Our personality assessment group judged the same faces on the basis of nice versus nasty, reliable or unreliable, intelligent or dull, and lively or stolid. In both cases subjects placed a mark on a 10 cm line indicating where along that dimension they would categorize each particular face.

Since we were anxious to avoid a situation where the subject would be simply recognizing one specific view of a particular face, we always tested in a different orientation from that presented, presenting all faces full face and testing in either a three-quarter or a profile view. Finally, we incorporated one other major variable, namely disguise. It could be argued that judgments in terms of personality might well be generally useful, but may be much more susceptible to disruption by disguise than would assessment based on physical dimensions such as shape of face and size of nose. We were anxious to avoid coming up with a strategy which could be easily disrupted in this way. We therefore tested our original target faces not only in their original mode, but also under various types of disguise. These included the addition or removal of a wig, the addition or removal of a beard, and the addition or removal of spectacles.

It proved to be the case that disguise was by far the most powerful variable. As Figure 7.2 shows, performance was extremely good when subjects attempted to recognize undisguised faces, but with each additional disguised feature performance dropped to a point at which subjects were only slightly above chance following a change in wig, beard, and spectacles. It will also be clear from Figure 7.2 that subjects who had originally seen a face in a frontal pose performed at a higher level when tested in three-quarter than when tested with a profile view. We shall return to this issue in the final section.

When subjects who had categorized the faces in terms of features were compared to the personality categorization group, we did observe the predicted advantage, with the 'deeper' processors discriminating reliably more effectively than the 'shallow' feature processors. However the effect was far from large (82% versus 76%) and certainly was not sufficiently substantial to encourage us to advocate this as a suitable training procedure.

At about this time, work on verbal memory was beginning to suggest that a more powerful factor in committing something to memory than depth of processing might be the degree and richness with which it was elaborated. For example, in a memory experiment where the subject is asked to remember the two words *man* and *watch*, linking them into a meaningful sentence such as *the*

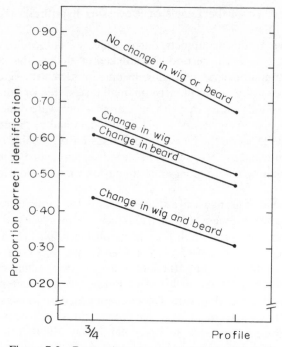

Figure 7.2   Proportion of correct identifications as a
function of changes in pose, wig, and beard

man dropped the watch would enhance learning. However learning would be even better if a richer and more elaborate relationship between the two words was generated, for example a sentence such as *the wizened old man hobbled across the room holding the gold watch which he dropped behind the chair*. We argued that if the same effect were to operate within the domain of face memory, then if we could associate a relatively rich background with the faces we presented to our subjects, it might make them much more memorable.

We therefore conducted an experiment in which we presented a number of photographs of young males. For one group, each photograph was simply accompanied by the person's name and age, while for a second group we accompanied the photograph with a biographical sketch. For example a particular person might be described as *a docker living in Wapping. Unmarried, fond of drinking and occasionally gets into fights*. Our subjects were shown a total of five such faces, and after a short interval during which they performed another unrelated task, were shown a sequence of 100 faces, comprising the 5 old faces twice, in different poses, and 90 new ones. They were asked to decide in each case whether or not the face had previously been presented, and if so to give the name if they remembered it. Subjects who had been given the character sketch together with the photographs recognized 66% whereas those given only the name and age recognized 61%, a difference that did not approach statistical significance.

While our results were not encouraging, it occurred to us that we might not have been giving the concept of elaboration a fair test. The character sketches and faces were presented at the same time, and it could be argued that the character sketch might have directed attention away from the face. Since the subject would spend less time looking at the face, he would be subsequently less likely to recognize it. In order to check out this possibility we ran another study, and on this occasion sandwiched the verbal description in between two presentations of the face. This time we also included a second control group in which the face was accompanied by a short but irrelevant passage which would distract the subject from continuing to think about the face, but would not be at all relevant to remembering it. Our results were very clear-cut. We obtained absolutely no difference between the three groups in accuracy of subsequent face recognition; giving an apparently rich and detailed personality to the face depicted seemed to have no effect on subsequent ease of recognition.

It seems clear from our results that the Levels of Processing approach with its emphasis on the 'deep' encoding of the face in terms of the underlying personality did not prove to be an effective way of enhancing face recognition. There is no doubt from many other studies that a small levels effect such as we obtained in our first study can readily be obtained. For example Winograd (1976) has shown that a whole range of ways of encoding a face ranging from personality to occupation may enhance recall. However it appears to matter little what the subject does with the face, provided he processes it as a person rather than simply a visual pattern. Consequently even asking the subject to estimate how tall the person depicted is likely to be, led to enhanced recognition. It appears then that the apparent effect of Levels of Processing in face-memory merely reflects the importance of encoding the face as a whole and as a person. Provided one does this, there is little evidence to suggest that more elaborate encoding will enhance performance.

GOOD AND BAD RECOGNIZERS

Our attempts to improve face recognition by inducing appropriate strategies, based on assumptions as to how faces are probably processed, turned out to be very unsuccessful. Our next strategy therefore was to try to select people who were particularly good at recognizing faces and see what we could learn from them. The first question this raises is whether there *are* consistent differences between people in how well they recognize faces. In an earlier unpublished study we had tested the ability of 90 members of our subject panel to memorize and subsequently recognize a set of 6 faces which appeared in 3 poses and were tested from a set of 108. At the same time as we tested them, we asked them to rate their face recognition ability on a scale ranging from 'Poor' to 'Very good'.

While we did observe a substantial range of performance, extending from 17% to 100% correct, the relationship between performance and the subject's own assessment of his face recognition ability was -0.05. It appears from our sample that either our measure of face recognition is not a very good one, or else people are very bad at assessing their own ability to remember faces, an issue of some significance in evaluating the attitudes of witnesses.

We decided to explore further the question of whether it is possible to select people who are particularly good or bad at face memory and with this in mind went through the records of the 400 subjects we had tested on one or other of our previous experiments. From this sample we selected 19 very good recognizers and 19 who had performed particularly poorly, and invited them back for further tests. The test battery we gave our subjects was that devised by Warrington (1974) for assessing the visual and verbal memory capabilities of brain damaged patients. The battery included three tests each of which involved presenting the subject with 50 items, followed by a test in which each of the items previously presented was paired with a new item, and in each case the subject was required to decide which of the two he had seen before. One of the tests involved presenting the faces of unfamiliar actors, a second involved presenting a series of paintings of objects and scenes, while a third involved presenting a series of unrelated words.

We hoped to answer three questions. First, are we able to select a sub-group of people who are consistently good at recognizing faces? Second, if a group of good face recognizers can be found, will this reflect good overall memory, with the same subjects also being good at paintings and words, or a good visual memory, with these subjects being good at paintings but not words, or will it reflect a specific memory for faces, with our good face recognizers not differing from the poor performers when tested on paintings or verbal material? The third question was again dependent on isolating a group of good recognizers. If we were to ask them how they committed faces to memory, would they be able to reveal new strategies to us which might perhaps help us devise a scheme for training others?

The results we obtained were very clear; those subjects we had selected as being good at recognizing faces did indeed prove to be significantly better than the poor recognizers (4% versus 15% errors). They also proved to be better at recognizing pictures, even though the pictures tended not to have human figures within them (1% versus 5% errors). However, there was no difference whatsoever between the two groups in ability to recognize words (4% versus 5% errors). This suggests that good face recognizers have a good general visual memory, and argues for a separation between the visual and verbal memory systems. It does not, however, suggest a separate facial memory system, as had sometimes been proposed.

Having verified the fact that it is possible to select good recognizers, what can they tell us about their strategies? Alas, once again the results were disappointing. When interviewed there were some slight differences between the two groups, but virtually the only difference between them in terms of reported strategies for remembering faces was that the good recognizers were slightly more inclined to say that they analysed individual features! No doubt Leonardo da Vinci and Jacques Penry would be pleased at this result, but it did not offer any very promising new training strategies. From a practical point of view, however, this study does at least have the comforting feature that it indicates that it should be possible to select people who are particularly good at recognizing faces for jobs that involve face recognition. It also suggests the much trickier option of subsequently evaluating the face recognition ability of a witness. Not a strategy that we would advocate on the strength of the available evidence, but one that might possibly be worth further exploration.

FACE RECOGNITION AND POSE

It may be recalled that our study exploring the effect of disguise on face recognition suggested that subjects who had originally memorized a face in full frontal pose did better at subsequently recognizing it in a three-quarter view than when it was presented in profile. The tendency for profiles to lead to poor performance had also cropped up in a number of our other studies, and raised the question of whether there is something particularly difficult about recognizing profiles or whether our results simply stemmed from a consistent tendency always to present the initial target in a frontal pose, as would be the case given a passport photograph. It could be argued that much of the information present in a profile view would not be obvious from a full-face view and vice versa. Our next experiment investigated the role of pose by presenting the original target in either a frontal, three-quarter or profile view and subsequently testing under each of these conditions.

Our subjects were presented with a total of six photographs of young men, of which two were presented in frontal pose, two in the three-quarter, and two in the profile view. After a delay of 15 minutes during which they performed an unrelated task, subjects were shown a total of 75 slides comprising examples of both target faces and new faces in all three poses. The question at issue was whether the previously observed poor performance on profiles would be once again observed or whether the best recognition view would depend on the view in which the target was originally presented.

Our results were very clear; regardless of initial pose, performance was best when that pose was presented again. Next best performance occurred with a transformation of 45° (frontal to three-quarter, profile to three-quarter or vice versa). Poorest performance occurred when a 90° change occurred between presentation and test pose (full face to profile and vice versa). This implies that the optimal view for generalizing to any possible subsequent pose is a three-quarter view, presumably because this combines information about the profile with information obtained from a frontal view. We decided to explore this further in a more complex study which also included frontal, three-quarter, and profile poses, together with the standard 'mugshot' condition of both frontal and profile poses, and a fifth condition in which all three poses were included. Subjects spent the same amount of time viewing each target face, regardless of whether a single view, two views or three views of that person were presented. When more than one view was presented they were placed side by side. The test involved presenting a series of individual views. In each case the subject was required to decide whether it was a target he had previously viewed or not.

The results are shown in Figure 7.3. Consider first the cases in which only a single target pose was presented during the learning phase. Once again we find an overall tendency for the three-quarter view to lead to better performance, with reasonably good recognition of targets presented in a three-quarter view regardless of whether they are tested in the frontal, three-quarter or profile pose. On further analysis we found that the frontal and profile views suffer badly when the test view is transformed through 90°. The traditional 'mugshot' view of profile and full face is no better than the single three-quarter view. However when a three-quarter view is added, thereby presenting all three poses, performance is best.

Our results suggest then that the conventional procedure of presenting only full-face views for passport photographs is probably sub-optimal. A three-quarter view appears to have the advantage of giving information about both a frontal and a profile view, with the possible additional advantages of inter-relating these two viewpoints. It seems likely that it is this capacity for showing the relationship between the frontal and profile views of a face which provides the additional information that makes the three-pose condition reliably better than the traditional two-pose 'mugshot'.

It occurred to us at this point that if indeed a three-quarter pose does convey more information than a frontal view, then this might be something known to traditional portrait painters. I therefore spent an afternoon in the National Portrait Gallery simply recording the angle of view used by portrait painters from the Tudors to modern times. The results of my rough categorization are shown in Table 7.2. It should be clear from this that up to and including the Edwardians, there was a very marked and consistent tendency for portrait painters to adopt a three-quarter view of their subject. Interestingly, however, the exhibition of modern portraits does not show this effect, indicating a very pronounced tendency for a frontal pose with the sitter gazing at the viewer. It is of interest to speculate on the meaning of this change in portrait style. So far as they go, our own results would support the traditional portrait painter in suggesting that a three-quarter pose is a consistently more informative way of conveying the characteristics of a face.

If our results are correct, then they do have some clear implications for a range of practical situations from the specification of passport photographs to taking family snapshots. However, all our studies have been concerned with

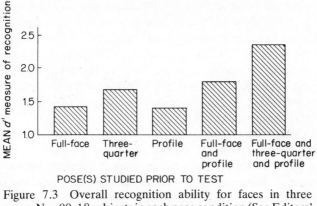

Figure 7.3 Overall recognition ability for faces in three poses. N = 90, 18 subjects in each pose condition (See Editors' Note, p. 54)

Table 7.2 Poses in the National Portrait Gallery

Period	Profile facing left	Three-quarter angled to left	Front facing	Three-quarter angled to right	Profile facing right
Tudor	2	16	2	13	0
Stuart	0	12	1	9	0
Civil War	0	20	2	19	0
Restoration	0	12	1	11	0
ⓒ & Georgian	1	17	13	12	2
Victorian/Edwardian	4	32	9	14	0
TOTALS	7	109	28	78	2
Contemporary	3	12	25	11	0
Jane Bown (photography)	0	10	20	4	0
TOTALS	3	22	45	15	0

presenting photographs and subsequently recognizing other photographs. Before advocating any major change in policy, it is clearly important that we establish that our pose results generalize to a situation in which memory for the photographed face is tested by presenting an actual person. We plan to carry out such an experiment shortly.

CONCLUSIONS

We began with two views of face perception, the feature based approach and the holistic personality based approach. We tried in turn to use each of these to enhance the encoding of faces in such a way that subsequent recognition would be improved. In each case we had minimal success. This suggests that the way in which we encode faces is so overlearned that there may be little we can do to affect it. However the possibility remains that if we understood more about the underlying process of face recognition then much more effective strategies might become available. Until we make such a breakthrough however, improving face recognition by teaching encoding strategies would appear to be a distinctly unpromising line of research.

Our investigations have shown up two potentially useful, if minor aids. The first is the demonstration that it is possible to select people who are extremely good at recognizing faces. While eyewitnesses can not usually be selected in advance, our result does suggest that for certain occupations where memory for faces would be advantageous, it should be possible to select appropriately. The second useful outcome from our work concerns pose, and suggests that a current preoccupation with a frontal viewpoint which seems to run right through from passport photographs to portraiture may well be misguided. The possible advantages of adopting a standardized three-quarter viewpoint certainly seem to merit further investigation.

REFERENCES

Bower, G.H. and Karlin, M.B. (1974). Depth of processing pictures of faces and recognition memory. *Journal of Experimental Psychology*, **103**, 751–757.

Craik, F.I.M. and Lockhart, R.S. (1972). Levels of processing: A framework for memory research. *Journal of Verbal Learning and Verbal Behavior*, **11**, 671–684.

Davies, G. Forensic face recall. This volume.

Patterson, K.E. and Baddeley, A.D. (1977). When face recognition fails. *Journal of Experimental Psychology: Human Learning and Memory*, **3**, 406–417.

Penry, J. (1971). *Looking at Faces and Remembering Them: A Guide to Facial Identification*. London: Elek Books.

Warrington, E.K. (1974). Deficient recognition memory in organic amnesia. *Cortex*, **10**, 289–291.

Winograd, E. (1976). Recognition memory for faces following nine different judgments. *Bulletin of the Psychonomic Society*, **8**, 419–421.

Woodhead, M.M., Baddeley, A.D., and Simmonds, D.C.V. (1979). On training people to recognize faces. *Ergonomics*, **22**, 333–343.

Evaluating Witness Evidence
Edited by S.M.A. Lloyd-Bostock and B.R. Clifford
© 1983 John Wiley & Sons Ltd.

Chapter 8

Lie Detection: Techniques and Countermeasures

Gisli H. Gudjonsson

Lying is a part of human behaviour that most people are undoubtedly familiar with. Most people have on occasion told lies or seen others being evasive. Through experience people may learn to detect such behaviour by interpreting outward verbal and non-verbal cues. This is possible because the act of lying is sometimes accompanied by behavioural and physiological changes that are detectable by the human sense organs. Indeed, studies have shown that un-aided by physiological instruments people are in general significantly better than chance at detecting deception (DePaulo and Rosenthal, 1979). However, detecting lies in others on the basis of various outward indications alone is problematic. For example, it has been found that, although overall detect-ability may be above chance level, many observers cannot easily detect deception from vocal and facial cues (Zuckerman *et al.*, 1979). Furthermore, the ability to detect deception appears to be a disparate set of skills, with observers being able to identify deception in members of one sex, but not necessarily in those of the other (DePaulo and Rosenthal, 1979). In view of this it is not surprising that people became interested in the 'instrumental' deter-mination of deception, where one could attempt systematically to record some of the subtle physiological changes that accompany lying.

The potential for psychophysiological detection of deception is of particular interest to the police because they frequently encounter people who may be being evasive. The possibility is not confined to suspects. The shrewd police officer also has to be aware of the possibility of deception by complainants and witnesses. Solicitors, judges, doctors, and many other professionals may also associate with people who are at times deceptive. Knowledge of when deception occurs may be important so that 'clients' can be appropriately dealt with.

This paper examines some of the background, principles, and application of the psychophysiological detection of deception, with particular reference to some of the countermeasure techniques.

HISTORICAL BACKGROUND

Throughout the centuries, detection of deception has been attempted by numerous methods. Torture and ordeals were commonly used in ancient times in an attempt to establish the truth and enforce the administration of justice (Larson, 1932). The idea behind ordeals was that guilt or innocence could be determined by observing the suspect's reactions when placed under severe stress. Although the ancients appear to have made some use of the physiological indicators of stress (e.g. sweating, dry mouth, blushing, etc.) the ordeals were undoubtedly based more on religious faith than on scientific understanding.

The human pulse was probably the first physiological system to be used directly to detect deception. It appears from historical accounts that as early as the Middle Ages deception was sometimes determined by feeling the pulse (Trovillo, 1939). However, it was not until the late nineteenth century that instruments for measuring and recording blood pressure and pulse rate were developed. Lombroso (1895) appears to have been the first person to use a scientific instrument for the detection of deception. He used some of the early methods of measuring blood pressure — pulse changes in experiments that he conducted on criminal suspects. Lombroso at times assisted the police by measuring suspects' physiological reactions to items of evidence placed suddenly and unexpectedly before their eyes (Trovillo, 1939). This suggests that Lombroso was not so much concerned with lying *per se*, but rather with suspects' physiological reactions to relevant (critical) stimuli.

Early in the twentieth century, Münsterberg, one of the founding fathers of forensic psychology, showed great interest in lie detection methods and encouraged one his students, William M. Marston, to follow the experimental work of Lombroso. Marston's early work was published in 1917 and dealt specifically with systolic blood pressure symptoms of deception (Marston, 1917). Marston's subsequent alleged discovery of a specific lie response and his extravagant claims (Marston, 1938) did much to exaggerate the forensic and commercial possibilities of the polygraph.

In 1921 John A. Larson constructed an instrument that simultaneously recorded blood pressure, pulse, and respiration. He worked as a police officer with the Berkeley police department and carried out many successful lie detection tests on criminal suspects (Larson, 1932). One of Larson's important contributions was to educate people about the practical value of the polygraph in the detection of deception during police investigations. However, Larson's original enthusiasm about the potential of lie detection in criminal cases gradually diminished as he became aware of its limitations and possible abuse. Larson was relying exclusively on the 'relevant–irrelevant' technique (see below) but subsequently more sophisticated techniques have been constructed and developed.

In 1926 Leonarde Keeler refined the instrument developed by Larson and added the electrodermal modality to the existing polygraph (Keeler, 1930). Keeler also introduced some new lie detection techniques, such as the 'card task' and the 'peak of tension test' (see below). Keeler's method of rechecking the responses of suspects by employing 'control' tests gave an important impetus to modern lie detection techniques.

At the present time there are a number of different polygraphs available for lie detection purposes but they are all based on similar principles. Since the beginning of this century polygraphs have continuously been refined although they have maintained some of their essential features. It is important to remember that these instruments were not developed for lie detection purposes. They were first intended for medical advances and only subsequently did people discover their potential in the field of lie detection. The polygraph does not detect lies. Early claims of a specific lie response (e.g. Marston, 1938) have not been substantiated. What is detected is a physiological response and the examiner must infer whether or not such reactions are indicative of lying.

The traditional polygraph consists of electrodermal, respiratory, and cardiovascular measures recorded simultaneously. In field contexts, the three measures are invariably used jointly, whereas experimentally electrodermal activity is commonly employed on its own. In the early 1970s two different instruments were devised specifically to measure 'stress' in the speaking voice. The original and more widespread of these is the Psychological Stress Evaluator (PSE). At first it seemed as if the PSE was going to be the first challenge to the traditional polygraph. Extravagant claims were made by the manufacturers which have not stood up to scientific scrutiny (Lykken, 1981).

TECHNIQUES

There are at present two fundamentally different methods available for the detection of deception. Lykken (1960, 1974, 1981) refers to these as 'lie detection' and 'guilty knowledge' techniques. Podlesny and Raskin (1977) have alternatively labelled them as 'deception' and 'information' tests. The former consists of any questioning technique that involves asking the subject one or more 'relevant' questions (e.g. Did you take the missing money?) and comparing the response with that to some 'irrelevant' question (e.g. Are you sitting down now?) or 'emotive control' question (e.g. Before the age of 18 did you ever steal anything?). Guilty knowledge tests are based on the assumption that the subject's awareness of certain information is capable of producing 'differential responsivity'. The method requires the examiner to establish certain facts that only the guilty subject will recognize as relevant. These facts can then be presented in the form of multiple-choice items, embedded in a set of a few alternatives that would seem equally plausible to an innocent subject. The basic assumption is that the guilty subject can be expected to show stronger physiological reactions to items he recognizes as significant than to the alternative items. Therefore, according to the assumptions of the guilty knowledge test, lying is not a necessary prerequisite for successful detection. The items need not even be in the form of questions to which the subject is required to give answers: the subject may simply be asked to listen to the presentation of the stimulus items.

However, in spite of the clear advantages of the guilty knowledge technique, it cannot often be used in practice because frequently there is not enough unpublished guilty knowledge material available to construct the test. For this reason the technique is rarely used in field examinations (Lykken, 1974). Police officers may also be reluctant to reveal critical information to suspects, even though it is embedded in a set of similar alternatives. Furthermore, in some instances police officers may unwittingly have provided suspects with significant information concering the crime in question (Irving and Hilgendorf, 1980). If this is the case then the value of the guilty knowledge technique is substantially reduced.

According to Lykken (1974) the assumptions of lie detection tests are not as straightforward as those of the guilty knowledge test. Some of the early workers in the lie detection field maintained that there was a distinctive pattern of physiological response which accompanied lying which could be distinguished from that accompanying truthtelling. Thus, Benussi (1914) stated that the respiratory ratio of expiration to inspiration increased after lying but decreased after a truthful answer. Marston (1938) believed that an increase in systolic blood pressure was certain evidence of lying. Such simplistic views of lie detection have not been substantiated. Indeed, the inference that physiological responses can indicate lying must be viewed with extreme caution since identical responses can be produced by many stimuli unrelated to lying (Burack, 1956; Dearman and Smith, 1963; Davidson, 1968). Furthermore, the detection of a critical item during a lie detection test does not appear to depend on the act of lying *per se*. For example, Kugelmass *et al.* (1967) asked subjects to answer the critical questions affirmatively (truthfully) and the control questions negatively (deceptively) during a standard card task procedure. The electrodermal responses to the critical cards were in general still larger than the responses to the irrelevant items even though the subjects were telling the truth. Orne *et al.* (1972) have interpreted such findings as suggesting that it is the deceptive intent rather than the overt lie that produces 'differential responsivity'.

Some of the most common lie detection tests that have been used are as follows:

Relevant-irrelevant tests

This technique was invented by Larson in the early part of this century and was the first standardized detection technique. The questions employed include some relevant questions and several irrelevant questions that are used for comparison purposes. Deception is indicated when the physiological responses to the relevant questions are larger and more frequent than those to the irrelevant questions. As Podlesny and Raskin (1977) point out, the relevant-irrelevant technique suffers from serious faults which relate mainly to inadequate control procedures, and bias against innocent subjects. For these reasons the technique is rarely used nowadays.

Peak-of-tension tests

As described in the literature (e.g. Reid and Inbau, 1977), the peak-of-tension technique consists in presenting a series of questions, only one of which is expected to elicit a lie from a guilty subject, after first showing him the sequence of the questions in advance. The name of the technique relates to the notion that a guilty subject will show increased physiological responsivity in anticipation of the relevant item and then a decline in responsivity after the item has passed. The test was invented by Keeler and is, strictly speaking not a lie detection test but is designed to detect 'guilty information'. In this respect the technique shares some characteristics with Lykken's guilty knowledge technique, although there are clear differences (Lykken, 1974).

Control questions tests

Following the realization of the limitations of the relevant-irrelevant techniques some more sophisticated lie detection methods have been devised. The control question technique was originally developed by John È. Reid (Reid, 1947) and is now the most commonly used field technique (Reid and Inbau, 1977). The technique involves asking control questions that are carefully constructed during a lengthy pretest interview. The questions are often of a similar nature to the relevant questions and are worded in such a way as to elicit a 'no' answer from the subject. However, they differ from the relevant questions in that they bear no direct relationship to the crime in question. The theory holds that an innocent subject will be more concerned about the control questions whereas the relevant questions will be stronger stimuli to the guilty subject (Raskin and Podlesny, 1979). The reason for this is that subjects are given subtle instructions which may affect the way they perceive the questions. For example, they are persuaded that the control questions are employed in order to evaluate their basic honesty which is relevant to their passing the test. The procedure is designed to create in innocent subjects concern about the control questions, whereas for guilty subjects the relevant questions will still represent a relatively greater threat. In addition to the attempt to elicit deceptive answers to the control questions in all subjects, the technique frequently involves use of a numerical scoring system that includes an 'inconclusive' category aimed to reduce false positive and false negative error.

The techniques discussed above are only a few of many that have been constructed and applied in field contexts. For further information about lie detection techniques and their assumptions see the books by Reid and Inbau (1977) and by Lykken (1981). It is probably true to say that only the guilty knowledge and control question techniques have reached acceptable scientific standards. The latter is not always practicable in the field.

VALIDITY

Lie detection techniques are currently being employed in many countries including the United States, Canada, Israel, and Japan, but have met with little enthusiasm in Europe. Lykken (1981) estimates that over 1 million polygraph tests are conducted annually in the United States by several thousand professional polygraphers. Most are carried out in commercial settings. In Great Britain lie detection techniques are rarely used in criminal cases but the author knows of one security firm that uses the Psychological Stress Evaluator regularly to detect deception and claims almost 100% success! Such extraordinary claims reveal a poor objective understanding of the complexities of human behaviour and of the limitations of instruments like the PSE. It is probably because of such unrealistic claims that the use of psychophysiological methods of detection is treated with suspicion by many people.

In the United States lie detection is one of the most important and controversial areas of applied psychology. The bitter disagreement between Lykken and Raskin over the validity of lie detection techniques is a matter of concern for those who are interested in the area. Both are eminent and reputable scientists. Raskin, who is a trained polygrapher and a psychophysiologist, claims a 90% success rate with the control question technique (Raskin and Podlesny, 1979). Lykken (1981), on the other hand, maintains that the polygraph test has an accuracy rate of between 64% and 72% (against a chance expectancy of 50%) when the scoring of the charts is done blind, and is uninfluenced by extrapolygraphic cues such as clinical impression. Furthermore, Lykken argues that the control question technique is particularly unreliable with innocent subjects because of the incriminating nature of the relevant questions.

In a laboratory setting there is usually a clearly defined criterion measure against which the results can be evaluated. Many experimental studies employing the guilty knowledge and control question techniques have reported over 90% success rate (Lykken, 1959, 1960; Davidson, 1968; Raskin and Hare, 1978). In field studies 'ground truth' is commonly difficult to establish because many crimes are never solved and a confession is not always a reliable index of the truth. Furthermore, subjects who subsequently confess are unlikely to be representative of deceptive subjects in general. Innocence and guilt have occasionally been evaluated by a panel of experts as in the study of Berch (1969). Field studies are thus generally difficult to evaluate due to inadequate criterion measures. There is no doubt however, that lie detection techniques are significantly better than chance at detecting deception, although the degree of accuracy is controversial. The exact validity of a particular technique may depend on such factors as the experience of the examiner and the care he has taken when constructing the test. The concept of lying is also problematic and lie detection tests may not be applicable to all situations where deception has occurred. Some of the techniques employed have not been adequately validated: it seems that the control question technique has been most thoroughly studied, and its validity has been empirically documented. Unfortunately, the guilty knowledge technique is difficult to apply but where applicable it seems highly effective and it is particularly useful in that it protects against false positive errors. However, the technique may be particularly prone to false negative errors (Podlesny and Raskin, 1978).

COUNTERMEASURES

Lie detection countermeasures are deliberate techniques that some subjects use to appear non-deceptive when their physiological responses are being monitored during a polygraph examination. Barland and Raskin (1973) point out that countermeasures imply deliberate action and must not be confused with 'accidental' false negatives or with psychological factors other than specific attempts to defeat the polygraph. For example, some subjects may be highly unresponsive during testing due to poor autonomic nervous system liability, although one should bear in mind that as far as electrodermal activity is concerned, significant detectability is possible at relatively low levels of reactivity (Kugelmass et al., 1973).

Subjects may by various methods try to 'beat' the lie detection test. Basically, however, there are two different ways of misleading the polygraph record:
1. Subjects can attempt to suppress their physiological responses to the critical questions/items and hence make differential responsivity minimal.
2. Subjects can attempt intentionally to produce physiological responses to the control questions/items so as to reduce the discriminative power of the critical item.

The latter method is considered to be more effective than the former (Gustafson and Orne, 1964; Lykken, 1981): the subject may concentrate on the control stimuli and emit responses that interfere with the efficacy of the technique. However, Gustafson and Orne (1964) point out that under field conditions this tactic is not likely to be successful because the subject's task would be to convince the examiner that he is innocent, and not that he is guilty of something else. Detection efficiency may also be improved by the subject's inability to control all the polygraph indices simultaneously (Cutrow *et al.*, 1972).

Some studies (e.g. Stern and Kaplan, 1967; Stern and Lewis, 1968) have shown that those subjects who are best able to control their electrodermal responses (response amplitudes and spontaneous fluctuations) usually report that their primary bodily response to real-life stress is sweating. Similar findings were reported by Stern more recently (Stern, 1973). However these studies were not concerned with lie detection and it is not known to what extent similar principles apply to the detection of deception.

Some of the countermeasure techniques employed by subjects to control their physiological responses and hence beat the polygraph are as follows:

Mental countermeasures

The subject may try to suppress or augment physiological responses by mental effort and strategies. One tactic might be mental dissociation where the subject attempts to ignore the content of the test and answer the questions automatically. He may focus his attention upon some irrelevant object or thought. It is probably comparatively easy for subjects to use mental dissociation on tasks like the peak-of-tension test, where they know the content and sequence of the questions and can try to answer them 'automatically' in a uniform way. Kubis (1962) refers to the mental dissociation countermeasure as 'modified yoga', but in his study it did not seem an effective countermeasure. A detection rate of 80% was obtained in the modified yoga group as compared with 75% in the control group. The expected detection rate by chance was 10%. Similar findings were obtained by More (1966).

Barland and Raskin (1973) suggest some counter-countermeasures which discourage the subject from employing dissociation tactics and make him more aware of the content of each question. For example, the subject may be required to repeat key words or read out the questions to ensure that he listens to the content.

'Rationalization' is another technique by which physiological responsivity might be suppressed. This technique may be effective if the subject believes the rationalization (Beattie, 1957). However, rationalization can only be considered to be a countermeasure if it is a deliberate and conscious strategy employed by the subject. For example, Flock (1950) and Reid and Inbau (1977) have expressed the opinion that some people can, by unconsciously employing defence mechanisms, rationalize their offence to the extent of producing false negative results.

Borkenstein and Larson (1957) imply that one way of reducing the effectiveness of rationalization is by using questions that deal with behaviour that is difficult to rationalize. Furthermore, a pretest interview, where questions are extensively reviewed before testing, emphasizes the intent of the questions and therefore reduces the possibility of rationalization (Barland and Raskin, 1973).

As mentioned above, another type of mental countermeasure is artificially to produce responses to the irrelevant questions by emotionally arousing thoughts (e.g. by reflecting back to an erotic or a painful experience). Kubis (1962) found this to be an effective countermeasure: detection was reduced from 75% in the control group to 25% in the experimental group. In More's (1966) study, however, exciting imagery was not found to be such an effective countermeasure: a detection rate of 95% was obtained in the control group as compared with 80% in the countermeasure group.

Barland and Raskin (1973) argue that it is difficult to counteract this type of countermeasure because of the difficulty involved in trying to establish when it is being employed: They further argue that creating a false response in the field situation can sometimes be done skilfully, especially when control question tests are used. The argument by Gustafson and Orne (1964) that it is not in the subject's interest artificially to create a response to control items in a field context, seems to hold true only when the relevant-irrelevant and peak-of-tension tests are employed. Exceptionally strong reactions to irrelevant questions would make a lie detection expert suspicious that countermeasures were being employed to distort the recording. Furthermore, many field examiners do not rely on the magnitude of responses alone but interpret the chart as a whole. On the peak-of-tension test, for example, a gradual increase in physiological responses would be expected as the critical item approaches, and then a decline thereafter. In order to be effective the subject would have to produce artificially responses of controlled magnitude. This is very difficult to do with regard to electrodermal activity.

In recent years there has been a growing interest in the extent to which subjects can be trained in using effective countermeasures. Lykken (1960) used sophisticated subjects and taught them that it was best to beat the machine by artificially producing responses to the irrelevant items. In spite of this, all deceptions were detected, employing the guilty knowledge technique. Suzuki et al. (1969) found that it was possible for subjects to enhance electrodermal responses to certain items by audio and visual biofeedback. However, there appears to have been only one published study that employed an extensive biofeedback programme as a mental countermeasure. Corcoran et al. (1978) administered a number of card tests to 30 subjects (19 males and 11 females). The 17 most responsive subjects were subsequently given training in either biofeedback or hypnosis. The goals of training were to teach the subjects to generate artificial responses and to suppress genuine responses. The training lasted 4 weeks. All 30 subjects were then retested and it was found that the 'trained' subjects were significantly better at deceiving the examiner than the controls. The authors did not draw any conclusion concerning the effectiveness of hypnosis versus biofeedback. Lykken (1981) reports having started carrying out a similar 'biofeedback' study during the 1960s. Although the study was never completed Lykken became convinced that some people can be trained to beat the lie detector test (Lykken, 1981, p. 238).

In a recent study, Dawson (1980) evaluated the effectiveness of actors in beating the polygraph. The actors had all been trained in the Stanislavsky method of using personal memories of sensory experiences in order to re-create emotional states. Half of the actors ($N = 12$) participated in a mock crime and the control question technique was used in order to establish their guilt or innocence. The technique was 100% effective with the guilty subjects but there were a number of false positive errors, which supports previous findings that false positive errors may occasionally occur with the control question technique (Barland and Raskin, 1973; Raskin and Hare, 1978; Rovner et al., 1979). Dawson (1980) suggests that instructing all subjects to use countermeasures may actually contribute to high false positive rates. It may be concluded from this that for an innocent subject an attempt to use counter-measures to establish his innocence could actually improve his chances of appearing guilty, particularly when the control question technique is used. In general, the studies by Lykken (1960), Rovner et al. (1979) and Dawson (1980) suggest that it is difficult for most people to learn how to beat the polygraph test by employing mental countermeasures.

The effectiveness of hypnosis as a countermeasure has been studied by a number of authors (Bitterman and Marcuse, 1947; Cumley, 1959; Germann, 1961; Tocchio, 1963; Weinstein, et al., 1970). It seems from these studies that hypnosis may only be marginally effective in misleading the lie detection expert.

Physical countermeasures

A number of physical manipulations can be used in an attempt to distort the polygraph recording. According to Barland and Raskin (1973), almost any voluntary contraction of a muscle group within the body may produce responses that resemble true physiological responses. Reid (1945) reports that it is possible to distort cardiovascular recording by tensing and relaxing the arm on which the cardic cuff is attached. Of course, the subject must select muscle manipulation that is not visible to the examiner. Some of the techniques that have been observed include pressing the toes against the floor (Smith, 1967) and pressing the thighs against the chair (Reid and Inbau, 1977). Lykken (1981) argues that people can be trained to employ such techniques. Barland and Raskin (1973) point out that such countermeasures will not be effectively applied by all subjects and may not even be consistently effective within a single individual over a period of time. Kubis (1962) found that asking subjects to press their toes against the floor reduced the detection rate from 75% to chance level (10%). However, More (1966), in his replication study of Kubis's findings, found no reduction in detectability caused by toe movements.

There are certain counter-countermeasures that can successfully reduce detection error. For example, Reid (1945) was able to record certain body movements by means of pneumatic sensors built into the back and seat of the subject's chair. One can also reduce the effectiveness of toe movements by using a reclining chair which removes the subject's legs from the floor and permits a better visual inspection of the legs. Barland and Raskin (1973) report that in some circumstances subjects may try to produce physical pain in an attempt to beat the lie detection test. One way this can be done is by concealing a drawing pin within the subject's shoe or under the tongue. Slight pressure may then by appropriately applied to produce considerable pain. Such techniques seem to be rarely applied in the field however. Intuitively it would seem rather difficult to apply these countermeasures since before the experiment the subject would presumable find it difficult to walk and talk naturally.

Another category of countermeasures involves the use of chemical and pharmacological agents. Arther (1971) reports that the use of an anti-perspirant on the hands prior to testing can diminish electrodermal reactivity. This countermeasure can be prevented from being effective by asking the subject to wash his hands with soap and water prior to the testing. With regard to pharmacological substances depressants appear potentially useful since they have been found to reduce autonomic reactivity (Berman, 1967). Alcohol has been shown to have a depressing effect on electrodermal activity (Smith, 1922; Smith, 1967). Davis (1961) considers alcohol, barbiturates, and possibly tranquillizers to have some potential as countermeasures, but as Reid and Inbau (1977) point out the amounts of drugs required to reduce responsivity sufficiently would produce noticeable behavioural abnormalities. However, recently Waid et al. (1981) showed that the tranquillizer Meprobamate successfully reduced detectability in college students when the guilty knowledge technique was used. Whether Meprobamate would also be effective in a highly motivating context and when the control question technique is used remains to be seen. Since the control question technique tends to be more emotionally arousing than the guilty knowledge technique the former may be more resistant to tranquillizers.

In summary, lie detection techniques are fairly resistant to countermeasure strategies, although some people can skilfully distort the polygraph recording and deceive the examiner. Errors are less likely to occur when more than one physiological measure is used and where the examiner evaluates obvious behavioural symptoms indicative of deliberate distortion techniques (e.g. breathing irregularly, deliberate movements, etc.) in addition to the chart.

A COUNTERMEASURE STUDY

It is apparent that there are a number of different countermeasures available which may differ in their effectiveness. The author has recently completed a study where 96 subjects (48 males and 48 females) were encouraged to 'beat the machine' during three traditional card tasks, while their electrodermal responses were recorded (for full details of the procedure see Gudjonsson, 1981). After each task the subjects were asked about the countermeasure technique they had employed. The subjects' replies could be classified into the following four groups according to the type of countermeasure they had used:

1. Here there was a deliberate attempt to *produce* physiological responses to the control/irrelevant items so as to reduce the discriminative power of the critical item. These only included mental effort and strategies; no subject reported having used physical manipulation such as voluntary contraction of a muscle group, although four subjects reported that they tried to take a deep breath immediately before the irrelevant items. The most common strategy was for people to concentrate on the irrelevant items or to reflect back to an erotic/pleasant or painful experience. Typical statements by subjects were as follows:

> 'I tried to react to number 7'
> 'I concentrated on April'
> 'I associated July with my girlfriend's month of birth'
> 'I tried to react to some other month'
> 'I made myself feel guilty to other numbers'

2. A number of people reported having made an effort to *relax* or to *control* their physiological responses to the critical/relevant items. Typical statements were as follows:

> 'I tried to relax as much as I could'
> 'I tried to keep my voice the same'
> 'I tried to control my breath'
> I tried to give the same reaction to all'
> 'I tried not to react to my number'

3. The third group of countermeasures involved a deliberate attempt to *distract* or *dissociate* away from the relevant items. Typical examples were as follows:

> 'I tried to forget the number I picked'
> 'I divorced myself from the task'
> 'I cut my mind off'
> 'I tried not to notice the month I had picked'
> 'I denied to myself that I had taken the number'

Some of the subjects reported that they found dissociation tactics difficult because they had to read out the items, which reminded them of the 'lie' stimuli.

4. There was a minority of subjects who reported not having made any attempt whatsoever to beat the machine, although they had been specifically encouraged to do so at the beginning of the experiment. When asked why they had not tried to beat the machine the subjects commonly stated that it was because they had not been interested, could not be bothered, or had too many things on their mind. Some of the subjects in this group complained about how boring they found the task.

The number of subjects in each of the four groups is shown in Table 8.1.

Countermeasure strategies in Group 2 were most commonly employed on all tasks. Only about 10% of the subjects reported having used no countermeasures at all. Tasks 1 and 2 were both number tasks and differed only in the numbers used and instructions given prior to the task. Task 3 was a traditional month-of-birth task (i.e. attempting to detect the subject's month of birth from his/her responses). Prior to Tasks 1 and 3 the subjects were told that they could use any countermeasure strategy they liked, whereas on Task 2 the subject was told that he/she could have drawn a blank card as opposed to a numbered one (although this was not the case), and therefore if he/she reacted to any of the numbers subsequently asked about then the experimenter would know that a number had been drawn. The subject was instructed that the only way to beat the machine on this task was to try not to react to any of the cards. This instruction was given in order to discourage subjects from intentionally producing physiological responses to the control items on one of the number tasks, so that a comparison between tasks could be carried out. In fact, both males and females showed significantly greater differential responsivity to Task 2 than on the other number task.

As shown in Table 8.1. the instructions given prior to Task 2 reduced the number of subjects employing the countermeasure strategies given in Group 1. Therefore, the instructions had the intended effects.

There was a marked sex difference however, in that all but one of the females (2.1%) reported that they followed the task instructions whereas ten of the males (20.8%) claimed not to have followed the instructions. In order to

Table 8.1   Number of subjects employing different countermeasure techniques

Group	Task		
	1	2	3
1	25 (26.0%)	11 (11.5%)	30 (31.2%)
2	36 (37.5%)	50 (52.1%)	40 (41.7%)
3	22 (22.9%)	27 (28.1%)	16 (16.7%)
4	13 (13.6%)	8 (8.3%)	10 (10.4%)
	96 (100.0%)	96 (100.0%)	96 (100.0%)

Table 8.2   The effects of countermeasure on detectability scores

Task	Countermeasure employed			No countermeasure employed			t-value	d.f.	$p <$
	N	Mean	SD	N	Mean	SD			
1	83	0.289	0.223	13	0.180	0.139	2.29	94	0.025
2	88	0.363	0.250	8	0.178	0.117	3.76	94	0.001
3	86	0.303	0.258	10	0.167	0.095	3.33	94	0.005

Note: The mean scores represent differential responsivity; that is, the skin resistance responses to the critical and control items were transformed in log $(1 + x)$ and the difference subsequently taken between them.

evaluate the sex difference a chi-square test was applied to the data; that is, males and females were compared on the number of times countermeasure 1 v. countermeasures 2 and 3 were used. The difference is statistically significant $(\chi^2 = 8.42, p (df = 1) < .01$, two-tailed test). When the 11 subjects were asked why they had not followed the instructions they generally reported that volitionally producing a physiological reaction to an irrelevant item was the only way they thought they could beat the machine.

Two types of predictions were made with regard to how countermeasures strategies might affect differential responsivity. These were as follows:
1. Employing a countermeasure should improve the detection rate. Group 4 showed less general interest in the tasks and would therefore be less likely to be detected (Orne et al., 1972; Day and Rourke, 1974).
2. Countermeasures 2 and 3 should be more effective than countermeasure 1. This would be expected from the views of Gustafson and Orne (1964) and Lykken (1981), in as far as they suggest it is more effective for subjects to beat the machine by attempting to augment responses to the irrelevant items rather than attempting to attenuate responses to the critical items.

Table 8.2 shows that subjects who reported having used no countermeasure at all (Group 4) were significantly less easily detected than the remaining three groups on all three tasks. This suggests that within an experimental context involvement in the task is associated with heightened detection.

Table 8.3 shows the difference in differential responsivity between Group 1 and Groups 2 and 3. The prediction was confirmed for one of the tasks only. This suggests that generally speaking, the most effective countermeasure strategy is for subjects intentionally to produce electrodermal responses to the control questions. However, there were clear individual differences. For example, one subject in the study was able to dissociate herself from the task to the extent of producing no measurable differential responsivity at all on any of

Table 8.3   Difference in effectiveness between countermeasures 1 v. countermeasures 2 and 3

Task	Countermeasure						t-value	d.f.	$p<$
	1			2 and 3					
	N	Mean	SD	N	Mean	SD			
1	25	0.204	0.164	58	0.325	0.236	2.68	81	0.005
2	11	0.403	0.361	77	0.366	0.243	−0.33	86	n.s.
3	30	0.268	0.268	56	0.314	0.236	0.45	84	n.s.

the tasks. The subject explained that before each task she 'accumulated a lot of energy and by determination cut herself off' from the demand characteristics of the task. It is interesting that her electrodermal chart was actually very consistent with her self-report; that is, a few seconds prior to each task there was a sudden decrease in her skin resistance level (increased arousal) and then there was a straight descending line (reduced arousal) throughout the task. Once the task was completed the skin resistance level returned to 'normal' and spontaneous fluctuations were resumed. This process was repeated identically on all three tasks. In fact, this subject was the only person out of the 96 participating in the study who was able to beat the machine on all three tasks. Other subjects also appeared able effectively to beat the machine on one or two of the tasks by using relaxation, control or dissociation strategies. Thus, there may be individual differences in the ability of subjects effectively to apply different countermeasure techniques.

CONCLUSION

Lie detection has become a booming business in the United States but it is rarely used in a criminal context in Great Britain. Professor Eysenck's early attempt to stimulate interest in lie detection in Britain (Eysenck, 1958) met with little enthusiasm. Recently Irving and Hilgendorf (1980) have written a review paper on lie detection and suggested that it is sufficiently reliable and valid for police forces to use it in conjunction with careful detective work. The authors further argue that with 'an error rate of 12 per cent, and 86 per cent reliability, the test cannot conform to the usual interpretations of beyond reasonable doubt'. It is implied that for this reason lie detection results should not be used as evidence in a court of law. The authors seem to overlook the fact that the 'burden of proof' in criminal cases relates to the whole of the evidence taken together and not to individual items. If each piece of evidence has to be interpreted as being 'beyond reasonable doubt' then most human testimony would not be admissible. The margin of error associated with polygraph results means that they should be required to be corroborated by other evidence, but not that they should never be admitted in evidence. It is abundantly clear from other papers in this book that in some cases eyewitness testimony may, in fact, be less reliable than lie detection results. However, some authors (e.g. Abbell, 1978; Lykken, 1981) consider that lie detection evidence does present special problems when it is proffered to the court. This is because of the objective, scientific, and sophisticated appearance of the polygraph apparatus. Lie detection results are almost invariably 'conclusive', although in recent years an 'inconclusive' category is sometimes used in cases of uncertainty. The jury may not be in a position to evaluate the subjective interpretation of the objectively derived scoring. In contrast to eyewitness testimony, the jury may have some difficulty evaluating lie detection evidence because it is based on measures that are not specifically related to lying. Unlike the experienced polygrapher, the jury has no knowledge of how to link psychophysiological responses to lying behaviour; it has to rely on the experience and opinion of the expert. The fear seems to be that the polygraph evidence will be accepted uncritically by the jury and may constitute a threat to the jury system. Such fears are not supported by the available empirical evidence (Barnett, 1973; Carlson *et al.*, 1977; Cavoukian and Heslegrave, 1980). Nevertheless, a polygraph evidence may be made inadmissible in a court of law due to such beliefs. This is precisely what happened recently when the author attempted to present the result of a polygraph test as evidence in a Crown Court case of Appeal in Oxford.

The author had administered a polygraph test to a young housewife who had been convicted in a Magistrates' Court of obtaining money by deception from a shop. The polygraph test showed the woman to be truthful regarding the offence. The case was successfully appealed and the barrister for the defence fought to have the evidence accepted in court. A lengthy legal battle over the admissibility of polygraph evidence in an English court of law took place. The judge objected to using such evidence on the basis that it had no precedence in English law and if accepted it would take over the function of judge and jury.

My argument is that polygraph evidence is sufficiently reliable and valid to be used when appropriate as a part of the totality of evidence in a court of law. The fear that the jury would place undue weight on such evidence is unsubstantiated. However, polygraph techniques clearly have inherent limitations and like most other sophisticated techniques are not appropriate in all cases and their use in commercial settings is very dubious. Even within a criminal context some subjects are not readily testable and in some situations the techniques are not applicable. Polygraph techniques are probably most suitably used as an investigative tool in police work. Indeed, a carefully constructed polygraph test can be an invaluable tool in selected cases, but employing such a technique routinely on all suspects and victims is to abuse its potential as an investigative tool. Furthermore, polygraph tests when inappropriately used can be potentially coercive and 'involuntary' confessions may occur (Lykken, 1981). It is also worth remembering that no polygraph technique is infallible. Errors do occur but these can be minimized by proper training and by employing the most up-to-date techniques. When the control question technique is used most reliance can be placed on truthful (non-deceptive) results but the reverse is true with the guilty knowledge techniques. Both techniques are gaining increased scientific acceptance and in the future it is likely that the reliability and validity of polygraph techniques can be further improved by the availability of computer facilities.

REFERENCES

Abbell, M. (1978). Polygraphic evidence: The case against admissibility in Federal Criminal Trials. *American Criminal Law Review*, **15**, 29–62.

Arther, R.O. (1971). The GSR Unit. *Journal of Polygraph Studies*, **5**, 1–4.

Balloun, K.D. and Holmes, D.S. (1979). Effects of repeated examination on the ability to detect guilt with a polygraph examination: A laboratory experiment with real crime. *Journal of Applied Psychology*, **64**, 316–322.

Barland, G.H. and Raskin, D.C. (1973). Detection of deception. In W.F. Prokasy and D.C. Raskin (eds), *Electrodermal Activity in Psychological Research*. New York: Academic Press, p. 417–477.

Barnett, F.J. (1973). How does a jury view polygraph examination results? *Polygraph*, **2**, 275–277.

Beattie, R.J. (1957). The semantics of question preparation. In V.A. Leonard (ed.), *Academy Lectures in Lie Detection*. Springfield: Thomas, p. 20–43.

Benussi, V. (1914). Die Atmungssymptome der Lüge. *Archive für die gesamte Psychologie*, **31**, 244–273.

Berch, P.J. (1969) A validation study of polygraph examiner judgments. *Journal of Applied Psychology*, **53**, 399–403.

Berman, M.A. (1967). Drugs versus the polygraph. *Journal of Polygraph Studies*, **1**, 1–3.

Bitterman, M.E. and Marcuse, F.L. (1947). Cardiovascular responses of innocent persons to criminal investigation. *American Journal of Psychology*, **60**, 407–412.

Borkenstein, R.F. and Larson, J.A. (1957). The clinical team approach. In V.A. Leonard (ed), *Academy Lectures in lie detection*. Springfield: Thomas, p. 11–19.

Burack, B. (1956). A critical analysis of the theory, method and limitations of the 'lie detector'. *Journal of Criminal Law, Crimonology and Police Science*, **46**, 414–426.

Carlson, S.C., Pasano, M.S., and Jannuzzo, J.A. (1977). The effect of lie detector evidence on jury deliberations. An empirical study. *Journal of Police Science and Administration*, **5**, 148–154.

Cavoukian, A. and Heslegrave, R.J. (1980). The admissibility of polygraph evidence in court: some empirical findings. *Law and Human Behaviour*, **4**, 117–131.

Corcoran, J.F.T., Lewis, M.D., and Garver, R.B. (1978). Biofeedback-conditioned galvanic skin response and hypnotic suppression of arousal: A pilot study of their relation to deception. *Journal of Forensic Sciences*, **23**, 155–162.

Cumley, W.E. (1959). Hypnosis and the polygraph. *Police*, **4**, 39.

Cutrow, R.J., Parks, A., Lucas, N., and Thomas, K. (1972). The objective use of multiple physiological indices in the detection of deception. *Psychophysiology*, **9**, 578–588.

Davidson, P.O. (1968). Validity of the guilty knowledge technique: The effects of motivation. *Journal of Applied Psychology*, **52**, 62–65.

Davis, R.C. (1961). Physiological responses as a means of evaluating information. In A.D. Biderman and H. Zimmer (eds), *The Manipulation of Human Behaviour*. New York: John Wiley & Sons, pp. 142–168.

Dawson, M.E. (1980). Physiological detection of deception: Measurement of responses to questions and answers during countermeasure manoeuvres. *Psychophysiology*, **17**, 8–17.

Day, D.A. and Rourke, B.P. (1974) The role of attention in lie detection. *Canadian Journal of Behavioural Science*, **6**, 270–276.

Dearman, H.B. and Smith, B.M. (1963). Unconscious motivation and the polygraph test. *American Journal of Psychiatry*, **119**, 1017–1020.

De Paulo, B.M. and Rosenthal, R. (1979). Telling lies. *Journal of Personality and Social Psychology*, **37**, 1713–1722.

Eysenck, H.J. (1958). *Sense and Nonsense in Psychology*. Harmondsworth: Penguin Books.

Flock, M. (1950). Limitations of the lie detector. *Journal of Criminal Law and Criminology*, **40**, 651–653.

Germann, A.C. (1961). Hypnosis as related to the scientific detection of deception by polygraph examination: A pilot study. *International Journal of Clinical and Experimental Hypnosis,* **9**, 309–311.

Gudjonsson, G.H. (1981). *Some psychological determinants of electrodermal responses to deception*. Unpublished Ph.D. dissertation, University of Surrey.

Gustafson, L.A. and Orne, M.T. (1964). The effects of task and method of stimulus presentation on the detection of deception. *Journal of Applied Psychology*, **48**, 383–387.

Irving, B. and Hilgendorf, L. (1980). *Police Interrogation: The Psychological Approach* (Royal Commission on Criminal Procedure). London: HMSO.

Keeler, L. (1930). A method for detecting deception. *American Journal of Police Science*, **1**, 38–44.

Kubis, J.F. (1962). Studies in lie detection: Computer feasibility considerations. Technical Report 62–205, prepared for Air Service Systems Command, Contract No: AF 30 (602) – 2270, Project No. 5534, Fordham University.

Kugelmass, S., Lieblich, I., and Bergman, Z. (1967). The role of 'lying' in psychophysiological detection. *Psychophysiology*, **3**, 312–315.

Kugelmass, S., Lieblich, I., and Ben-Shakhar, G. (1973). Information through differential GSRs in Bedouins of the Israeli Desert. *Journal of Cross-Cultural Psychology*, **4**, 481–492.

Larson, J.A. (1932). *Lying and its Detection: A Study of Deception and Deception Tests*. Chicago: The University of Chicago Press.

Lombroso, C. (1895). L'Homme Criminal (2nd French edn); cited in P.V. Trovillo, A history of lie detection. *Journal of Criminal Law, Criminology and Police Science*, **29**, 848–881.

Lykken, D.T. (1960). The validity of the guilty knowledge technique: The effects of faking. *Journal of Applied Psychology*, **44**, 258–262.

Lykken, D.T. (1959). The GSR in the detection of guilt. *Journal of Applied Psychology*, **43**, 385–388.

Lykken, D.T. (1974). Psychology and the lie detection industry. *American Psychologist*, **29**, 275–739.

Lykken, D.T. (1981). *A Tremor in the Blood: Uses and Abuses of the Lie Detector*. London: McGraw-Hill Book Company.

Marston, W.M. (1917). Systolic blood pressure symptoms of deception. *Journal of Experimental Psychology*, **2**, 117–163.

Marston, W.M. (1938). *The Lie Detector Test*. New York: R.R. Smith.

More, H.W. (1966). Polygraph research and the university. *Law and Order*, **14**, 73–78.

Orne, M.T., Thackray, R.I., and Paskewitz, D.A. (1972). On the detection of deception. In N.S. Greenfield and R.A. Sternbach (eds.), *Handbook of psychophysiology*. New York: Holt, Rinehart and Winston.

Podlesny, J.A. and Raskin, D.C. (1977). Physiological measures and the detection of deception. *Psychological Bulletin*, **84**, 782–799.

Podlesny, J.A. and Raskin, D.C. (1978). Effectiveness of techniques and physiological measures in the detection of deception. *Psychophysiology*, **15**, 344–359.

Raskin, D.C. and Hare, R.D. (1978). Psychopathy and detection of deception in a prison population. *Psychophysiology*, **15**, 126–136.

Raskin, D.C. and Podlesny, J.A. (1979). Truth and deception: A reply Lykken. *Psychological Bulletin*, **86**, 54–59.

Reid, J.E. (1945). Simulated blood pressure responses in lie detection tests and a method for their detection. *Journal of Criminal Law, Criminology and Police Science*, **36**, 201–214.

Reid, J.E. (1947). A revised questioning technique in lie detection tests. *Journal of Criminal Law, Criminology and Police Science*, **37**, 542–547.

Reid, J.E. and Inbau, F.E. (1977). *Truth and Deception. The Polygraph ('Lie-Detector') Technique*. Baltimore: The Williams & Wilkins Company.

Rovner, L.I., Raskin, D.C., and Kircker, J.C. (1979). Effects of information and practice on detection of deception. *Psychophysiology*, **16**, 197–198 (Abstract).

Smith, B.M. (1967), Polygraph. *Scientific American*, **216**, 25–30.

Smith, W.W. (1922). *The Measurement of Emoton*. London: Kegan Paul, Trench, Trubner & Co. Ltd.

Stern, R.M. (1973). Voluntary control of GSRs and reports of sweating. *Perceptual and Motor Skills*, **36**, 1342.

Stern, R.M. and Kaplan, B.E. (1967). Galvanic skin response: Voluntary control and externalization. *Journal of Psychosomatic Research*, **10**, 349–353.

Stern, R.M. and Lewis, N.L. (1968). Ability of actors to control their expression of emotion. *Psychophysiology*, **4**, 294–299.

Suzuki, S., Watanabe, T., and Shimizu, K. (1969) Effects of visual feedback by skin potential response. *Japanese Journal of Psychology*, **40**, 59–67.

Tocchio, O.J. (1963). Lie detection under hypnosis. *Police*, Sept/Oct., 9–11.

Trovillo, P.V. (1939). A history of lie detection. *Journal of Criminal Law, Criminology and Police Science*, **29**, 848–881; **30**, 100–119.

Turner, W.W. (1968). *Invisible Witness: The Use and Abuse of the New Technology of Crime Investigation*. New York: Bobbs-Merrill.

Waid, W.M., Orne, E.C., Cook, M.R., and Orne, M.T. (1981). Meprobamate reduces accuracy of physiological detection and deception. *Science*, **212**, 71&73.

Weinstein, E., Abrams, S., and Gibbons, D. (1970). The validity of the polygraph with hypnotically induced repression of guilt. *American Journal of Psychiatry*, **126** 1159–1162.

Zuckerman, M., De Frank, R.S., Hall, J.A., Larrance, D.T., and Rosenthal, R., (1979). Facial and vocal cues of deception and truth. *Journal of Experimental Social Psychology*, **15**, 378–396.

PART III

FACTORS INFLUENCING THE QUALITY OF MEMORY

Evaluating Witness Evidence
Edited by S.M.A. Lloyd-Bostock and B.R. Clifford
© 1983 John Wiley & Sons Ltd.

Chapter 9

The Malleability of Eyewitness Accounts

Elizabeth F. Loftus and Katherine E. Ketcham

Sigmund Freud believed that memories are held permanently in the brain. These 'true' memories lie deep in the unconscious and remain undisturbed by surface mental activities, Freud insisted, somewhat like huge fish resting in the cool bottom of a very deep pond. Never lost or completely forgotten, they are 'only inaccessible and latent, having become part of the unconscious' (Freud, translation, 1967). To call these memories up, Freud advocated the technique of free association. By merely encouraging people to think about past episodes in their lives, Freud believed they could dig up long-forgotten but important memories from their past.

But how did Freud know that his troubled patients were remembering the truth? Did he ever consider that his patients' versions of events in their past might be twisted or merely fabricated? New insights in the field of human memory leave no doubt that people can have 'memories' for things that never happened and that the 'true' memories Freud believed in and searched for may, in fact, be complex blendings of fact and fiction. Memory, it appears, is extremely fragile and can be supplemented, altered, or even restructured by as simple an instrument as a strong verb, embedded unnoticed in a question about the event concerned.

BASIC FINDINGS

The extraordinary malleability of memory has been recently demonstrated in our laboratory (see Loftus, 1979a, for a review of this work). Consider a typical experiment in which college students were presented with a film of an auto-mobile accident and immediately afterwards asked a series of questions about the accident. Some of the questions were designed to present misleading information — that is, to suggest the existence of an object that did not in fact exist. Half the subjects were asked 'How fast was the white sports car going when it passed the barn while travelling along the country road?' In fact, no barn existed. The remaining subjects were asked, 'How fast was the white sports car going while travelling along the country road?' Later, all subjects were asked if they had seen a barn. When questioned again about the accident a week later, more than 17% of those exposed to the false information about a barn said they had seen one (Loftus, 1975). Apparently, the assumption of a barn during the initial questioning caused many subjects to incorporate the non-existent barn into their recollections of the event. Moreover, a subsequent experiment showed that simply asking people whether they had or had not seen a barn — a question to which they usually answered 'no' — was enough to increase the likelihood that they would later instate a barn into their memories of an accident. We argued that the false information had become integrated into the person's recollection of the event, thereby supplementing his memory of that event.

Yet new information can do more than simply supplement a memory: it can apparently alter or transform the memory. In another study (Loftus et al., 1978), subjects saw a series of 30 colour slides depicting successive stages in an accident involving an automobile and a pedestrian. A red Datsun was travelling along a side street towards an intersection at which there was a stop sign for half the subjects and a yield sign for the remaining subjects. The remaining slides show the Datsun turning right and knocking down a pedestrian crossing the street.

Immediately after viewing the slides, the subjects answered a number of questions about them. One of the questions presupposed the existence of either a stop sign or a yield sign. For half the subjects the presupposed sign was consistent with what they had actually seen; for half it was inconsistent. The subjects then performed a distracting task for 20 minutes, after which a final recognition test began. For this final test subjects saw 15 pairs of slides and were asked to choose the one slide out of each pair that they had seen before. When the critical question asked earlier had presupposed a traffic sign consistent with what the subjects had actually seen, they chose the correct sign 75% of the time; when the earlier question presupposed an inconsistent traffic sign, however, the subjects chose the correct slide only 41% of the time. This experiment suggests that presuppositions are capable of transforming memory as well as merely supplementing it.

Memory can, in fact, be moulded by so subtle an instrument as a strong verb. In another experiment (Loftus and Palmer, 1974), subjects were shown films of automobile accidents and then answered questions about events in the films. Subjects estimated a higher speed when the question 'About how fast were the cars going when they smashed into each other?' was asked than when the verb 'smashed' was replaced with the verb 'collided', 'bumped', 'contacted' or 'hit'. When tested 1 week later, those subjects who had been given the verb 'smashed' were more likely to answer 'yes' to the question 'Did you see any broken glass?' — even though broken glass was not present in the film. By using the word 'smashed', the experimenter supplies a new piece of information — namely, that the cars 'smashed' into each other — and the subject has a memory representation of an accident that was more severe than it was in fact. Since broken glass is associated with a severe accident, the subject is more likely to 'remember' that broken glass existed.

These experiments, along with many others using similar procedures, confirm the elasticity of memory. False information can be introduced into a person's recollection, whether that recollection is measured by a recall or a recognition procedure. Further, the information can supplement the previously acquired memory (as in the case of the barn), or transform it (as in the case of the stop sign/yield sign or the creation of broken glass).

Once we made the initial discovery that memory could be influenced in these ways, we decided to study this phenomenon in more detail. The next six sections represent our most recent work on the malleability of memory.

COMMITMENT OR CONSCIOUS THOUGHT

One question we asked was whether it matters whether or not a person has made a commitment to a particular version of the event. A reasonable hypothesis was that misleading information would have less of an impact if the witness had already verbalized his or her opinion about a certain detail. To test this hypothesis, we conducted two experiments on memory for the colours of objects (Loftus, 1977). In these experiments subjects saw a series of colour slides depicting an accident involving an automobile and a pedestrian. In the series a green car drives past the accident but does not stop. Some time after viewing the accident, some of the subjects were exposed to the misinformation that the car that had passed was blue. Finally, all subjects saw a colour wheel containing 30 colour strips and had to choose the colour that best represented their memory of the car that drove past the accident.

We found that most of the subjects given the 'blue' information tended to pick a blue or bluish-green as the colour of the car that passed the accident. But, more to the point, subjects who had committed themselves by recalling various object colours before being exposed to the misleading information showed greater resistance to that information. These subjects, relative to those who had not committed themselves publicly, reported much 'greener' recollections. This experiment indicates that information to which we have committed ourselves is particularly resistant to change. If we publicly state that we remember a particular detail to be one way, it is difficult for subsequent suggestions to cause us to change our minds.

BLATANTLY FALSE INFORMATION

There appears to be a limit, then, to how far our recollections can be swayed. A further question we hoped to answer was: For a non-existent item to be incorporated into a person's recollection, must that item somehow be plausible and consistent with the event witnessed? Or could a person be convinced that he had seen something as implausible as an alligator scuttling across a living room rug?

We began to design experiments to answer these questions. In our first attempts, implausible misleading information was embedded in questions asked of a person who had seen an incident and whose recollection would ultimately be tested. We found out very quickly that even though this misleading information might be embedded cleverly in a presupposition, many subjects noticed it. This 'trick' constituted proof that we were trying to put something over on them, and their subsequent suspiciousness made it hard to obtain useful data from them.

We thus needed to introduce misleading information into a person's recollection in a way that would be less likely to arouse suspicion about the purpose of the study. In one experiment (Stotts, cited in Loftus, 1979b), subjects were shown a set of unrelated slides, a description was given to them that was ostensibly produced by a college professor who had viewed the slides three times as long as the subjects had. The professor's description contained both non-existent items that were plausible within the context and non-existent items that were implausible. For example, some subjects read a version with a telephone booth in a farm scene (implausible) or a water pump in that same scene (plausible). If a subject noticed something peculiar, he could attribute it to error rather than crafty manipulation on the part of the experimenter.

After reading the 'professor's' description, the subjects were given a yes/no recognition test, asked to give their answers a confidence rating, and urged to say 'yes' only to items they remembered seeing. Not surprisingly, the subjects said they had seen the non-existent objects much more often if they were plausible rather than implausible. Furthermore, the implausible items were almost never recognized on the test when they had not been mentioned, but when they had been mentioned, the likelihood that a subject reported he had seen them increased substantially.

Another experiment was constructed to answer a related question: What would happen if a piece of false information was introduced that blatantly contradicted a clearly perceived detail? Here we found a slightly different result. The subjects viewed a series of slides showing the theft of a large, bright red wallet from a woman's handbag (Loftus, 1979b). Between the incident and the test, the subjects read a version of the event that was allegedly written by a professor who had looked at the slides for a much longer period than they had. Two versions of the 'professor's' description were constructed. One contained an erroneous description of four critical items, for example, a green notebook was referred to as blue. A second version contained, in addition, erroneous mention of a very obvious object: it referred to the red wallet taken by the thief as dark brown.

Few subjects accepted the blatantly false suggestion that the wallet was brown. In fact, this clumsy lie made it harder to sway witnesses' recollections about other objects, such as the colour of the notebook.

TIMING OF SUBSEQUENT INFORMATION

Another question we asked was this: Does information introduced subsequent to an event have a differential impact depending upon whether it is introduced immediately after the event or later? To determine this, the experiment described at the beginning of this chapter was extended using over 600 participants (Loftus *et al.*, 1978). The subjects were shown the same series of 30 slides, including the slide of the red Datsun stopped either at a stop sign or a yield sign. A questionnaire was then administered, followed by a forced-choice test. The questionnaire contained either information that was consistent with what they had seen (e.g. they actually saw a stop sign and were told it was a stop sign), inconsistent information (e.g. they actually saw a stop sign but were told it was a yield sign), or no relevant information. The forced-choice test was given either immediately after the questionnaire or 20 minutes, 1 day, 2 days, or 1 week later. Half the subjects filled out the questionnaire about the incident immediately after viewing the slides, and the other half were given the questionnaire just before the forced-choice test. When no information was introduced during the retention interval, performance on the critical test was quite high immediately after the slide sequence — almost 90% correct. As the interval between the slide sequence and the test increased, performance dropped gradually, and by the time 2 days had passed, subjects were performing at about the chance level of 50% correct. This is consistent with the usual finding that people are less accurate when tested after a long interval than after a short one.

Subjects given consistent information, however, were correct over 70% of the time after a 2 day interval. This result supports the idea that mentioning an object which has in fact been seen enhances a person's memory for that object.

When misleading information is presented immediately after the viewing of the event, the subjects were correct about half the time (chance). When a week's interval passed between the event and the misleading information and subjects were tested soon thereafter, they were correct a mere 20% of the time. Misleading information clearly, then, had a greater impact on performance when it was delayed. Why? When misleading information is introduced immediately after the accident viewing, both the misleading information and the incident have faded after a week's interval. When tested, the subject can only guess, and he is, as would be expected, correct about half the time. If the misleading information is given a week later, just before the test is given, however, the original event information has faded and the newly introduced misleading information is strong. Thus, the subjects tend to remember the incorrect information and consequently 80% of them perform incorrectly on the test.

QUESTION COMPLEXITY

After an event has occurred, post-event information can be introduced into a person's recollection, sometimes supplementing the previously acquired memory and sometimes altering it. The attachment of new information to an earlier memory, which we have termed 'mental bonding' (Loftus, in press), is proposed to occur fairly automatically unless the information is tagged as being inappropriate. Can inappropriate or implausible information be bonded, however, if the subject's attention is partially diverted such that a minimum amount of attention is devoted to the critical piece of misinformation — enough so that it is processed but not so much that it is scrutinized?

In previous experiments we may have stumbled — almost by accident — upon an optimal procedure for inducing bonding. Recall the structure of the questions that we used to introduce misinformation in previous experiments. In one study, the question was: How fast was the white sports car going when it passed the barn while travelling along the country road? In another study, the question was: Did another car pass the red Datsun while it was stopped at the stop sign?

In both cases, the questions are rather complex, and the misleading information is embedded in a clause. In both cases, the question focuses the attention of the respondent on some aspect of the situation that is unrelated to the misleading detail. Does the complex wording of these questions contribute to the bonding that we observe? In a recent doctoral dissertation, Kenneth Johnson (1979) examined variations in question wording and the extent to which these influenced the likelihood that a piece of misinformation would later be recalled erroneously by a subject. Johnson's results indicate that subjects were most likely to indicate erroneously that they had seen a particular detail when that detail had been embedded in a complex question.

A follow-up experiment attempted to replicate Johnson's findings using different subjects and materials (Loftus, in press; Loftus and Greene, 1980). In this experiment, subjects were asked only one critical question that contained a piece of misinformation, in order to minimize the chances that subjects would become suspicious about the presence of misleading details. In this study, too, subjects were later asked whether they had actually seen various objects, including the critical one. Finally, they were tested for their memory for the intervening questions — something Johnson had not done. The study thus addressed an additional question: To what extent would subjects remember having read about the misinformation on their intervening questionnaire? Would memory for this be different depending on whether the information was introduced via a complex versus a simple presupposition?

The subjects in this study were 147 students who were enrolled in an undergraduate psychology course. During an ordinary class period, two men abruptly came into the classroom. One of them stood by the door while the other interrupted the class to pick up a book that he had left on a table in the front. The taller one had a brief argument with the professor and both of them left. About 40 minutes later, the students were given a questionnaire designed to test their memory for the incident. The questionnaire contained 15 questions, the tenth of which was critical. For each question the subject responded by checking a space for 'yes', 'no', or 'I don't know'. Unknown to the subjects, two versions of question 10 were constructed, both of which falsely presupposed that the intruder had a moustache: Was the moustache worn by the tall intruder light or dark brown? Did the intruder who was tall and had a moustache say anything to the professor?

One-third of the subjects were asked the question with the simple presupposition; one-third were asked the question with a complex presupposition, and the remaining third were asked a control question about the tall intruder's eyebrows.

One day later, the subjects were given an additional questionnaire that contained 10 new questions of the form 'Did you see?' The ninth question asked whether or not the subjects had seen a moustache on the tall intruder.

Only 4% of the subjects in the control condition claimed to have seen a moustache on the intruder. When the moustache had been mentioned via a simple presupposition, that percentage rose to 26%. When the moustache had been mentioned via a complex presupposition, the percentage falsely saying yes was even higher at 39%. Although the difference between the simple and complex presuppositions was only marginally significant, the result is none the less supportive of the notion that the complex presupposition is better able to influence the recollection.

The final result concerned memory for what was mentioned on the initial questionnaire. Almost none of the control subjects (1%) incorrectly claimed to have read about the moustache on their questionnaire. However, many of the other subjects correctly remembered the mention of the moustache: 20% of the subjects who had been given the simple presupposition definitely remembered the moustache being mentioned, whereas only 8% of those given the complex presupposition definitely remembered reading about the moustache. One point of interest about these data is that they seem to indicate that less processing of critical information eventuates in greater memory for that information. This is contrary to the ideas expressed in the 'levels of processing' view (see Craik and Lockhart, 1972), and probably indicates the need for considering more carefully the distinction between information presented for influence purposes and information presented for verbatim memory purposes.

These results, in conjunction with those of Johnson (1979), suggest that misinformation embedded in more complex questions is likely to have a greater effect on memory than that same information conveyed in simpler questions. The complex question seems to work because it focuses the subject's attention on something other than the critical information. Further evidence that subjects do not pay as much attention to the critical object when it is deeply embedded comes from the final memory test: subjects were less likely to remember having read about the critical object when it appeared in a complex rather than a simple presupposition. It is plausible that the complex questions have a greater impact in part because they convey a stronger belief in the existence of the critical object. How much of their impact is due to this quality rather than the diverting of attention remains a matter for further research.

ARE FACES SPECIAL?

If memory for types of objects, colours of objects, presence of objects and so on can be so easily influenced, what about memory for faces? People generally have no trouble picking out the face of a friend in a crowded room; it is a task that usually seems quite easy, relative to other sorts of recognition tasks. Using standard recognition memory designs, several investigators have reported very little forgetting of faces over reasonably long retention intervals (see Clifford and Bull, 1978, pp. 92–93, for numerous examples).

Some researchers have suggested that face recognition generally involves a special recognition system (Yin, 1969), whereas others have noted that 'it is only because we have constant practice that face recognition usually seems so easy' (Glass et al., 1979, pp. 68–69). In fact, the argument has recently been advanced that faces are special in their lack of susceptibility to interference from other faces (Davies et al., 1979), a claim that seems to have received some support from others (e.g. Carr et al., 1979). In this latter research, subjects looked at human faces for 5 seconds apiece. These subjects were actually better at discriminating targets from new distractors 2 weeks after the original viewing than they were 2 minutes afterwards. Thus, there appeared to be an improvement in performance rather than the decline that is typically observed with landscapes, common objects, and other materials. Although these results are only preliminary, they do suggest that something interesting may be happening when it comes to perceiving and remembering faces.

If there is something special about faces, particularly those seen in an eyewitness simulation, then it may be rather difficult deliberately to alter a witness's recognition or reconstruction of a face, despite the ease with which this can be done with other kinds of information. This was the basic hypothesis guiding our experiments designed to study the extent to which memory for faces can be altered. In a pilot study, subjects viewed a face and then heard a description of that face ostensibly written by another witness. For some subjects the other witness inaccurately described one facial feature. For example, a target person who actually had light-coloured straight hair, was described as having 'light-coloured curly hair'. After hearing the other witness's description, the subject had to write his or her own description of the face, and then reconstruct the face by using an Identi-Kit. (The Identi-Kit contains transparent line drawings of numerous alternatives of different facial features). The results showed that when freely describing the faces they had seen, subjects adopted the verbal expressions of another witness even when those expressions were in error. Furthermore, subjects who heard a misleading detail had a tendency to incorporate that detail into their reconstructions of the original face; subjects who did not hear the misleading detail rarely did so. These findings were further explored in three larger scale experiments (Loftus and Greene, 1980).

In these experiments, subjects viewed a target individual in a photograph, in a film, or live. Subsequently, some subjects were exposed to misleading information, either via a version of the target individual ostensibly given by another witness or via a misleading question. The major results were as follows: (1) Experiment 1: If another witness referred to a misleading feature, over one-third of the subjects included that detail in their own description, using the exact wording that the other witness had used. Control subjects rarely did so (5%); (2) Experiment 2: If the other witness referred to a misleading detail, nearly 70% of the subjects later 'recognized' an individual with that feature. Control subjects did so far less often (13%); and (3) If subjects were asked leading questions containing misinformation about a critical feature (moustache), over 30% indicated that they had seen the critical feature. Control subjects rarely did so (4%).

These results show that memory for faces is affected by the introduction of subsequent misleading information about that face, contradicting the view that faces are special in their lack of susceptibility to interference (from either other faces or information of any kind). The idea that faces are subject to distortion in memory obviously occurred to Martin Cruz Smith, who wrote in the novel 'Gorky Park': 'What good is a witness? Their memories are indistinct after a day. After three months, frankly, I could get them to recognize anyone I wanted to.' The experiments on memory for faces have important implications for police practices regarding eyewitness recognition. For example, since witnesses will easily pick up the verbal expressions used by others, investigators should take care not to put words into the mouths of witnesses. In one recent unreported case a witness described her assailant as having a thin moustache. An investigator later remarked: 'You said it was a pencil-thin moustache, didn't you?' From that time forward, the witness described the moustache as being pencil-thin. An awareness of the phenomenon of verbal contagion can perhaps aid us in avoiding its potentially nasty consequences in the future. The generality of this effect has also been found by Clifford and Hollin (1982) in conformity experiments in eyewitnessing, where 'leaders' (experimental stooges) were primed to give specifically worded wrong answers. Subjects were found not only to change their propositional recall but also their mode of verbal expression concerning these recalls in line with those of the stooges.

DO WARNINGS HELP?

The experiments discussed in this chapter clearly demonstrate that misleading information presented after a witnessed event may become incorporated into a person's memory and either supplement or alter the original memory. Would a warning about the possibility of future misinformation increase people's resistance to that misinformation? To answer this question, four experiments were designed involving 216 subjects (Green *et al*., 1982). A major interest of these experiments was the extent to which a warning could confer resistance to post-event information. In these experiments, subjects first viewed a complex event, and were then exposed to post-event information that occasionally included some erroneous details. Finally, the subjects were tested on their own memory of the event.

It seemed reasonable that warning a subject that he or she might receive misleading post-event information could effectively reduce the impact of that information for a variety of reasons. First, the warning might cause subjects to process the initial event more deeply and thoughtfully as it was being shown to them. Such deep processing might lead to enhanced memory (Craik and Lockhart, 1972), and subsequent ability to resist misleading suggestions. Second, warning might cause subjects to rehearse the event after it had already been presented to them. Third, the warning might cause greater scrutiny of the post-event information while it was being processed. And finally, the warning might be effective because it induces more careful test taking, which could include a more careful reviewing of the event and/or the post-event information at the time the test is taken.

Taken together, the results of these studies indicate that exposure to a warning just prior to the presentation of the misinformation caused subjects to read the information more slowly, and resulted in a slightly greater resistance to its suggestive effect. Warnings given at other times, particularly after the misinformation had already been processed, had no effect. To our surprise, a warning given before the event itself had minimal effect. These findings suggest that warnings work by causing greater scrutiny of the post-event information while it is being processed, rather than causing deeper processing of the event as it is being witnessed, rehearsal of the event after it is over, or more careful retrieval of past information while being tested. In short, the major effect of warnings is on the processing of the post-event information that they precede.

CONCLUSIONS AND IMPLICATIONS

As these experiments demonstrate, human memory is a fragile and elusive creature. It can be supplemented, partially restructured, or even completely altered by post-event inputs. It is susceptible to the power of a simple word. This is not to imply that all memories are changed and no original memories remain intact. Perhaps it is the case that some memories are modified by subsequent inputs while others are not. If so, then a major question that confronts the memory theorist is this: Under what circumstances does one process rather than the other occur? As a start towards answering this question, Loftus and Loftus (1980) have suggested that the mechanism responsible for updating memory both seeks efficiency and takes account of real-world constraints. In some situations memories may not be tampered with by subsequent input, and these may last essentially forever. In other cases, new inputs which cannot logically coexist with earlier ones may cause an alteration to occur. In such instances, economy may dictate that one memory be dismissed in favour of another, much as a computer programmer will irrevocably destroy an old program instruction when a new one is created.

A recent distinction has been made between active and and inactive memory (Lewis, 1979). Active memory (AM) is a subset of inactive memory (IM) and contains either newly formed memories or established retrieved memories or both. A body of evidence suggests that while in AM, memories are particularly open to disruption either by amnesic agents or through other forms of interference. Most of this evidence derives from the animal memory literature, yet it leads to the strong speculation that human memory may have to be evoked for it to be altered or distorted. Active memory is considered to be a changing subset of all permanent memories possessed by an organism. Over the course of time, numerous memories may become activated, and these may be especially subject to change. Yet, at any given time many of the permanent memories, which have the potential of being active, are in a relatively inactive state and have little effect on current behaviour. Some of these memories may never be brought into an active state, and thus may never be subject to interfering events that could potentially cause their alteration or distortion. This is, of course, impossible to test.

The fact that some of our memories are subject to alteration or distortion cannot be denied. Thus, the notion that all of our memories are intact — like the venerable old fish waiting patiently at the bottom of the pond for a lure to probe deep enough — is almost certainly a myth. Much of what we remember is, in actuality, a complex blend of fact and fiction. When gaps appear in our memory, we unconsciously fill them in with bits and pieces that may or may not be based in reality. All the things that alter memory fuse with experience, and we become sure that we saw or said or did what we remember.

Yet Freud's influence dies hard. Despite the overwhelming evidence that memory is malleable, most people — scientists and laymen alike — continue to believe in and promote the inherent truthfulness and integrity of memory. Memory is given a sacrosanct position in our society, and nowhere is this more apparent than in the legal system's heavy reliance on eyewitness testimony. Few things, outside a smoking pistol, carry as much weight with a jury as the testimony of an actual witness. In fact, eyewitness testimony is so powerful that it can sway a jury even after the testimony has been shown to be false (Loftus, 1979a; Cavoukian, 1980).

People in general and jurors in particular are so ready to believe eyewitness testimony because for the most part our memories serve us reasonably well. But precise memory is rarely demanded of us. When a friend describes a vacation, we don't ask 'Are you sure your hotel room had two chairs, not three?' Or, after a movie, 'Are you sure Warren Beatty's hair was wavy, or was it curly?' But precise memory suddenly becomes crucial in the event of a crime or an accident. Small details assume enormous importance. Did the assailant have a moustache, or was he clean-shaven? Was the light red, yellow, or green? Did the car stop at a stop sign or a yield sign? To be mistaken about details is not the result of a bad memory, but of the normal functioning of human memory. As we have seen, human remembering does not work like a videotape recorder or a movie camera. When a person wants to remember something, he or she does not simply pluck a whole memory intact out of a 'memory store'. The memory is constructed from stored and available bits of information; any gaps in the information are filled in unconsciously by inference. When these fragments are integrated and make sense, they form what we call a memory.

Clearly, eyewitness testimony should not be considered the solid, ironclad evidence it has sometimes been in the past. But mistakes in eyewitness testimony can teach us a great deal about the workings of human memory. Perhaps the most important lesson is to remain sceptical about the precision of that vital but frequently unreliable resource, the human memory. We also need to discover under precisely what circumstances the memory works best and what circumstances are likely to distort or alter memory. The workings of stress, fear, and prejudice, for example, are all important in the study of memory. Finally, it is time to start figuring out how to put our malleable memories to work in ways that can serve us well. Now that we are beginning to understand the malleability of human memory, new research may begin to tell us exactly how to control it.

NOTES

We are grateful to the National Science Foundation which has supported our research over the last several years. Please address all correspondence to Elizabeth Loftus, Department of Psychology, University of Washington, Seattle, Washington 98195, USA.

REFERENCES

Carr, T.H., Deffenbacher, K.A., and Leu, J.R. (1979). Is there less interference in memory for faces? Paper presented at the meeting of the Psychonomic Society, Phoenix, Arizona.

Cavoukian, A. (1980). Eyewitness testimony: The ineffectiveness of discrediting information. Presented at the American Psychological Association annual meeting, Montreal.

Clifford, B.R. and Bull, R. (1978). *The Psychology of Person Identification*. London: Routledge & Kegan Paul.

Clifford, B.R. and Hollin, C.R. (1982). Conformity effects in eyewitnessing. *Journal of Applied Social Psychology*, in press.

Craik, F.I.M. and Lockhart, R.S. (1972). Levels of processing: A framework for memory research. *Journal of Verbal Learning and Verbal Behavior*, **11**, 671–684.

Davies, G., Shepherd, J., and Ellis, H. (1979). Effects of interpolated mugshot exposure on accuracy of eyewitness identification. *Journal of Applied Psychology*, **64**, 232–237.

Freud, S. (1967). Introductory lectures on psychoanalysis, trans. by James Trachley. New York: Liveright, pp. 178–179.

Glass, A.L., Holyoak, K.J., and Santa, J.L. (1979). *Cognition*. Reading, Mass.: Addison-Wesley.

Greene, E., Flynn, M.S., and Loftus, E.F. (1982). Inducing resistance to misleading information. *Journal of Verbal Learning and Verbal Behavior*, in press.

Johnson, K.A. (1979). *The leading question: Isn't there an effect?* Unpublished doctoral dissertation, University of Washington, Seattle.

Lewis, D.J. (1979). Psychobiology of active and inactive memory. *Psychological Bulletin*, **86**, 1054–1083.

Loftus, E.F. (1975). Leading questions and the eyewitness report. *Cognitive Psychology*, **7**, 560–572.

Loftus, E.F. (1977). Shifting human color memory. *Memory and Cognition*, **5**, 696–699.

Loftus, E.F. (1979a). *Eyewitness Testimony*. Cambridge Mass.: Harvard University Press.

Loftus, E.F. (1976b). Reactions to blatantly contradictory information. *Memory and Cognition*, **7**, 368–374.

Loftus, E.F. Mentalmorphosis: Alterations in memory produced by the mental bonding of new information to old. In J.B. Long and A.D. Baddeley (eds), *Attention and Performance*, IX, in press.

Loftus, E.F. and Greene, E. (1980). Warning: Even memory for faces may be contagious. *Law and Human Behavior*, **4**, 323–334.

Loftus, E.F. and Loftus, G.R. (1980). On the permanence of stored information in the human brain. *American Psychologist*, **5**, 409–420.

Loftus, E.F., Miller, D.G., and Burns, H.J. (1978). Semantic integration of verbal information into a visual memory. *Journal of Experimental Psychology: Human Learning and Memory*, **4**, 19–31.

Loftus, E.F. and Palmer, J.C. (1974). Reconstruction of automobile destruction: An example of the interaction between language and memory. *Journal of Verbal Learning and Verbal Behavior*, **13**, 585–589.

Stotts, cited in Loftus 1979b.

Yin, R.K. (1969). Looking at upside-down faces. *Journal of Experimental Psychology*, **81**, 141–145.

Evaluating Witness Evidence
Edited by S.M.A. Lloyd-Bostock and B.R. Clifford
© 1983 John Wiley & Sons Ltd.

Chapter 10

Identification After Long Delays

J.W. Shepherd

The fallibility of eyewitnesses has been acknowledged for many years by legal authorities both in the UK and in the USA. An English Committee of Inquiry as long ago as 1904 observed that 'evidence as to identity based on personal impressions, however bona fide, is perhaps of all classes of evidence the least to be relied upon, and therefore, unless supported by other facts, an unsafe basis for the verdict of a jury' (Watson, 1924).

The Committee of Inquiry had been set up as a result of the celebrated case of Adolf Beck. This unfortunate man had been approached in the street by a woman who accused him of having stolen some jewellery from her some $2\frac{1}{2}$ weeks previously. Beck's complaint about the woman resulted in his being arrested on the basis of her accusation. At the local police station nine other witnesses, who had made similar complaints of theft and fraud picked him out from a group of other men in the prison yard, and as a result he was convicted and sentenced to seven years' penal servitude.

Some time after his release from prison he was again charged with fraud and theft, and with only identification evidence against him was again convicted. Before he could be sentenced the true culprit was apprehended on other charges, and Beck's innocence was established for all the offences of which he had been convicted.

Beck's case occurred as long ago as 1896, but there are certain features of the case which are pertinent to the present topic. First, all the witnesses expressed complete certainty that Beck was the guilty man when they saw him among a group of other men in the prison yard. Second, these identifications occurred at intervals varying from 5 months to 13 months after the last date on which Beck had allegedly been seen by the witnesses. Third, the circumstances under which they had observed him might be considered optimal for subsequent recognition — a highly congenial meeting lasting for up to 45 minutes, during which the witnesses in no way suspected that they were victims of crime.

Surprisingly, perhaps, the defence made nothing of these lengthy delays between incident and identification, but argued that the high excitement of the women at the first meeting and their later intense disappointment was the basis for their error. The error was without doubt genuine, and understandable, perhaps, in view of the similarity in appearance of Beck and the true culprit (see Watson, 1924, pp. 208, 222).

Since this very early case there have been many other instances of wrongful conviction based upon eyewitness identification, but when these verdicts have been overturned by higher courts, the question of delay has seldom been one of the points at issue. Nevertheless, legal and judicial authorities have drawn attention to the possible effects of delay on identification accuracy (Woocher, 1977).

Wall, in his book *Eyewitness Identification in Criminal Cases* (1965), lists a number of 'danger signals' to be considered in identification evidence, and says of lapse of time, 'it is common knowledge that memory and sense impressions fade with the passage of time. Consequently no purpose would be served by citing cases which deal with this danger signal.' (p. 127)

The problem with 'common knowledge' is that it lacks precision in defining the limits of its rules. It may indeed be true that memory fades with the passage of time, but how long is it likely to be until it fades to a level of complete unreliability? This difficulty is exemplified in the Devlin Committee Report, which also regarded the lapse of time between incident and parade as a matter to which the judge, in his summing up, should draw attention. Yet, in discussing this point, the Committee expressed some scepticism about its importance. 'We have considered', they said, 'whether in a substantial number of cases a witness's memory may be impaired by the lapse of time between the obser- vation of the offence and the subsequent observation of the offender, however it was made. While this must be true in certain instances, such evidence as is available suggests that it is not a significant factor in the great majority of cases.' (Devlin, 1976, p. 74)

Although the available evidence is not presented in the text, there are a few pointers in the discussion as to what determined the Committee's opinion. Of the 36 cases of misidentification reviewed by Devlin, 60% involved delays of less than 7 days. In these cases, which comprised the majority of those con- sidered, the delay may not have been sufficient to have had a significant effect. Three cases, however, had delays of over 100 days, averaging 255 days; but of these the Committee had little to say, except that in one case two boys identified a man as having indecently assaulted them 8 months previously — an offence to which another man confessed. On the basis of 'common knowledge' one might consider that such a long delay would give ample time for the memory to fade, and on this basis the evidence might be very doubtful. What we do not know is at what stage between these extremes the delay might be regarded as a significant element in evaluating the identification evidence.

The more recent case of Biggers in the US Supreme Court (1972) raises just such a question. The appeal in this case was based primarily on the violation of due process in holding a showup — in which the witness confronted only the accused, instead of an identification parade. In passing judgment, however, the

Court did acknowledge that the identification had taken place 7 months after the offence, a rape, and that 'this would be a seriously negative factor in most cases'. Nevertheless, they discounted the delay factor on the grounds that the witness had spent a considerable time in the presence of the culprit (cf. Beck above), had not identified anyone in previous showups and parades, and expressed a high level of certainty in her identification. The Court thus seemed to have assumed that even a long delay will have little effect if the conditions at original viewing are good; that confidence is correlated with accuracy; and that intervening attempts at identification will produce no interference.

EXPERIMENTAL STUDIES OF RETENTION

Most experimental psychologists would, I suspect, challenge the first of the Supreme Court's assumptions. Numerous studies, beginning with Ebbinghaus in 1885, have demonstrated that retention of material diminishes with the passage of time since the original experience, and the rate of forgetting is generally most rapid in the first few hours of the retention period. Much of this evidence, however, is based upon experiments in verbal memory using recall rather than recognition as a measure of performance. Since we are concerned with the ability of witnesses to *recognize* — i.e. pick out a suspect from a parade — rather than *recall* the suspect's appearance — i.e. provide a verbal description from memory or construct a pictorial likeness — we should restrict our consideration to studies of pictorial or person memory which have used recognition as a measure.

Pictorial stimuli generally show higher rates of recognition than verbal stimuli, but nevertheless show a similar pattern of forgetting over time. Shepard (1967) presented over 600 pictures to his subjects, and on subsequent tests used 68 pairs comprising one old and one new picture. Identification rates fell from 100% after 2 hours to 93% after 3 days, 92% after a week and 57% — which represents chance performance — after 4 months. Gehring *et al.* (1976) used line drawings of common objects to test recognition after delays varying from 10 minutes to 3 months and also found relatively rapid forgetting over shorter delay intervals, followed by a much less steep decline in recognition for delays greater than 1 week.

Among pictorial stimuli, recognition studies of photographs of faces would appear to be most relevant to the issue of identification performance. The procedure in these studies is similar to that in other recognition studies, and usually takes the form of presenting subjects with a series of photographs or slides, usually about 20, and then on a later occasion presenting the same series randomly mixed with a number of new faces. The subject's task is to decide for each face whether it is a new or old stimulus.

Only a few studies have examined the effect of delay on recognition performance on faces. Chance *et al.* (1975) compared recognition rates after 48 hours with immediate recognition and found no significant decline, while Shepherd and Ellis (1973) found that after a week's delay, performance was no worse than on immediate testing. After 35 days, however, performance did decline significantly, except on faces judged most attractive and least attractive. Very recently, Deffenbacher *et al*. (1981) compared recognition at 2 weeks with recognition after 2 minutes' delay and found a small but significant decline in performance for the longer delay.

Thus research into facial recognition using multiple targets has provided further support for the common-sense view that identification becomes less reliable with the passage of time, although the effects for faces seem to be weaker than for other classes of stimuli, and the delays have typically been relatively short.

The experimental research which deals specifically with the question of identification evidence is that which tests the identification performance of witnesses to a staged incident. In these experiments the procedures are slightly different from those used in other studies of memory. An event using one, or, occasionally, two live targets is usually staged in the presence of witnesses who often are not expecting the incident. On a later occasion the witnesses are asked to try to pick out the target from a photographic lineup or a live parade comprising from five to eight people. The subject is usually *not* instructed to attend to the target at the initial presentation, and does not expect to be asked to recognize him later on.

If there is a considerable delay between incident and identification, there may be other differences between identification studies and face recognition experiments. The subject may have to recognize the target in a different mode — a photograph instead of in the flesh. The target's clothing and facial expression may be very different from when he was first seen, and with very long delays he may undergo major changes in appearance as a result of the passage of time or fluctuations of fashion. He may grow a beard, change his hair style, gain or lose weight, all of which may undermine the accuracy of the witness, and for research purposes make difficult the interpretation of delay effects.

So far, these problems have not been acute in published research. Very few studies have used delays greater than 8 weeks, and these have used photographic parades. One study, by Egan *et al*. (1977) tested delay effects in identification performance. They forewarned their audience that they were about to see two live targets whom the subjects were to imagine had just been involved in an armed robbery. The targets appeared for 15 seconds. Subjects were recalled after delays of 2 days, 21 days or 56 days and were asked to try to select either of the targets from a photographic parade or a live parade of five men, on which only one target appeared. Subjects were not informed of how many targets were on the parade, nor were they told how many they were to select. Although identification rates were higher for live parades than for photographs, the rate of correct identification (hits) did not vary across the three delay intervals. Overall 90% of subjects selected a target. However, the percentages of subjects selecting a non-target (false alarms) increased with delay from 48% at 2 days to 62% at 21 days and 93% at 56 days. Expressed in another way, *error-free* performance, selecting a target with no false alarms, was achieved by 45% of subjects at 2 days, 29% at 21 days, and only 7% at 56 days.

These results are consistent with those published in two studies by Malpass and Devine (1981a, 1981b). They staged a spectacular and, for the audience, unexpected act of vandalism in a lecture hall, and on the three following days held live five man identity parades which included the vandal. Eighty three % of their subjects correctly identified the vandal, and none made a false identification. After a delay of 5 months, Malpass and Devine recalled further members of the same audience and asked them to select the target from a photographic version of the original five man live parade. The identification rate and false alarm rate in the relevant condition in this study were 36% and 35% respectively. Even allowing for the different mode of parade, this represents a substantial drop in identification performance over the 5 month delay interval.

These results do seem to suggest that the lapse of time reduces the chances of errorless identification. If this is so, we should expect criminal cases in which there was a long delay between the offence and identification parade to show more disagreement among witnesses and lower rates of identification than those in which the delay was much shorter. Unfortunately, we do not have these data; but we do have some evidence from experimental studies of identification performance among which the delay before testing has varied although the delay interval may not have been part of the design. These experiments do vary, of course, in many respects, and it may be argued that they cannot sensibly be compared with each other. But they vary a lot less than do real-life crimes, and the circumstances under which parades are held by different police forces. We can, furthermore, reduce the variation among the experiments by selecting results from particular conditions. First, by selecting only incidents involving one or two persons and lasting less than 2 minutes, the difficulty of the initial observation can be held relatively constant. Second, by considering only experiments in which subjects have to select one target from a live or photographic parade of five to eight people, the difficulty of the identification task can be roughly equated across experiments. Third, false alarms typically increase if the instructions to subjects encourage guessing, or if the subject has been exposed to photographs or another lineup before the parade. Results from such experimental conditions have not been considered.

We have found seven experiments which meet these requirements, and the hit and false alarm rates for these are listed in Table 10.1. The delay between the incident and testing in these experiments varies from a few minutes to 5

Table 10.1   Hit and false alarm rates for studies which vary in delay interval between incident and parade

	Delay		Hits (%)	False alarms (%)
Leippe *et al.* (1978)	Immediate		31	not given
Lindsay and Wells (1980) Dissimilar parade	Immediate		71	12
Lindsay and Wells (1980) Similar parade	Immediate		58	29
Wells *et al.* (1979)	Immediate		58	20
Malpass and Devine (1981a)	1, 2, 3 days		83	0
Dent and Stephenson (1979) Expt. 1	7 days		21	16
Dent and Stephenson (1979) Expt. 2	7 days	Photos	29	30
		Live	12	30
Malpass and Devine (1981a)	5 months		36	35

months. But it will be noted that none of these studies has a 100% hit rate, even with immediate testing. Second, although there is some indication that studies with immediate testing might have higher hit rates than studies with delayed measures, there is little evidence of a decline in hit rate with increasing length of this delay. Table 10.1 shows the false alarm rates for the same set of studies. Here there is no evidence for any increase in false alarm rates with greater delay, and the immediate test rates are no lower than those for subjects tested after delay.

Clearly, with so few studies only very cautious inferences can be drawn from these data. Nevertheless, the trend of the results gives little support to the hypothesis that performance declines with the delay, and certainly indicates that immediate testing does not ensure reliable identification. It is also clear, however, that none of the studies has set out to test the simple hypothesis that delay impairs identification parade performance.

In our own research we planned to test this hypothesis with delays of up to a year. This gave rise to the possibility of attrition of parade members, which would alter the task of the subjects at different delay intervals in that the composition of the parade would vary. There was, furthermore, the possibility that the appearance of the target would change in the course of a year. One solution to this problem is to use photographs, but we considered that a closer approximation to live parades could be achieved by the use of video tapes. These, in our view, would provide a satisfactory compromise between the static, two-dimensional, photographic parade and the more dynamic, three-dimensional live parade.

In the video parade an attempt was made to simulate the course of a witness at a live parade. First, a long shot of the entire parade was set, so that the relative height of the men on the parade could be judged; then a camera tracked along the parade, stopping in front of each member for 12 seconds before moving on. In this way, the witness got a life-size view of the head of each man on the parade, and a changing perspective on his appearance as the camera tracked and panned. The sequence ended with a second long shot of the parade. The recordings were made in colour, in a television studio with a professional production team.

Experiment 1 — The effect of parade mode

The equivalence of live and VTR parades was established in a preliminary experiment in which witnesses observed a live target for 2 minutes: 2 weeks later the witnesses returned and were asked to try to select the target from one of four kinds of parade: *live*, in which the target plus eight other men stood along a wall; *video*, which video recorded the live parade in the manner described above; *colour stills*, in which a full face, profile, and a full length photograph of all the parade members were mounted on a board; and *monochrome stills*, where an identical arrangement, but in monochrome was prepared.

As Table 10.2 shows, the identification rates were high in all conditions, with the video parade being as high as the live parade. We therefore felt justified in using video parades.

Table 10.2 Results of Experiment 1. Identification rates after 2 weeks' delay (Number in each condition in parentheses)

	PARADE MODE			
	Live (19)	Video (20)	B/W Still (16)	Colour (13)
Per cent hits	89	95	81	92

Experiment 2 — Delay and parade performance

The first experiment to test the effects of delay used subjects drawn from the local non-university population. They were asked to attend the psychology department ostensibly to carry out a series of paper and pencil tests. While they were being briefed about these, a young man burst into the laboratory and demanded to know who owned a car with a particular number, since this car had scratched his own and was in addition blocking his exit from the car park. The owner of the car did not volunteer himself, and the irate complainant, after a few more angry words, retired from the scene. In total the intervention lasted approximately 45 seconds. Subjects were not informed about the true nature of the incident, and after completing their tests, which were in no way related to the incident, they were told they would be asked to return later to complete another series of tests.

Different groups of subjects were recalled after 1 week, 1 month, 3 months, and 11 months. On this occasion they were given the task of identifying the interloper at the previous session on a nine man video parade. The instructions to the subjects were modelled on those recommended in the Devlin Report, which explicitly warn the witness that the target may not be present on the parade, and ask for an identification only if the witness is certain he is present.

Four different targets were used, balanced across delay intervals, and separate parades were constructed for each target, the foils being selected by police officers from a large pool of volunteers.

Table 10.3 shows the percentage of subjects at each delay interval who (a) correctly identified the target (hit), (b) selected a non-target member of the parade (false alarm), and (c) failed to select anyone (miss). The difference between the hit rate at 11 months and that at each of the other delay intervals is significant, but there is no difference among the rates at 1 week, 1 month, and 3 months, in spite of the steady decline. The marked drop in hit rate from 50% at 3 months to 10% at 11 months is associated with a corresponding increase in misses (no identification) over the same period, but there is no increase in the false alarm rate across the four delays. The very large increase in misses at the 11 month delay might be interpreted as reflecting an unduly cautious criterion among those subjects, who with a less timid approach might have produced more hits. In other words, our cautionary instruction may have led to a trade off in which targets were missed in order to avoid more false alarms. We have some evidence pertinent to this hypothesis, because after the initial parade, those subjects who failed to pick out anyone were asked to say who on the parade

Table 10.3   Percentage of subjects who identified (hits) misidentified (false alarm) or failed to make a selection (miss) at four delay intervals

Per cent	DELAY INTERVAL			
	1 week	1 month	3 months	11 months
Hits	65	55	50	10
False alarms	15	20	20	15
Misses	20	25	30	75
	(20)	(20)	(20)	(20)

Note: numbers in parentheses are n for each delay condition.

most resembled the target. For the first three delay intervals there is an approximately equal division of these subjects between those selecting the target and those selecting a foil. After 11 months, however, 87% select a non-target. The poor hit rate at this interval thus appears truly to reflect forgetting among the subjects rather than an exceptionally cautious criterion.

The results of this experiment, then, seem to suggest that relatively little forgetting occurs between the end of the first week and the third month, but that at some time after this, considerable loss occurs by the eleventh month.

The design of this experiment was very simple. Once the incident had occurred, no further reference was made to it until the identification parades were held. In subsequent experiments we went on to examine the effects of various procedural alterations on identification after different delay intervals.

Experiment 3 — Interpolated activity and delay

In our next experiment, then, we introduced a recognition or recall activity shortly after the staging of the incident in an attempt to simulate the procedure of questioning witnesses about the appearance of a suspect, or having the witness look through a photograph album to try to identify the culprit.

There is very little evidence from previous research from which to predict the effect of providing a description. Dent and Stephenson (1979) suggest, from the results of a study they conducted with children, that there was a trend for those who provided a description of a target to be worse at identifying him on a parade a week later than those not providing a description. Williams (1975) also reports that witnesses to a filmed mugging who provided a description made more choices but were less accurate than those who gave no description. In a previous experiment, however, Davies et al. (1978) found no substantial effect of constructing a Photofit picture of a target on recognition of the target after a delay of 3 weeks.

The photographic search condition was introduced because of its common use in criminal cases. The use of photographs in the investigative stage of the procedure was accepted as a necessary and valuable aid by the Devlin Committee. The Committee was aware, however, of the potential danger of a witness picking out on a parade someone he had seen among the photographs rather than the true culprit. This phenomenon has been demonstrated experimentally by Brown et al. (1977), who found that a non-target on a parade who had appeared in a previous photographic display was as likely to be picked out at the parade if the target was absent, as the target when he was present.

Our interest was in a different kind of interference — namely, the effect on subsequent recognition of the target of searching through a set of photographs. Quite simply, would exposure to a fairly large number of faces shortly after the incident and in a similar setting interfere with the clarity of the witness's impression of the target? The evidence from research into face memory is equivocal with respect to this problem. In some cases exposure to a large number of faces has led to a reduction in hit rate for one target (Laughery *et al.*, 1971) or three targets (Davies *et al.*, 1979). On the other hand, Deffenbacher *et al.* (1981) have recently shown that faces are less susceptible to the effects of an immediate interference series if there is a delay of 2 weeks before testing, than on immediate testing.

Our next experiment, therefore, tested the possible effects of interpolated activity at two delay intervals. Once again members of the general public were invited to attend a 'testing' session at which they were supposedly to see a video tape. As they waited expectantly, a loud crash occurred in the corridor outside the laboratory, and an embarrassed technician came in to announce that a mishap had occurred and that there would be no video show. Subjects then completed a personality inventory, which took about 20 minutes after which they were debriefed about the true nature of the incident, and were assigned to one of three treatment groups. One group looked through a set of 40 black and white photographs to try to identify the technician (who was not among them); a second group provided a description of the target, while the third group answered a general questionnaire about how good they believed their memory to be.

Subjects were recalled after an interval of 1 month or 4 months to attend a live parade of nine men, of which one was the target. Instructions were identical to those used in the previous experiment.

The different interpolated tasks had no effect on identification performance measures at either 1 month or 4 months, and results for these different treatments were therefore combined. The combined results showed that there was no overall effect for delay on any of the three measures. Hit rate after 1 month was 21% and after 4 months 27%. False alarms were 25% at 1 month, 35% at 4 months, and no selection was made by 54% at 1 month and 38% at 4 months. None of these rates differs significantly between 1 and 4 months. When the subjects who had made no selection were forced to select the person who 'most resembled' the target, equal numbers selected the target and a foil, as in the previous experiment.

Overall, hit rates were lower than in the previous experiment, and false alarm rates ran generally at about the same level, the tendency being for the no selection (miss) rate to be higher. This experiment thus replicated the absence of any delay effects for delays of 1 month and 4 months from the previous experiment with a hit rate at half the level of the first study, using live parades instead of video parades.

Experiment 4 — Variations in parade composition

In all the experiments so far the subjects always had a chance to identify the target because he was always present on the parade. This together with very conservative instructions, may account for the absence of false alarm increases with delay.

Egan *et al*. (1977) presented subjects with two targets but only one appeared on the parade. They found a sharp increase in false alarms with delay, although no change in hit rate. Other studies, for example by Malpass and Devine (1981a), have found that parades from which the target is absent produce higher false alarm rates than parades on which he is present. In one study they had a 33% false alarm rate with the target absent, compared with 0% rate when he was present with testing within 3 days. Taking these results together the false alarm rate should be expected to increase with the absence of the target, and the rate should rise with increasing delay since the event.

In the next experiment an incident involving two targets was staged. On a later occasion witnesses attended a parade on which both, only one or neither of the targets were present.

For this study, further groups of local citizens attended for 'pencil and paper tests'. Just before they began their session, there was a loud knocking at the door of the laboratory, and two young men entered in front of the group and called to the person in charge to direct them to the computer laboratory. They were given directions and walked across the front of the class to exit by a door at the opposite side of the room from where they had entered. The incident lasted some 20 seconds.

One minute after this incident the subjects were informed about its true nature, and were given a questionnaire concerning the dress and behaviour of the two targets during the incident. No questions were asked about the facial features of the targets. Four different targets were used in all possible combinations of pairs at different sessions.

Subjects were recalled after a delay of either 1 month or 4 months, and were shown a video taped parade. Instructions were the same as in the other experiments, except that subjects were warned explicitly that the parade might have both targets, one target or neither target present, and that they were not to make an identification unless they were quite sure.

Some subjects saw a parade on which only one target was present. This was of the same form as parades in the previous experiments — comprising the target in addition to eight foils. Other subjects saw the same parade, but neither of the targets they had seen appeared in the parade. A third group saw parades on which both targets appeared. These parades were slightly different from the other parades. The Devlin Committee recommended that where more than one suspect was on a parade, there should be an additional foil for each additional suspect. To slightly reduce the probability of a chance identification ten foils were used with two targets.

Identification rates are obviously relevant only for parades on which targets were present. On the two target parades 30% of witnesses identified at least one target at 1 month's delay, and 39% after 4 months' delay. However, only 1 out of 41 witnesses combined across both delays was able to identify both targets. Clearly, the variation in delay had no effect on hit rates. For the one target parade, 30% of witnesses identified him at 1 month's delay and 9% after 4 months. In spite of the apparent size of the difference a statistical test indicated that there was no significant effect for length of delay ($\chi^2 = 2.19$). Once again, then, a difference in delay of 3 months had no significant effect on hit rates; nor, in this study, did the presence of two targets on a parade increase the hit rate over the one target parades.

The effect of mounting a blank parade might be expected to increase the false alarm rate since any selection on a blank parade must be an error. False alarm rates overall averaged 35%. However, neither delay nor the number of targets on the parade had a significant effect on the number of false alarms (Table 10.4), although there was a marked variation among conditions.

To summarize briefly the results of these three experiments, we have failed to find significant effects on hit rates or false alarm rates for variations in delay ranging from 1 week to 4 months. These results have occurred with different targets and different incidents, with hit rates varying across experiments from 50% to 25%. Intervening recall tasks, and the presentation of two targets have not affected these results. Parades on which no target appeared did not have higher false alarm rates than those on which a target was present. Only after a delay of 11 months was any substantial reduction in hit rate found, but this was not associated with any increase in false alarms.

These results conflict with findings in other areas of research into memory, and with what one might expect on common-sense grounds. It might be argued that delays of 1 month and 4 months would not show the effect unless they were compared with a control group tested immediately after the incident because most forgetting would occur in the first few days. But we failed to find any effect in our first experiment with delays of 1 week, 1 month and 3 months, and research in face memory has found little decline in performance in the course of a week.

Hit rates do vary across experiments, however. The incidents in different experiments varied somewhat, and in particular in length, from about 40

Table 10.4   Percentage of subjects identifying a target at each delay interval, and making a misidentification in parades with 2, 1, or 0 targets

Delay	Per cent identification*	Per cent misidentification		
		2 target	1 target	0 target
1 month	30	39 (23)	30 (30)	52 (23)
4 months	23	39 (18)	23 (22)	32 (19)

* 2 target and 1 target conditions combined.
Note: numbers in parentheses are n per cell.

seconds to about 20 seconds. They also varied in the amount of attention they commanded. In a supplementary experiment video taped recordings of the three different incidents were shown to fresh groups of subjects, who were asked to rate them on vividness, memorability, and degree of interest. The first incident, which had by far the highest hit rate, was consistently rated highest on all these measures. Not surprisingly, then, the likelihood of the target attracting the attention of the witness may be an important factor, and possibly a more important factor than delay in its effect on identification. In this respect, laboratory studies of identification differ from experiments in face memory. In fact memory studies subjects are explicitly told to attend to the targets, and sometimes even to try to memorize them. In identification experiments no such instructions are given. In our own series, when we did tell our subjects to attend to the target, as in Experiment 1, we obtained hit rates of 90% after 2 weeks' delay.

False alarms did not increase with lapse of time, and even at 11 months the rate was no higher than it was after a week. Nevertheless, the fact that some 35% of subjects made a false identification is disturbing in view of our emphasis to them that they should not make an identification unless they were quite sure that they could recognize the target, together with the explicit warning that the target might not be present on the parade. False alarms did not increase when we used blank parades on which no target appeared, but we did not deliberately include a suspect who resembled the target for these parades. In the case of a police parade, the suspect could appear on a parade because he resembled a witness's description of the target, a condition we might expect to increase the rate of false alarms.

There is some evidence which suggests that subjects who made false identifications were not only guessing but knew they were guessing and were not genuinely confusing the appearance of the target with one of the parade. For example, there was no consistency in the foil who was wrongly chosen, the selections being distributed across nearly all other members of the parade. Second, subjects who made false identifications were consistently less confident than subjects who scored hits, a result which held across all delays. This relationship between accuracy and confidence has not always been found in other studies (see Deffenbacher, 1980), but there are two elements in our studies which may have contributed to the relationship. Subjects were discouraged from guessing, and in addition, those who did guess had only a one in nine chance of being correct. It is thus very likely that those who did recognize the target were confident of their accuracy, a confidence which did not vary with delay. Even after 11 months, identifiers were as confident as those at a week, and were probably making a true identification.

However, these differences in confidence are based upon averages for groups. The *certainty* of a witness is not a reliable indicator of his accuracy for legal purposes, since many witnesses who were *wrong* expressed as high a degree of certainty as the most confident of those who were right.

The question of how widely our results can be generalized arises, and in particular whether they are relevant to criminal cases. It has been argued that for experiments to be of forensic value, they need to be realistic, and involve some kind of simulated crime or deviant action. We do not know whether staged criminal incidents would have produced similar results. However, the hit rates and false alarm rates we obtained fall well within those found in 'realistic' experimental studies. It should also be borne in mind that identification witnesses are not always witnesses to a crime, but sometimes witnesses that a particular person was in a particular place at a certain time. The case which Devlin reviewed of Laszlo Virag and George Payen had a number of such witnesses.

Finally, I have frequently mentioned the low hit rate and high false alarm rate we obtained. Our instructions stressed the need for accuracy; subjects were under no external pressure to choose someone; and had no personal interest in trying to get a conviction, as, for example, Beck's counsel suggested was the motive behind the witnesses in his case. Eyewitness identification witnesses are fallible. We could look at our results and conclude that up to a delay of 4 months, identification performance does not decline. We could equally look at the same results and conclude that even with short delays of a week or so, misidentifications are as likely as they would be after 3 months.

NOTE

The research reported in this paper was carried out in collaboration with G.M. Davies, H.D. Ellis, and J. Freeman, and was financed by the Home Office Research Unit.

REFERENCES

Brown, E., Deffenbacher, K.A., and Sturgill, W. (1977). Memory for faces and the circumstances of encounter. *Journal of Applied Psychology*, **62**, 311–318.

Chance, J., Goldstein, A.G., and McBride, L. (1975). Differential experience and recognition memory for faces. *Journal of Social Psychology*, **97**, 243–253.

Davies, G.M., Ellis, H.D., and Shepherd, J.W. (1978). Face identification: the influence of delay upon accuracy of Photofit construction. *Journal of Police Science and Administration*, **6**, 35–42.

Davies, G.M., Shepherd, J.W., and Ellis, H.D. (1979). Effects of interpolated mug-shot exposure on accuracy of eyewitness identification. *Journal of Applied Psychology*, **64**, 232–237.

Deffenbacher, K.A. (1980). Eye witness accuracy and confidence. *Law and Human Behavior*, **4**, 243–260.

Deffenbacher, K.A., Carr, T.H., and Leu, J.R. (1981). Memory for words, pictures and faces: retroactive interference. *Journal of Experimental Psychology, Human Learning and Memory*, **7**, 299–305.

Dent, H.R. and Stephenson, G.M. (1979). Identification evidence: experimental investigations of factors affecting the reliability of juvenile and adult witnesses. In

D.P. Farrington, K. Hawkins, and S.M. Lloyd-Bostock (eds), *Psychology, Law and Legal Processes*. London: Macmillan.

Devlin, Rt. Hon. Lord Patrick (1976). Report to the Secretary of State for the Home Department of the Departmental Committee on evidence of identification in criminal cases. London: HMSO.

Ebbinghaus (1885) trans. H.A. Ruger and C.E. Bussenius (1913). *Memory*. New York Teacher's College, Columbia University.

Egan, D., Pittner, M., and Goldstein, A.G. (1977). Eyewitness identification: photographs vs. live models. *Journal of Law and Human Behavior*, **1**, 199–206.

Gehring, R.E., Toglia, M.P., and Kimble, G.A. (1976). Recognition memory for words and pictures at short and long retention intervals. *Memory and Cognition*, **4**, 256–260.

Laughery, K.R., Alexander, J.V., and Lane, A.B. (1971). Recognition of human faces: effects of target exposure time, target position, pose position and type of photograph. *Journal of Applied Psychology*, **55**, 477–483.

Leippe, M.R., Wells, G.L., and Ostrom, T.M. (1978). Crime seriousness as a determinant of accuracy in eyewitness identification. *Journal of Applied Psychology*, **63**, 345–351.

Lindsay, R.C.L. and Wells, G.L. (1980). What price justice? Exploring the relationship of line-up fairness to identification accuracy. *Law and Human Behavior*, **4**, 303–313.

Malpass, R.S. and Devine, P.G. (1981a). Eyewitness identification: line up instructions and the absence of the offender. *Journal of Applied Psychology*, **66**, 482–489.

Malpass, R.S. and Devine, P.G. (1981b). Guided memory in eyewitness identification. *Journal of Applied Psychology*, **66**, 343–350.

Neil v. *Biggers* 409 US 188.

Shepard, R.N. (1967). Recognition memory for words, sentences and pictures. *Journal of Verbal Learning and Verbal Behavior*, **6**, 156–163.

Shepherd, J.W. and Ellis, H.D. (1973). The effect of attractiveness on recognition memory for faces. *American Journal of Psychology*, **86**, 627–633.

Wall, P.M. (1965). *Eyewitness Identification in Criminal Cases*. Springfield: Thomas.

Watson, E.R. (1924). *The Trial of Adolf Beck*. Edinburgh: Hodge.

Wells, G.L., Lindsay, R.C.L., and Ferguson, T.J. (1979). Accuracy, confidence and juror perceptions in eyewitness identification. *Journal of Applied Psychology*, **64**, 440–448.

Williams, L. (1975). Application of signal detection parameters in a test of eyewitnesses to a crime. Center for Responsive Psychology, Report No. CR-20.

Woocher, F.D. (1977). Did your eyes deceive you? *Stanford Law Review*, **29**, 969–1030.

Evaluating Witness Evidence
Edited by S.M.A. Lloyd-Bostock and B.R. Clifford
© 1983 John Wiley & Sons Ltd.

Chapter 11

Memory for Voices: The Feasibility and Quality of Earwitness Evidence

Brian R. Clifford

On June 12, 1967, the United States Supreme Court decided three landmark cases (*Stovall* v *Denno; United States* v. *Wade*; and *Gilbert* v. *California*), all of which were held to raise a problem concerning the constitutionality of certain legal practices and procedures in obtaining eyewitness identifications. What is not often acknowledged is the fact that in the first two cases voice identification also played a major part in conviction. In the Wade case, Billy Joe Wade was arrested for a bank robbery and at the lineup all participants were required to wear strips of tape over their faces and to say 'Put the money in the bag'. A bank employee identified Wade. In the *Stovall* v. *Denno* case the accused was held to have entered the home of a doctor, stabbed him to death and then attacked the doctor's wife inflicting multiple stab wounds. Two days later the accused was presented at the hospital bed of the wife and asked to say a few words for voice identification purposes. Stovall was identified, convicted, and sentenced to death.

Now while these cases contained other types of evidence, especially visual evidence, it is conceivable that several criminal situations, such as obscene phone calls, bomb hoaxes, ransom demands, hooded rape or muggings, may result in the perpetrator's *voice* being the only tangible piece of evidence available to facilitate police investigation and court conviction.

The fact that most research into witness testimony and identification has been conducted in the visual realm reflects the fact that most identification situations normally involve a witness in using a variety of visual cues. It is unfortunate, however, that this preponderance of research also serves to obscure the fact that there are many instances when both visual and auditory information is available and yet others where only auditory cues may exist.

It was the awareness of the latter two types of criminal situation which convinced the present writer that research into human abilities to recognize voices should be pursued with all reasonable speed. This chapter is designed to give an impetus to this needed research by providing a review of existing voice memory research illustrated by our own work carried out over the last 4 or 5 years. Because there has been little concerted research in this field our research

189

will be seen to be mainly exploratory in nature, concerned with 'baseline performance' under fairly optimal conditions of listening and testing.

To set the scene it may be instructive to draw a parallel with visual identification. The starting point for judgments about voice identification feasibility may be seen to be the same as that for eyewitness judgments: the common-sense belief based upon personal experience that voice identification can be very good. No doubt readers will be able to recall occasions where, for example, they picked up the phone and immediately recognized the voice of an old friend whom they had not talked to, nor interacted with, for many years. This finding is legion and underpins the common-sense belief that voice identification is valid and reliable and supports the easy transposition of such a belief into cultural consciousness which, enshrined in law, allows such identification to stand as evidence of a 'special nature' (similar to visual identification) in courts of law. Identification testimony based on the sound of a person's voice is regarded as direct evidence of identity and therefore admissible as evidence.

Now as with visual identification the *fact* of occasionally excellent voice identification (such as in the above telephone example) is not at issue: there is no doubt that recognition of familiar voices over very long periods of time does occur. What is in doubt is the interpretation of, and the extrapolation from, these occurrences in terms of forensically relevant witness testimony. The key point to note is that 'surprising' voice recognition is always of familiar voices — just the type of voice which is not the usual case in criminal situations. The point to make is that while long-term voice recognition of familiar voices is theoretically puzzling and therefore interesting it cannot be used to shore up a common-sense justification for over-credulity in the powers of witnesses who testify to the identity between a previously heard unfamiliar voice and a currently presented voice: the two situations are just not comparable. Identification of familiar and unfamiliar voices constitutes two entirely different classes of phenomenon.

This failure to disentangle cases where voice identification is predicated upon hearing familiar voices, from cases where such identification is of unfamiliar voices largely explains the observed discrepancy in potentially relevant empirical studies where opinions cover the whole spectrum of acceptance/rejection. Thus while some hold that 'the ability of human listeners to identify speakers from their voices has long been known' (Atal, 1972) others opine that long-term speaker identification must be treated with 'the utmost caution' (Saslove and Yarmey, 1980). This division of opinion should serve to sensitize us to the fact that the state of the art is still rudimentary. In fact, few if any of the putatively important areas have been adequately investigated, far less settled (see Clifford, 1978, 1980a; Clifford and Bull, 1978).

Given this perception of the qualitative and quantitative nature of research into voice identification a 'baseline performance' approach seemed advisable.

It was considered that the 'ideal type' (Weber, 1949; see Twining, this volume) of voice identification situation involved a witness or a victim hearing an unfamiliar voice during the commission of a crime and being asked, at some later time, to attend a voice 'lineup' in order to assert whether a suspect's voice was the same voice as that heard previously. This ideal type, or 'most common situation', rules out investigation of two other approaches to voice identification currently in use in forensic psychology. One such approach is that of expert testimony, whereby a phonetic or linguistics expert listens to at least two tape recordings, one being of a suspect, and judges whether they are from the same person or from different persons. The second, excluded, approach is that of voice print or other electromechanical methods of voice matching. At base, expert (phonetic) testimony and voice print analysis both require tapes of voices, a requirement not easily satisfied in the vast majority of criminal cases. In addition, it is not clear that these two methods can advance our knowledge of how everyday human listeners encode, store, and retrieve voices under a number of criminally relevant situations.

Thus our research strategy was designed to approximate as closely as possible the usual situation which exists in cases where voice identification evidence has been used in real-life criminal procedures. This strategy was qualified by two tactical decisions: to operate optimal listening and testing conditions wherever possible and to exercise maximum experimental control to allow fairly clear specification of the feasibility of voice identification, and its quality.

With these perceptions of the status of extant research and given the orienting assumptions of how to progress most advantageously, the methodology employed involved listeners hearing between one and six unfamiliar taped voices and then a few minutes later asking these listeners to try to identify the previously heard (target) voice when that voice was re-presented among 4 to 11 other non-target (distractor) taped voices. To make the recognition or identification tests sufficiently hard the target and distractor voices were selected on the basis of, first, being devoid of any regional accent or speech defects, and, second, being fairly homogeneous in terms of speech characteristics. The similarity eventually obtained in our voice banks (based on ratings by non-experimental subjects and colleagues) was certainly greater than would be obtained in an actual police voice parade composed in a way analogous to the guidelines which exist for visual identification parades. While this basic paradigm was modified in particular experiments (to be detailed below), when different factors were under investigation, it was felt that it best approximates optimal conditions of listening, while achieving correct identification rates which avoided floor and ceiling effects due to the employment of artificially difficult or easy testing conditions. In this way a fairly definite indication of just whether voice identification was possible and how it could be augmented or decremented was felt to be possible.

That voice identification may be seen as an important aspect of information in any and all aspects of the criminal justice system was underlined in the UK, by the Devlin Committee's Report (1976), whose brief was to investigate identification evidence (in all its forms) in criminal cases in Great Britain. While mainly concerning itself with visual identification this Report did state that as far as the Committee was concerned there had been no scientific research into voice identification questions but that research should proceed as rapidly as possible. Now while I have been critical of this blanket statement (Bull and Clifford, 1976) it is true that little directly relevant research had been conducted and formal study and experimentation are a fairly recent development. The Devlin Committee's statement could thus be seen as an overly-drawn conclusion of the research effort as of 1976. The situation is a little better at the time of going to press.

While voice experimentation has a fairly long history, that history is of a sporadic rather than of a continuous and progressive kind. From the beginning, however, researchers have always been aware of the possible application of their work. In fact one of the earliest and best known studies resulted directly from the celebrated Lindbergh case in America in 1935. Because of the furore created by that case McGehee (1937) set out to determine the extent to which unfamiliar voices could be recognized after varying intervals of time. Her basic procedure was to have a concealed speaker read out a fairly extensive passage to listeners and then have these listeners attempt to select the original reader when that reader again read a passage aloud but this time when distractor speakers also read before and after the target. That is, listeners had to select the target voice from among a variable number of other readers all reading the same passage. A chief focus of this study was any possible difficulty created by increasing the time between initially hearing the target voice and eventually trying to pick it out from among several other voices. McGehee found that identification accuracy was 83% at 2 days, 68% at 2 weeks, 35% at 3 months, and 13% at 5 months. Further study in 1944 by McGehee broadly confirmed that: (a) voice identification was possible; (b) recognition rates were quite high; and (c) delays of about 2 weeks did not decrement performance too drastically. These two studies further suggested that the greater the number of target voices initially heard the poorer was eventual identification (one target voice producing 83% accuracy while more than three target voices reduced identification to 50%). Men seemed to be better ear witnesses than women (84% and 59% accurate respectively) but the sex of the voice heard seemed not to be important in terms of future identification.

This early 'blunderbuss' investigation served to spawn numerous later 'rapier'-like experiments which focused on one or other of the several original findings and attempted to go beyond the 'grass trampling' operation of the progenitor by testing to destruction the particular finding of interest. What follows is a review of these latter experiments, classified under a number of headings which could be of value to the criminal justice system, informed where appropriate by my own published and unpublished work. When the dust clears it should be clear which findings are wheat and which merely chaff.

LENGTH OF SPEECH SAMPLE HEARD

An important consideration in estimating the likelihood of a witness providing accurate voice identification in criminal cases would seem to be how long the criminal talked for or was kept talking. The common-sense assumption here is that the greater the exposure to a voice the better that voice can be remembered. In eyewitness research Laughery *et al.* (1971) found in a laboratory setting that longer exposure to face-photographs led to better later recognition than shorter exposure, while in a field setting Clifford and Richards (1977) found that policemen's recall of visual information about a target person was more accurate after 30 seconds of interaction than after 15 seconds. The question of 'exposure duration' is an important one because the Devlin Committee suggested that it be one of the factors raised by judges in warnings to the jury.

Exposure duration has received a fair amount of attention from experimental psychologists but unfortunately not always under ecologically valid conditions. In addition to this, the issue of the quantity versus quality of the speech sample heard is seen to be problematic. Lastly, the question of criterion performance within an applied perspective has still to be adequately addressed.

Three studies have produced evidence which relates to the quantity v. quality issue but all three are flawed by ecological invalidity. In one study Pollack *et al.* (1954) found that the larger the speech sample heard the more accurate were identifications, this effect being due to the greater speech repertoire present in the longer samples since repetition of short samples did not increase the number of correct identifications. The forensic relevance of this study is questionable, however, because the voices used were of friends of the listeners. Much the same criticism can be levelled at Bricker and Pruzansky's (1966) study which examined the same topic. They unfortunately used voices of people who worked with the listeners. Notwithstanding, they found 98% correct identification when spoken sentences were produced, 84% for syllables, and 56% for vowel excerpts. These researchers stressed that the different number of phonemes contained in the speech samples, rather than duration *per se*, provided the better explanation of their findings. A similar conclusion was drawn by Murray and Cort (1971) who used school children as their subjects. They found that repetition of the same speech sample did not lead to any increase in identification accuracy whereas increasing the speech repertoire available in a speech sample by lengthening a sentence was sufficient for identification performance to reach an asymptote and they concluded that at least for their subjects a 15 syllable sentence provided sufficient cues for voice identification. Once again, however, the voices being identified were those of familiar classmates.

Allowing for the problem of generalizability from familiar to unfamiliar voices these studies do fairly unambiguously stress that it is the quality of the speech sample (in the sense of variability) which is critical, rather than the sheer quantity. The possible generalizability of research on familiar voices to unfamiliar voices is in fact hinted at in a recent paper by Legge *et al.* (in press) which compared the effect of unfamiliar voices uttering 6, 20, 60, or 120 second speech samples on later identification. While these authors talk of reading an 'identical passage' under all conditions it is unclear whether for example the voices under the 120 second condition read the same 6 second passage 20 times (quantity manipulation) or simply read more of the same passage (quality manipulation). Notwithstanding this unclarity they found a significant ($<$ .01) effect for sample size such that while 6 second samples eventuated in chance performance only (50%), 60 second samples produced a 70% hit rate. Paradoxically, 120 second samples resulted in below 60% correct identification. In sum then — no more than a hint at generality.

What about the case, however, when only quantity is allowed to vary? Can voice identification rise above chance level when the amount of speech heard is extremely short? And if it can, how short is short?

In terms of familiar voices it has been shown that above chance performance in voice identification has resulted from exposures as short as 25 milliseconds (Compton, 1963) and single utterances of isolated vowels (La Riviere, 1972). In terms of unfamiliar voices Doehring and Ross (1972) found subjects could identify which of three voices speaking a nonsense syllable matched the speaker of a sample vowel. In a more applied paradigm Goldstein *et al.* (1981) presented listeners with a one word utterance ('impossible') and then tested their identification powers by presenting the target speaker among four other speakers in a test array where each speaker uttered the same six word sentence but which did not contain the critical word 'impossible'. The mean correct identification score was 50% whereas chance performance would be 20%.

These studies serve to indicate that voice identification of both familiar and unfamiliar speakers is possible under extremely impoverished speech sample duration, and that this performance is not achieved solely on the basis of primitive, and very short-term, matching. This would seem to be a fairly important finding for forensic psychology. However a strong conclusion that the extent of the voice sample heard is unimportant would be wrong on a number of counts. First, the above research has been couched in terms of comparison with chance level performance, an inappropriate comparison standard in criminal cases. Second, the above findings' generality has still to be established under more criminally-relevant contexts. Third, there is some evidence that the greater the amount of speech initially heard the better the eventual recognition.

Thus while Rousey and Holzman (1967) found no difference in recognition accuracy following either a 1-second or a 3-second long speech sample and Clarke *et al.* (unpublished) failed to find any difference in accuracy following exposure to either three-, five-, seven-, nine- or eleven-syllable speech samples, other research exhibits different findings. For example, Stevens *et al.* (1968) have shown an appreciable decrease in error scores for identification of a two- or three-syllable speech sample compared with a one-syllable sample. Additionally, simple repetition of an utterance has sometimes been shown to lead to large improvements in performance (Haggard, 1973).

Because of the suggestion of some irreducible minimum above which increasing the speech sample heard eventuates in little appreciable improvement and because of the importance of this possibility to forensic concerns our own research included this in its checklist of topics for investigation. In designing the relevant experiments we were very conscious of the weakness of several of the above studies and attempted to correct them, believing that the extant research was conflicting and less than clear.

The first experiment we performed involved 134 adult subjects who were randomly allocated to one of three conditions, the conditions being determined by the amount of speech initially heard. One group of subjects heard six target voices (one per trial) uttering a speech sample of four sentences in length, a second group heard the same voices uttering two of the four sentences, and a third group heard the target voices uttering one of the four sentences. Each voice in the test parade, which comprised the target and five distractors, was heard to utter one and the same sentence. In terms of results, across the three speech sample length conditions the mean recognition accuracy performance was 78%, with one sentence producing 75.2% correct identification; two sentence samples, 77%; and four sentence samples producing 81.6% correct identification. Statistical analyses revealed, however, a non-significant difference between any of the group means.

In a second experiment 132 subjects aged 12–16 years were again randomly allocated to one of three conditions: one-half sentence, one sentence, and two sentence speech samples. The design was similar to that of the experiment reported above. The results for this experiment differed from those of the previous one. First, the accuracy scores were much lower (41%, 36%, and 49% for half, one, and two sentence speech samples, respectively) and this most probably reflects the differential perceptual accuracy of the children used in this study as opposed to adults (who were used in the previous study). Second, in this experiment, unlike the previous one, there was a statistically significant difference between the three speech sample conditions ($p < .025$), which is best accounted for by the difference between the one and two sentence speech sample conditions (Scheffé, $p < .025$.

A third experiment in this series looked for a possible interaction between the length of speech sample heard and the number of distractors employed at recognition by presenting independent groups of subjects with either one or eight word speech samples and testing for identification of target voices placed within either 5 or 11 distractors. One hundred and twenty-four adult subjects were randomly allocated to the four resulting cells and a two-way analysis of variance (ANOVA) was applied to the mean correct accuracy scores. This analysis revealed that the only significant main effect was size of speech sample initially heard, with identification being better for eight word samples ($p <$ .01). No interactions attained significance.

From this series of studies it would appear that support is offered, at least with adults, for the extant finding that the length of the speech sample initially heard makes little difference to later identification providing that at least one sentence is presented. With children, however, this does not seem to be the case; they seem to be able to benefit from increased speech sample exposure.

A few cautionary points should perhaps be made explicit before any hasty, applied, implications are drawn. The accuracy levels were not impressive in any of our three studies reported here, despite the fact that memory was tested over very short time intervals. Thus only further research can establish whether there is a general and genuine non-effect of speech sample size and if so, what length of sample is required for optimum identification performance.

THE EFFECT OF VOICE DISGUISE

The concept of disguise connotes some deliberate intention to alter or modify one's appearance or voice in such a way as to mislead those concerned to establish a truthful identification. This conscious intent on the part of a perpetrator has always been known by the criminal justice system. In voice identification, however, there is, in addition, an unintentional dimension to disguise, modification or alteration. This stems from the fact that, undoubtedly, crime commission is an arousing activity and such arousal can create distortion in the way people speak. The problem is compounded by the possibility that physiological and cognitively determined voice alterations may differ in important respects; although this speculation still awaits experimental investigation. The present, pressing problem for forensic psychology is that we know little or nothing about the effects of disguise (whatever its source) upon later voice identification accuracy, although the weight of evidence from voice print research suggests that following disguise manipulations voice recognition is considerably less accurate.

For example, it has been shown that the acoustical components of speech can be significantly altered by persons speaking with a freely chosen disguised voice (McGlone et al. 1977), and that only 23.3% of visual inspections of such voice prints were correct (Hollien and McGlone, 1976). Using similar procedures, Reich et al. (1976) compared normal voice identification with identification of voices disguised by means of affecting old age, hoarseness, slow speech rate, or free disguise. Accurate identification dropped from 57% correct spectral matching with normal voices to 22% correct matching for freely disguised voices.

These voice print results seems to replicate with human aural identification. Thus, in 1979 Reich and Duke investigated the effect of six different voice mode disguises (normal, slow, aged, hoarse, hypernasal, free disguise) upon speaker identification by human listeners. The listeners' task was to decide whether two taped voice samples, the first of which was undisguised, the other either disguised or not, were uttered by the same or different speakers. For naive listeners the nasal and free disguise were the most effective modes of disguise in reducing performance (59% and 61% respectively) while the undisguised condition led to significantly higher accuracy than any of the other conditions (92%). The reasons for the differential effectiveness of the various disguise modes are unclear but it seems likely that the different disguises permitted differential concealment of the most salient vocal or speech features employed in voice identification or recognition.

A frequently quoted disguise mode used by criminals would seem to be some variant of whispering. Unfortunately this seems to be quite effective! Pollack et al. (1954), using 16 familiar talkers obtained only 30% accurate identification when these talkers were heard whispering, compared to 95% correct identification for 1 second of normal speech. Pollack et al. in fact found that the sample of whispered speech needed to be heard for three times as long as normal speech before comparable identification levels were achieved.

A few studies have employed voice manipulations which could more correctly be called voice alterations than disguise — but the results have been the same as those in which true disguise has been employed. Thus Saslove and Yarmey (1980) altered the tone of a heard voice between initially hearing and later identifying. The actual alteration was from an angry to a normal tone. These researchers found a strong and reliable effect for this change in voice tone, such that identification accuracy dropped from a mean of 5.15 correct identification under no tone alteration to a mean of 2.37 under tone alteration conditions. It thus seems that even a relatively simple change in the voice can cause substantial decrement in the recognition accuracy of human listeners. This pessimistic assessment is supported by a study by Clifford and Denot (unpublished) which will be discussed more fully below under another heading. For our purposes here suffice to note that in one condition subjects heard a live stooge speaking a fairly extensive speech sample in an angry tone and were later required to identify that voice when speaking calmly whereas other subjects heard the same stooge speaking calmly both initially and eventually (at the recognition stage). Those subjects who had to recognize the changed voice produced 33% accurate identification while those who were presented with an unaltered voice scored 50% correct identification, with chance being 10% correct.

From these studies then it would seem that intentional disguise, or even changes in tone which are not designed as intentional disguise, greatly reduce identification accuracy even under short-term and ideal conditions of listening and identifying. Further evidence from our own laboratories correcting for certain artificiality and ecological validity do nothing to attenuate this conclusion.

In one fairly complex experiment a total of 216 members of the general public took part, being divided into three groups (16–20, 20–40, and 40–70 years of age) with equal numbers of males and females in each group. Half the subjects received disguised voices, half received the same persons talking in their natural voices. The basic procedure was to have subjects hear a target voice, either disguised or not, and then have them attempt identification of that target voice, always speaking naturally, in a recognition set of four, six or eight distractor voices. The target voice was always present in these recognition sets, and recognition sets were carefully controlled and compiled to have a very high degree of similarity (as assessed by non-experimental subject raters). This was facilitated by having pools of target and distractor voices which had no strong accents or speech defects.

Six trials were given to each subject with three of the trials involving female target voices and three involving male voices; the recognition set voices always being of the same sex as the target voice. The recognition phase of each trial began 10 seconds after the offset of the target voice, and both the target and each of the distractor voices were heard to utter the same 13 word sentence. The disguised targets were instructed to disguise their voice in 'any way you choose'. The results were clear. Disguising a target voice greatly decreased recognition accuracy compared to that following a non-disguised target voice ($p < .001$) with mean respective accuracy 26.4% and 53.7%. In addition to this major finding several interesting first and second order interactions reached significance. (For full details the interested reader should consult Rathborn *et al.*, 1981.) Thus while increasing the number of distractors employed in the disguised voice condition had a very clear effect no such clear effect was found in the non-disguised condition. This means that as one attempts to meet at least one criterion of lineup fairness (see Malpass and Devine, this volume), viz. size, the probability of correctly identifying an initially disguised voice drops dramatically. In addition while females were significantly better than males at recognizing voices overall ($p < .025$) further analysis revealed that this significance lay solely in identification trials with non-disguised voices, there being no difference between males and females with disguised voices. Of interest and perhaps importance was the fact that the sex of the disguised voice had no effect whatever on listener's accuracy.

From all of the studies quoted above the conclusion seems fairly clear: if we have reason to believe that voice disguise was employed by a crime perpetrator then our estimation of the accuracy of listener identification should assume some low value. This conclusion is driven by research from voice print; from work with humans recognizing familiar voices; and from humans recognizing unfamiliar voices.

DELAY

As was indicated at the beginning of this chapter several key (American) criminal cases, usually described from a visual identification point of view, have served to raise the whole issue of the validity and therefore value of witness testimony. It was also pointed out there that, although not always acknowledged, voice identification was also critically involved, and in addition often after appreciable time delays: after several months in one case. This issue of delay was also argued to have been one of the chief stimuli to voice identification research, in particular the Lindbergh case. Perhaps *the* critical question, not yet answered unequivocally, is whether delay does have an appreciable effect on voice recognition accuracy and further, if so, whether there is some critical cut-off point after which no credence can or should be placed upon proffered identification.

We have already detailed the results of the two early studies by McGehee (1937; 1944) in which accuracy of voice identification was approximately 83% at 2 days, but between 69% (1937) and 48% (1944) at 2 weeks, and 51% (1937) to 47% (1944) at 4 weeks. The two studies therefore become somewhat discrepant over longer periods of delay with, further, the 1937 study indicating decrement to 35% correct identification at 3 months and 13% correct identification at 5 months, while the later (1944) study suggested little decrement over comparable time spans. Thus the two studies agree closely on short-term delays (2 days) but begin to conflict from 2 weeks onwards. It should perhaps be made explicit here that, because of the sensitivity of actual scores to listening and testing conditions, it is the pattern of data rather than their absolute values which carry information for psychologists although the criminal justice system may wish to take issue with this assertion.

In one of the more recent researches into the voice identification capabilities of humans, Saslove and Yarmey examined the effects of a short delay interval (24 hours) upon voice recognition accuracy. The listeners initially heard a voice uttering a 10 second sentence and were then required to pick out that voice from among four others. Some listeners were tested immediately, whereas others were tested after a delay of 24 hours. For those listeners tested immediately recognition performance was 60% accurate, and for those tested after a delay of 24 hours it was 70%. Thus, a 24 hour delay had no deleterious effect on performance. This non-effect of delay was found to apply both when subjects were 'informed' and 'non-informed' as to the fact that their recognition accuracy would be tested; or, when the target voice changed or did not change in tone between the initial hearing and later recognizing phases. Surprisingly, though Saslove and Yarmey did not investigate the effects of delays greater than 24 hours, they stated that 'long-term speaker identification must be treated by the criminal justice system with suspicion and caution'.

In the previously mentioned recently completed study by Legge *et al.* (submitted) in which they looked at speech sample size, they also investigated the effect of various retention intervals on learning unfamiliar voices. Their stimuli were 20 recorded voices uttering passages from Grimm's Fairytales. The retention intervals employed were 15 minutes and 10 days. They also varied the size of speech sample spoken having nominal durations of 6, 20, 60, and 120 seconds. While they found a significant main effect for speech sample size such that increasing voice sample duration from 6 seconds to 60 seconds led to improved voice recognition they found no main effect for delay. That is they found voice recognition was little affected by increasing the delay in identifying from 15 minutes to 10 days. Unfortunately, while not scrutinized in their originally submitted paper, there was a significant first order interaction between sample size and retention interval which does require qualifications to be entered in any discussion of main effects. At best then this result is equivocal and offers only tentative support to the idea that voice identification may not be adversely affected by delays of up to 10 days.

The three sets of studies reviewed above seem to contradict each other over the effects of both short and long delay intervals upon voice recognition accuracy. Partly as an attempt to resolve this issue Clifford and Denot (unpublished) had subjects partake of a simulated real-life incident in which they were seated quietly at a number of galvanic skin response (GSR) machines having been deceived into believing that they were taking part in a psychophysiological experiment which required the establishment of initial values on GSR. While being so deceived they witnessed a live incident in which a stooge entered a room, had a brief (aggressive or neutral) conversation with the experimenter, and then left. The witnesses' voice and face recognition powers were tested at 1, 2, or 3 weeks later. For voice recognition, after a delay of 1 week correct identification performance was 50%, after 2 weeks it was 43%, and after 3 weeks it was at the chance level of 9%. Statistical analysis of these data revealed that there was no difference in performance between delays of 1 and 2 weeks, but there was a significant drop in performance with a 3 week delay.

To summarize these studies so far, little or no decrement appears to occur in voice identification over a 24 hour delay period, but from 2 to 4 weeks' accuracy may or may not drop. Because of the importance of this topic to real-life criminal issues and because previous research by no means offers a clear prediction concerning the effects of either short (e.g. hours) or long (e.g. days and weeks) delay intervals upon voice identification accuracy, my research team undertook a series of studies into delay effects, several of which are reported here.

Subjects were presented with tape recorded male and female target voices which, from previous experimentation (see Clifford *et al.*, 1981) could be objectively defined as either 'high-recognition voices' or 'low-recognition voices' (i.e. voices which had in previous studies been found to lead to high or low recognition scores). Identification of these target voices placed among a number of distractor voices was then attempted after an interval of either 10, 40, 100, or 130 minutes. The recognition set comprised 22 voices of which 20 were distractors and 2 were targets (1 male, 1 female). The recognition set contained equal numbers of male and female voices, and the target and distractor voices were randomly allocated to serial position in the set. The order of male and female target voice in the learning set was counterbalanced within and across conditions.

The distractors and targets were selected from a large pool of voices in such a way that a fairly high degree of similarity within the recognition sets was obtained (as confirmed by independent raters). Voices were so selected as to have no marked accents or unusual vocal characteristics.

All target voices uttered a semantically identical one-sentence speech sample, as did the distractors: 'I will meet you outside the National Westminster Bank at 6 o'clock tonight.' Actual speech duration was constant (± 2 seconds) across all targets.

A between-subjects design was employed such that each subject performed under only one testing delay and type of voice ('high-' and 'low-recognition') treatment combination, with 64 female subjects taking part.

The results indicated that identification accuracy was better at 10 minutes' delay (mean = 56.25%) than at all other delays ($p < .025$) which did not differ significantly among themselves (mean = 41.67%). The low- and high-recognition voice factor did not interact with delay indicating that well recognized voices were as much affected by delay as were objectively defined, poorly recognized voices. For a further discussion of this experiment see Clifford *et al.* (1981). Overall these results suggest that while delay does have an effect it is not massive. However the relatively short durations tested in this experiment render any firm conclusions extremely tentative given the usual time lapse between hearing or seeing a criminal and later trying to identify him (see Devlin, 1976 for UK estimates of delay in real cases). The next experiment took this point into account and ran basically the same design but this time with intervals of 10 minutes, 24 hours, 7 days, and 14 days.

One hundred and twelve trainee nurses took part in the experiment, each subject performing under only one delay × type of voice (well or poorly recognized) treatment condition. The only significant effect was for delay interval, with 10 minutes leading to better identification ($p < .025$) than any of the other delays which themselves did not differ, the mean percentage correct being 55%, 32%, 30%, and 37% respectively. While not significant the well and poorly recognized voices did behave differently under different delay conditions such that, while recognition of the former type of voice was best at 10 minutes and 14 days' delay and poorest at 1 and 7 days, the latter type of voice eventuated in a steady decline in accuracy as the delay interval increased. Possible reasons for the bowed curve for well recognized voices under delay manipulation have been discussed elsewhere (Clifford *et al.*, 1981) but for the moment the safest, most valid, general conclusion is perhaps that while delay does have a detrimental effect that decrement is far from catastrophic. A definitive statement on delay and accuracy thus still awaits further research.

In an unpublished study (Clifford, in press) designed to investigate further the somewhat noisy delay data which seem to characterize this aspect of voice recognition work an experiment was run in which some subjects performed under only one delay interval while other subjects performed under all delay intervals. This was done to rule out the possibility that non-linear trends across delay intervals could be due to faulty sampling and random allocation of subjects to conditions. In the event this possibility was ruled out. The between-subject data pattern (and absolute levels) was mirrored by the within-subject pattern — and it was still noisy. That is, whether subjects were acting as their own controls or not, a clear decrement with increase in delay was not evident.

VOICE PARADES — THEIR SIZE, NATURE, AND COMPOSITION

The Devlin Committee (1976) stated that 'research should proceed as rapidly as possible into the practicality of voice parades'. The reasoning here no doubt was that, if identification by voice was to become an accepted part of criminal and civil evidence then the holding of voice parades comparable to visual identification parades would be the preferred mode of establishing such evidence. This explicit stress on voice parades may reflect the discussion in the legal world generally concerning the critical question of the number of non-suspects that should be present in any identification procedure. The Devlin Committee, along with many others, argued that the use of 'showups' (i.e. lineups containing only one person — the suspect) should be avoided at all costs or wherever and whenever possible and practical, although theoretically, and I stress theoretically, testing recognition memory without distractor items in the test phase is supportable as a legitimate procedure, as Wallace (1980) has argued recently.

There can be little doubt that the discussion currently underway in the eyewitness literature concerning the number of non-suspects and their function in eliminating bias (Lindsay and Wells, 1980; Loftus, 1979; Malpass and Devine, this volume) is equally applicable to earwitness situations and voice parades.

Additionally, a question not yet adequately addressed is that of the number of distractors that should be involved in testing if and when the number of targets (perpetrators) is greater than one, in either eye witnessing (Clifford and

Hollin, 1981) or in earwitnessing situations (McGehee, 1937). This question has not yet received any comprehensive study and the pragmatic suggestions concerning such cases (for example the Devlin Committee's suggestions concerning increasing the number of non-suspect paraders, or splitting the lineups) are simply that — pragmatic. What is required is an extension of the analysis along the lines sketched by Malpass and Devine (this volume) to the case where the number of targets is greater than one. However because this is for the future the present review will concentrate upon those cases where there is only one target to be identified.

The rationale for employing a number of distractors has been explained by Malpass and Devine (this volume) and therefore will not be repeated here. Instead certain issues which arise when persons, or, in this case, voices other than the suspect appear in a parade will be discussed.

One such issue is the question of target placement. That is, does the location in the parade of the to-be-identified target have an effect upon recognition accuracy? It should be noted that one of the few freedoms that the suspect can exercise in lineup situations is a choice of where to stand in a parade. In visual identification Laughery et al. (1971) found, in 'mugshot' searching, that recognition performance was an inverse function of the position of the target face in the search set; this effect being found, however, only when the non-target faces had a high degree of similarity to the target faces (Laughery et al., 1974). The theoretical explanation for this effect could be some form of interference based upon similarity, although, without safeguards, build-up of interference is confounded with delay and thus, possibly, decay.

Concerning earwitnessing, Doehring and Ross (1972) had subjects match a previously heard speaker of a vowel to one of three voices speaking a nonsense syllable. They found a significant though small effect of target placement in the testing array with the target voice being recognized 65% of the time when in first position, 62% when in position two, and only 56% of the time when placed in position three. A similar effect was found in the study by Clarke and Becker (1969) in which listeners heard a target voice utter a few syllables and were then required to pick it out from an array of four speakers. They found that the percentage correct responses declined linearly from 70% to 48% as the number of intervening distractors increased from none to three.

These three studies strongly suggest then that the number of distractors employed is important, and further that they may be important because either they cause interference or because they create time gaps between presentation and re-presentation of the target voice that allow decay of a very fragile and fast decaying memory trace to take place. For a number of reasons chief among which are the fact of very good long-term memory for familiar voices, our own research with unfamiliar voices, and the extremely short retention intervals employed by the above studies, memory decay does not seem a very plausible alternative. If it were, with the intervals employed above (a matter of a few seconds), voice identification could be ruled out as a viable type of evidence in criminal and civil cases.

While the theoretical underpinnings of the putative placement effect documented above is important for theoretical psychologists they are not a central concern in forensic applications. Much more important is their validity. The study by Carterette and Barnaby (1975) sheds a little light on this more important question. These researchers had subjects listen to either 2, 3, 4 or 8 speakers saying 'You all be' and then in an immediate test, consisting of 4, 6, 8 or 16 voices, they were required to indicate which voices they had heard previously. Unlike the previous two studies mentioned Carterette and Barnaby employed two dependent variables: correct recognition (hits) and incorrect recognition (false alarms). They found that although there was a linear decline in correct recognitions as the number of voices in the test array increased this was only of the order of 2% per voice. Thus the hit rate appeared to be almost independent of the number of voices in the recognition set. The false alarm rate, however, increased noticeably as the number of voices increased from 4 to 16.

Overall then it seems that previous research is unable to answer many important questions concerning the number of speakers that a voice lineup should contain for it to be seen to be fair. For example, the studies by Doehring and Ross (1972) and Clarke and Becker (1969) failed to evidence an asymptote and thus imply that voice identification parades of less than five speakers may not be employing enough distractors. This being the most important practical question implicit in voice parade research we decided to examine it in our own research, both directly (by treating 'number of distractors' as a factor) and indirectly (by looking at it in a *post hoc* fashion, across experiments).

In one of the studies designed to look at the effect of speech sample heard on later recognition accuracy, targets initially uttering either one or eight words were placed in test arrays containing 5 or 11 distractors. We found that this latter variable had no statistically significant effect upon performance: with the smaller speech sample correct recognition was 36% with 11 distractors and 38% with 5. With the eight word utterance correct recognition was 49% and 53% with 5 and 11 distractors respectively. These performance levels it should be noted were well above chance (9% in the 11 distractor condition) thus floor effects cannot be evoked to explain the absence of effects for the number of distractors.

Now while this result seemed to fly in the face of extant research in verbal memory where it can be seen that as the number of similar distractors increases so performance decreases, it is possible that some asymptotic performance (in terms of number of distractors) had been discovered. That is, it may be that while performance may decrease with increased number of distractors there may be a point where this relationship ceases to hold. If so then we may have an operational definition of the 'required number' of distractor voices in a voice parade. The lack of difference between 5 and 11 distractors in our speech sample studies and our delay studies suggested that this may lie somewhere about four or five distractor voices (cf. Doehring and Ross, 1972; Clarke and Becker, 1969). To test this we ran a number of experiments which varied the number of distractors as a factor, employing four, six or eight distractors, as the vast majority of real-life visual parades employ this number of non-suspects for several very practical reasons.

In one of the experiments 108 members of the general public attempted to recognize a once heard voice uttering a 13 word sentence when it was placed within either four, six or eight other distractor voices which had all been rated by non-experimental subjects as 'very similar' to the target voice on a five point scale. The focus of the experiment was an answer to the question of whether the number of distractor voices used in an identification set influenced the accuracy of identification of a target voice placed within that set and further, whether there was some point at which decrement no longer occurred. We found that recognition accuracy was significantly better under the four distractor condition (64%) than under either the six or eight distractor conditions which did not differ between themselves (48% and 49% respectively). The overall finding suggested that identification performance did not decrease uniformly as parade size increased while the latter finding suggested an asymptotic performance from six distractors onwards.

To check this finding a second experiment was conducted with 27 subjects who, this time, performed under all three parade size conditions. This within-subject replication was designed to control as much as possible individual differences by having each subject act as his own control. In the event essentially identical results were obtained, with a significant difference between the four and six distractor conditions (73% and 58% respectively) and no difference between the six and eight conditions (58% and 62%). The slightly higher overall performance in the second study may be accounted for by the fact that undergraduate, and therefore test-sophisticated subjects, were employed. The most noticeable fact, however, is the strong agreement in pattern of results between the two studies. It therefore seems that in highly optimal conditions, in which subjects are warned that they will be asked to recognize later a target voice, which utters a fairly extensive, non-disguised speech sample, six distractors are all that is required to attain a 'reasonable and fair' voice parade.

This, however, can afford no more than a baseline consideration because actual criminal situations frequently lack these optimal conditions. This has been shown in our own experiments where, for example, when a target voice has been disguised, a significant monotonic decline in performance has been found as the number of distractor voices was increased from four through six to eight.

Regarding the secondary question of target placement in a test array comprising more than the suspect, we have found little evidence supportive of the questionable data cited at the start of this section. Specifically, whenever we have used a variable number of distractors we have taken steps to observe whether the location of the target voice correlated with its recognizability. No such correlation (positive or negative) has been found to pertain.

PREPAREDNESS

Criminal situations in general may be characterized as dynamic, rapid, unexpected, and of sudden on-set and off-set. As such, witnesses or victims are almost always taken unawares. This common-sense understanding was the basis of an issue raised by Clifford (1978, 1981) in a general critique concerning the relevance to real-life criminal evidence of eyewitness testimony research conducted in the laboratory: the issue of preparedness.

In this critique it was argued that for witnesses to be forewarned of what was to happen and of what was expected of them was to favour the engagement of a whole constellation of cognitive sets which encompassed maximally efficient processing and encoding strategies not necessarily, or even likely to be, evoked in real-life witnessing situations. If there is a disjunction between the sets of strategies employed in these respective situations then perhaps the belief that laboratory studies talk to real criminal cases is somewhat naive: perhaps we should not expect a concordance between the indices of accuracy recorded in each. This pessimistic view can be seen to be supported in visual identification (Clifford, 1978), is it also supportable in the earwitness field?

In one study into earwitnesses' ability Saslove and Yarmey (1980) looked at voice identification under conditions where some subjects were warned that at some point in the experiment they would hear a voice over a telephone and that they would be tested on their ability to recognize that voice at a later date. Other subjects were given no warning whatever concerning the presence of an initial or eventual voice factor in the experiment. These researchers found a highly significant difference between the warned and unwarned groups on later voice recognition, with the informed group performing better than the uninformed group. From this study it would seem that, as with eyewitnessing, preparedness also has an effect upon voice recognition accuracy.

In a more realistic type of experiment Clifford and Denot (unpublished) had subjects taking part in what they believed to be a psychophysiological (galvanic skin response — GSR) experiment during which the subjects were exposed to a stooge who behaved in a friendly or a very aggressive way towards the (female) experimenter. When the cover (psychophysiological) experiment had run its course all the subjects were required to offer testimony and identification on visual, verbal, and action aspects of the staged (covert) event. Thus, throughout, the witnesses were totally unaware of the true nature of the experiment, and were unprepared for either the appearance of the stooge in the experiment or the later testing sessions. Thus we had a situation fairly analogous to the context pertaining in real criminal situations. For our purposes here correct identification of the stooge's voice was 49% at 1 week's delay (chance being 10%), 41% at 2 weeks, and 8% at 3 weeks. In terms of comparability of voice and face identification, visual identification was 83% correct at 1 week, 50% correct at 2 weeks, and 34% correct at 3 weeks (chance again was 10%). Although there was no adequate control in this experiment for voice identification under warned conditions, because it formed only a part of a much larger experiment (see Clifford and Denot, unpublished) it is instructive to compare the above hit rates with those obtained in our other baseline performance experiments (this chapter; Clifford et al., 1980). In these latter experiments an overall estimate of voice identification capabilities lies between 60% and 70% accuracy. By comparison then the conclusion seems to be forced that voice identification under incidental (unprepared) conditions is low. This conclusion is strengthened by the fact that in the Clifford and Denot study the listeners heard a fairly extensive speech sample (48 words) being delivered in a fairly uniquely accented voice (Iranian), and the recognition set comprised a heterogeneous set of accented voices which eventuated in a functional lineup size of only three.

In another study Clifford and Fleming (unpublished) were interested in the voice and face identification capabilities of shopkeepers and bank clerks,[1] following a low-key, innocuous interaction sequence such as could occur in a counterfeit, a fraud or a confidence trick situation. A male stooge entered either a bank or a shop, approached the clerk or shopkeeper and introduced himself by name and then explained that he had lost his cheque book and card and was seeking clarification on the procedure to be gone through in such a situation.

Either immediately, 1 hour, 4 hours or 24 hours later the female experimenter approached the clerk or shopkeeper concerned and, having gained his/her acceptance, ran him/her through a visual (face photographs), and a voice (taped) identification protocol, and a testimony checklist on physical actions and descriptions of the relevant incident. Again, for our purposes here, only the voice identification data will be discussed. By 4 hours voice identification was no better than chance! Correct identification at immediate testing was 41% correct; at 1 hour, 24%; at 4 hours 4%, and at 24 hours no correct identifications were made at all.

Once again then the conclusion seems clear: if the witness is unaware that a crime is being perpetrated and thus he or she is not attempting to fixate the voice for later possible identification purposes any identification that is offered should be treated with the utmost caution. The fact that the absolute scores in the Clifford and Fleming study are so much worse than in the Clifford and Denot research tentatively suggests that the problems caused by unpreparedness are exacerbated by the 'significance' ('noticeableness') of the unexpected event; the more innocuous the incident the poorer the memory for that incident.

POSSIBLE TRAINING EFFECTS IN VOICE IDENTIFICATION

A number of researchers have looked at the nature and number of different ways in which a given voice may be perceived as different from another voice. Shearme and Holmes (1959) argued that there are some features of a voice which we can say from experience contribute to recognition and discrimination — the most obvious being laryngeal frequency characteristics, rate of speaking (Goldman-Eisler, 1954), accent, and idiosyncrasies in speaking (e.g. hesitancy). However even among speakers where all these features are similar recognition is still possible by a property which is difficult to define but which is encompassed by what we call 'voice quality'. The complexity of voice identification is indicated by Bordone-Sacerdote and Sacerdote (1969) who affirm that while voice recognition could make use of general utterance patterns produced by pause, rhythm, cadence, nasal propensities, and duration of phonemes, or regional accents, all these factors are subject to modifiability as a function of maturation and emotional, physiological, and psychological changes.

Using factor analytic techniques Voiers (1964) has extracted the four factors of clarity, roughness, magnitude, and animation as contributing most to voice discriminability, while Holmgren (unpublished) extracted the four factors of intensity, quality, pitch, and rate. Now while there is some overlap between these two groups of factors it is true that when these characteristics have been used as encoding dimensions in voice identification studies they have not been found to be very relevant (e.g. Carterette and Barnaby, 1975).

A more relevant, and perhaps practically useful, approach is one suggested by Fahrmann (personal communication), which may also have implications both for questioning procedures and voice Identi-Kit construction. The major principle of Fahrmann's approach is to move from a global to a discrete description, that is from overall qualities to individual peculiarities of voice or manner of speech. This would also seem to have implications for training would-be witnesses. Under 'overall voice quality' Fahrmann groups dialect, faults in speech (stuttering, lisping), and general impression. Under 'individual peculiarities of voice' he suggests pitch, strength, tempo, rhythm, and accentuation.

As part of our overall research strategy Clifford and McCardle (unpublished) sought to investigate whether subjects could verbally describe a voice and whether these descriptions were consistent over time, and third, whether the descriptions formed had any relation to identification accuracy. Fifteen student subjects were presented with 10 voices of which 5 were male and 5 female. All 10 voices were heard over a tape recorder reading out a 33 word paragraph. After each voice was heard the subjects were asked to give a written description of the heard voice using any criteria they wished. A number of questions were addressed in this initial part of the study: whether subjects could supply composite descriptions of voices; whether these descriptions could be grouped into meaningful categories; and whether the descriptions exhibited any sex differences. The question of the relationship between voice descriptions and identification accuracy was addressed in a later part of the study.

The results suggested that subjects had no great difficulty in describing voices and that generally speaking the same broad categories were employed by all subjects. These involved sex of speaker, class or accent of the voice, physical characteristics of the talker, and emotional–personality extrapolations. However, within these categories there was little consensus — thus the same voice was variously described as 'motherly' and 'bossy' or 'nervous' and 'assured'. Interestingly the most frequently employed category related to the speaker's character rather than the voice *per se*. Broadly speaking males and females did not differ in the types of adjectives used in describing voices although there was a suggestion that female listeners were more prepared to commit themselves to an 'emotional' interpretation (e.g. 'warm'/'cold') whereas the males relied more on 'factual' data such as age, sex or class.

In terms of consistency over a 3 month gap it was found that the subject's description of the different voices was highly reliable ($p < .01$).

One day after having rated the 10 target voices subjects underwent an unannounced identification test for these 10 voices when placed in a recognition set consisting of 20 other distractor voices. While an overall hit rate of 62% was obtained (with a miss rate of 38%) these were found to be unrelated to either the quantity or the quality of the description given for the voices.

Summarizing the above then we found: (a) that people categorized unfamiliar voices consistently; (b) that these categorizations involved going 'beyond the information given' in a voice *per se* to character, emotional and personality ascriptions; and (c) such categorizations did not seem to relate, positively, to future identification accuracy.

The juxtaposition of (a) (b) and (c) is unfortunate because given (a) and (b), (c) should have followed if voice and visual identification are comparable. This should be so because several studies in facial recognition have shown that the more meaningful (deep) the processing of a stimulus face at presentation the better the eventual recognition or recall is found to be (Bower and Karlin, 1974; Clifford and Prior, 1980; Patterson and Baddeley, 1977, but cf. Baddeley and Woodhead, this volume; Winograd, 1978). The bridging assumption for voice is that to have categorized a voice as 'friendly' would be to have processed it more deeply than would be required to have categorized it as 'nasal'.

Following the above negative study by Clifford and McCardle subjects were randomly allocated to one of six groups defined by the levels of processing (depth of processing) to be performed on the target voices, and which formed a subjective continuum from superficial to deep processing. The superficial processing tasks involved judging the age and sex of the speakers while deeper processing tasks involved judging the emotional and character status of the talkers. In the event no significant differences were found between any of the six group means.

In a second experiment 209 subjects were randomly allocated to four levels of processing, again reflecting a continuum from superficial to deep. The actual encoding levels were 'judge the sex of the speaker's voice', 'judge the speaker's age', 'judge the warmth of the speaker' and finally 'judge whether the voice reminds you of anyone' (a manipulation based on Pear's (1931) observation that the effect of a voice on a listener may be to consciously or unconsciously conjure up a famous or significant person's voice, see Clifford, 1980a). However, once again statistical analysis revealed no differences between any pairs of means, or overall.

While theoretical reasons for these specific null findings have been discussed elsewhere (see Clifford, 1980a) the overall practical conclusions from all the studies are relevant here — and they are essentially negative. While such conclusions may have been anticipated (Clifford and McCardle) they would not have been predicted from depth of processing research on facial identification (but cf. Baddeley and Woodhead, this volume). What must not be concluded, however, is the utter impossibility of any training effects: we have, for example, found that blind listeners outperform sighted listeners (Clifford *et al.*, 1980), and McGehee (1944) found that a 'music' group produced better performance than 'non-music' groups in picking out a once-heard voice from a distractor set containing that target voice. Likewise Haggard and Summerfield's (unpublished) results contain implications for training: although in their study improvement would lie unequivocally at the retrieval rather than the encoding end of the total memory process because they show that a basic difference between good and poor voice identifiers is 'identifying criteria' differences, i.e. the witness's proclivity to say 'yes' or 'no' when presented with a target voice at testing.

In short then, the possibility of training a would-be witness in voice identification remains an open question. It is both an immensely complex, and a fundamentally important area of research for those psychologists at the psycho–legal interface and as such should not be ignored simply because of a crop of initially negative studies into encoding processes.

WITNESS CONFIDENCE–ACCURACY RELATIONSHIPS

The question of just how jurors, magistrates or police go about evaluating witness testimony which is essentially uncorroborated is an intriguing question which is only beginning to be investigated (see Wells and Lindsay, this volume). One possible and possibly plausible source of evaluation would seem to be the confidence with which the witness proffers his or her testimony. The common-sense assumption here is that it would seem intuitively plausible that a person is more likely to be correct when he or she espouses certainty of being correct. That this easy assumption may be made by those whose task it is to evaluate testimony seems to have empirical support from the study by Wells *et al.* (1979) in which they found that lay jurors (undergraduates) seemed to believe in a positive relationship between accuracy and confidence, in that they relied heavily on confidence to determine the credibility of a witness.

The problem is that the objective relationship between accuracy and confidence has not always been shown to be positive, especially in eyewitness testimony. In fact, the weight of evidence seems to suggest the absence of any relationship (Clifford and Scott, 1978; Deffenbacher *et al.* 1978; Yarmey, 1979), or even a negative relationship (Buckhout, 1974; Buckhout *et al.*, 1974; Loftus *et al.*, 1978). Even in those cases of eyewitness testimony or identification where a positive relationship has been found the researchers concerned have been at pains to stress the fact that little weight should be placed on such findings. A case in point is Lipton (1977) who, despite finding a +.44 correlation between accuracy of testimony concerning a filmed sequence in which a man was shot and robbed and an overall confidence rating of correctness on a seven-point scale, felt obliged to remark that 'in many cases a witness may be very certain about his testimony yet inaccurate, or be uncertain and accurate' (p. 94).

In studies of voice identification the same entering of caveats following the finding of a positive correlation can be seen. Saslove and Yarmey (1980) uncovered a +.26 correlation between accuracy in identifying voices and stated confidence in being correct in that identification. They went on to suggest that 'the importance of this relationship should not be unduly emphasized . . . [and] should be accepted with caution. Certainty of response is unlikely to be a good predictor of speaker identification in any practical sense.' (p. 115)

In the light of a review of extant research conducted prior to 1978 Deffenbacher (Deffenbacher *et al.*, 1978) concluded that 'witness confidence is not a reliable predictor of either recognition or recall accuracy across eye witness and task variables' and altered this assessment little in his 1980 review, although there he argues that the predictability of accuracy from overtly expressed confidence varies directly with the degree of optimality of information-processing conditions during encoding of the witnessed event.

One problem with evaluating the numerous studies which have looked at this critical correlation is their multifarious nature: some have used live events, some have used film or video material while others have simply used facial photographs. Another problem is the way in which the various researchers have calculated the relevant correlations. Some have simply used a gross tally of overall confidence and overall accuracy while others have predicated the correlation coefficients upon individuals' scores on both measures. Until these two sources of methodological diversity are either equated or evaluated for generality a clear and definitive answer cannot be given to those of the legal profession who would wish an unequivocal statement.

The intent of this section is not to offer such unequivocal statements but rather to provide further material, from voice identification research, which will have to be weighed in the balance before any final, definitive, answers can be given.

Contrary to many visual identification studies, in our voice studies we have consistently found positive and significant correlations between confidence and accuracy. In our delay study which involved delays up to 14 days we found that a significant correlation ($p < .025$) existed across subjects, and within subjects ($p < .001$). Again, in the speech sample length experiment which involved a comparison between one and eight words, a positive correlation was found across subjects ($p < .05$) and within subjects ($p < .01$). In another experiment not reported here (see Rathborn et al., 1981) in which we investigated voice recognition over the telephone across-subject and within-subject accuracy and confidence was again found to be positively and significantly related ($p < .05$ and $p < .01$) respectively. Finally, in our otherwise negative studies into possible training effects in voice identification we found that within the different encoding conditions employed significantly positive accuracy–confidence correlations materialized ($p .01$).

In summary then in all our voice memory experiments in which we took confidence ratings, positive relationships were found. In addition because most studies involved multi-trials we could go beyond gross computation of accuracy–confidence correlations to look at individual correlations, and once again most of these were found to be positive and significant. To put these findings into perspective, however, it should be acknowledged that in most of our experimentation subjects knew that a target was definitely present — a situation not necessarily true of a real lineup situation — though in our own defence it should be noted that witnesses do tend to have a strong belief that the perpetrator is actually present at a police lineup (Clifford and Bull, 1978). Another, possibly serious, objection to putting too much faith in the presence of a positive correlation in the above studies is that they all fall within what Deffenbacher (1980) would call 'high optimality conditions', a situation almost certainly non-representative of real criminal episodes.

Notwithstanding the above possible objections to the research quoted these are encouraging results and in the light of these initial findings research in voice identification should proceed as rapidly as possible to establish their reliability and generalizability. The further testing of such results is somewhat imperative given that the putative relationship between confidence and accuracy seems to be assumed and acted upon by 'jurors' in attempting to evaluate testimony from eyewitnesses and is likely to pertain in earwitness assessment also.

CONCLUSION AND PROGNOSIS

In our British Home Office Report (Clifford *et al.*, 1980; Clifford *et al.*, 1981) we outlined over 188 cases which had involved voice identification or testimony in some form at some stage in the criminal justice process. Because we were not trained legal researchers or archivists there can be little doubt that this number represented only the tip of an iceberg. As such it is our belief that voice identification evidence is much more prevalent than one may assume. Before the 1960s little empirical evidence existed on just how reliable this type of evidence was or could be. The courts and police had to proceed on hunches that were undoubtedly informed by common-sense awareness concerning voice identification. Since the 1960s, however, research on this topic has been, very slowly, gaining momentum and the picture has now become a little clearer.

A wide range of possibly important areas of concern for the legal system has now been explored, some of which have not been reported in detail here. For completeness we may note that the sex of a speaker is usually very accurately deduced by earwitnesses even from very short speech samples (e.g. Coleman, 1971; Coleman and Lass, 1981; Hartman and Danhauer, 1976; Ingemann, 1968; Lass *et al.*, 1978), and under conditions of unpreparedness (e.g. Cole *et al.*, 1974; Craik and Kirsner, 1974; Hintzman *et al.*, 1972). In addition, unlike the situation in eyewitnessing (but cf. Lindsay and Wells, this volume) there seems to be little evidence of cross-racial problems in speaker identification (e.g. Goldstein *et al.*, 1981) although this conclusion may depend upon the extensibility of the speech sample initially heard (Goldstein *et al.*, Exp. 3). Another area of research not detailed here is that of the age of the witness. Some research suggests that very young and quite old listeners are inferior to middle-aged witnesses (e.g. Mann *et al.*, 1979) and our own research supports this conclusion (see Bull and Clifford, in press; Clifford, 1980a). Again, sex effects in voice identification have been observed which parallels, at least partially, those found in the eyewitness literature. Our own research strongly suggests that, other things being equal, females will make the better witnesses. However other things are rarely equal and this general effect may need to be qualified in terms of consistency v. quantity (Yarmey, 1979); violent v. non-violent situations of witnessing (Clifford and Hollin, 1981; Clifford and Scott, 1978); and the nature of the information to be recalled (Loftus, 1979), as it has had to be modified in eyewitness research.

In terms of what has been discussed at some length in this chapter what can we conclude concerning the central issue posed? That issue, it will be remembered, was whether voice recognition was feasible and reliable or not. At the most general level there can be little doubt that under very favourable conditions such recognition is possible but will almost always be less good than facial recognition.

The aspect of voice identification which creates most concern is the susceptibility of this form of identification to the reduction of optimality. We discussed how disguise, of any form, generally reduced recognition accuracy dramatically. Similarly staging an unannounced event or presenting a voice unexpectedly served to reduce greatly the level of accuracy obtained. It is this fragility and susceptibility to conditions which counsels caution in the use of voice identification or testimony as 'evidence' in all but the case building sphere. And perhaps not even there!

Some positive conclusions can perhaps be drawn concerning the size of the speech sample initially heard by a witness and that witness's later evidence. The common-sense belief that the greater the speech sample heard the better the eventual identification will be is not substantiated by the weight of evidence, although there is room for argument. Because of our closeness to the answer this is an important area in which to try to establish really rock-solid conclusions, because what or how much was heard has been known to decide the direction of police enquiries: whether to abort or to continue a line of investigation.

Another fairly positive finding is the fact that delay has no simple decremental effect on accuracy. While the overall evidence (especially our own) is characterized by 'noise' it would seem that delay *per se* should not be an *a priori* ground for rejection of potential voice identification information. The interaction with disguise and with preparedness is, however, another question altogether. Here delays longer than 3 to 4 weeks would appear to be good grounds for rejection of proffered testimony.

In summary then the data reviewed in this chapter, while holding out some hope for the validity of voice identification evidence, predominantly sound a warning note. While voice memory is a demonstrable fact, good voice memory under all but super-optimal conditions of encoding, storage, and retrieval, is the exception rather than the rule. The implication for the criminal justice system is thus fairly straightforward: voice identification by a witness concerning a stranger should be treated with the utmost caution, both in its informational and its evidential aspects. As there seem to be no qualitative differences between eye- and earwitnessing the framework of evaluation currently being erected to vet all aspects of visual identification seems to be an admirable attitudinal target for 'cultural borrowing', providing that it is applied even more stringently to the quantitatively inferior case of earwitnessing.

NOTE

1. The police had been approached to take part in this experiment but Scotland Yard had declined access to local stations.

REFERENCES

Atal, B.S. (1972). Automatic speaker recognition based on pitch contours. *Journal of the Acoustical Society of America*, **52**, 1687–1697.

Baddeley, A.D. and Woodhead, M. Improving face recognition ability. This volume.

Bordone-Sacerdote, C. and Sacerdote, G.C. (1969). Some spectral properties of individual voices. *Acustica*, **21**, 199–210.

Bower, G. and Karlin, M. (1974). Depth of processing pictures of faces and recognition memory. *Journal of Experimental Psychology*, **103**, 751–757.

Bricker, P. and Pruzansky, S. (1966). Effects of stimulus content and duration on talker identification. *Journal of the Acoustical Society of America*, **40**, 1441–1449.

Buckhout, R. (1974). Eyewitness testimony. *Scientific American*, **231**, 23–31.

Buckhout, R., Alper, A., Cherns, S., Silverberg, G., and Slomovits, M. (1974). Determinants of eyewitness performance in a line-up. *Bulletin of the Psychonomic Society*, **4**, 191–192.

Bull, R. and Clifford, B.R. (1976). Identification: The Devlin Report, *New Scientist*, **70**, 307–308.

Bull, R. and Clifford, B.R. Earwitness voice recognition accuracy. In Wells, G. and Loftus, E. *Eyewitness Testimony: Psychological Perspectives*, in press.

Carterette, E. and Barneby, A. (1975). Recognition memory for voices. In A. Cohen and G. Nooteboom (eds), *Structures and Processes in Speech Perception*. New York: Springer.

Clarke, F. and Becker, R. (1969). Comparison of techniques for discriminating among talkers. *Journal of Speech and Hearing Research*, **12**, 747–761.

Clarke, F., Becker, R. and Nixon, J. (1966). Characteristics that determine speaker recognition. (Report ESD-TR-66-636), Air Force Systems Command, Hanscom Field (unpublished).

Clifford, B.R. (1978). A critique of eyewitness research. In M. Gruneberg, P. Morris, and R. Sykes (eds), *Practical Aspects of Memory*. London: Academic Press.

Clifford, B.R. (1980a). Voice identification by human listeners: on earwitness reliability. *Law and Human Behavior*, **4**, 373–394.

Clifford, B.R. (1980b). Psychologist as expert witness in cases of disputed identification. *Legal Action Bulletin*, July, 154–157.

Clifford, B.R. (1981). Towards a more realistic appraisal of the psychology of testimony. In S. Lloyd-Bostock (ed.), *Psychology in Legal Contexts*. London: Macmillan.

Clifford, B.R. *Long Term Memory for Voices*. In press.

Clifford, B.R. and Bull, R. (1978). *The Psychology of Person Identification*. London: Routledge & Kegan Paul.

Clifford, B.R., Bull, R., and Rathborn, H. (1980). Voice identification, Report (Res. 741/1/1) to the British Home Office.

Clifford, B.R., Bull, R., and Rathborn, H. (1981). Human voice recognition. *Home Office Research Bulletin*, **11**, 18–20.

Clifford, B.R. and Denot, H. Visual and verbal testimony and identification under conditions of stress. Manuscript submitted for publication.

Clifford, B.R. and Fleming, W. Face and voice identification in a field setting. Manuscript submitted for publication.

Clifford, B.R. and Hollin, C. (1981). Effects of the type of incident and the number of perpetrators on eyewitness memory. *Journal of Applied Psychology*, **66**, 364–370.

Clifford, B.R. and McCardle, G. Memory for Voices. Manuscript submitted for publication.

Clifford, B.R. and Prior, D. (1980). Levels of processing and capacity allocation. *Perceptual and Motor Skills*, **50**, 829–830.

Clifford, B.R., Rathborn, H., and Bull, R. (1981). The effects of delay on voice recognition accuracy. *Law and Human Behavior*, **5**, 201–208.

Clifford, B.R. and Richards, V.J. (1977). Comparison of recall by policemen and civilians under conditions of long and short durations of exposure. *Perceptual and Motor Skills*, **45**, 503–512.

Clifford, B.R. and Scott, J. (1978). Individual and situational factors in eyewitness testimony. *Journal of Applied Psychology*, **63**, 352–359.

Cole, R., Coltheart, M., and Allard, F. (1974). Memory of a speaker's voice: Reaction time to same- or different-voiced letters. *Quarterly Journal of Experimental Psychology*, **26**, 1–7.

Coleman, R. (1971). Male and female voice quality and its relationship to vowel formant frequencies. *Journal of Speech and Hearing Research*, **14**, 565–577.

Coleman, R. and Lass, N. (1981). Effect of prior exposure to stimulus material on identification of speaker's sex, height and weight. *Perceptual and Motor Skills*, **52**, 619–622.

Compton, A. (1963). Effects of filtering and vocal duration upon the identification of speakers, aurally. *Journal of the Acoustical Society of America*, **35**, 1748–1752.

Craik, F. and Kirsner, K. (1974). The effect of speaker's voice on word recognition. *Quarterly Journal of Experimental Psychology*, **26**, 274–284.

Deffenbacher, K.A. (1980). Eyewitness accuracy and confidence: Can we infer anything about their relationship? *Law and Human Behavior*, **4**, 243–260.

Deffenbacher, K., Brown, E. and Sturgill, W. (1978). Some predictors of eyewitness memory accuracy. In M. Gruneberg, P. Morris, and R. Sykes, (eds), *Practical Aspects of Memory*, London: Academic Press.

Devlin, Lord P. (1976). Report to the Secretary of State for the Home Department of the Departmental Committee on the Evidence of Identification in Criminal Cases. HMSO.

Doehring, D. and Ross, R. (1972). Voice recognition by matching to sample. *Journal of Psycholinguistic Research*, **1**, 233–242.

Goldman-Eisler, F. (1954). On the variability of the speed of talking and on its relation to length of utterance in conversation. *British Journal of Psychology*, **45**, 94.

Goldstein, A., Knight, P., Bailis, K., and Conover, J. (1981). Recognition memory for accented and unaccented voices. *Bulletin of the Psychonomic Society*, **17**, 217–220.

Haggard, M. (1973). Selectivity versus summation in multiple observation tasks: Evidence with spectrum parameter noise in speech. *Acta Psychologica*, **37**, 285–299.

Haggard, M. and Summerfield, Q. (1980). Sample size and perceptual parameters in speaker verification by human listeners. Submitted for publication.

Hartman, D. and Danhauer, J. (1976). Perceptual features of speech for males in four perceived age decades. *Journal of the Acoustical Society of America*, **59**, 713–715.

Hintzman, D., Block, R., and Inskeep, N. (1972). Memory for mode of input. *Journal of Verbal Learning and Verbal Behaviour*, **11**, 741–749.

Hollien, H. and McGlone, R. (1976). An evaluation of the voice print technique of speaker identification. *Proceedings Canadian Conference on Crime Counter-Measures*, pp. 39–45.

Holmgren, G.L. (1963). Speaker recognition: Final report prepared for Air Force Cambridge Research Laboratories, USA May 1963.

Ingemann, F. (1968). Identification of speaker's voice from voiceless fricatives. *Journal of the Acoustical Society of America*, **44**, 1142–1144.

La Riviere, C. (1972). Some acoustic and perceptual correlates of speaker identification.

In A. Rigault and R. Charbonneau (eds), *Proceedings of the Seventh International Congress of the Phonetic Sciences*. New York: Mouton.

Lass, N., Mertz, P., and Kimmel, K. (1978). The effect of temporal speech alterations on speaker race and sex identification. *Language and Speech*, **21**, 279–291.

Laughery, K., Alexander, J., and Lane, A. (1971). Recognition of human faces: effects of target exposure, target position, pose position and type of photograph. *Journal of Applied Psychology*, **55**, 477–483.

Laughery, K., Fessler, P., Lenorivitz, D., and Yoblick, D. (1974). Time delay and similarity effects in facial recognition. *Journal of Applied Psychology*, **59**, 490–496.

Legge, G.E., Grosmann, D., and Pieper, E. Learning unfamiliar voices. Submitted to *Journal of Experimental Psychology: Learning Memory and Cognition*, in press.

Lindsay, R. and Wells, G. What do we really know about cross-race identification? This volume.

Lindsay, R. and Wells, G. (1980). What price justice? Exploring the relationship of lineup fairness to identification accuracy. *Law and Human Behavior*, **4**, 303–313.

Lipton, J. (1977). On the psychology of eyewitness testimony. *Journal of Applied Psychology*, **62**, 90–95.

Loftus, E. (1979). *Eyewitness Testimony*. Cambridge: Harvard University Press.

Loftus, E., Miller, D.G., and Burns, H.J. (1978). Semantic integration of verbal information into a visual memory. *Journal of Experimental Psychology: Human Learning and Memory*, **4**, 19–31.

Malpass, R. and Devine, P. Measuring the fairness of eyewitness identification lineups. This volume.

Mann, V., Diamond, R., and Carey, S. (1979). Development of voice recognition: Parallels with face recognition. *Journal of Experimental Child Psychology*, **27**, 153–165.

McGehee, F. (1937). The reliability of the identification of the human voice. *Journal of General Psychology*, **17**, 249–271.

McGehee, F. (1944). An experimental investigation of voice recognition. *Journal of General Psychology*, **31**, 53–65.

McGlone, R., Hollien, P., and Hollien, H. (1977). Acoustic analysis of voice disguise related to voice identification. *Journal of the Acoustical Society of America*, **62**, 31–35.

Murray, T. and Cort, S. (1971). Aural identification of children's voices. *Journal of Auditory Research*, **11**, 260–262.

Patterson, K. and Baddeley, A. (1977). When face recognition fails. *Journal of Experimental Psychology: Human Learning and Memory*, **3**, 406–417.

Pear, T. (1931). *Voice and Personality*, New York: Wiley.

Pollack, I., Pickett, J., and Sumby, W. (1954). On the identification of speakers by voice. *Journal of the Acoustical Society of America*, **26**, 403–406.

Rathborn, H., Bull, R., and Clifford, B.R. (1981). Voice recognition over the telephone. *Journal of Police Science and Administration*, **9**, 280–284.

Reich, A. and Duke, J. (1979). Effects of selected vocal disguise upon speaker identification by listening. *Journal of the Acoustical Society of America*, **66**, 1023–1028.

Reich, A., Moll, K., and Curtis, J. (1976). Effects of selected vocal disguise upon spectrographic speaker identification. *Journal of the Acoustical Society of America*, **60**, 919–925.

Rousey, C. and Holzman, P. (1967). Recognition of one's own voice. *Journal of Personality and Social Psychology*, **6**, 464–466.

Saslove, H. and Yarmey, A. (1980). Long term auditory memory: Speaker identification. *Journal of Applied Psychology*, **65**, 111–116.

Shearme, J.N. and Holmes, J.N. (1959). An experiment concerning the recognition of voices. *Language and Speech*, **2**, 123–131.

Stevens, K., Williams, C., Carbonell, J., and Wood, B. (1968). Speaker authentication and verification: A comparison of spectrographic and auditory presentations of speech materials. *Journal of the Acoustical Society of America*, **44**, 1596–1607.

Twining, W. Identification and misidentification in legal processes: Redefining the problem. This volume.

Voiers, W.D. (1964). Perceptual basis of speaker identity. *Journal of the Acoustical Society of America*, **36**, 1065–1072.

Wallace, W.P. (1980). On the use of distractors for testing recognition memory. *Psychological Bulletin*, **88**, 696–704.

Weber, M. (1949). *The Methodology of the Social Sciences*. Translated by G.A. Shils and H.A. Finch. Glencoe, 111: The Free Press.

Wells, G.L. and Lindsay, R.C.L. How do people infer the accuracy of eyewitness memory? Studies of performance and a metamemory analysis. This volume.

Wells, G.L., Lindsay, R.C.L., and Ferguson, T.J. (1979). Accuracy, confidence and juror perceptions in eyewitness identification. *Journal of Applied Psychology*, **64**, 440–448.

Winograd, E. (1978). Encoding operations which facilitate memory across the life span. In M. Gruneberg, P. Morris, and R. Sykes (eds.) *Practical Aspects of Memory*. London: Academic Press.

Yarmey, A. (1979). *The Psychology of Eyewitness Testimony*. New York: The Free Press.

Evaluating Witness Evidence
Edited by S.M.A. Lloyd-Bostock and B.R. Clifford
© 1983 John Wiley & Sons Ltd.

Chapter 12

What Do We Really Know About Cross-Race Eyewitness Identification?

R.C.L. Lindsay and Gary L. Wells

Recent books and reviews by Clifford and Bull (1978), Ellis (1975), Loftus (1979), Wells (1978), and Yarmey (1979) each reviewed the rapidly growing literature on eyewitness identification. All discussed the problem of cross-race eyewitness identification and reviewed the literature in this area. All concluded that cross-race eyewitness identifications are less accurate than same-race eyewitness identifications. We argue that this conclusion was premature and based on an oversimplified view of the impact of race on identification accuracy. To support our arguments, our review of the cross-race identification literature highlights inconsistencies in the results, limitations of the methods used (i.e. the failure of researchers in the area to use ecologically valid manipulations and experimental designs), and the failure of researchers in the area to ask forensically relevant questions.

Previous reviews have concluded that no hypothesis[1] accounting for the cross-race facial recognition effect is adequately supported by the existing evidence. Thus, the first problem with generalizing about the influence of cross-race facial identification is apparently agreed upon by all concerned: we have no firm theoretical understanding of the phenomenon. Since we are not going to discuss theory, all that remains is to focus upon the empirical evidence. Before we discuss the empirical studies we must define exactly what we mean by 'the cross-race effect'. The most popular view of this phenomenon is that people recognize faces of their own race better than faces of other races. Taken literally this would be revealed in data as a complete crossover interaction. Specifically, people of any race should recognize and be recognized by members of their own race significantly better than they recognize or are recognized by members of other races.

Consider some of the possible patterns that a race of witness by race of suspect interaction could assume and the criminal justice recommendations that would follow from each. Figure 12.1 illustrates three patterns that the race of witness by race of suspect interaction could assume. The complete crossover is illustrated at the top of Figure 12.1. This pattern represents the cross-race effect as most (if not all) researchers and reviewers have described it. Each race is better at recognizing faces of its own race and each race is recognized better by members of its own race. If this pattern accurately reflects cross-race facial recognition, then it is reasonable to assume that cross-race eyewitness identifications are less likely to produce accurate identifications of the guilty party than are same-race eyewitness identifications.

The second pattern of interaction (middle panel of Figure 12.1) is an incomplete crossover. Once again both races identify faces of their own race better than faces of the other race. However, only whites are recognized better by their own than by the other race. Blacks are recognized equally well by either race. Based on this pattern, we could recommend that white witnesses are more likely than black witnesses to identify the guilty party if the criminal is

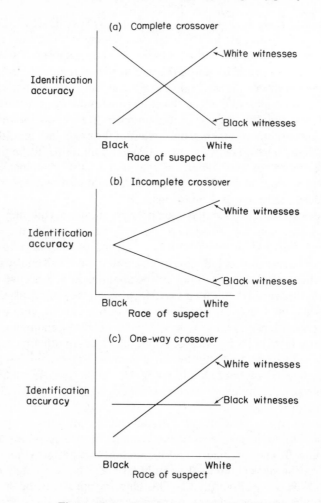

Figure 12.1   Cross-race witness identification

white. Either race of witness is equally likely to be able to identify the guilty party if the criminal is black. Thus the race of the witness only matters if the criminal is white.

The third pattern of interaction (bottom panel of Figure 12.1) is described as a 'one-way' crossover because the interaction is produced by the change in identification accuracy of white witnesses across black and white suspects: black witnesses reveal no effects due to the race of the suspect. The one-way crossover shares some characteristics with the complete crossover pattern. As for the complete crossover, white witnesses are more likely to identify a guilty white and less likely to identify a guilty black than are black witnesses. However, unlike the complete crossover pattern, the one-way crossover indicates that the race of the suspect is only relevant if the witness is white. Black witnesses are equally likely to be accurate for either race of suspect.

Table 12.1 Pattern of race of subject by race of face interactions from studies cited in Clifford and Bull (1978), Ellis (1975), Loftus (1979), Yarmey (1979) and/or Wells (1978)

	Interaction Pattern†			
	Complete crossover	One-way crossover	Incomplete crossover	No interaction
Brigham and Barkowitz, 1978			X	
Chance, Goldstein and McBride, 1975	X			
Cross, Cross and Daly, 1971		X		
Feinman and Entwisle, 1976	X			
Galper, 1973	X			
Goldstein and Chance, 1976				X
Luce, 1974	X			
Malpass, 1974 overall*				X
Condition 1			X	
Condition 2				X
Malpass and Kravitz, 1969 Overall*		X		X
Howard sample			X	
Illinois sample	X			
Malpass, Lavigueur and Weldon, 1973	X			
Shepherd, Deregowski and Ellis, 1974			X	
TOTAL‡	6	1	4	2

† See Figure 12.1 for an illustration of each interaction pattern.

‡ 'Overall' patterns were not included in the totals.

INCONSISTENCY OF THE DATA

What evidence do we have to support the cross-race hypothesis? To explore the empirical basis of the cross-race effect we examined all of the published studies cited by Clifford and Bull (1978), Ellis (1975), Loftus (1979), Wells (1978), and Yarmey (1979)[2]. Some studies were eliminated from the current review because they used only one race of subjects (e.g. Billig and Milner, 1976; Elliott et al., 1973; Seeleman, 1940) or used only one race of faces to be identified (Lavrakas et al., 1976). Another study was eliminated because it did not involve facial recognition (Ellis et al, 1975). This left 11 empirical studies that had more than one race of subject identifying faces of their own and other races thereby having the design required to demonstrate the cross-race effect. All but one of the studies obtained a race of observer by race of face interaction, for at least part of the sample.

The pattern of results for each study is summarized in Table 12.1 Two of these studies (Malpass, 1974; Malpass and Kravitz, 1969) are divided into two separate samples in Table 12.1 because the results for the two samples are quite different. Thus, there is a total of 13 published empirical samples in which the cross-race facial recognition effect could have been found. Less than half of the studies (6 of 13) found the cross-race effect as defined by a full crossover pattern.

Chance et al. (1975), Feinman and Entwisle (1976), Luce (1974), and Malpass et al (1973) obtained very clear complete crossover interactions for their black and white subjects identifying black and white faces. Blacks were better at identifying black faces than white faces and blacks were better than whites at identifying black faces. Similarly whites were better at identifying white faces than black faces and whites were better than blacks at identifying white faces. Recognition of Oriental faces, however, does not produce a similarly clear pattern. Chance et al. (1975) found that both black and white subjects had most difficulty identifying Orientals. Luce (1974) found that blacks had equal difficulty identifying whites or Orientals but, contrary to the cross-race hypothesis, whites could identify Orientals almost as well as their own race. Further complications arise from Luce's data for Oriental subjects who could recognize blacks almost as well as their own race but performed relatively poorly at recognizing whites. Thus the Luce study supported the cross-race effect only for blacks and whites. The data for Orientals was contradictory.

Galper (1973) also found a complete crossover effect for black and white subjects' recognition of black and white faces but only if the white subjects were drawn from the general pool of subjects. White subjects drawn from a black studies programme recognized black faces better than faces of their own race. Apparently all people who share the visible, physical characteristics that are generally referred to as 'race' may not respond in the same manner to a facial recognition task involving faces of their own and/or other 'races'. Galper argued that the white subjects from the black studies programme identified with blacks and thus performed as blacks did on the recognition task. Regardless of the merits of this interpretation of the data, such results complicate any advice that psychologists could give to criminal justice authorities. Even if we assume that the complete crossover is the best description of cross-race facial recognition, the Luce and Galper studies give us reason to question its generality.

Malpass and Kravitz (1969) collected data at both Howard University and the University of Illinois. The two samples produced quite different results.[3] The Illinois sample generated a complete crossover while the Howard sample produced an incomplete crossover. Combined, the data most closely resemble the one-way interaction. This widely cited study (the only paper cited by all five reviews of the literature) provides an excellent example of the inconsistencies in the data: this single study generates all three patterns of interaction.

Four studies generated data most closely resembling the incomplete crossover interaction (Brigham and Barkowitz, 1978; Malpass, 1974 condition 1; Malpass and Kravitz, 1969; Shepherd et al., 1974). The Shepherd et al. study is flawed by the confounding of race with culture since all of the black subjects were African and all of the white subjects were European. The Brigham and Barkowitz and the Malpass studies appear to be well designed and executed. Why these studies produced a different pattern of results from the complete crossover is not clear. A one-way crossover pattern was found by Cross et al. (1971). Once again, there is no flaw apparent in the design or execution of this study that would explain the failure to obtain a complete crossover interaction. The remaining study (Goldstein and Chance, 1976) failed to obtain any interaction between race of face and race of subject.

What can we conclude from these studies? Race clearly has some influence on facial recognition, but the pattern of that influence varies across studies. Perhaps the most consistent finding is that white witnesses identifying white faces produce the highest rate of accuracy. The order of the remaining race of witness and race of face combinations is not clear. Even this conclusion is not consistent with all of the data. For example, in one of Malpass's (1974) conditions an incomplete crossover pattern was obtained in which whites were identified equally well by either race and blacks were identified better than whites in general. Furthermore, some studies indicate that cross-race facial recognition effects can be modified and possibly eliminated by certain experiences. Elliott et al. (1973) demonstrated that white subjects' identification of Oriental faces improved with training such that whites identified either race equally well after but not before training. Lavrakas et al. (1975) produced a similar improvement in the identification of blacks by whites after training but found the effect did not persist over time. Malpass et al. (1973, Exp. 2) also successfully eliminated differences between the identification of black and white faces by white subjects with a training procedure. These three studies suggest that some type of experience may eliminate any cross-race effect that does exist. Until we explore this phenomenon further, we cannot be sure that the cross-race effect occurs for all or under what circumstances it may be reduced or eliminated.

We conclude that the cross-race facial recognition literature is far from consistent. The complete crossover interaction is the most common finding but the prevalence of other patterns brings into question the generality of 'the cross-race effect'.

HOW IMPORTANT IS THE CROSS-RACE EFFECT?

So far we have argued that there is insufficient evidence available to support the conclusion that the complete crossover, cross-race effect is an accurate description of the impact of race on identification accuracy. Setting aside that issue for the moment and assuming that the complete crossover is the best description (because it is the most frequent result), we can question the importance of the cross-race effect on other grounds. First, the research to date has focused on the *existence* of the cross-race effect but ignored its *size*. None of the studies cited has found that any racial group is *unable* to recognize faces of any particular other group. In other words, facial recognition scores have indicated that blacks do recognize whites reasonably well though perhaps not quite as well as whites recognize whites. Even if the differences found in this literature are statistically significant, are they sufficiently large to be important?

Examination of the data from only the six studies that obtained complete crossover effects (presumably the best evidence for the cross-race effect) reveals that both blacks and whites identified same and other race faces accurately about 50% to 65% of the time. False alarms (see Editors' Note, p.000) which are not always reported appear to occur about 10% of the time for same-race identifications and *no more than* 25% of the time for cross-race identifications. Even if the evidence were entirely consistent, we could only report that cross-race identifications would be inaccurate in about 15% more cases than same-race identifications.

Furthermore, we have virtually no data on the impact of cross-race identifications in the courtroom. Do triers of fact already discount cross-race identifications to some extent? The study by Yarmey and Jones (this volume) is one of the few empirical investigations of the views of experts (both psychological and legal) and laymen of the perceived impact of race and other factors on identification accuracy. In the absence of such information, it is not clear that the courts are in need of advice with regard to the accuracy of cross-race identifications.

Finally, the data reviewed have all been collected in laboratories employing memory paradigms. The validity of conclusions drawn from these data and generalized to real-world situations is not clear. This issue is worthy of detailed discussion.

LIMITATIONS OF THE MEMORY PARADIGM

Clifford (1979) described the problems of employing laboratory memory paradigms to investigate forensic eyewitness identification. His critique focused on the differences between laboratory studies and real-world crimes and questioned the generalizability of the laboratory studies. Clifford recommended a paradigm shift to staged crimes (forensic paradigm). By describing in detail the issue of cross-race eyewitness identification, we hope to convince our colleagues that research employing forensic paradigms is a *necessary* step before any strong conclusions can be drawn on a forensic issue. Thus employing a forensic paradigm is not merely useful, it is imperative!

Before discussing their relative merits, we should point out that the distinction between memory and forensic paradigms describes a continuum rather than a dichotomy. At one end is the classic memory for faces paradigm. In this paradigm, experimental subjects are forewarned that they must remember the faces they will be shown. A sequence of slides of faces is then shown to the subjects with each slide exposed for a fixed duration and with a constant inter-trial interval. Shortly after this first exposure the subjects are shown a larger set of slides including those they had already seen. The subject indicates for each slide whether the face is 'old' (seen before) or 'new' (not seen before). As Clifford (1979) and many others have pointed out, identification of faces under these conditions is dramatically different from eyewitness identification. At the other end of the continuum are studies such as Malpass and Devine (1980). In this experiment an act of vandalism occurred in front of a large audience who were unaware that the crime had been staged for their benefit. Later, police officers arrived and took statements from the witnesses. On subsequent days the police staged lineups from which the witnesses attempted to identify the vandal. At the time the subjects made their identification decisions they were still unaware that they were participating in an experiment and had every reason to believe they were involved in a genuine criminal identification procedure. Obviously the results of studies such as that by Malpass and Devine are much more likely to reflect the responses of real eyewitnesses in real-world identification situations. Unfortunately such elaborate deceptions produce strong reactions in the communities on which they are perpetrated (as Roy Malpass can attest) and the number of such studies that can be run is quite limited. Less elaborate paradigms must be used for the bulk of our research.

Previous studies seem to indicate that even minor modifications in the memory paradigm can radically alter results and hopefully improve generalizability. For example Brown *et al.* (1977) employed the classic memory for faces paradigm with one slight modification: one-half of the original set of faces was seen in one room, the other half in a distinctly different room. The subjects were informed that they should remember not only the faces but also in which room each face was viewed. Brown *et al.* (1977) found that overall memory for faces was high as is typical in the memory paradigm but that memory for where the face had been seen was only slightly above the chance level. Thus, a minor modification of the memory paradigm produced results indicating that the task of eyewitness identification, which involves placing the suspect at the scene of the crime, is considerably more difficult than simply recognizing a previously seen face. Loftus (1976) employed still pictures of faces with an audio-taped story of an incident. Her subjects were subsequently asked to identify the face of one of the characters in the taped story from a picture array. Wells and Lindsay (1980) reanalysed Loftus's data and found a pattern quite similar to the results of a staged crime study (Lindsay and Wells, 1980). Thus any modification of the classic memory paradigm to resemble more closely the forensic paradigm seems rapidly to approximate the results obtained in staged crime experiments.

Although the cross-race area has received a great deal of researchers' attention, there are no published studies in the area that have employed a forensic paradigm. All of the cross-race facial recognition studies discussed above employed some version of the classic memory paradigm. Even if the cross-race data had consistently supported the complete crossover interaction, the lack of data from studies employing a forensic paradigm should lead us to be cautious of drawing conclusions about the impact of race on real-world eyewitness identifications. The relevance of our data to criminal justice issues should increase as the use of staged crime paradigms increases.

ASKING FORENSICALLY RELEVANT QUESTIONS

Two years ago the first author was describing the results of some of our research at a department party. A memory researcher in the group expressed concern that we must be doing something wrong. Our procedures must be in error. He could cite half a century of research clearly proving that facial recognition was highly accurate yet we were claiming that minor situational differences could produce large changes in identification accuracy. Of course, the data he referred to were collected with the classic memory paradigm. Results from the memory paradigm can be quite misleading when generalized to real-world identification issues. The memory paradigm misleads because the researcher using it frequently fails to ask *forensically relevant questions*. Although memory studies do indicate how well faces can be remembered under ideal conditions, the criminal justice system is interested in memory for faces under conditions which are far from ideal.

Consider the issue of lineup construction. If we employed a memory paradigm to test the impact of having foils in a lineup who were similar in appearance to the suspect, what would we find? Assume that we first had our subjects look at a target face (the criminal), and then asked them to identify the target from a set of six pictures (lineup) one of which was the original target. If none of the five remaining pictures (foils) resembled the target we would expect an extremely high rate of accurate identification. As we add more foils who resemble the target, we would expect some subjects to identify these look-alikes producing a decrease in identification of the target or less accurate identifications. Generalizing from such findings to real-world identifications, we would recommend that lineups should contain only one person who looks like the criminal, namely the suspect. Of course the flaw in this reasoning is quite obvious: what happens if the suspect is innocent and just happens to resemble the criminal? In other words, what if the criminal is not in the lineup? Would subjects select a replacement for the original target who looked somewhat like the target? Certainly legal authorities and psychological researchers have suspected that this may be the case.

Studies by Doob and Kirshenbaum (1973) and Wells *et al.* (1979) have indicated that police lineups may frequently be constructed in such a way that the people in them do not all look alike. In particular, the foils or distractors in lineups may not resemble the suspect. Both studies discuss such lineups as biased or unfair because an innocent suspect who happens to resemble the true criminal is more likely to be identified from a lineup containing no foils resembling the criminal. Wells and Lindsay (1980) defined lineup diagnosticity, a measure of identification accuracy, as the ratio of identifications of the suspect when the suspect is the criminal to identifications of the suspect when the suspect is not the criminal; that is, the ratio of correct to false identifications. Since we can rarely be certain of the true guilt or innocence of a suspect, diagnosticity cannot normally be measured for real lineups. However, the impact of various lineup practices can be estimated by measuring the diagnosticity of lineups in staged crime studies in which the experimenter manipulates the presence or absence of the criminal (or guilt or innocence of the suspect) in the lineup. Lindsay and Wells (1980) demonstrated that the diagnosticity of a lineup increases as the similarity of the lineup foils to the suspect increases in spite of the fact that accurate identifications of the guilty party were reduced.

Lineups produce superior evidence when the foils resemble the suspect because the distribution of incorrect identifications is not a random event.[4] Assuming that there is only one suspect in the lineup and that the suspect at least resembles the criminal, eyewitness identifications of the suspect are quite likely regardless of the guilt or innocence of the suspect. As foils resembling the suspect are added to the lineup, identifications of the suspect decrease. However, identifications of guilty and innocent suspects do not decrease at the same rate. Since the innocent suspect resembles but is not the criminal, the addition of foils resembling the suspect spreads identifications across the lineup members. The eyewitness is presented with an array of innocent people and several of these people (i.e. not just the suspect) resemble the criminal. If the eyewitness makes an identification in this situation, he or she must guess and these guesses should distribute more or less randomly across all lineup members closely resembling the criminal. If the suspect is the criminal, the addition of foils resembling the suspect will draw some identifications away from the criminal but the distribution of identifications should not be random. Since the criminal was the person actually seen by the eyewitnesses, the criminal will continue to draw a relatively large proportion of choices compared to foils who simply resemble the criminal. As lineup members look more alike: (1) the rate of identification of innocent suspects declines more rapidly than the rate of identification of guilty suspects; (2) as a result, the probability that an identified suspect is actually guilty increases; and (3) the quality of the evidence obtained from the lineup procedure increases. Thus both data and common sense indicate that lineups are fairer and more valid sources of evidence if 'they all look alike'.

THE RELEVANCE OF THE PRECEDING ARGUMENT TO THE CROSS-RACE ISSUE

Let us return to the issue of cross-race identification. We have already seen that there is no solid theoretical explanation for the cross-race effect nor are the data supporting the effect consistent. Because of these problems it is difficult to make any recommendations to criminal justice authorities about the impact of race on identification accuracy. If we are unable to agree on recommendations based on these data, is there anything that we can agree on? Yes, there is. Most researchers in this area agree that the cross-race effect (whatever form it takes) is based on the psychological 'feeling' that other-race faces 'all look alike' to witnesses (e.g. Goldstein and Chance, 1979). Although Goldstein (1979a, 1979b) has demonstrated that races do not differ significantly in the variability of many facial features, people often refer to the perception of similarity in other race faces (consider, for example, the titles of the cited papers by Brigham and Barkowitz, Goldstein and Chance, or Luce). What are the implications of other-race faces looking alike? Most researchers have assumed that other-race eyewitness identifications must be less accurate. But is this so? Lindsay et al. (1981) hypothesized that cross-race eyewitness identifications from lineups should be more accurate (or at least more diagnostic) than same-race identifications from the same lineups. A lineup containing only people of another race should be fairer because all members of the lineup would *psychologically* look more alike than if the eyewitness was of the same race as the lineup members. Just as increasing the physical similarity of the lineup foils in the Lindsay and Wells (1980) study improved the diagnosticity of identifications, we expected changing from same-to-cross-race identifications would *increase* the apparent similarity of the lineup foils and thus the diagnosticity of the lineup. Thus our prediction was based on the assumption that cross-race eyewitnesses would make somewhat fewer correct identifications of the guilty party but considerably fewer identifications of the innocent suspect.

Since the Lindsay *et al.* (1981) study is unpublished, we will describe it in some detail here. To test our hypothesis we staged a theft for Caucasian and Oriental subjects. Following our usual procedure, each subject was instructed to sit alone in a small, well lit cubicle and wait for the experimenter to return. Shortly after the experimenter left, a female Caucasian confederate entered posing as a subject arriving late for the experiment. The confederate interacted with the subject for approximately 30 seconds. She then 'found' a calculator in the cubicle and left with it. The experimenter returned about a minute later and informed the subject that he (she) had just witnessed a staged theft. Each subject-witness subsequently attempted to identify the Caucasian thief from a photospread containing a picture of the thief or from an identical photo spread except that the picture of the thief was replaced with a picture of someone who resembled her. The results of our study supported our predictions. As the data in Table 12.2 reveal, the diagnosticity of identification decisions was considerably greater for cross-race than for same-race eyewitness identifications. Same-race eyewitnesses were slightly more likely than cross-race eyewitnesses to identify the guilty party as predicted from the memory paradigm. Unfortunately same-race eyewitnesses were also much more likely to identify an innocent suspect who simply resembled the thief. The cross-race identifications produce a higher level of diagnosticity because the *ratio* of correct to false identifications is greater for the Oriental subjects. We have argued that this higher diagnosticity level means that, compared to same-race identifications, cross-race identifications are more informative about the guilt or innocence of the suspect and thus better evidence (Lindsay and Wells, 1980; Wells and Lindsay, 1980).

Table 12.2 Percentage of correct identifications/false identifications, and resultant diagnosticity ratios from a crime staged for Caucasian and Oriental Subjects (Lindsay *et al.*, 1981)

| | Identifications | | |
	Guilty suspect	Innocent suspect	Diagnostic ratio
Caucasian subjects	83	45	1.84
Oriental subjects	77	15	5.13

Lindsay, Wells and Rumpel (1981).

Using a forensic paradigm to ask a forensically relevant question has led to a different conclusion from that drawn from memory paradigm studies. By asking what the consequences of cross-race identification would be if the target were absent (or the suspect innocent), we have demonstrated that the relationship of race to identification accuracy is neither 'clear' (Ellis *et al.*, 1977) nor 'obvious' (Malpass and Kravitz, 1969) as previously assumed.

What recommendations should we make based on these new data? The Lindsay *et al.* (1981) data indicate that cross-race eyewitness identifications are superior to same-race eyewitness identifications. The results logically follow from the generally agreed upon assumption that other-race faces psychologically 'all look alike'. Perhaps we should recommend that cross-race identifications are superior to same-race identifications.

It would appear we have come full circle. We have recommendations that cross-race identifications should be considered both more and less accurate than same-race identifications. Which recommendation should we make? We could argue that the Lindsay *et al.* study is more ecologically valid because we more closely simulated real-world conditions as recommended by Clifford (1979) and thus recommend cross-race identifications as superior. To make such a recommendation we would have to ignore several limitations of our study: (1) the study has not been replicated; (2) we had neither a Negro nor an Oriental confederate so we can make no claims of generality; (3) we assumed only one suspect would appear in a lineup; (4) we employed a lineup rather than a showup or mugshot procedure.[5] These and many other problems make any recommendation premature. What the Lindsay *et al.* study shows is that the cross-race issue is complex. *Considerable doubt exists about the impact of race on identification accuracy!*

SUMMARY AND RECOMMENDATIONS

Our summary of the cross-race issue is rather negative. There is no theory of cross-race identification effects that is well supported by the data. The empirical literature reveals more inconsistency than reviewers have previously described. Studies in the area have failed to employ forensic paradigms and, as a result, frequently failed to address forensically relevant issues. Because of these problems, we will make no recommendations to criminal justice authorities about the influence of race on identification accuracy. Instead we will conclude with a recommendation to researchers in the area of psychology and law.

We emphasize to psychologists interested in the application of laboratory eyewitness and/or facial recognition research to real-world problems that we have a responsibility to be cautious in our recommendations. There is no doubt that the criminal justice system needs guidance with regard to the limitations of eyewitness identification (Yuille, 1980). However, no one will benefit if the guidance we give is premature and misleading. At the moment, we can only say that any relationship that does exist between race and identification accuracy is weak and inconsistent. More research is required to clarify when, and if, the race of suspects and witnesses will lead to an increased likelihood of false identifications. Research is required to determine the extent to which cross-race identifications are differently weighted as evidence by triers of fact. In brief, it will be some time before we can make definitive statements about the impact of race on eyewitness identification accuracy. With regard to other issues more positive statements are reasonable. Identification procedures should involve as many foils resembling the suspect as is reasonably possible. Eyewitness confidence should not be employed as a criterion of accuracy. Memory for events can be distorted by the method of interrogation.

Psychologists are increasing knowledge of the factors influencing eyewitness identification and testimony. This knowledge has enormous potential for guiding legal practice and reform. However, we must avoid overzealous errors of generalization. Only a few arguments and retractions would be necessary to discredit our entire area as a source of valid information for the criminal justice authorities. One of the best ways to avoid such errors is to insist upon testing *any* relevant finding using a forensic paradigm *before* suggesting to the courts that we can provide useful recommendations.

NOTES

1. Proposed hypotheses have included greater physical homogeneity of faces of some races, differential exposure to faces of own versus other race, and greater perceived similarity of other-race faces.
2. A decision to include the five unpublished studies cited (Berger, 1969; Dowdle and Settler, 1970; Goldstein, 1975; Scott and Foutch, 1974; Yarmey and Beihl, 1977) would not have altered our conclusions.
3. The fact that Howard University is a predominantly black campus while the University of Illinois is a predominantly white campus may have contributed to the differences in the obtained results. Previous studies have failed to support the hypothesis that amount of association with people of other races consistently influences facial recognition (Berger, 1969; Billig and Milner, 1976; Luce, 1974; Malpass and Kravitz, 1969). In addition, any systematic differences between the two universities would strengthen rather than weaken our argument since it would provide a rationale for predicting the lack of generality of the cross-race effect.
4. The non-random distribution of false alarms in facial recognition studies has been documented by Goldstein *et al.* (1977).
5. Using either a showup or mugshot procedure involves an identification procedure in which everyone who can be identified is at least potentially a suspect. The Lindsay *et al.* (1981) data reveal that same-race witnesses are *less* likely than cross-race witnesses to make any identification when the 'criminal' is absent from the lineup. Thus same-race identification might be expected to be more accurate in situations involving showup or mugshot identifications. Clearly we cannot generalize from any one identification procedure to others without testing the implications of each type

of procedure. The majority of evidence collected by psychologists to date is relevant to lineup identification but may or may not be generalizable to other identification procedures.

REFERENCES

Berger, D. (1969). *They all look alike to me*. Unpublished doctoral dissertation, Vanderbilt University.

Billig, M. and Milner, D. (1976). A spade is a spade in the eyes of the law. *Psychology Today*, **2**, 13–15, 62.

Brigham, J.C. and Barkowitz, P. (1978). Do 'they all look alike'? The effect of race, sex, experience, and attitudes on the ability to recognize faces. *Journal of Applied Psychology*, **8**, 306–318.

Brown, E., Deffenbacher, K., and Sturgill, W. (1977). Memory for faces and the circumstances of encounter. *Journal of Applied Psychology*, **62**, 311–318.

Chance, J., Goldstein, A.C., and McBride, L. (1975). Differential experience and recognition memory for faces. *Journal of Social Psychology*, **97**, 243–253.

Clifford, B.R. (1979). A critique of eyewitness research. In M. Gruneberg, P. Morris, and R. Sykes (eds), *Practical Aspects of Memory*. London: Academic Press, pp. 199–209.

Clifford, B.R. and Bull, R. (1978). *The Psychology of Person Identification*. London: Routledge and Kegan Paul.

Cross, J.F., Cross, J., and Daly, J. (1971). Sex, race, age, and beauty as factors in recognition of faces. *Perception and Psychophysics*, **10**, 393–396.

Doob, A.N. and Kirshenbaum, H.M. (1973). Bias in police lineups— partial remembering. *Journal of Police Science and Administration*, **1**, 287–293.

Dowdle, M.D. and Settler, J.M. (1970). Recognition memory and prejudice. Paper presented at the annual meeting to the Midwestern Psychological Association, Cincinnati.

Elliott, E.S., Wills, E.J., and Goldstein, A.G. (1973). The effects of discrimination training on the recognition of white and oriental faces. *Bulletin of the Psychometric Society*, **2**, 71–73.

Ellis, H.D. (1975). Recognizing faces. *British Journal of Psychology*, **66**, 409–426.

Ellis, H.D., Davies, G.M., and Shepherd, J.W. (1977). Experimental studies of face identification. *National Journal of Criminal Defense*, **3**, 219–234.

Ellis, H.D., Deregowski, J., and Shepherd, J. (1975). Descriptions of white and black faces by white and black subjects. *International Journal of Psychology*, **10**, 119–123.

Feinman, S. and Entwisle, D.R. (1976). Children's ability to recognize other children's faces. *Child Development*, **47**, 506–510.

Galper, R.E. (1973). 'Functional race membership' and recognition of faces. *Perceptual and Motor Skills*, **37**, 455–462.

Goldstein, A. (1975). Implications of differential face recognition data. Paper presented at the Midwestern Psychological Association Symposium on Faces: How do we Perceive and Remember Them? Chicago.

Goldstein, A.G. (1979a) Facial feature variation: Anthropometric data II. *Bulletin of the Psychonomic Society*, **13**, 191–193.

Goldstein, A.G. (1979b) Race-related variation of facial features: Anthropometric data I. *Bulletin of the Psychonomic Society*, **13**, 187–190.

Goldstein, A. and Chance, J. (1976). Measuring psychological similarity of faces. *Bulletin of the Psychonomic Society*, **7**, 407–408.

Goldstein, A., and Chance, J. (1978). Intra-individual consistency in visual recognition memory. Paper presented at the annual meeting of the American Psychological Association, Toronto.

Goldstein, A.G. and Chance, J. (1979). Do foreign faces really look alike? *Bulletin of the Psychonomic Society*, **13**, 111–113.

Goldstein, A.G., Stephenson, B., and Chance, J. (1977). Face recognition memory: Distribution of false alarms. *Bulletin of the Psychonomic Society*, **9**, 416–418.

Lavrakas, P.J., Buri, J.R., and Mayzner, M. (1975). The effects of training and individual differences on the recognition of other-race faces. Paper presented at the American Psychological Association Conference.

Lavrakas, P.J., Buri, J.R., and Mayzner, M. (1976). A perspective on the recognition of other-race faces. *Perception and Psychophysics*, **20**, 475–481.

Lindsay, R.C.L., and Wells, G.L. (1980). What price justice? Exploring the relationship of lineup fairness to identifcation accuracy. *Law and Human Behavior*, **4**, 303–313.

Lindsay, R.C.L., Wells, G.L. and Rumpel, C.M. (1981). Cross-race eyewitness identification: it may be better if they all look alike. Unpublished manuscript, University of Alberta.

Loftus, E.F. (1976). Unconscious transference in eyewitness identification. *Law and Psychology Review*, **2**, 93–98.

Loftus, E.F. (1979). *Eyewitness testimony*. Cambridge, Mass.: Harvard University Press.

Luce, T.S. (1974). Blacks, whites, and yellows: They all look alike to me. *Psychology Today*, Nov., 105–108.

Malpass, R.S. (1974). Racial bias in eyewitness identification. *Personality and Social Psychology Bulletin*, **1**, 42–44.

Malpass, R.S. and Devine, P. (1980). Realism and eyewitness identification research. *Law and Human Behavior*, **4**, 347–358.

Malpass, R.S. and Kravitz, J. (1969). Recognition of faces of own and other race. *Journal of Personality and Social Psychology*, **13**, 330–334.

Malpass, R.S., Lavigueur, H., and Weldon, D.E. (1973). Verbal and visual training in face recognition. *Perception and Psychophysics*, **14**, 285–292.

Scott, W.C. and Foutch, V. (1974) The effects of presentation order and ethnicity on facial recognition. Paper presented at the Oklahoma Academy of Science, Duran.

Seeleman, V. (1960). The influence of attitude upon the remembering of pictoral material. *Archives of Psychology*, **36**, 1–64.

Shepherd, J.W., Deregowski, J.B., and Ellis, H.D. (1974). A cross-cultural study of recognition memory for faces. *International Journal of Psychology*, **9**, 205–211.

Wells, G.L. (1978). Applied eyewitness-testimony research: System variables and estimator variables. *Journal of Personality and Social Psychology*, **36**, 1545–1557.

Wells, G.L., Leippe, M.R., and Ostrom, T.M. (1979). Guidelines for empirically assessing the fairness of a lineup. *Law and Human Behavior*, **3**, 285–293.

Wells, G.L. and Lindsay, R.C.L. (1980). On estimating the diagnosticity of eyewitness nonidentifications. *Psychological Bulletin*, **88**, 776–784.

Yarmey, A.D. (1979). *The psychology eyewitness testimony*. New York: Free Press.

Yarmey, A.D. and Beihl, H. (1977). The influence of attitudes and recall of impressions on memory for faces. Paper presented at the annual meeting of the Psychonomic Society, Washington, D.C.

Yarmey, A.D. and Jones, H. (1982). Is eyewitness identification a matter of common sense? This volume.

Yuille, J.C. (1980). A critical examination of the psychological and practical implications of eyewitness research. *Law and Human Behavior*, **4**, 335–345.

Evaluating Witness Evidence
Edited by S.M.A. Lloyd-Bostock and B.R. Clifford
© 1983 John Wiley & Sons Ltd.

Chapter 13

The Influence of Arousal on Reliability of Testimony

Kenneth A. Deffenbacher

As long ago as 1928 Hutchins and Slesinger opined in a *Columbia Law Review* article that greater levels of arousal or excitement impaired accuracy of eyewitness observation. Slesinger, being a psychologist, was aware of turn-of-the-century findings demonstrating that increases in excitement past a certain point served to decrease the accuracy of eyewitness report (this research tradition had been reviewed by G.M. Whipple in a series of articles appearing virtually every year in the *Psychological Bulletin* from 1909 to 1918).

Although Hutchins and Slesinger's comments have been echoed from time to time by legal scholars (by James Marshall in his 1966 book *Law and Psychology in Conflict*, for example) American criminal court judges seem typically to have subscribed to the opposite theory. This is at least implicit in certain *voir dire* decisions. When forced to rule on the admissibility of expert testimony by psychologists concerning the effects of heightened stress on witness perception and memory, many have ruled that such testimony does not relate to a proper subject matter. As Suggs (1979) has pointed out, these decisions have been of two types. The first view has been that the proffered expert testimony concerning stress effects is a matter of common understanding and is therefore unnecessary and possibly prejudicial (e.g. the 1975 California case of *People* v. *Guzman*). A second view has been that such testimony invades the province of the jury in that it would be for the purpose of discounting the credibility of the eyewitness, and it has been traditionally the jury's task to determine witness credibility (e.g. the 1973 9th Circuit US Court of Appeals decision in the case of *United States* v. *Amaral*).

But what is the common understanding regarding the effect of high arousal on fidelity of witness memory? In the United States at any event, legal doctrine in this matter appears to reflect a generalization of the *res gestae* exception to the inadmissibility of hearsay evidence rule. Subdivision 2, Rule 803 of the *Federal Rules of Evidence* (1975) provides that certain excited utterances are not excluded by the hearsay rule. An excited utterance is 'A statement relating to a startling event or condition made while the declarant was under the stress of excitement caused by the event or condition.' The theory is simply that nervous excitement will make for a spontaneous, sincere, and trustworthy response, one free of fabrication because high arousal temporarily stills the capacity of reflection. Hence American judges apparently believe that high stress or arousal facilitates veridical perception.

American criminal court judges also apparently hold the view that heightened arousal increases accuracy of memory as well as that of perception, however inappropriate a generalization this may be. Holding to such a belief would help to explain why judges still typically do not admit expert testimony concerning effects of high arousal on memorial processes. Though Rule 704 of the Federal Rules has now abolished legal grounds for excluding expert testimony on the grounds that it might usurp the jury's province, Rule 403 still provides for the exclusion of evidence that wastes time, confuses the issues, or misleads the jury. A judge believing that it is common-sense knowledge that large increases in stress facilitate memory might well indeed feel that a psychologist claiming the contrary would needlessly confuse and mislead.

It would appear, however, that common understanding regarding the influence of arousal on the reliability of testimony is not so clear-cut. The legal profession has made no empirical assessment of what constitutes the layperson's (juror's) understanding of the effects of stress on memory, but several psychologists have. In four different samples of data collected by Deffenbacher and Loftus (1982) never more than 25% of laypersons have indicated that extreme stress experienced as a crime victim should increase one's ability to perceive and recall details of the criminal event. In fact, only 5% of a sample of 43 persons with criminal trial jury experience in the previous 5 years responded in agreement with the prevailing judicial theory. Even American trial attorneys are far from complete agreement. Brigham (1981) has recently surveyed 235 of them, and found that 82% of criminal defence attorneys felt that high arousal leads to poorer facial recognition. Fully 32% of their prosecutorial colleagues felt likewise, and only 47% of prosecutors subscribed to the notion that high arousal leads to better facial recognition.

It would seem at least arguable that the currently accepted view of stress effects on memory held by the American criminal court judiciary may be in some difficulty. Notwithstanding difficulties posed by possibly inappropriate extension of the theory behind *res gestae*, and, by the lack of a truly common understanding of the matter, the ultimate arbiter ought to be the results of empirical tests of the effects of increased arousal levels on eyewitness memory. However, a cursory examination of the relevant research reveals a good deal of inconsistency of findings. Indeed there is a body of recent psychological investigations whose results, taken at face value, suggest that situational increases in arousal or chronically higher personal arousal levels increase eyewitness accuracy, or at least do not decrease it. But there is a greater number of recent studies of forensically relevant visual memory producing just the opposite results. Both sets of studies will be cited and discussed at length later in this review.

This inconsistency of findings is more apparent than real, however. It should not lead the legal profession to conclude that psychology is a horribly inexact science. It should not, therefore, lead attorneys and judges to conclude that these research efforts have served only to muddy the waters — thereby in any way justifying continued belief in the theory that high arousal promotes greater fidelity of visual memory. It turns out that a rather venerable set of psychological principles nicely encompass the seemingly discrepant results.

A THEORETICAL RESOLUTION OF THE CONFLICTING RESEARCH FINDINGS

The rather venerable set of psychological principles in question are those subsumed by the Yerkes–Dodson Law: (1) There is an optimum level of arousal for every task. (2) For a task of any real complexity, there is a curvilinear relation between arousal and performance, with optimal performance level being associated with intermediate arousal levels. (3) Optimum arousal level and task complexity are inversely related. Figure 13.1 nicely illustrates these assumptions.

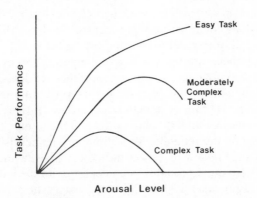

Figure 13.1   The curves show how performance is affected by arousal and task difficulty. Note that optimal performance is lower for more complex tasks

The Yerkes–Dodson Law has received remarkably varied experimental confirmation. Tasks have ranged from brightness discriminations to memorization of verbal materials. Means of inducing changes in arousal level have included stressors such as electric shock, air deprivation, sleep deprivation, noise, temperature, and ego-involving anxiety manipulations. Species have included mice (Yerkes and Dodson, 1908), chickens (Cole, 1911), kittens (Dodson, 1915), rats (Broadhurst, 1957), and humans. In the instance of *Homo sapiens*, Michael Eysenck (1979) has noted in a recent review that some

13 studies dealing with the relationship of anxiety and performance have obtained the interaction predicted by Yerkes–Dodson Law. High anxiety improved performance on the easy task in all 13 studies, while high anxiety impaired performance on the difficult task in 11 of the studies.

Research on the effects of so-called stressors such as noise, temperature, and sleeplessness has suggested that there may be more than one central nervous system mechanism mediating the relationship of arousal and performance (compare, for example, Broadbent, 1971). Indeed, a number of individuals have proposed various theoretical accounts of the empirical relations described by the Yerkes–Dodson Law. Easterbrook (1959) proposed that task complexity be defined in terms of the number of cues that must be utilized simultaneously to achieve appropriate task behaviour. Increases in arousal serve to reduce the range of cues monitored, aiding performance at first by excluding peripheral, task-irrelevant cues, but impairing performance later as further narrowing of the range of cues employed excludes more and more central, task-relevant cues. Building on both Easterbrook's and Broadbent's efforts, Michael Eysenck (1979) has developed a new theoretical treatment of the effects of anxiety on processing effectiveness and working memory capacity. Walley and Weiden (1973) have even supplied a speculative physiological underpinning for Easterbrook's hypothesis — proposing that higher arousal levels produce cognitive masking that then reduces the likelihood of more efficient shared or parallel processing by the brain.

Nevertheless all these attempts at explaining the Yerkes–Dodson Law should not detract from its very obvious importance. It does indeed appear to reflect some fundamental property of higher vertebrate central nervous systems in their response to task demands and stress. It, therefore, might be expected to have some heuristic value in sorting out the research relating to the influence of arousal on the reliability of testimony. The heuristic value is just this: The studies I shall review that show facilitation of eyewitness memory by arousal increases have quite probably been dealing with the left-hand portion of the Yerkes–Dodson curves, while the studies suggesting just the opposite have quite probably been operating on the right-hand portion. This of course assumes that eyewitness tasks are at least moderate in difficulty level.

REVIEW OF THE LITERATURE

Some 21 studies have been completed that assess the relation between arousal level and the fidelity of eyewitness memory. Ten of them have produced results that suggest that higher arousal levels increase eyewitness accuracy — or at least do not decrease it. Six of them used experimentally manipulated increases in arousal (Hosch and Cooper, 1980; Johnson and Scott, 1976; Leippe et al., 1978; Majcher, 1974; Shepherd et al., 1980; Sussman and Sugarman, 1972), while four used higher levels of individually assessed arousal (Brigham, et al.,

1982; Deffenbacher *et al.*, 1978; Miller *et al.*, 1978; Mueller *et al.*, 1979b)[1]. A majority of these particular experiments have tested memory for only one type of stimulus. Five studies test facial memory only, while two test only memory for landscapes or settings. But it is also the case that a majority of the experimenters involved have increased the ecological validity of their studies by employing live event methodology (Clifford, 1978). I shall have occasion a bit later, however, to argue that live events or not, subjects in these experiments were not aroused to levels typical of a great many criminal situations.

The remaining 11 studies have produced just the opposite result — lower accuracy of memory was yielded by experimentally manipulated increases in arousal (Brigham, *et al.*, 1980; Clifford and Scott, 1978; Clifford and Hollin, 1978; Clifford and Hollin, 1981; Giesbrecht, 1979; Loftus and Burns, 1981) or higher individually assessed arousal levels (Buckhout *et al.*, 1974; Mueller *et al.*, 1979a; Nowicki *et al.*, 1979; Siegel and Loftus, 1978; Zanni and Offermann, 1978). While only one of these studies involves a live event, five others include realistic film presentations, and one rather laboratory-bound experiment has produced levels of physiological arousal that are in my opinion not only at ethical limits but also at levels not unrepresentative of many rather violent forensic situations. The forensic applicability of this latter body of studies is further increased by the fact that all but four of them test more than one kind of visual memory. That is, lineups are employed and/or recall tests of details such as suspect physical description, suspect actions, and nature of the setting are given. And, as I shall be arguing shortly, these particular studies would seem to have tapped arousal levels more appropriate to criminal justice situations involving assault, homicide, rape, robbery, and the like.

In order to evaluate whether these varying results arise because they relate to different portions of the Yerkes–Dodson curves, it is necessary to examine the actual experiments in closer detail. The studies are reviewed in four groups depending on the direction of the results, i.e. whether memory was facilitated or debilitated; and on whether arousal was experimentally manipulated or individually assessed.

Witness memory facilitated by greater arousal

Increases in experimentally manipulated arousal

In the published literature concerning eyewitness behaviour there has been only one empirical report in recent years that could be interpreted as showing that manipulated increases in arousal may facilitate eyewitness memory (Leippe *et al.*, 1978). Occasionally one does indeed find commentators echoing the conclusion reached by Whipple in his 1915 review of turn-of-the-century eyewitness research, to wit, '. . . excitement improves observation and memory of witnesses up to a given point . . .' (e.g. Levine and Tapp, 1973). But thus far there has been only the one specific attempt to replicate and extend any of the 70–80 year old results that might have given birth to Whipple's conclusion. However, whether the work has been designed specifically to test Whipple's assertion or not, there are four additional studies that are supportive of it. These are the reports by Hosch and Cooper (1980), Johnson and Scott (1976), Majcher (1974), and Shepherd et al. (1980). Finally, Sussman and Sugarman (1972) have obtained results that suggest that while increased arousal may not facilitate memory, neither is it particularly injurious. Let us now examine the methodology and results of these other studies as well as those of Leippe et al. (1978).

Leippe et al. set out to manipulate arousal level within an ostensibly low arousal situation, namely introductory psychology students fulfilling a course requirement by showing up for an experiment in 'personality assessment'. There were three experimental conditions, a staged theft of an unknown person's calculator (high serious theft), a staged theft of the same un-known person's cigarettes (low serious theft), and a no-theft control. Witnesses learned of the stolen object's value either before or after the theft. Recognition memory was tested within minutes using a six-person photo spread. At least when witnesses knew the value of the stolen object beforehand, accuracy was much better in the presumably more aroused high serious theft condition, 56% versus 19% in the low serious theft group. Manipulation checks revealed that persons in the high serious condition did indeed perceive the crime to be more serious and the value of the stolen object to be much greater, $46.44 versus $1.49. Quite possibly, modest arousal increases in the high serious condition served to reduce attention to more peripheral, task-irrelevant cues, thereby facilitating later recognition of the culprit's face.

Hosch and Cooper's (1980) experiment involved a similar staged theft methodology, with there being subjects observing a target person stealing an unknown person's calculator, or viewing the theft of their very own watch, or observing no theft on the target person's part. Presumed increases in arousal in the watch and calculator theft groups improved the rate of accuracy on a six person photo spread relative to the no-theft control condition (71%, 67%, and 33%, respectively). Interestingly, these increases in arousal and accuracy were associated with increases in the amount of variance accounted for by self-monitoring (SM) ability as measured by Snyder's Self-Monitoring Scale (Snyder, 1979). For the control, calculator theft, and watch theft conditions the Pearson r's relating eyewitness accuracy and SM were +.09 ($p < .21$), +.30 ($p < .07$), and +.43 ($p < .02$), respectively. High SM persons are more con-cerned than low SM ones with observation and control of their own expressive behaviour and self-presentation and that of others. It may well be that within a relatively low arousal situation that modest arousal increases can serve to potentiate an individual difference variable having to do with the degree of attention paid to expressive behaviour in others.

Witnesses in Johnson and Scott's (1976) study sat in a waiting room, ostensibly waiting for a psychology experiment to occur. After a few minutes, half the witnesses overheard an innocuous conversation about an equipment failure. A target individual then appeared holding a pen in grease-covered hands, muttered a single line about broken machines, and left. The other half overheard a hostile interaction replete with breaking bottles and crashing chairs. The target persons in this higher arousal condition then dashed into the waiting room while clutching a bloodied letter opener, uttered a single line, and again exited after about 4 seconds. Testing was done immediately or after a week and included a free narrative report, a controlled narrative, and a mug-shot test. Witnesses for the most part rated their arousal in the lower half of the arousal scale used. Under the relatively more high arousal conditions, how-ever, males did show both higher recall and recognition. Females likewise did better under high arousal conditions on tests of memory for the setting and the target's actions, only doing worse under higher arousal on tests of memory for facts about the target person. Perhaps the latter result is due to 'weapon focus' or 'person avoidance' being greater for females than males when confronted by a violent-acting, weapon-bearing male. Perhaps females in this particular condition of the study passed beyond the optimal arousal level as soon as the male target person emerged upon the scene.

Majcher (1974) manipulated level of physiological arousal by exposing one group of subjects to the rather intense sound of 100 dB white noise while they were viewing slides of college student faces. Though their recognition memory rate in terms of absolute magnitude of effect was not a great deal higher than that of a no-noise control group, the difference was nevertheless statistically significant. Pretesting had indicated that presence of the noise did indeed raise the galvanic skin response, a peripheral measure of physiological arousal.

Shepherd et al. (1980) conducted a series of five experiments, of which Experiments 2, 3, and 4 were concerned, among other matters, with the effects of length of retention interval (i.e. time elapsed since witnessing the incident) on recognition memory for target persons who had been viewed by witnesses during three different staged incidents whose duration ranged from 20–45 seconds. Strikingly, absolute accuracy of memory in Experiment 2 was 20–50% higher than in Experiments 3 and 4, at delays of both 1 month and 3–4 months. Suspecting that the incident staged in Experiment 2 had engendered more emotional arousal than the incidents staged in the other two experiments, Shepherd et al. videotaped a careful simulation of each of the three staged incidents and had a new group of subjects view them in counterbalanced order before answering a 12 item questionnaire asking them how they would have felt about each incident. These persons said they would have been significantly more embarrassed and would have felt significantly more upset in the situation of Experiment 2. Though statistically significant, these differences in expressed arousal were all within the lower half of the scales used ('not at all', 'slightly', 'fairly'). Nevertheless, being 'fairly' aroused may have helped persons to focus on the target's face and body more than being 'slightly' aroused or 'not at all' aroused.

Witnesses in Sussman and Sugarman's (1972) study viewed either a violent or a non-violent film of a robbery. The violent version involved the robbery victim being threatened with a gun and being beaten about the head with much bleeding the result. Those viewing the non-violent version were spared the blood, the gun, and the violence. There was no statistically reliable difference between the two groups in identification accuracy. It should be pointed out, however, that witnesses in both groups had been forewarned of the nature of the to-be-witnessed event and of the tasks to be performed afterwards. This particular lack of ecological validity may have been responsible for the null difference finding. Knowing that they would need later to be able to identify a culprit who would be engaged in rather violent behaviour, the one group of witnesses may have been able to steel themselves to spend more time than otherwise in observing the culprit's face. So Sussman and Sugarman's result may well have been artefactual, and their witnesses of the violent event may actually have had arousal levels characteristic of the right-hand portion of a Yerkes–Dodson curve (cf. later in this chapter Clifford and Hollin, 1981; Loftus and Burns, 1981).

Higher individually assessed arousal levels

Though the evidence here is weak, there are four studies which seem to show that ostensibly higher individually measured arousal levels increase or at least do not decrease fidelity of eyewitness memory. Two assess memory for faces (Brigham *et al.*, 1982; Deffenbacher *et al.*, 1978) while two assess memory for scenes (Miller *et al.*, 1978; Mueller *et al.*, 1979b).

Brigham *et al.*'s eyewitnesses were 9 black and 64 white convenience store clerks. Two experimental confederates, one black and one white, interacted separately with each clerk for 3 to 4 minutes in a set but somewhat unusual routine such as paying for cigarettes in pennies and then asking for directions. Two hours later, witness memory was tested with two, six-person photo spreads, one of blacks and one of whites. Looking only at identifications attempted, black clerks were accurate 69.2% of the time (66.7% for white target, 70.8% for black target), while white clerks were accurate only 39.9% of the time (40.8% for the white target, 39% for the black). How might one account for the greater accuracy of the black clerks? Brigham has suggested that given the demographics of many large American cities, it would not be surprising if the black clerks had lived and worked in higher crime areas, perhaps thereby promoting in them at least a higher work-hours level of vigilance and attention to more central, more relevant detail. On this interpretation, Brigham's study relates greater accuracy of witnesses to higher personal arousal levels.

The remaining three studies in this set have found either zero correlation of face recognition memory and a measure of trait anxiety (Deffenbacher et al., 1978) or no relationship between scene recognition memory and measures of both trait and state anxiety (Miller et al., 1978; Mueller et al., 1979b). It should be pointed out that at least in the latter two studies attempts were made to assure that state arousal differences were maximized by the giving of ego-involving instructions. So for scene memory, anyway, increases in arousal may not facilitate on average but neither do they debilitate.

Witness memory debilitated by greater arousal

Increases in experimentally manipulated arousal

Writing some 5 years ago, Hastie et al. (1977) commented that laboratory manipulations of arousal had likely not yet produced arousal levels typical of more violent crimes. It would now seem, however, that we do indeed have evidence as to the probable effects of rather high arousal levels. Results of some six experiments not yet completed at the time of their review or unavailable to Hastie et al. have shown that increases in arousal past some ill-defined point definitely do reduce the fidelity of eyewitness memory (Brigham et al., 1980; Clifford and Hollin, 1978, 1981; Clifford and Scott, 1978; Giesbrecht, 1979; Loftus and Burns, 1981). These findings confirm another of Whipple's (1915) observations, namely that increases in excitement past a certain point impair witness memory.

The Brigham et al. study defined low, moderate, and high arousal groups in terms of the frequency with which they received electric shocks on study trials, trials on which they were exposed to slides of college student faces for 3 seconds each. Low arousal witnesses received no shocks — in fact shock was never mentioned. The arousal level of these persons was low only relative to that of persons in the other conditions of this experiment, however. A reasonable estimate of their arousal level would be that it was close to the optimum level, probably a bit less than the optimum.[2] Moderate and high arousal witnesses were told 'safe but uncomfortable shock' would be used and had stimulating and recording electrodes attached. Discomfort thresholds were individually determined with low, medium, and high intensity shocks being defined as 0.50, 2.25, and 4.50 times the discomfort thresholds, respectively. High arousal persons received a shock on 12 of the last 24 study trials, 4 low, 4 medium, and 4 high intensity shocks. Moderate arousal persons, on the other hand, received a medium intensity shock on the first trial but received no further shocks after this trial — in fact, the stimulating electrode was removed at this point.

Given the extremely aversive quality of electric shock for human subjects, it is not at all surprising that facial recognition declined dramatically in the two higher arousal groups.[3] Mean d' scores (see Editor's Note, p. 000) for low, moderate, and high arousal conditions were 1.60, 1.09, and 0.65, respectively, where a d' of 0.00 would imply complete inability to discriminate faces seen before from those never seen. All subjects had also been asked to give a ratio-scale estimate of their arousal on each trial, and significant decreases in recognition accuracy were also mirrored by significant increases in reported arousal, at least for females. If one were indeed to assume that the 'low arousal' persons were at a little below optimal arousal level, at a point just to the left of the inflection point on a Yerkes–Dodson curve for a moderately difficult task, then Brigham *et al*. have provided a nice confirmation of the Yerkes–Dodson Law. Even if one were to assume that Brigham *et al*.'s group-tested subjects were actually at optimum, there remains clear support for predictions from the right-hand segment of the Yerkes–Dodson curve.

The two experiments by Clifford and Hollin used different means to increase arousal in eyewitnesses but yielded similar results. In Clifford and Hollin (1981), arousal was manipulated by varying the level of violence of episodes in which videotaped targets were viewed. Validity checks showed that the more violent episodes received significantly higher violence ratings than did the non-violent ones and that violent episodes generated expected differences in galvanic skin response, which is, as mentioned previously, a peripheral measure of physiological arousal. Though the less accurate photographic identification of a suspect under more violent viewing conditions was not statistically significant (23.3% v. 30.0%), the lower rate of recall of his personal characteristics under more violent conditions was (20% v. 32.4%). Furthermore, the latter decrease in accuracy was exacerbated by the presence of greater numbers of perpetrators. It is also interesting that the optimality hypothesis proposed by Deffenbacher (1980) would have predicted a significant correlation of identification accuracy and eyewitness confidence only for the non-violent episodes. The point biserial correlation of accuracy and confidence was indeed significant at $+.41$ under non-violent conditions but was not significant under violent ones. Finally, Clifford and Hollin may well have found support for Easterbrook's (1959) narrowing of attention interpretation of the Yerkes–Dodson Law. Recall of personal characteristics of the female subject in the two episodes was nearly identical for both violent and non-violent groups. But then she had been viewed in the same non-arousing situation at the beginning of both videotapes, prior to the entry of any male perpetrators.

In the Clifford and Hollin (1978) experiment, white noise-induced arousal decremented both recall and recognition of target persons relative to that of a non-arousing noise control group. Giesbrecht (1979) likewise used arousing white noise, finding that increased arousal interfered with facial recognition at longer retention intervals, particularly under less than optimal conditions, such as being exposed to non-distinctive target faces.

Clifford and Scott (1978) also varied arousal levels by varying violence level. Their witnesses viewed either a videotape of a 1 minute violent episode (physical assault of a bystander by one of two policemen) or a non-violent one (verbal exchange among a bystander and two policemen with a number of weak restraining movements being executed by one of the policemen). Within minutes witnesses gave either a brief narrative, free report emphasizing physical descriptions and actions, or a brief interrogative report of the same. A few minutes after this, all witnesses answered a 40-item questionnaire covering both descriptions and actions. Accuracy was poorer under violent conditions (35% overall, 32% for descriptions, 38% for actions) than under non-violent ones (46% overall, 41% for descriptions, 51% for actions) for both sexes, but the decline was greater for women. Under violent viewing conditions, they showed a statistically significant but rather small inferiority in absolute terms; their mean recall accuracy was 33.6% as compared with 36.4% for men. Consonant with this difference, women rated the violent film as significantly more violent than did the men. If personal characteristics of the episode participants are judged as more central, while their actions are judged to be more peripheral, then with this experiment we again have support for Easterbrook's (1959) interpretation of the Yerkes–Dodson Law. Viewers of the violent episode suffered from less accurate recall of both physical descriptions and actions, but their memory for the actions of the target persons suffered significantly more so.

Witnesses in Loftus and Burns's (1981) study saw either a violent or non-violent film of a bank robbery, a film that is part of an American bank's training programme designed to teach employees how to react during a holdup. Those exposed to the violent version, in which a young boy is brutally shot in the face, showed poorer recall for and recognition of film details. Furthermore, Loftus and Burns showed that the memory impairment was due to the mentally shocking nature of the violent episode and not to its merely being unexpected.

Higher individually assessed arousal levels

Some five studies have yielded findings of a detrimental effect on eyewitness accuracy of higher levels of trait anxiety and/or higher levels of state anxiety (Buckhout et al., 1974; Mueller et al., 1979a; Nowicki et al., 1979; Siegel and Loftus, 1978; Zanni and Offermann, 1978). The Mueller et al. and Nowicki et al. experiments have assessed the effects of greater experienced arousal levels on face recognition alone. The other three teams of investigators have examined the detrimental effects of higher personal arousal levels on memory for additional aspects of the target situation, personal details of target persons other than their faces, their clothing and actions, characteristics of the surrounding environment, and so forth.

Buckhout *et al.* did not attempt to relate scores on a standard psychometric measure of anxiety to performance on an eyewitness task. Instead, they created an arousing purse-snatching incident in front of two unsuspecting college classes and had witnesses simply indicate on a seven-point scale how much stress they felt right after the incident. As opposed to unsuccessful witnesses, those witnesses successful on a videotaped lineup given 3 weeks later were those who felt significantly less stress at the scene of the 'crime'. The lineup-successful witnesses also were more accurate in their estimate of incident duration and the 'criminal's' weight on two recall measures given a few minutes after the arousing incident. So although the arousing incident did involve creation of an object focus, the purse-snatching itself, it appears that those experiencing more situational stress were more susceptible to this focus — thereby paying less attention to the suspect's personal details as well as to cues predictive of incident duration — details peripheral to the stolen object but somewhat central to the eyewitness's task.

As mentioned above, Mueller *et al.* and Nowicki *et al.* related recognition memory for previously unfamiliar faces in a laboratory setting to scores on certain paper-and-pencil measures of anxiety. Mueller *et al.* established extreme groups, high anxiety persons being significantly higher than low anxiety persons on the Sarason Test Anxiety Scale (trait anxiety), the State Anxiety Inventory, the Thayer Activation–Deactivation Adjective Checklist (state anxiety), and self-rated state anxiety. High anxiety persons showed an impaired ability to discriminate faces seen once before from those never before seen (lower d' scores). Nowicki *et al.* did not use an extreme group's design, but simply correlated scores on the Adult Nowicki–Strickland Internal–External Locus of Control Scale with d' scores on an announced face memory task. For their male subjects, at any rate, locus of control and d' correlated significantly at $-.32$. Since locus of control typically correlates $+.70$ with trait anxiety, those scoring high on locus of control (externality) also tend to be chronically more anxious. Therefore Nowicki *et al.* may also have shown that higher anxiety tends to be associated with lowered capacity for face recognition.

Both the Siegel and Loftus (1978) and Zanni and Offermann (1978) experiments employed a similar methodology. Either a short slide sequence (Siegel and Loftus) or a short film (Zanni and Offermann) of a real-life event were viewed and then followed by a questionnaire testing memory details. Siegel and Loftus found significant negative correlations of $-.20$ to $-.26$ between eyewitness ability and three separate measures of state anxiety. Zanni and Offermann included in their recall questionnaire five questions pertaining to aspects of the viewed event that were not actually present. Errors (false alarms) were defined as 'yes' responses to these questions concerning absent items. In two separate experiments, Zanni and Offermann found that the tendency to commit false alarm errors and neuroticism score on the Eysenck Personality Inventory were fairly well correlated. Correlation coefficients were

+.51 in the one case and +.41 in the other. Here we have some of the strongest empirical evidence to date that chronically higher arousal levels (high neuroticism) may be associated with lowered eyewitness accuracy.[4]

Conclusions

Regardless of national origin, criminal court judiciaries should be informed that there is no empirical support for the notion that relatively high levels of arousal facilitate eyewitness testimony. I refer here to arousal levels engendered by crimes of violence, arousal levels typical of the right-hand portion of a Yerkes–Dodson curve. In addition, American criminal court jurists ought to be informed that this notion does not square with the common-sense understanding of jurors and trial attorneys, either. Furthermore, the American judiciary may inappropriately have extended the theory behind res gestae to the situation of the witness testifying from his or her long-term memory.

This is not to say that all increases in arousal may serve to decrement reliability of testimony. If the witness's initial arousal level were relatively low, a very modest increase could add to the reliability of report. Certainly there could be real-life situations such as that set up in the convenience store study by Brigham et al. where a witness would be unaware at the time that it might be important to remember details concerning some other person or event. In such an instance, a person who had had a good night's sleep and had been at his or her daily tasks for 1 hour would be more highly aroused and more nearly at an optimal level of vigilance than a person who had missed a night's sleep and had been on the job for 8 hours. The latter individual would be too little aroused.

But this point should not detract from the fact that arousal levels engendered by crimes of violence, homicides, rapes, assaults, armed robberies, are almost invariably going to be greater than the Yerkes–Dodson optimum, given the reasonably high complexity of the task expected of eyewitnesses. Hence the probability that any given peripheral detail of a criminal event will be remembered accurately is assuredly lower for a violent event than for a criminal event where there is little immediate threat to life and limb. Furthermore, even the probability of a more central aspect of a violent situation being accurately remembered is an inverse function of the degree of emotional arousal engendered by the event.

Thus a weapon focus induced by an armed robbery would quite likely reduce the amount of processing of the culprit's facial cues by the victim/witness. The gun would become the centre of the perceptual field and would receive a disproportionate amount of processing time. Unfortunately, the rather high arousal level engendered by the armed robbery would seriously reduce the range of cues that could be monitored effectively, thereby reducing the probability of the witness being able to switch attention sufficiently to the robber's face and other distinguishing physical characteristics. Whether because of situational or personality factors, arousal could rise to a point where even the centre of the perceptual field would not be monitored adequately. At this point the witness might not even be processing sufficient accurate information to be able later to describe the weapon in adequate detail. All this suggests that a jury should not be allowed to convict a person of a violent crime on eyewitness evidence alone unless there are exceptional circumstances such as evidence that the defendant is well known to the victim/witness and/or had been *carefully* observed for an extended period of time (compare, for example, Devlin, 1976, p. 150).

NOTES

1. The distinction made here concerning manipulation versus assessment simply reflects the approaches of two different traditions in psychology, the experimental and the psychometric. The former approach would attempt to manipulate arousal level by exposing one group of subjects to greater amounts of electric shock, higher white noise levels, a higher level of 'crime' seriousness or violence, etc., than another similar group. The assumption would be that such manipulations would increase the average arousal level. Often experimenters check on this assumption by monitoring measures of physiological arousal and verbal reports from these persons. The latter approach typically assesses chronic differences in predisposition to be emotionally aroused (trait anxiety differences) and/or transient differences in situationally experienced emotional arousal (state anxiety differences). State anxiety is a product both of trait anxiety level and the degree of situational stress, whether produced by nature or deliberate action of the experimenter. Assessment of these differences is by paper-and-pencil rating scales, adjective checklists, or true–false inventories, and the investigator is interested in knowing how much of the variance in performance on an eyewitness task is accounted for by these individual differences in emotional arousal.

2. This surmise is based on the assumption that the college student actually engaged in a laboratory task typically is trying to do his/her best and will be at or near optimal arousal level. (This is not the case, of course, with the college student subjects of the staged crime studies, who were simply sitting around waiting for the ostensible experiment to begin. The presumption here is that such individuals would be somewhat less than optimally aroused). It is very possible, however, that the 16 subjects in the 'low arousal' condition of Brigham *et al.*'s study were a bit less than optimally aroused. Their group d' score was 1.60, less than the 1.97 average score obtained by 22 college student subjects in a very similar experimental condition of the Chance *et al.* (1980) study. Both groups were exposed to slides of same and other race faces with similar study and test trial exposure times; in both studies memory was measured by a yes/no recognition task. Both groups of subjects were college adults at similar calibre universities.

3. Since ethical and legal considerations prevent the experimenter from staging the ultimate in crime simulation, pulling a gun on the unsuspecting subject, and the like, stimulation by electric shock may be the most emotionally arousing substitute available. Indeed, psychologists generally recognize the powerful unlearned motive in humans to avoid painful stimulation and to have fear responses elicited by it. The 60 Hz a.c. stimulus used in this study delivers an 'ugly', 'digging' pain even at moderate intensities. The perception of shock intensity grows as a power function of

shock current level, with an exponent as high as 3.50 having been reported (Stevens, 1961). Unless it be the fear and arousal elicited by situations threatening life and limb, there would seem to be no more arousing stimulus in human experience. After all, even the exponent of the power function relating perception of thermally induced pain and corresponding temperature increase is only 1.00.

4. The personality dimension neuroticism–stability appears to be much the same as the dimension high anxiety–low anxiety measured by the various tests of trait anxiety already cited. Correlations between neuroticism scores and trait anxiety scores have been reported in the range from .40 to .80 with a typical correlation being about .70 (Eysenck and Eysenck, 1968). Furthermore, Eysenck (1967) has theorized that persons high in neuroticism have very low thresholds for emotional arousal, such arousal produced as a result of action of the limbic system of the brain and its outflow to the autonomic nervous system. This is very similar to the theory behind trait anxiety, namely that high trait anxious persons are predisposed to perceive a wide range of objectively non-dangerous situations as threatening and to respond with autonomic arousal.

REFERENCES

Brigham, J.C. (1981). The accuracy of eyewitness evidence: How do attorneys see it? *The Florida Bar Journal*, November, 714–721.

Brigham, J.C., Maas, A., Snyder, L.D. and Spaulding, K. (1982). The accuracy of eyewitness identifications in a field setting. *Journal of Personality and Social Psychology*, in press.

Brigham, J.C., Snyder, L.D., Spaulding, K., and Maas, A. (1980b) The accuracy of eyewitness identification in a field setting. Unpublished manuscript, Florida State University.

Broadbent, D.E. (1971). *Decision and stress*. London: Academic Press.

Broadhurst, P.L. (1957). Emotionality and the Yerkes–Dodson law. *Journal of Experimental Psychology*, **54**, 345–352.

Buckhout, R., Alper, A., Chern, S., Silverberg, G., and Slomovits, M. (1974). Determinants of eyewitness performance on a lineup. *Bulletin of the Psychonomic Society*, **4**, 191–192.

Chance, J.E., Turner, A.L. and Goldstein, A.G. (1980). Developmental effects in differential recognition of own- and other-race faces. Paper presented at the Psychonomic Society meeting, St Louis, Missouri.

Clifford, B.R. (1978). A critique of eyewitness research. In M.M. Gruneberg, P.E. Morris, and R.N. Sykes (eds), *Practical Aspects of Memory*. London and New York: Academic Press.

Clifford, B.R. and Hollin, C.R. (1978). Experimentally manipulated arousal and eyewitness testimony. Unpublished manuscript, North East London Polytechnic.

Clifford, B.R. and Hollin, C.R. (1981). Effects of the type of incident and the number of perpetrators on eyewitness memory. *Journal of Applied Psychology*, **66**, 364–370.

Clifford, B.R. and Scott, J. (1978). Individual and situational factors in eyewitness testimony. *Journal of Applied Psychology*, **63**, 352–359.

Cole, L.W. (1911). The relation of strength of stimulation to rate of learning in the chick. *Journal of Animal Behavior*, **1**, 111–124.

Deffenbacher, K.A. (1980). Eyewitness accuracy and confidence: Can we infer anything about their relationship? *Law and Human Behavior*, **4**, 243–260.

Deffenbacher, K.A., Brown, E.L., and Sturgill, W. (1978). Some predictors of eyewitness memory accuracy. In M.M. Gruneberg, P.E. Morris, and R.N. Sykes (eds), *Practical Aspects of Memory*. London: Academic Press.

Deffenbacher, K.A. and Loftus, E.F. (1982). Do jurors share a common understanding concerning eyewitness behaviour? *Law and Human Behavior*, **6**, in press.

Devlin, L.P. (1976). Report to the Secretary of State for the Home Department of the Departmental Committee on Evidence of Identification in Criminal Cases. London: HMSO.

Dodson, J.D. (1915). The relation of strength of stimulus to rapidity of habit formation in the kitten. *Journal of Animal Behavior*, **5**, 330–336.

Easterbrook, J.A. (1959). The effect of emotion on the utilization and organization of behavior. *Psychological Review*, **66**, 183–201.

Eysenck, H.J. (1967). *The Biological Basis of Personality*. Springfield, Illinois: Charles C. Thomas.

Eysenck, H.J. and Eysenck, S.B.G. (1968). *The Manual to the Eysenck Personality Inventory*. San Diego, California: Educational and Industrial Testing Service.

Eysenck, M.W. (1979). Anxiety, learning, and memory: A reconceptualization. *Journal of Research in Personality*, **13**, 363–385.

Federal Rules of Evidence for United States Courts and Magistrates. St Paul, Minn.: West Publishing Company, 1975.

Giesbrecht, L.W. (1979). *The effects of arousal and depth of processing on facial recognition*. Doctoral dissertation, Florida State University *Dissertation Abstracts International*, 40/09, 4561-B. (University Microfilms No. 8006257).

Hastie, R., Loftus, E.F., Penrod, S., and Winkler, J.D. (1977). The reliability of eyewitness testimony: Review of the psychological literature. Unpublished manuscript, Harvard University.

Hosch, H.M. and Cooper, D.S. (1980). Victimization and self-monitoring as determinants of eyewitness accuracy. Unpublished manuscript, University of Texas at El Paso.

Hutchins, R.M. and Slesinger, D. (1928). Some observations on the law of evidence: Spontaneous exclamations. *Columbia Law Review*, **28**, 432.

Johnson, C. and Scott, B. (1976). Eyewitness testimony and suspect identification as a function of arousal, sex of witness, and scheduling of interrogation. Paper presented at meetings of the American Psychological Association, Washington DC.

Levine, F.J. and Tapp, J. (1973). The psychology of criminal identification: The gap from Wade to Kirby. *University of Pennsylvania Law Review*, **121**, 1079–1131.

Leippe, M.R., Wells, G.L., and Ostrom, T.M. (1978). Crime seriousness as a determinant of accuracy in eyewitness identification. *Journal of Applied Psychology*, **63**, 345–351.

Loftus, E.F. and Burns, T.E. (1981). Mental shock can produce retrograde amnesia. Paper presented at meetings of the Psychonomic Society, Philadelphia.

Majcher, L.L. (1974). Facial recognition as a function of arousal level, exposure and duration and delay interval. Unpublished MA thesis, University of Missouri.

Marshall, J. (1966). *Law and Psychology in Conflict*. Indianapolis: Bobbs-Merrill.

Miller, D.J., Mueller, J.H., Goldstein, A.G., and Potter, T.L. (1978). Depth of processing and test anxiety in landscape recognition. *Bulletin of the Psychonomic Society*, **11**, 341–343.

Mueller, J.H., Bailis, K.L., and Goldstein, A.G. (1979a). Depth of processing and anxiety in facial recognition. *British Journal of Psychology*, **70**, 511–515.

Mueller, J.H., Miller, D.J., and Hutchings, J.L. (1979b). Anxiety and orienting tasks in picture recognition. *Bulletin of the Psychonomic Society*, **13**, 145–148.

Nowicki, S., Winograd, E., and Millard, B.A. (1979). Memory for faces: A social learning analysis. *Journal of Research in Personality*, **13**, 460–468.

People v. *Guzman* (1975). 47 Cal. App. 3d 380, 385; 121 Cal. Rptr. 69, 71.

Shepherd, J.W., Davies, G.M., and Ellis, H.D. (1980). Identification after delay. Final report for Grant RES 522/4/1 awarded by the Home Office Research Unit to the Department of Psychology, University of Aberdeen.

Siegel, J.M. and Loftus, E.F. (1978). Impact of anxiety and life stress upon eyewitness testimony. *Bulletin of the Psychonomic Society*, **12**, 479–480.

Snyder, M. (1979). Self monitoring processes. In L. Berkowitz (ed.), *Advances in Experimental Social Psychology* (Vol. 12). New York: Academic Press.

Stevens, S.S. (1961). The psychophysics of sensory function. In W.A. Rosenblith (ed.), *Sensory Communication*. Cambridge, Mass.: MIT Press.

Suggs, D.L. (1979). The use of psychological research by the judiciary: Do the courts adequately assess the validity of the research? *Law and Human Behavior*, **3**, 135–148.

Sussman, E.D. and Sugarman, R.C. (1972). The effect of certain distractions on identification by witnesses. In A. Zavala and J.J. Paley (eds), *Personal Appearance Identification*. Springfield, Ill.: Charles C. Thomas.

United States v. *Amaral* (1973). 488 F 2d 146 (9th Cir.).

Walley, R.E. and Weiden, T.D. (1973). Lateral inhibition and cognitive masking: A neuropsychological theory of attention. *Psychological Review*, **80**, 284–302.

Whipple, G.M. (1909). The observer as reporter: A survey of the 'psychology of testimony'. *Psychological Bulletin*, **6**, 153–170.

Whipple, G.M. (1910). Recent literature on the psychology of testimony. *Psychological Bulletin*, **7**, 365–368.

Whipple, G.M. (1911). The psychology of testimony. *Psychological Bulletin*, **8**, 307–309.

Whipple, G.M. (1912). Psychology of testimony and report. *Psychological Bulletin*, **9**, 264–269.

Whipple, G.M. (1913). Psychology of testimony and report. *Psychological Bulletin*, **10**, 264–268.

Whipple, G.M. (1914). Psychology of testimony and report. *Psychological Bulletin*, **11**, 245–250.

Whipple, G.M. (1915). Psychology of testimony. *Psychological Bulletin*, **12**, 221–224.

Whipple, G.M. (1917). Psychology of testimony. *Psychological Bulletin*, **14**, 234–236.

Whipple, G.M. (1918). The obtaining of information: Psychology of observation and report. *Psychological Bulletin*, **15**, 217–248.

Yerkes, R.M. and Dodson, J.D. (1908). The relation of strength of stimulus to rapidity of habit formation. *Journal of Comparative Neurology and Psychology*, **18**, 459–482.

Zanni, G.R. and Offermann, J.T. (1978). Eyewitness testimony: An exploration of question wording upon recall as a function of neuroticism. *Perceptual and Motor Skills*, **46**, 163–166.

PART IV

FUTURE DIRECTIONS

Evaluating Witness Evidence
Edited by S.M.A. Lloyd-Bostock and B.R. Clifford
© 1983 John Wiley & Sons Ltd.

Chapter 14

Identification and Misidentification in Legal Processes:
Redefining the Problem

William Twining

In recent years the problem of misidentification, especially in criminal cases, has attracted a good deal of attention from the media, lawyers, psychologists, and others. One influential, but by no means universally held, view of the problem might be stated in some such terms as these:

> From time to time an innocent man is convicted by a jury of a crime he did not — or probably did not — commit, on the basis, mainly or entirely of eyewitness testimony relating to identification. Typically this testimony is honest, but mistaken. It may be only half-a-dozen or so chaps a year who suffer such miscarriages of justice and some of these are professional criminals who might well have been put inside for some other offence; no system of criminal justice can be expected to eliminate all mistakes, but our legal tradition and public opinion place a high value on safeguarding the innocent, even at the price of letting some, but not an unlimited number, of criminals go free. The problem peculiar to identification is that the value of the evidence is exceptionally difficult to assess. The task is to reduce the risk of error by taking measures to improve the law and procedure governing *evidence* of identification.

In this view the main relevance of psychology to the problem of misidentification is thought to relate to the cognitive processes of individual witnesses (notably perception, attention, memory, bias, and suggestion) rather than to cognitive processes of other participants and interactive aspects of legal processes.

The purpose of this paper is to suggest that this orthodox view presents an artificially narrow definition of the problem and that future research and public debate about the problem of identification in legal processes would benefit from being set in the context of a comprehensive model of legal processes, and of a clearly articulated, integrated, theoretical framework; that information about the identity of a person or persons thought to be involved in some event or situation has a bearing not solely on adjudication of guilt or innocence, but on a wide variety of decisions each of which may have potentially harmful or unpleasant consequences for persons who are objects of identification; that such information needs to be regarded not only as evidence, but also as potential evidence and as information relevant to other decisions; and that the ways in which it is 'processed' and used and the operation of factors which affect its reliability or completeness (or other 'validity') need to be considered at every stage in the process. Finally, I shall argue that redefining the problem of misidentification in this way raises questions about the scale and distribution of the phenomena as they have been perceived in the *Devlin Report on Evidence of Identification in Criminal Cases* (Devlin, 1976) and the debate surrounding that report.

The paper proceeds as follows: in the first section I shall consider the implications for perceptions of the problem of identification of adopting one of two different perspectives, which can crudely be designated as 'expository' and 'contextual' approaches to law. I shall argue that there are certain general tendencies and biases in the expository tradition that are reflected in part in the standard legal literature on the law of evidence, in contrast with most contemporary writing about legal processes which tends to be more in tune with a contextual approach; and I shall examine the extent to which these biases are found in the literature on identification. In the following section I shall sketch, in the form of an ideal type, a profile of a standard case of the problem of misidentification that reflects some of the biases both in the expository literature and in official or orthodox definitions of the problem — I shall argue that a broader 'information model' of misidentification may provide the basis for a more systematic and more realistic approach to the topic. In the final section the main elements of the problem of misidentification are re-examined in the light of the previous discussion and some implications of adopting a broader perspective in this context are suggested.

The analysis takes as its starting-point the *Devlin Report* and three very useful books on the psychological aspects of eyewitness testimony and identification (Clifford and Bull, 1978; Loftus, 1979; and Yarmey, 1979). Those four works, together with the chapters in the present volume, adequately survey the literature and provide a convenient basis for taking stock and considering future directions: for the purpose of this chapter these works will be taken as representative of the literature on identification. It is part of the thesis of this chapter that *some* discussions of identification have been influenced by some of the biases in the expository approach — notably a tendency to concentrate on adjudicative decisions in contested criminal cases and to view information about identity largely, if not solely, in terms of admissible evidence presented to a jury. However, it is important to emphasize at the outset that by no means all writers on the subject have taken so narrow a view of the subject. In particular this chapter should not be read as a critique of recent contributions by psychologists to the study of eyewitness identification and related problems. The psychological literature has not been entirely free of some of the narrow assumptions that are criticized here; but the main thrust of the chapter is to warn against some tendencies in legal literature and to sketch the basis for a broader perspective on the subject.

TWO PERSPECTIVES ON LAW AND LEGAL PROCESSES

At some risk of oversimplification it is convenient to postulate two contrasting approaches to the study of law which are current in the United Kingdom and, with some more or less significant variations, in the United States and other parts of the English-speaking world. Each approach suggests a differing perspective on the problem of identification and hence on the potential contribution of psychologists, and others. The first, which I shall refer to as the Expository Tradition, is sometimes known as 'legal formalism' or 'the black letter approach'. It has, at least until recently dominated academic law in the United Kingdom during this century and it is exemplified by such standard works as Cross on *Evidence*, Smith and Hogan on *Criminal Law*, and Salmond on *Torts*.[1] In this view, the study of law consists predominantly of the exposition, analysis and, to a lesser extent, criticism of the rules of positive law in force in a given jurisdiction. Its protagonists would readily concede that history, the social sciences, and other disciplines are relevant to an understanding of law, but they tend to treat them as marginal and not really part of the specialized study of law. Thus the subject-matter of evidence is the *rules* of evidence; Cross on *Evidence* for example, scarcely makes any reference to the logical, mathematical, epistemological, scientific, psychological or other 'nonlegal' aspects of evidence and proof. Cross sharply differentiates the law of evidence from the law of procedure and from substantive law. Much legal writing about evidence proceeds on the assumption that if there were no rules of evidence there would be nothing for lawyers to study. Similarly, within the Expository Tradition, even the study of procedure has been largely confined to the rules of procedure. Few legal scholars have adhered rigidly and consistently to this view, but its influence has nevertheless been both pervasive and profound. It has not merely influenced legal education and legal scholarship, but has also provided the main underlying basis for the ways of thought and discourse about law of most practising lawyers and judges, even in the context of debates about reform.

An alternative approach (only one of several alternatives) I shall refer to here as the Contextual Approach.[2] The central unifying tenet of this approach is that rules are important — indeed a central feature of law — but for the purposes of understanding, criticizing or even expounding the law, the study of rules alone is not enough. Rather, legal rules, institutions, procedures, practices, and other legal phenomena need to be set in some broader context. What constitutes an appropriate context depends on the purposes of the study or other discourse in question. For example, if one is concerned to study the law of evidence in action, the rules of evidence need to be viewed in the context of the legal processes in which they in fact operate and those processes may need to be seen in the context of other social processes. In this view, the rules of evidence are only one small part of the subject of evidence and proof.[3] The rounded study of evidence, as part of the study of law, would include logical, philosophical, psychological, processual, and other dimensions. In order to make such a study coherent and manageable an overarching theory of evidence (or evidence and proof) is needed which provides a unifying conceptual framework, and, at the very least, maps the connections between these various aspects or dimensions (see Twining, 1979).[4]

It is not necessary to canvass the much-discussed merits and limitations of these two different approaches (see Twining, 1974, 1979 for a fuller discussion); but it is relevant to consider briefly certain tendencies or biases in the Expository Tradition that are to be found in some of the legal literature that has a bearing on the present subject. In its extreme form the Expository Tradition tends: (i) to be rule-centred; (ii) to pay disproportionate attention to the decisions of appellate courts; (iii) to treat jury trials as the paradigm of all trials; (iv) to concentrate on events in the courtroom, to the exclusion of pre-trial and post-trial events; (v) to adopt a rationalistic and aspirational approach to problems of evidence rather than an empirical perspective; and (vi) in discussing reform, to take existing rules and devices as the starting-point for response to problems, with a consequent tendency to be rather thin on diagnosis.

All of these tendencies are to be found to a greater or lesser extent in expository legal literature, as exemplified by orthodox treatments of the law of evidence; they are less marked in recent legal literature on judicial processes. I shall suggest that examples of some, but not all, of these tendencies have spilled over into recent discussions of identification.

(i) Rule-centredness

We have seen that there is a tendency in the Anglo–American literature to treat the rules of evidence as constituting all, or nearly all, of the subject of evidence. It happens to be the case that the Anglo–American systems have by and large turned away from trying to regulate questions of *cogency* (or weight) and questions of *quantum* (amount) of evidence by means of rigid rules. (One of the few exceptions to this are the rules requiring corroboration in certain limited situations). The great bulk of evidence doctrine is concerned with the rules of admissibility and exclusion — that is to say, rules governing what evidence may or may not be presented in what form and by whom to the decision-maker. This represents a partial victory for Jeremy Bentham, who argued that there should be *no* formal rules of evidence (Bentham, 1827). Since the middle of the nineteenth century there has been a general, if slow, trend in the direction of de-regulating evidence along the lines advocated by Bentham. However, as is well known, his victory has not been complete, especially in the United States.[5] What is significant in the present context is the fact that many aspects of presenting and weighing evidence are not governed by formal rules at all and that it is widely recognized that changes in the law of evidence represent only one of a number of possible strategies for tackling problems of misidentification. Thus, the Devlin Report conspicuously rejected the idea of a formal rule requiring corroboration of eyewitness identification testimony or of excluding such evidence; and it was generally sceptical as to whether much could be achieved by changing legal rules, except perhaps rules governing procedures of identification parades.

The literature on identification is not strikingly rule-centred in the sense of focusing on formal rules: more attention has been paid to techniques for improving reliability of identification and to warnings about the pitfalls and dangers of eyewitness identification, independently of the formal rules of evidence. Nevertheless, some writers have from time to time talked as if this is part of the *law* of evidence. For example, Professor John Kaplan in his introduction to Elizabeth Loftus's *Eyewitness Testimony* treats the book as 'a contribution to the *law* of evidence' and implies it is strange that 'there are virtually *no* rules which govern what witnesses may say they saw with their own eyes' (Loftus, 1979, p. vii). This is a harmless example of rule-centred talk. Ironically, Professor Kaplan himself has made a pioneering contribution to the discussion of probabilities and proof (Kaplan, 1968), another topic concerned with evidence where significant steps have been taken away from the rule-dominated treatment of evidentiary issues in recent years. Elizabeth Loftus herself, in considering possible responses to the problem of unreliability of eyewitness testimony explicitly rejects formal rules of exclusion or of corroboration as remedies; she is dubious about the efficacy of cautionary instructions to the jury and she advocates, as the most important remedy, a more widespread use of psychologists as expert witnesses (Loftus, 1979). Suffice to say here that problems of misidentification are only marginally concerned with the formal rules of evidence and that this has by and large been recognized in the literature.

(ii) 'Appellate court-itis'

The American jurist Jerome Frank identified one of the major diseases of legal formalism as 'appellate court-itis' — that is, a tendency to concentrate far too much attention on the work of appellate courts and disputed questions of law (as exemplified by the commanding position in legal literature occupied by law reports), with a corresponding almost total neglect of the work of trial courts and of disputed questions of fact (Frank, 1949). Not surprisingly, the literature on eyewitness identification is largely free of this bias; for example, the Devlin Committee cited barely a dozen appellate cases, while devoting nearly 60 pages to the detailed analysis of the total process involved in the cases of *Dougherty* and *Virag*, in striking contrast with most orthodox legal literature.[6] Elizabeth Loftus quite legitimately devotes a section to Supreme Court decisions on eyewitness testimony but fully recognizes that legal doctrine developed by the court is only a small part of the whole story (Loftus, 1979, pp. 180–187).

(iii) Jury-centredness

The first step away from 'appellate court-itis' is to shift attention from appellate to trial courts. There is a tendency in the orthodox literature on evidence to treat the contested jury trial as the paradigm case of all trials. This is under-standable, though misleading, if only because the history and rationale of the rules of evidence are intimately bound up with the institution of the jury. Moreover rules of evidence tend to be applied more strictly in jury trials than in other proceedings. Nevertheless, this concentration on the jury has been strongly challenged by some writers. The American scholar, Kenneth Culp Davis has suggested that nearly all literature and discourse about evidence is dominated by 'jury thinking' and that this is inappropriate since only a tiny minority of all trials are jury trials (Davis, 1964). The jury is less important in England than it is in the United States; an even smaller proportion of criminal cases, albeit many of the more serious ones, are tried by juries. The jury has almost completely atrophied in civil cases in this country and is on the decline in the United States.[7]

Apart from the obvious reason that juries tend to deal with more serious and more spectacular cases, another reason for the dominance of 'jury thinking' in much legal literature and public debate is that a high proportion of the con-tributors are judges and senior barristers, whose experience — at least their recent experience — has tended to be confined to jury trials. In the past academic lawyers have also tended to be prone to the biases of 'jury thinking', but recently increased academic attention has been paid to magistrates courts and to tribunals.

Much of the literature on identification has been jury-centred. Psychologists writing on the subject such as Loftus, Yarmey, and Clifford and Bull, (see also, Saunders, Vidmar, and Hewitt, this volume) although they occasionally use examples from non-jury trials and other proceedings, sometimes seem to *assume* that eyewitness testimony of identification is presented to a jury. Even more striking is the fact that the Devlin Committee devoted only 3 pages out of nearly 200 to magistrates courts and explicitly decided to limit their recom-mendations ('for the time being' [*sic*]) to trials on indictment. The main reason given for this was that disputes as to identity and disputes involving alibi evidence are rare in summary proceedings, but no evidence was advanced for these statements.[8] Thus it is fair to say that the bulk of literature about identification is strikingly jury-centred; whether this is justifiable will be considered below.

(iv) Court-centredness

The shifts from appellate courts to jury trials and from jury trials to all trials represent important steps in broadening the focus of attention of legal studies in the direction of a more balanced and realistic treatment of legal processes generally. An even more important advance has been to face the fact that what takes place in open court represents only one small part of legal processes and to follow through the implications of this perception. We all know that only a small minority of cases ever reach the stage of being contested in court and that the outcomes of contested cases are heavily influenced by events and decisions that have occurred before trial. Yet to an extraordinary extent orthodox legal literature and discourse have disguised these facts and their implications. This can be illustrated by contrasting standard works on evidence and on procedure. To put the matter in simplified form: the bulk of Anglo–American literature on *evidence* still tends to assume that the contested jury trial is the paradigm and to concentrate on events in the courtroom; on the other hand, nearly all modern Anglo–American literature on *procedure* considers total legal processes, starting with some initial situation or triggering event and following through a variety of stages of different kinds of process, often beyond formal adjudicative determinations of guilt or liability (or other determinations) to post-adjudicative decisions and events, such as sentencing, parole, and the enforcement of civil judgments.

During the past decade broader approaches have gained much wider acceptance in the United Kingdom, with the result that the dominance of the Expository Tradition has been quite successfully challenged, although first class expository work is still, quite rightly, accepted as a respectable form of legal scholarship. This movement is quite neatly illustrated by the differences between three reports which have dealt, *inter alia*, with criminal evidence and procedure in recent years. The Eleventh Report of the Criminal Law Revision Committee (1972), which concentrated almost entirely on contested trials on indictment and on the operation of rules of evidence in court, is a fairly typical product of the Expository Tradition. In sharp contrast the recent *Report of the Royal Commission on Criminal Procedure* (Philips Report, 1981) devoted more attention to police powers and pre-trial events and decisions than to proceedings at trial and was almost as much concerned with summary proceedings as with trials on indictment. The Philips Report in many respects is based on a contextual approach. Viewed thus, the Devlin Report can be treated as an example of a half-way house, combining features of both approaches; its analysis of the cases of *Dougherty* and *Virag* represents excellent case studies based on a total process model and, in some respects, it took into account a variety of considerations; yet the Report is not entirely free of the biases and hidden assumptions of the Expository Tradition, as is illustrated by its concentration on contested jury trials and its failure to explore the scale and distribution of cases of misidentification.[9]

In so far as the debate on misidentification has concentrated on eyewitness *testimony*, and has treated identification parades solely as evidence-generating devices, it has tended to be court-centred. However, a shift towards a broader perspective is discernible in recent writings as exemplified by some of the contributions to this volume.

(v) Optimistic and complacent rationalism

Anglo–American evidence scholarship since the time of Jeremy Bentham has been remarkably homogeneous, not least in respect of its acceptance of the idea that modern methods of adjudication are 'rational'.[10] The dominant approach has been expository, as exemplified by the works of writers such as Starkie, Greenleaf, Taylor, Stephen, Phipson, MacCormick and Cross. But Bentham's writings on evidence (Bentham, 1827), Thayer's *A Preliminary Treatise on Evidence of Common Law* (1898), Michael and Adler's *The Nature of Judicial Proof* (1931), and Eggleston's *Evidence, Proof and Probability* (1978), are leading examples of an alternative tradition in which attempts have been made to go beyond exposition of the rules to deal with historical, logical, psychological, and other dimensions of evidence and proof. The greatest evidence scholar, the American, John Henry Wigmore, straddled both perspectives; his ten volume *Treatise on Evidence* (Wigmore, 1940) is generally regarded as one of the major achievements of expository scholarship; on the other hand, the historical aspects of the *Treatise* and his *Principles of Judicial Proof as Given by Logic, Psychology and General Experience* (later *The Science of Judicial Proof*) (Wigmore, 1937) remain the single most important attempt since Bentham to establish a Science of Proof, based on a coherent general theory which covers both the rules of evidence and the non-legal aspects of probative processes.

Some of the best legal minds have contributed to this dual tradition of evidence scholarship. What is particularly striking about it is the remarkable homogeneity of the basic underlying assumptions of what may be termed the Rationalist Tradition of evidence scholarship (Twining, 1982). Almost without exception the leading Anglo–American scholars have, either explicitly or implicitly, adopted a view of adjudication which treats it as a rational process directed towards rectitude of decision, that is the correct application of valid substantive laws through accurate determination of the truth about past facts in issue (i.e. facts material to precisely specified allegations expressed in categories defined in advance by law).[11] This applies both to expository writers such as Phipson and Cross and those who were also interested in broader perspectives on evidence and proof, such as Wigmore.

The claim that the modern system of adjudication is 'rational' is best treated as a statement of what is considered to be an *aspiration* of the modern system; the aim is to maximize the rationality and accuracy of fact-finding in adjudication, so far as this is feasible and is compatible with other, overriding social values. Such aspirational rationalism does not necessarily involve a commitment to the view that the aspiration is always or even generally realized in practice. It is commonplace within the classical rationalist tradition to criticize the existing practices, procedures, rules, and institutions in terms of their failure to satisfy the standards of this aspirational model. Nor within this general framework of assumptions is there a general consensus on all particular issues; the intellectual history of Anglo–American scholarship and discourse has had its share of long-running debates,[12] but there has been an extraordinarily high degree of consensus within the tradition about the objective of maximizing rationality and accuracy in determination of questions of fact and about the underlying assumptions as to what this involves. To be an aspirational rationalist of this kind can reasonably be construed as involving a degree of optimism about the feasibility of the aspiration; in evaluating and considering possible improvements in existing legal rules, institutions, and practices it does not make sense to postulate completely unattainable goals. Optimism easily spills over into complacency and, with some notable exceptions (including Bentham himself), nearly all leading Anglo–American evidence scholars have not only been optimistic about the feasibility of their ideals, they have also tended to be complacent about the basic design of the system and its actual workings and effects in practice. It is as if they had said: 'It is a poor show that a dozen or so chaps a year get gaoled or executed on the basis of unreliable identification evidence; we need to take steps to reduce the number of mistakes, but, after all, it is only a dozen or so. . . .'

It is important to notice that the Rationalist Tradition is not only rationalistic and optimistic, with a tendency to complacency. It is also aspirational and unempirical. The focus of attention in discussions of the logic of proof, and in debates about probabilities as part of those discussions, is on how people *ought* to reason in arguing, deciding, and justifying their decisions; it is not on how they in fact argue, decide, and justify. The study of logic is the study of what constitutes valid arguments; it is not the study of actual mental processes. One of the main reasons, I suspect, for the perennial uneasiness of relations between law and psychology is that, quite understandably, legal discourse is predominately normative, while the dominant intellectual tradition of psychology is empirical. Lawyers, both academic and practising, are not primarily concerned with systematic description, explanation or understanding of events in the real world. Even in debates about the reform of particular rules a standard pattern is to move directly from the existing rule to a recommendation for 'improvement', with at best only highly impressionistic and superficial notions of its operation in practice. The dominant intellectual tradition in psychology being scientific — that is primarily concerned with systematic description, explanation and understanding and with the establishment and testing of empirical generalizations — it is conversely strong on the empirical and less concerned with the normative aspect.

The Rationalist Tradition of evidence scholarship is also unsceptical. Within legal discourse there is, however, a contrasting, but somewhat diverse strain of apparent scepticism. Rabelais' Bridlegoose threw dice to decide cases; Jerome Frank's 'Fact-Scepticism' emphasized some of the obstacles to predictability in judicial decision-making; many lawyers view the adversary process more as a controlled form of battle in which the main objective of the contestants is to win rather than as a form of procedure designed to maximize the pursuit of truth through dialectical debate or disputation; contrasts between 'the law in books' and 'the law in action', between 'theory' and 'practice', and terms like 'the forensic lottery' are clichés in legal discourse. Before Karl Marx, Jeremy Bentham launched a full-scale attack on the mystifying devices of English law and procedure. Modern radical critics have carried on the tradition, arguing that many of the most cherished safeguards are merely a form of ideological façade and that 'adversary' proceedings are for a large part a myth. This alternative strand in legal thought is more in tune with the warnings by psychologists about the potential unreliability of various kinds of testimony than is optimistic rationalism. Yet as I have suggested elsewhere, many critical or seemingly sceptical writers tend to invoke the standards of prescriptive rationalism when criticizing existing practices or pointing to contrasts between aspiration and reality (Twining, 1981).

(vi) The way of the baffled medic: prescribe first, diagnose later — if at all

In the Expository Tradition the existing rules of positive law are the natural starting point for almost all legal discourse. There is a core of sense in the notion that one needs to know what the law is before starting to evaluate or to criticize it. But it is very easy to slide from this kind of attitude into a view of rules as things-in-themselves; once posited the law is the law independently of its origins or purposes. An alternative view of rules is to see them as responses to problems, or as instruments designed to further certain purposes or policies. In this view it is almost always sensible to see particular rules or bodies of rules in the context of perceived problems to which they were a response or of the purposes which led to their creation. In evaluating or criticizing rules it is a good rule of thumb to identify and diagnose the problem before moving on to consider the adequacy or otherwise of the rule as a response to it. To study rules without reference to problems is like studying remedies without reference to diseases. Orthodox discussions of law reform follow the Way of the Baffled Medic in so far as they substitute one prescription for another without any serious attempt to diagnose the problem.

The literature on reform of the law of evidence is replete with examples of this tendency. The standard weakness is to assume that the nature of the problem is self-evident and that the scale of its central factors is either well known or irrelevant. Thus the CLRC (Criminal Law Revision Committee) managed to treat professional criminals manipulating technical rules of evidence as typical of the behaviour of all persons accused of crimes. Nowhere in the literature on identification is there a full analysis of the nature, scale, and epidemiology of 'the problem of identification'. Typically the problem is *assumed* to be something to do with the unreliability of eyewitness testimony in jury trials; sometimes, as in the case of the *Devlin Report*, the nature of the problem is asserted with little by way of evidence or analysis. I shall endeavour to show below that the nature, scope, and scale of the problem of misidentification is by no means self-evident.

Many early discussions of identification parades provided, in a less obvious way, further examples of the operation of the fallacy of the Way of the Baffled Medic. So much attention has been focused, at least until recently, on this particular device that it has sometimes appeared as if the problem of identification is perceived as being co-extensive with some acknowledged defects and limitations of parade or lineup procedures and that the only, or at least the central, question is: how can the reliability of identification parades be improved? This is an interesting and legitimate question, but on its own it suffers from at least two limitations; it focuses on only one possible response to the problem of identification, assuming that one knows what the problem is; and it suggests that the only use of such procedures is to produce *evidence* of identification — whereas a study of decisions when and whether to hold parades might show that in some police areas there may be other objectives or uses; for example, the elimination of suspects or a decision to drop a case for want of evidence, or to persuade a suspect that the game is up. Where the identification parade is the starting point of discussion there has perhaps been a tendency to take too much for granted both about the problem of identification and about the uses of the device, to focus rather narrowly on a limited range of cases and to consider other possible devices, such as the use of photographs, too much in contrast with parades rather than to consider their potential in a variety of contexts. Starting from existing solutions, concentrating on only one of a possible range of devices, and not asking demographic questions about the phenomena under consideration are standard biases associated with the Expository Tradition.

TWO MODELS OF MISIDENTIFICATION

The contrast between the expository and contextual approaches to law may be reflected, at least in part, by contrasting views of what constitutes a standard case of misidentification. The analogy is not exact because, as we have seen, the orthodox definition of the problem does not simply reflect the tendencies and biases of an expository approach in its purest form. Nevertheless, it is possible to postulate a standard case, which is a fair reflection of the narrow view of the problem that was stated at the start of this paper. It may be helpful to depict this as an ideal type, consisting of a number of elements and to note some possible variants in respect of each element, as in Table 14.1.

Table 14.1   Ideal type or standard case of misidentification and possible variants

Standard case	Some possible variants
A *witness* (W) of indeterminate age, sex, class, race, and occupation	W was middle-aged, male, myopic, middle class, white, bank clerk or immigration officer
sees	contact was by telephone or involved a combination of visual, aural, and other impressions
an *incident*	W alleges that O was present in a particular vicinity, e.g. a theatre, a bar, a bed
of *short duration*	over a period of hours or longer
which becomes the subject of *criminal* proceedings	the issue of identification arose in a civil proceeding or a tribunal hearing or a non-legal proceeding, such as a university disciplinary hearing
in a *contested* case	the case was not contested, for example O pleaded guilty or the case was settled out of court or proceedings were dropped
tried before a *jury*	the (contested) hearing took place before a bench of magistrates or a professional judge or a court martial or other tribunal
in which W *willingly*	W was coerced or bribed or compelled to testify
gives *evidence*	the information given by W was used for purposes other than forensic evidence, e.g. as information leading to suspicion or investigation, or to neglect or elimination of a line of enquiry
of the *identity*	it was sufficient for the purposes of the enquiry that O was placed within a certain class of people rather than was identified as a unique individual
of the *accused* (O)	the object of identification was a *thing* (e.g. a car, a typewriter or a gun) or an *animal*

Standard case	Some possible variants
a person of *indeterminate* age, sex, class, race, and occupation	O was a black, male youth or a one-legged elderly woman
who was a *stranger* (i.e. previously unknown to W)	the subject was well known to W
W's evidence is unsupported by other evidence of identification	W's evidence was corroborated or denied by other testimonial or circumstantial evidence
and is *unreliable*	several factors in the particular situation enhanced the probability that the identification was reliable — e.g. W was an experienced or trained observer, the period of observation was substantial, O was already known to W, and so on
but *results*	the information or evidence of W was not believed by the jury or other relevant participant(s)
in the *conviction* of O	the *mischief* of the alleged misidentification was not that the subject was wrongly convicted or acquitted, but that he or she suffered *vexation* and/ or *expense* and/or *delay* (with consequential injury) through being suspected or arrested or interrogated or charged or sued, or suffered some *other* serious damage, such as injury to reputation or loss of a job.

Three points about Table 14.1 deserve comment. First, the standard case shares some, but not all, of the tendencies associated with the Expository Tradition (especially as illustrated by orthodox writings on evidence). In particular, it concerns an *incident* leading to a *contested case* tried before a *jury* in which the main role of the witness (W) is to provide *admissible evidence* of identification. The emphasis is on the objective reliability of evidence presented in *court*, and on *conviction* of innocent persons as the sole mischief of misidentification.

Second, in so far as psychologists and other writers on identification have tended to concentrate on examples which share all or most of the features of the standard case, they have also — perhaps unwittingly — shared some of the biases of the Expository Tradition. However, some researchers and commentators have pursued one or more variants of the standard case. For example, a good deal of attention has been paid to possible differentiating characteristics of witnesses, such as age, sex, and race: rather less attention has been paid to differentiating characteristics of subjects, except in regard to race (see Lindsay and Wells, this volume). Similarly as Baddeley and Woodhead have pointed out (this volume), identification of persons may have special practical significance for certain occupations such as immigration officers, bank clerks, prostitutes, and the police. This raises questions both about the possibilities of improving the performance of such persons in providing reliable information and whether training or experience significantly improves capacity to identify. However, the crucial point here is that investigation of such variants has proceeded neither on a systematic basis nor in the context of some general theoretical framework. At best, it has tended to be *ad hoc* and uneven.

Third, the variants on the standard case point in a variety of possibly divergent directions. This raises the question whether what is needed is not a single polar ideal type, contrasting with the standard case, so much as a flexible model which can accommodate a variety of types of processes, of types of decisions within each process and of types of cases, including both the standard case and at least the more important variants of the kind indicated above. This involves a shift of perspective to a higher level of generality than is postulated by the standard case. What I wish to suggest is that the basis for such a perspective is to hand in a way that combines elements of contextual perspectives on legal process and some notions about information processing borrowed from cognitive psychology and information theory: the result might be a composite 'information model', which is broader than, but incorporates, the traditional evidentiary model that is assumed in the standard case.

Let me revert briefly to the contrast between Expository and contextual perspectives on law. Although the intellectual history of Anglo–American legal scholarship has not followed a single neat line of development, it is possible to pull out one thread which forms something of a pattern: this is a steady broadening of the focus of attention beyond disputed questions of law, represented by the standpoint of appellate court judges, through steadily wider conceptions of different legal processes to a view of law in the context of society as a whole and, indeed, of humankind and of the universe. To put the matter simply: the focus shifted from disputed questions of law in appellate courts to disputed questions of fact tried before juries, to contested cases tried before courts without juries (and before other tribunals and arbitrators) to other methods of dispute settlement. This broadening of the focus of attention to include other *arenas* was paralleled by a perception that even the most formal kind of legal process involved a sequence or *flow of decisions and events* involving a variety of *participants*. Such total processes, like stories, have no finite beginnings and endings other than those points selected, often arbitrarily, as suitable for the particular purpose at hand by the particular expositor, story teller or whatever. In its most comprehensive and systematic version, as presented by Lasswell and McDougal (e.g.: Lasswell and McDougal, 1967; McDougal and Reisman, 1981), the physical universe is the universe of discourse and any particular legally significant decision or event needs to be considered in the context of some larger legal process which in turn belongs to a broader totality of social processes.

Such contextual models of legal processes are, of course, quite commonplace today, even within legal scholarship. They are explicitly used, or assumed by implication, in most contemporary writing about identification. But the potential of such models has not been consistently and fully exploited in treatments of identification. A particularly revealing example is to be found in a recent book by a psychologist. In his chapter on 'Evidence and Truth in the Criminal Justice System', addressed to non-legal readers, Yarmey presents a model of 'Major Events and Proceedings Involved in a Criminal Prosecution' (Figure 14.1).

This flow-chart was designed to provide a general introduction to criminal process as one context in which eyewitness evidence is important. It is interesting in that some of the categories it uses — 'facts gathered', 'theories constructed', 'data analysed', 'evidence presented', 'facts', 'truths'— could equally well be fitted into an information processing model of a kind that is to be found in books on cognitive psychology (e.g. Lindsay and Norman, 1977) or on information theory (e.g. Willmer, 1970). This suggests that it might be relatively easy to integrate a more sophisticated model of typical criminal processes (and models of other legal processes) with one or more standard models of information processing, borrowed from other contexts.

For the purpose of a detailed analysis of problems of identification and misidentification, Yarmey's flow-chart would need to be expanded and refined in a number of ways. First, it is important to bring out the fact that by the time a witness comes to testify at the trial he or she has typically 'presented' at least some of his or her information on several previous occasions, for example in informal conversation, in interviews with the police and possibly with one or more lawyers, in depositions, perhaps at committal proceedings and so on. This is one reason why it is useful to think in terms not merely of witnesses testifying (*evidence*) but of the creating and processing of *information*. An adequate model for the purposes of the study of identification should indicate at least standard points in the process at which eyewitnesses report what they think they saw, what stimulated them to report, to whom, in what context and for what purposes.

It is also important to remember that information provided by eyewitnesses is relevant to a number of other decisions in criminal process — for example, the decision to hold an identification parade, the decision to prosecute, the decision to charge, the decision to plead guilty or not guilty, the decision whether or not to call a particular witness and so on. Such decisions should not be seen merely as stages on the way to a jury verdict: they can have other direct consequences, some of which can surely be called 'consequences of identification'. Again an adequate model would include all the standard decisions and events which might have such consequences.

Yarmey's model follows convention in depicting standard processes as following a single linear pattern. A crime is committed— the police investigate — a suspect is identified, located, arrested, and charged— a case is prepared—

and the evidence is presented in court. As readers of detective fiction will know, criminal processes do not follow a single pattern: in particular, the stages of an investigation follow in no set sequence and may overlap to a greater or lesser extent with preparation of the case against (or on behalf of) a particular suspect. Sometimes the story could be said to begin with a policeman seeing someone behaving suspiciously: if the starting-point is the finding of a dead body, it may or may not be clear at the outset that death was due to a criminal act and this can readily affect the sequence of investigation. Similarly police enquiries, formal 'interviews', identification parades and so on do not follow a single sequence — there are at least several different patterns. The immediate significance of this is that eyewitnesses play a variety of roles at different stages of pre-trial processes and this may have very significant impacts both on their own mental processes and on how information provided by them is treated or used.

The above analysis suggests that an 'information model' as a basis for a systematic approach to the subject of identification and misidentification in legal processes would need to satisfy the following conditions: it would need to accommodate all the main types of legal processes, rather than merely criminal processes; it would need to cover the main stages in each type of process, rather than concentrate on events in the courtroom; and it should be able to identify different points at which information relating to identification is provided, by whom and to whom, and how that information is processed and is used in a variety of types of decisions by different participants at different stages in the process. Furthermore it would need to point to the consequences of such decisions — especially the actual and potential mischiefs for the objects of identification. Finally, in deciding on the practical importance of particular research strategies, reforms, etc., some estimate would need to be made of the typicality and scale of the more important phenomena involved.

To produce such a comprehensive model would be an ambitious enterprise, which is beyond the scope of this chapter. However it may help to concretize the discussion and suggest some possible ways forward by taking a fresh look at the problems of identification in the light of such considerations.

REDEFINING THE PROBLEM OF (MIS)IDENTIFICATION

It is a truism that the characterization, definition, and diagnosis of a practical problem depend on the standpoint, perceptions, concerns, and objectives of those doing the defining. 'The problem of identification' as it emerges from the literature has certain obvious characteristics. It is seen as a practical rather than a scientific or intellectual problem: the underlying concern is to improve legal processes rather than solely or even mainly to understand them better. It is seen mainly as a problem of design; and the standpoint is 'official' — not in any pejorative sense of that term — but, like Bentham's legislator, the standpoint is

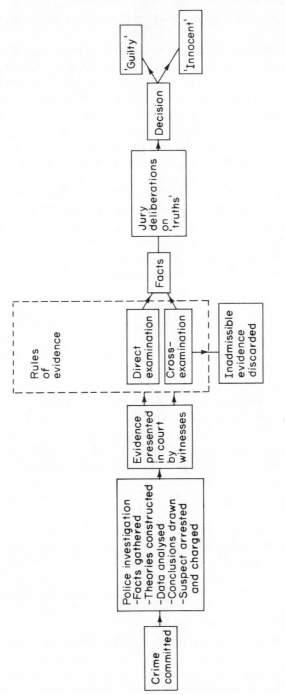

Figure 14.1 Major events and proceedings involved in a criminal prosecution (From Yarmey: *The Psychology of Eyewitness Testimony*, 1979. Reproduced with permission)

primarily of those responsible for the design and healthy operation of the system.

Eyewitness identification can, of course, be studied from a variety of other standpoints. It can, for example, be looked at from the point of view of the victim — as was done in part by Peter Hain (1976). It could be looked at from the point of view of police investigators or detectives or of prosecution or defence lawyers preparing cases, or of witnesses or of judges or jurors or of other participants in legal processes. It is also quite possible that the study of eyewitness testimony may produce insights, hypotheses, and findings which might be of theoretical significance in general psychology or in our understanding of legal processes.

To date, however, the primary focus has been on the practical problem of reducing the incidence of misidentification in the administration of justice; this is also the focus of this chapter. From that point of view, I wish to suggest that the problem has been defined in an artificially narrow way and that, while some of the limitations are justifiable on grounds of keeping the subject manageable, others are not. Accordingly let us look at some of the main ingredients of the 'problem' in turn.

The notion of identity

Wigmore, in what remains one of the best theoretical discussions of evidence of identity, stated:

> Identity may be thought of as a quality of a person or thing — the quality of sameness with another person or thing. The essential idea is that two persons or things are for the moment conceived as existing, but that one is alleged, because of common features to be the same as the other; so that there is in fact only a single person or thing . . .
> The process of constructing an inference of identification . . . consists usually in *adding together a number of circumstances*, each of which by itself might be a feature of many objects, but *all of which together can most probably, in experience, co-exist in a single object only*. Each additional circumstance reduces the chances of there being more than one object so associated. (Wigmore, 1937, pp. 258–259).

In the present context it is not necessary to start, let alone to chase, any philosophical hares about the notion of 'sameness'. At least in respect of identification of persons such puzzlements rarely, if ever, raise any issues of practical consequence. However, it is worth noting that in some legal contexts the problem of what constitutes identity (of, for example, ideas, transactions, or things) is both familiar and important, as students of copyright, passing off, and Roman law will know. So long as the problem of identification is confined to persons, the notion of identity may be taken for granted; if the subject is extended to things, then the matter may not always be so straightforward. Alger Hiss's typewriter either was or was not the one on which the documents were typed; but that may not be true of a stolen car that has been dismantled or a metal object, such as a piece of silver plate, that has been melted down.

'Identifying'

If one looks at the 'problem of identification' in the context of legal process as a flow of decisions and events, it is obvious that a complex variety of mental processes and human actions are involved: seeing, hearing; acquiring, storing, interpreting, and retrieving information; recognizing; believing; asserting, communicating, describing, persuading; deciding; and so on. It is also obvious that the mental processes and actions of a variety of individual participants are involved and that they interact in complex ways. In the light of this it is worth noting two points about the concept of 'identification'. First, in the context of phrases like 'the problem of identification' it covers a complex range of mental processes and actions that need to be differentiated. Second, in some contexts statements of the kind 'X identified Y' may be ambiguous: such a statement could mean 'X *recognized* Y' or 'X formed the *belief* that Y was the same as Z' or 'X *decided* that Y was probably the same as Z' or 'X *asserted* that Y was the same as Z'.

It would not be appropriate here to attempt a systematic analysis of the main concepts and distinctions involved. But it is worth making the point that a systematic theory of identification in legal processes requires a quite elaborate conceptual framework which would need to draw on the language of both law and psychology. It would, for example, be necessary to integrate concepts and terminology from cognitive psychology (such as acquisition, retention, and retrieval of information) and from information theory (such as 'noise', 'signal', 'coding', and 'active'/'passive' information). Some standard concepts from decision theory and social psychology may also be useful, in addition to concepts and distinctions from legal discourse such as materiality, relevance, admissibility, and receivability; quantum, cogency, and admissibility of evidence; *factum probans* and *factum probandum*; and the whole panoply of standard procedural concepts. This is not intended as a plea for the jargonization of identification; rather it is to emphasize the truism that in this as in other spheres of interdisciplinary work an important step towards an integrated approach is the harmonization of concepts from the relevant disciplines.

A further point about psychological aspects of the subject is suggested by the foregoing: several different branches of psychology are relevant to the study of identification. In recent years the psychology of eyewitness identification has spread beyond concentration on the cognitive processes of one actor, the witness, to include other established lines of psychological enquiry. Saks and

Hastie (1978), for example, have been praised for directing attention to other actors, but have been criticized for concentrating too much on individual actors while neglecting 'the intricate web of relationships that bind and define different actors' (Loh, 1981). Clifford and Bull have pointed to several areas of social psychology that are directly relevant to the relatively narrow topic of person identification in contested jury trials. Broaden the perspective and other areas may become relevant as well. This suggests that there is already in existence a substantial accumulation of concepts, theories, and findings in psychology, and elsewhere, some of which have not yet been perceived to be relevant to the subject of identification, at least in any sustained and systematic manner.

Identity of what?

The 'ideal' case and nearly all of the literature on eyewitness identification concentrates on what Clifford and Bull (1978) referred to as 'person identification'. However, Loftus (1979; this volume) reports on some experiments in which identification and recognition of cars were involved and other examples are to be found in the literature. Cases of eyewitness identification of objects or of animals can arise in practice and some of the psychological processes involved may be similar, if not identical. For many purposes it may be perfectly justifiable to focus primarily or exclusively on identification of persons — as I shall do from now on — but it is worth bearing in mind that many of the same considerations apply to identification of things; furthermore people are often identified or recognized through their close association with distinctive things, such as clothes.

Identification by what means?

Identity may be proved in court by circumstantial or testimonial evidence or by a combination of the two. As forensic science has developed, technological improvements such as fingerprinting, blood grouping, microanalysis of traces and the like have increased in practical importance; eyewitness identification may over time become correspondingly less important. Nevertheless it is likely to continue to have a role to play in investigation and in litigation, both civil and criminal, for the foreseeable future.

So far as analysing the problem is concerned only a few brief comments about means are needed. One point worth noting is that recognition is not solely visual; it is in theory possible to recognize another person by any one of the five senses; as a practical matter, as has often been acknowledged, identification may involve a *combination* of two or more senses, most commonly sight and hearing (Clifford and Bull, 1978; Clifford, this volume). Accordingly, it may be artificially narrow or misleading to define the problem strictly in terms of *eye*witnesses.

Another form of combination needs also to be borne in mind. The paradigm case postulates that identification is based on the testimonial evidence of one or two eyewitnesses alone. However, the question of reliability of this kind of testimony remains in cases where there is a combination of testimonial and circumstantial evidence, especially where the circumstantial evidence alone is not sufficient to settle the issue. Thus even a rule requiring corroboration of eyewitness evidence of identity in certain kinds of case would not eliminate the need for guidance as to the likely reliability of a particular item of testimonial evidence in a given case. It is also worth noting that the problem of combining convergent evidence of different types has also puzzled logicians and other theorists of evidence (e.g. Cohen, 1977, 1980; Eggleston, 1978, 1980; Glanville Williams, 1979).

Finally it is worth remarking that much more attention has been given to date to evaluating the reliability of existing methods of eyewitness identification, such as confrontations, dock identifications, identification parades and the like than to inventing new devices or radically improving existing ones. In particular, discussions of the use of photographs seem on the whole to be rather unimaginative about the possibilities, perhaps because they dwell on the limitations of the photograph and the dangers of existing uses to which they are put rather than concentrating on how their advantages — especially cheapness, convenience, and flexibility — can be exploited and how procedures can be devised which offset or mitigate some of the acknowledged dangers and limitations.

The mischiefs of misidentification: who are the victims?

The paradigm case in nearly all of the literature on identification assumes that the only mischief arising from misidentification is the conviction of the innocent. Even if one extends this to other mistaken adjudicative decisions (such as the wrong person being held liable or even erroneous acquittals) this is an extraordinarily narrow conception of the mischiefs involved. Suppose, for the sake of argument, that Roger Orton was indeed the real Roger Tichborne, what where the consequences of the mistake? He was not only convicted of perjury and imprisoned: he lost his inheritance, his reputation and a good deal else besides; he was subjected to considerable expense and mental agony; and, in a sense, he even lost his identity. Peter Hain was acquitted of a charge of armed robbery, but can one seriously claim that he was not a victim of misidentification, given the anxiety, the expense, and the potential damage to his reputation that he suffered, in addition to what he refers to as 'the indignity and injustice of being hauled through the courts' (Hain, 1976, p. 29)? Hain wrote a vivid account of his experience; he also described a number of cases in which misidentification led to evils short of conviction, thereby reminding us that even to be suspected, interrogated, arrested or threatened with prosecution can be an unpleasant, even traumatic, experience with a whole range of possible harmful consequences, financial, psychological, and otherwise. To treat mistaken adjudicative decisions as the only evils of misidentification is symptomatic of a narrow kind of formalism. Conviction and punishment of the innocent are among the great social evils; but they are not by any means the only ones. Add to Bentham's notions of the collateral pains of procedure — vexation, expense and delay — the notion of other harmful consequences, direct and indirect, of being involved as a party in legal processes and one has a more comprehensive conceptual basis for assessing the mischiefs of misidentification.

To broaden the enquiry in this way has important implications: it forces us to look at the consequences for the object of identification (and for others) at every step in legal process; it also transforms our estimates of the likely scale of the problem, for under 'victims' of misidentification are now included all those who have fallen under suspicion, who have been interrogated, harassed, arrested, charged, paraded, or have been involved in other unpleasant experiences in civil, criminal or other proceedings or in expense as a result of information derived from a witness. While the number of people wrongly convicted by a jury as a result of eyewitness identification may be as few as ten or a dozen over a year, the number who have suffered other evils of misidentification may number hundreds or even thousands. By broadening the notion of victims our perception of the nature and scale of the problem is transformed.

Two objections to this move need to be considered. The first is that it is reasonable to concentrate on mistaken *adjudicative* decisions, because these represent at once the most serious consequences of misidentification and the most easily remedied. No amount of improvement of the system can prevent innocent people falling under suspicion or being the subject of false allegations. A second possible objection is that to broaden the definition of the problem in this way renders it unmanageable.

To which one may reply: first, which is the greater social evil: an estimated ten or a dozen convictions of innocent persons each year or hundreds, perhaps thousands, mistakenly subjected to the vexations, expense, and other consequences of being involuntary involved in legal processes? Even if one concedes that wrongful conviction of the innocent is necessarily always the worst evil — which is debatable — surely the potential scale of the wider problem is such as to demand at least as much attention.

Second, from several points of view it is artificial to isolate one harmful consequence of being involved unwillingly in legal processes from the other consequences. What the consequences that flow from a single, wrongful or mistaken identification are in a particular case is largely a matter of chance. For the individual victim the evil consequences tend to cumulate, whether or not the formal outcome is an unfavourable adjudicative decision. From the point of view of improving the system, almost any measure affecting the adjudicative stage, will also affect other stages in the process: for example, there is a widely held view that one of the most important ways of avoiding wrongful convictions is to exercise more careful control over decisions whether or not to prosecute — but clearly measures affecting how such decisions are made have many potential ramifications in addition to the likely effect on wrongful convictions. The costs and benefits of almost any measure designed to deal with problems of identification cannot be rationally assessed by looking only at adjudicative outcomes.

Third, to broaden the definition of 'the problem of identification' may lead to a more realistic appraisal of the complexities of the situation, but this does not make it any less manageable than other important topics in legal process, such as confessions, plea-bargaining, and settlement out of court. Of course, there is need for specialized lines of research — for example into police identification of juveniles in some particular kinds of situation — but any particular research project and the evaluation of the significance of its findings need to be set in the context of some broader total picture.

Identification for what purposes?

In the orthodox view it is common to treat the information provided by eyewitnesses solely as *evidence* to be presented at trial. If, however, one looks at criminal process as a whole one is likely to find that such information is used in a variety of ways: eyewitness accounts and descriptions may provide the first leads for identifying a suspect or, anterior to that, for searching for potential suspects who correspond to a description; at a later stage information provided by the witness may lead to the elimination of particular suspects during the course of investigation and, as was dramatically illustrated by the Yorkshire Ripper investigation, false or misleading information may lead to the premature elimination of a suspect. As we have already seen, identification parades need not be solely evidence-generating devices; they may also be used to eliminate suspects or they may lead to the discontinuance of a case for lack of potential evidence. Even if evidence of positive identification at a parade were not generally admissible, or were inadmissible in a particular case because of some defect in the procedure, occasional parades might still be useful as part of the process of detection. Information provided by eyewitnesses also represents *potential evidence* which may have an important bearing on a number of pre-trial decisions, such as decisions to hold a parade, decisions to prosecute, decisions whether or not to plead guilty, and decisions whether to elect for summary trial or trial by jury. Thus in considering problems of identification in the context of criminal processes as a whole it is important to distinguish between the uses of information from eyewitnesses as *investigative inform-*

ation, as *potential evidence*, and as *evidence actually presented* in court. There are no doubt other uses of such information in criminal processes and analogous distinctions also need to be drawn in the context of non-criminal processes. It is useful to see evidence and potential evidence as species of information provided by eyewitnesses, for that should serve as a reminder that the phenomenon under consideration is a particular form of human information processing in a rather complex kind of social process.

REDEFINING THE PROBLEM

If one draws together the main strands in the foregoing analysis the following picture emerges: the starting-point of the process is a triggering event or situation in which one person, the witness, sees or hears another person, thing or animal, which on some subsequent occasion or occasions he or she is asked to describe or to state is the same as an object presented to his or her senses either directly, as in a parade, or through some representation such as a film, a photograph, a recording, a drawing or a description. It is generally recognized that a variety of factors tend to make such statements unreliable, even where the witness is disinterested. From this certain practical problems arise — for example, how to differentiate reliable from unreliable statements and how to improve the reliability of such statements.

Up to this point there is no difference of substance between the orthodox definition of the problem and the perspective advocated in this paper. It can readily be conceded that for certain purposes it is reasonable to confine the definition of the problem to *eye*witness identification of *persons* in *criminal* processes, so long as it is recognized that the processes of identifying other objects, by other means (such as voice or a combination of sense data) in other legal and similar processes are in many respects closely analogous. At the next stage, however, significant differences flow from the orthodox and broader perspectives. The former concentrates on identification statements as *evidence*, while the latter also includes the uses of such statements as *potential evidence* and as *information* relevant to a *variety of decisions* and other purposes. Similarly, if it is accepted that wrongful convictions are only one of the harmful consequences (*mischiefs*) that tend to flow from mistaken or dubious identification statements, then the population of *victims* is very substantially increased and attention is inevitably focused on *the whole process*, including events and decisions before and after trial. From this perspective it would be artificial to distinguish sharply between cases which are contested before a jury and other proceedings which take place before some other court or tribunal or which never reach the stage of a trial of the issue of identity. Even if a particular study concentrates on the trial stage in criminal proceedings, it will almost certainly be necessary to consider the trial in the context of the process as a whole.

The substitution of an explicit and broadly gauged 'information model' for the narrower, typically implicit, jury lawyer's 'evidentiary model' has a number of practical and theoretical implications for future research, for public debate and for practical action relating to the topic of identification in legal processes. First, at the level of theory, the information model may provide a better conceptual basis for an integrated multidisciplinary approach to the topic. Second, this kind of perspective fits rather more easily with much contemporary research and writing about legal processes than does the evidentiary model. This in turn may help cross-fertilization between several bodies of literature that have to some extent developed separately. For example, it may point to connections between psychological literature about eyewitness testimony and sociological, legal, and other literature about plea bargaining and guilty pleas or about juvenile courts. It may also serve as a constant reminder of the enormous complexity of legal processes. Third, this broader perspective may indicate new lines of research for psychologists and others; it may also suggest that some existing bodies of research and literature have a more direct bearing on the study of identification, and vice versa, than has hitherto been generally perceived. Thus, on the one hand, relatively little is known about such specific matters as decisions to hold, or not to hold, identification parades and the consequences of such decisions or about the special features of juveniles as objects of identification. On the other hand, the potential broader implications of identification have yet to be systematically explored. Fourth, the 'information model' may provide the basis for a diagnosis and evaluation of the mischiefs of misidentification in legal processes that is at once more systematic and more realistic than that presented by the Devlin Report and similar policy documents. It may also open the way for a more free-ranging and imaginative approach to improving and inventing procedures, techniques, and rules for reducing the evils of misidentification in legal processes.

Since all this might seem rather ambitious, it is appropriate to end with some disclaimers. All I have tried to do in this chapter is to suggest that a fresh look needs to be taken at the problem of misidentification from a broader perspective than has generally been adopted in the past. A systematically constructed 'information model' (or series of models) has yet to be developed in this context and this paper does no more than suggest some of the factors that might be taken into account in such an enterprise, for which, as a jurist, I have no special qualifications. Similarly a comprehensive, empirically based restatement of the problems of misidentification in England, or more generally, has not been attempted. Nor should anything that has been said here be taken as denigrating the very substantial advances in the study of the subject that have been made in recent years, especially by psychologists. All I have tried to suggest is that in so far as recent writings — as exemplified by the Devlin Report and the books by Yarmey, Loftus, and Clifford and Bull — have been influenced by 'the evidentiary model' of identification statements, some of the tendencies and biases of the expository tradition of academic law and jury-oriented practitioners have crept into the literature; in so far as they have broken away from the narrow focus of this model — as in many respects they have — the development of a broadly conceived 'information model' might provide a general perspective on the subject which is at once systematic and close to the empirical realities of the operation of legal processes.

NOTES

This paper is a by-product of a general study of theoretical aspects of evidence and proof in adjudicative processes. I am grateful to Peter Twining for assistance with an early draft, and to the editors and Michael King for helpful criticisms and suggestions. I am particularly indebted to the Social Science Research Council for a Personal Research Grant during 1980–1981, which enabled me to work full-time on the general study.

1. Recent editions are Cross (1979); Salmond (1981); and Smith and Hogan (1978).
2. It might equally be referred to as Legal Realism, except that this term is often associated with a number of fallacies of which few, if any, leading Legal Realists were in fact guilty — such as the belief that talk of rules is a myth or that law can be defined in terms of prediction.
3. Broadening one's perspective typically requires redefining the scope of the subject and the choice of a new organizing category — in this context, the substitution of 'Evidence, Proof and Fact-Finding' (or something similar) for 'Evidence'. Wigmore divided the study of Evidence into two parts: The Science of Proof and the Trial Rules of Evidence; this, however, underemphasizes the procedural dimensions.
4. Such theories have been attempted in the past, for example by Jeremy Bentham and John Henry Wigmore, but they have not caught on, partly because of the dominance of the Expository Tradition and partly because they are defective as theories in important respects. Nevertheless there is sufficient in the heritage of the literature on evidence and on judicial processes to provide a starting-point for a broader approach to the study of identification.
5. The most important survivals are some exclusionary rules, such as those governing privilege, evidence of disposition and character, improperly or illegally obtained evidence (including confessions), and hearsay. There are also important rules governing presumptions, standards and burdens of proof, judicial notice and opinion evidence.
6. The Devlin Report's analysis of the stories of Dougherty and Virag provides two case studies that deserve to become classics. Each follows the process from the initial crime through trial and appeal to the activities which eventually led to official acknowledgements that an error had been made and the payment of modest *ex gratia* compensation to the two men. The main focus in both accounts is on what went wrong and each reveals a catalogue of mistakes, accidents, and coincidences calculated to hearten inefficiency theorists, if no one else. In both cases misidentification played an important part, but they illustrate vividly how a series of mishaps and mistakes by different participants can combine to contribute not only to a wrongful conviction, but to failures to rectify errors on appeal and afterwards. The Report concludes that *R. v. Dougherty* was so badly bungled that it 'will never be a leading case on misidentification', whereas Virag's was nearly a

'copy book case' in which misidentification was not only the main factor, but 'was itself a cause of some contributory errors'.

These two case studies could be said to be based on an implied rather than an express, total process model. They clearly illustrate the complex interactions between events and decisions during different stages in the process, the contributions of different participants, and the importance of setting alleged examples of misidentification in the context of the story as a whole. However, it is debatable whether the rest of the Devlin Report gave adequate weight to all the implications of the lessons of these two case studies—especially in respect of some of the crucial decisions taken prior to trial in each case. Moreover, as had already been observed, by failing to make adequate demographic estimates of the main factors and actors in the situation, the Report provides no adequate basis for judging the typicality of the cases of Dougherty and Virag, except perhaps in respect of the importance of misidentification as a source of error as against other factors.

7.   In England and Wales the number of civil jury trials is rarely more than 15–25 a year. In 1973 47% of those sent to prison were sent by Crown Courts, 43% were sent by magistrates, and 10% were tried by magistrates and sentenced by Crown Courts. The great majority of these pleaded guilty. See generally Zander (1980, especially pp. 1–5, 311–313).

8.   When a defendant can choose between summary trial or trial by jury, he is likely to be advised to opt for the latter in cases where there is a dispute about evidence of identity. Thus most contested cases of the kind in which a potential prison sentence is at stake are probably tried by Crown Courts. Against this must be set uncontested cases, cases tried before magistrates, in Juvenile Courts and in other tribunals and cases which never reach trial, but in which a suspected or accused person has suffered substantial vexation and/or expense. No reliable statistics about the extent of such cases are at present available.

9.   The reasons for these differences are complex and cannot be explored in detail here; they are in part due to the differences in composition of the two bodies; in part to the narrowness of the traditional definition of 'evidence' as a subject; and in part to a generally heightened awareness that even questions about the admissibility of evidence at criminal trials can only sensibly be discussed when they are viewed in the broader context of some conception of criminal process as a whole. The differences in the definition of the problem of each report, including the way the terms of reference were drafted, reflected in large part a significant shift in perspectives.

10.   Perhaps the *locus classicus* is Thayer's dictum: 'What was formerly "tried" by the method of force or the mechanical following of form is now tried by the method of reason' (Thayer, 1898, pp. 198–199).

11.   The underlying epistemology is cognitive rather than sceptical; a correspondence theory of truth is generally preferred to a coherence theory; statements of fact are seen as representations of past events; the mode of decision-making is 'rational' as contrasted with 'irrational' modes such as battle, compurgation and ordeal; decisions are supposed to be taken on the basis of relevant evidence presented to the decider; since the evidence is often incomplete and unreliable, decisions about the truth of the material allegations have to be made on the basis of probabilities, but whether such probabilities are in principle always mathematical is a matter of controversy; the characteristic mode of reasoning in this context is induction, deduction playing a limited and subsidiary role; the pursuit of truth in adjudication as a means to justice under the law demands a high, but not necessarily an overriding priority as a social value: for Bentham, for example, the primary

objective of adjudication, rectitude of decision, was subject to the secondary objectives of avoiding or minimizing vexation, expense, and delay, the priorities in each case to be determined by preponderant utilities. For many civil libertarians, on the other hand, the pursuit of truth in adjudication should be subject to additional constraints based on principles independent of utility, such as principles of due process and absolute prohibitions on torture and coercive means of interrogation (see generally Twining, 1982).

12.   For example, debates about the privilege against self-incrimination, about illegally or improperly obtained evidence, about the nature of forensic 'probabilities', and about the rationales of the hearsay rule and its exceptions.

REFERENCES

Baddeley, A. and Woodhead, M. Improving face recognition ability. This volume.

Bentham, J. (1827). *Rationale of Judicial Evidence* (ed. J.S. Mill). London: Hunt and Clarke.

Clifford, B.R. Memory for voices: The feasibility and quality of earwitness evidence. This volume.

Clifford, B.R. and Bull, R. (1978). *The Psychology of Person Identification*. London: Routledge.

Cohen, L.J. (1977). *The Probable and the Provable*. Oxford: Clarendon.

Cohen, L.J. (1980). The logic of proof. *Criminal Law Review*, 91–103.

Criminal Law Revision Committee (1972). Eleventh Report, Evidence (General), Cmnd. 4991, London: HMSO.

Cross, R. (1979). *Evidence* (5th edn) London: Butterworths.

Davis, K.C. (1964). An approach to rules of evidence for nonjury cases. *American Bar Association Journal*, **50**, 723–727.

Devlin, Lord, P. (1976). Report to the Secretary of State for the Home Department of the Departmental Committee on Evidence of Identification in Criminal Cases (the Devlin Report). London: HMSO.

Eggleston, R. (1978). *Evidence, Proof and Probability*. London: Weidenfeld and Nicolson.

Eggleston, R. (1980). The probability debate, *Criminal Law Review*, 678–688.

Frank, J. (1949). *Courts on Trial: Myth and Reality in American Justice*. New Jersey: Princeton University Press.

Hain, P. (1976). *Mistaken Identity*. London: Quartet Books.

Kaplan, J. (1968). Decision-theory and the factfinding process, *Stanford Law Review*, **20**, 1065–1092.

King, M. (1981). *The Framework of Criminal Justice*, London: Croom Helm.

Lasswell, H. and McDougal, M. (1967). Jurisprudence in policy oriented perspective. *Florida Law Review*, **19**, 486.

Lindsay, P. and Norman, D. (1977). *Human Information Processing: An Introduction to Psychology* (2nd edn). New York and London: Academic Press.

Lindsay, R.C.L. and Wells, G. What do we really know about cross-race eyewitness identification? This volume.

Loftus, E.F. (1979). *Eyewitness Testimony*. Cambridge, Mass.: Harvard University Press.

Loftus, E.F. and Ketcham, K. The malleability of eyewitness accounts. This volume.

Loh, W.D. (1981). Psycho–legal research. *Michigan Law Review*, **79**, 659–707.

McDougal, M. and Reisman, W.M. (1981). *International Law Essays*. New York: Foundation Press.

Michael, J. and Adler, M. (1931). The nature of judicial proof. (unpublished, preliminary edition, Columbia University, New York).

Philips Commission (1981). Report of the Royal Commission on Criminal Procedure. London: HMSO.

Saks, M.J., and Hastie, R. (1978). *Social Psychology in Court*. New York: Van Nostrand Rheinhold.

Salmond, J. (1981). *Torts* (18th edn, edited by R.F.V. Heuston and R.S. Chambers). London: Sweet and Maxwell.

Saunders, D., Vidmar, N., and Hewitt, E. Eyewitness testimony and the discrediting effect. This volume.

Smith, J.C. and Hogan, B. (1978). *Criminal Law* (4th edn). London: Butterworth.

Thayer, J.B. (1898). *A Preliminary Treatise on Evidence at Common Law*. Boston: Little Brown.

Twining, W. (1974). Some jobs for jurisprudence. *British Journal of Law and Society*, **1**, 149–174.

Twining, W. (1979). Goodbye to Lewis Eliot. *Journal of the Society of Public Teachers of Law (N.S.)*, XV, 3–19.

Twining, W. (1981). Some scepticism about some scepticisms. Unpublished paper, Wolfson College, Oxford.

Twining, W. (1982). The Rationalist Tradition of evidence scholarship (forthcoming).

Wigmore, J.H. (1937). *Science of Judicial Proof* (3rd edn). Boston: Little Brown.

Wigmore, J.H. (1940). *Treatise on Evidence* (3rd edn). Boston: Little Brown.

Williams, G. (1979). The mathematics of proof. *Criminal Law Review*, 297–308, 350–54.

Willmer, M.A.P. (1970). *Crime and Information Theory*. Edinburgh: University Press.

Yarmey, D. (1979). *The Psychology of Eyewitness Testimony*. New York: Free Press. London: Collier Macmillan.

Zander, M. (1980). *Cases and Materials on the English Legal System* (3rd edn). London: Weidenfeld and Nicolson.

Chapter 15

Witness Evidence: Conclusion and Prospect

Brian R. Clifford and Sally M.A. Lloyd-Bostock

The focus of this collection of papers was Witness Evidence. The question that must now be asked is what the book as a whole offers of benefit to this area of concern and whether the international conference from whence, eventually, this book evolved, was worth while. The editors are in no doubt that it was although the gain was diverse and multifaceted rather than linear and unitary. Thus not only was new knowledge communicated and therefore made available and fed into the educative process of all concerned with psycho–legal issues, but questions of the most fundamental nature were raised about the adequacy, comprehensiveness or applicability of past, present, and future empirical data in this area. In editing the book we did not try to conceal the disagreements between contributors on some or all of these problems. Thus we should note the, perhaps implicit, criticism of certain prevailing paradigms and orienting assumptions in eyewitness evidence research. Explicitly, the validity of whole data bases concerning specific issues, from which psychologists have gone to court in the past, was questioned. Overall the consideration shown or not shown by researchers for realism and/or ecological validity (and they are not the same) was a key feature of these presentations. We believe that these critical appraisals of one's own and others' work testifies to the increasing maturity of this most important area of work.

Individually and collectively the contributors have served to advance the study of witness evidence in all its forms. The fact that the conclusions of some of the reported research are essentially negative should not be taken to mean impotence — it merely means that blind alleys have quickly been seen for what they are and that more powerful and fruitful lines of psychological enquiry or criminal procedure should be engaged. In practice (and in theory) research which shows what is not the case is every bit as useful as that which shows what is the case.

Looking at the contributions as a whole we think that a number of lines of future development have been clearly signposted. These developments have to do with the improved understanding of the witness as evidence provider; the juror and jury as evidence evaluator; and the social and structural features of the total criminal justice system as evidence elicitor. Another, continuing, concern is the relationship between empirical data and legal theory and practice: that is, the question of whether, and if so, how, psychological research should inform legal policy.

There can be little doubt that eyewitnesses (and earwitnesses for that matter) play a key role in the criminal justice system — both in the apprehension and in the conviction of criminal suspects. As such it seems likely that much future research in witness evidence will continue to focus on the witness *per se*. However within this volume there are indications that while this focus may remain the attitude to what is proper subject-matter may exhibit a difference in emphasis. The earlier work in the eyewitness field was essentially negativistic. It was concerned with showing the witness's fallibility and his inability to recall accurately physical actions, person descriptions or verbalizations, and his inability to identify unequivocally a once seen person when that person is presented in a lineup, photo spread or mugshot book. In short, the witness was shown to be a somewhat pathetic figure in the face of extramemorial factors occurring at encoding, during storage or at retrieval. Hopefully however this negativity will be a characteristic of the history of eyewitness research, and not of its future. A fundamental insight (see Clifford and Bull, 1978) most clearly articulated and demonstrated by Malpass and Devine (1981) is that correct identification is a joint function of the witness's ability to distinguish old from new events (e.g. the offender from look-alike foils) and the level of their identification criterion. That is the decision as to whether or not to identify someone is conceptually distinct from their actual ability to be accurate. Eyewitness testimony is a psycho–social phenomenon: as such, future research must begin to untangle those psycho–social factors and processes which influence the decision to choose, from those more strictly speaking cognitive factors and limitations which influence the potential accuracy of the choice.

When this is done counter-intuitive findings may eventuate. To take an example. Working on the assumption that the perceived value to witnesses of their response (to choose someone or say 'don't know') can change independently of the information the witnesses actually have and can independently affect their willingness to make an identification, Malpass *et al.* put a common objection to the test. The common objection was that subjects in the laboratory frequently know that their decisions to choose someone will have no important impact. Malpass *et al.* staged a vandalization incident and with the help of the local police maintained the deception right through to identification. The witnesses were informed (by surreptitious means) that the suspect, if identified, would either go to jail or get a 'good talking to'. Those informed about a heavy sentence made identification choices 83% of the time; those informed of a light sentence identified only 26% of the time. Thus research designed to get 'inside the skull' of a witness is a highly desirable future direction which should be encouraged.

The data provided by Saunders, Vidmar, and Hewitt in this volume also suggest that a desirable line of future research would be a similar approach to jurors and juries. Evidence suggests that the presentation of expert testimony causes the jury to give more consideration to proffered eyewitness testimony. Such a finding is not terribly surprising. What is surprising is the fact that such evidence causes increased evaluation of other — non-eyewitness related — evidence. This finding is non-intuitive and certainly important. Thus research should proceed rapidly into juror's 'implicit eyewitness theory' and few better leads can be given than that by Wells (this volume). Not only does this chapter document the fact that jurors have expectations of how accurate and inaccurate eyewitnesses differ but it also uses that data as input to an embryonic theory of juror behaviour when confronted with evidence of an eyewitness kind. Once we have some idea of how jurors evaluate testimony or identification evidence we can begin a new round of educative communication directed at indicating to them which facets of their 'theory' have empirical support and which do not.

Another important aspect of jury behaviour that should fall within the eyewitness researchers' interests is the relationship of judicial warning to the juror's accuracy in evaluation of fact (e.g. Turnbull directive). Do such directions help, hinder or simply not articulate with the jurors and jury? We really do not know: but we should.

In terms of the structural and procedural features of the criminal justice system the chapters by Malpass and Devine, and Davies should be productive of reasoned questioning of current procedures. If one can accept that one purpose of eyewitness identification research is to contribute to the solution of the practical problems of obtaining accurate criminal identification by assisting *inter alia* law makers in formulating procedures for developing valid eyewitness evidence then it follows that lineups or identification parades will continue to be a form of future research. The development of heuristics or algorithms in this area which have practical and practicable embodiments are greatly to be encouraged. The perception of fairness in lineups comprising both size and bias conceptions is a move in that direction. However much remains to be done.

Perhaps the greatest challenge the future holds for witness researchers is that of the validity of their data and hence its applicability to legal issues and policy. At base all researchers have a deep and genuine concern and consideration for their work and its impact on the judicial system in all its multifarious forms. We do not wish to see changes in policy predicated upon shaky or invalid data. The difficult question, however, is how to achieve firm and valid findings? If truth be told it is a fairly simple matter to get valid or invalid data accepted by the courts — either in its adjudicative or its legislative context (See Davis, 1955). This is because either (in Davis's adjudicative context) the rules of evidence ask the wrong questions (qualifications, proper subject-matter, conformity with a generally accepted explanatory theory, probative value) or because psycho-logical research is presented summarily and not subject to cross-examination

(Davis's legislative context). Thus in a very real sense we as the researchers are thrown back on our own integrity.

The way forward has been indicated in this book. Where nothing but common-sense speculation prevails 'baseline' research (e.g. Clifford, this volume) is required to ascertain the warrantability of common-sense beliefs. This may be sufficient to indicate that research should not be pursued further. Where further research is indicated it should then be of a different type. Broadly this research takes two forms.

The first form is to work backwards from the naturally occurring situation to, if needs must, laboratory simulation, experimenting as early in this backward extrapolation as possible. This is basically the request for ecologically valid research called for by Clifford (1978). For this type of research it is essential that the conceptual distinction be drawn between realistic research method-ology and ecologically valid research methodology. The first requires only sensitive perception and common-sense understanding of the situation being simulated (e.g. because criminal episodes are dynamic, face photograph re-search is inappropriate). The latter requires deep and true knowledge of what actually happens in the to-be-simulated situations. This requires frank and full information exchange between researchers and those personnel located in all aspects of the criminal justice system. Given all interlocutors supposedly have a common end this ought not to be a problem — but it is! Problems, however, should not inhibit research thinking, they should merely make it more creative.

Thus if we are driven to run laboratory based studies, for example to test some abstract psychological theory or as a theory of legal behaviour, before 'going public' on it we should be concerned to monitor its generalizability by running analogue realistic and/or ecologically valid studies. No longer can we luxuriate in the belief that generalizability can or ought to be settled by intuition. Now that we are partially accepted by the legal profession this settling must be done in the court of empiricism.

Lest there be readers who doubt that credibility is a major problem it should be noted that Lord Devlin's Committee (1976) concluded that 'the stage seems not yet to have been reached at which the conclusions of psychological research are sufficiently widely accepted or tailored to the needs of the judicial process to become the basis of procedural change' (p. 73).

The second, different but related, approach to external (and internal) validity is what Saunders, Vidmar, and Hewitt have called 'conceptual repli-cation', or what Campbell and Jackson (1979) call 'intergroup conceptual replication'. This basically refers to the substantiation of a finding across a number of different subject populations, different but conceptually related treatments, and different outcome measures. This approach is seen in action in the Saunders et al. chapter where they address the 'discrediting failure effect' hypothesis. It is our belief that this approach can usefully be applied to many other areas of evidence research.

It should perhaps become the norm that routinely, before communication with legal personnel, any finding should be shown to be impervious to the use of different subject populations, different research settings, different experimental materials, and different research designs or methodologies. This multi-method approach would greatly increase our confidence in any conclusions we would wish to draw. This of course is the ideal, the practice is likely to be much more problematic — as indeed it was seen to be with the 'discrediting failure hypothesis'. We think, however, that the position is clear: in the search for 'certainty' a conflicting or contradictory set of findings based on a multi-method approach is to be preferred to a 'clear' finding based on only one method of study, since conclusions based on the clear finding may be wrong but this may go undetected. Liberty and freedom are just too important for it to be otherwise. We must, as scientists with a social responsibility, be more prepared to admit frankly that 'we don't know yet', when in fact we may have a good hunch that we do, rather than to state that 'we do know' when in fact we have not as yet adequately or fully tested the boundary conditions of the effect under discussion.

In all these areas the contributors to this volume have not only indicated the desirability of advance but have begun to chart its implementation. Whereas the psychologists in the book perceived difficulties both in the nature of the psychological research conducted and in their findings which may limit practical application, Twining, as an academic lawyer, questioned whether psychologists (and lawyers) in general had adequately defined the problem or problems they were investigating. The broadening of perspectives beyond a courtroom focus and to new types of question which is apparent throughout the book becomes a major theme in Twining's chapter. There he shows how differing traditions within legal scholarship imply different roles for the psychologists, and that legal sources (such as the Devlin Report, and various texts on Evidence) which have been influential in directing the attention of psychologists to particular issues are themselves the product of particular bodies of legal thought. There are therefore serious pitfalls for the unwary psychologist who comes into contact with only selected parts of the legal literature. Psychologists need to be aware at least of certain major legal traditions and debates. Twining suggests in particular that most psychological research on witness reliability has been dominated by a view of the problem as primarily one of *evidence* in the legal sense, which will eventually be presented in court. This perspective is compatible with a particular, rather narrow legal tradition and has proved very resilient in the psychological literature on identification. While as Twining acknowledges many psychologists have moved their focus of attention away from the courts, he still feels they frequently retain elements of this perspective, as shown, for example, by references to the view that the courts might take of certain evidence, or what a jury would make of it; or implying that the function of an identity parade is to generate evidence. Indeed, this tendency is illustrated in this book: most of the contributors indicate the legal relevance of their work by reference to legal questions about evidence, courts or juries, or slip into the equation of legal settings with court settings. To the extent that these references are more than expository devices employed by psychologists to communicate their commitment to the area being investigated, Twining's admonitions are timely and fundamental. He suggests that psychologists and lawyers working in the area need explicitly to free themselves from this 'evidence model' and the habits of thought that go with it, and replace it with a broader 'information model' which substitutes the notion of information for that of evidence, and which takes a very broad view of 'legal' processes and the 'problem' of misidentification. At the same time he calls for a comprehensive and articulated theoretical framework to provide coherence to work within this very wide and complex area.

Here then we have a reflective legal mind throwing down a gauntlet to empirical psychologists: there can be little doubt that it is a 'gauntlet with a gift in't'. The question is whether the gift will be seen in its full potential. Certainly, Twining's paper deserves the closest scrutiny by all applied psychologists in the witness field.

Whether or not Twining's actual thesis proves fruitful, there is another sense in which, 'he that comes last is commonly best'. It is important in the sense that it most clearly succeeds in representing, at the most general level, the focus of the present book: a prospective rather than a retrospective focus. In this sense, if this book is useful not simply as a static state-of-the-art document but as a dynamic, positive progenitor of the next wave of advance in witness research then it, and the conference in Oxford which spawned it will have achieved its objectives. This, however, is for the reader and more particularly the future to determine.

REFERENCES

Campbell, K.E. and Jackson, T.T. (1979). The role of and the need for replication research in social psychology. *Replication in Social Psychology*, **1**, 3–14.
Clifford, B.R. (1978). A critique of eyewitness research. In M. Gruneberg, P. Morris, and R. Sykes (eds), *Practical Aspects of Memory*. London: Academic Press.
Clifford, B.R. and Bull, R. (1978). *The Psychology of Person Identification*. London: Routledge and Kegan Paul.
Davis, J. (1955). Judicial Notice. *Californian Law Review*, **55**, 945–954.
Devlin, Lord P. (1976). Report to the Secretary of State for the Departmental Committee on Evidence of Identification in Criminal Cases. HMSO.
Malpass, R.S. and Devine, P.G. (1981). Eyewitness identification: Line up instructions and absence of the offender. *Journal of Applied Psychology*, **66**, 482–489.
Malpass, R.S., Devine, P.G. and Bergen, G.T. (1980). Eyewitness identification: Realism vs. the laboratory. State University of New York, Plattsburgh Behavioral Science Programme.

Name Index

291

Subject Index